ACTIVE AGEING

Voluntary work by older people in Europe

Edited by Andrea Principi, Per H. Jensen
and Giovanni Lamura

First published in Great Britain in 2014 by

Policy Press
University of Bristol
6th Floor
Howard House
Queen's Avenue
Clifton
Bristol BS8 1SD
UK
t: +44 (0)117 331 5020
f: +44 (0)117 331 5369
pp-info@bristol.ac.uk
www.policypress.co.uk

North America office:
Policy Press
c/o The University of Chicago Press
1427 East 60th Street
Chicago, IL 60637, USA
t: +1 773 702 7700
f: +1 773-702-9756
sales@press.uchicago.edu
www.press.uchicago.edu

British Library Cataloguing in Publication Data
A catalogue record for this book is available from the British Library

Library of Congress Cataloging-in-Publication Data
A catalog record for this book has been requested

ISBN 978 1 44730 720 4 hardcover

Cover design by Andrew Corbett
Printed and bound in Great Britain by CPI Group (UK)
Ltd, Croydon, CR0 4YY
Policy Press uses environmentally responsible
print partners

Contents

List of tables and figures

Tables

Figures

Notes on the contributors

Paula Aleksandrowicz was born in Wrocław, Poland, and graduated in sociology and English studies at the University of Mannheim, Germany. Her doctoral thesis at Jacobs University Bremen was on the impact in Poland and Germany of retirement legislation on companies' personnel policy and practice in dealing with older workers. She has published on issues of old-age pension policy, age management in companies and demographic change in small trade. Paula is currently working as a senior expert on demography at German Social Accident Insurance.

Per-Åke Andersson is a research fellow at the Department of Economics in the School of Business, Economics and Law at the University of Gothenburg, Sweden. He holds a PhD in economics. His main research areas are development economics, economic growth, international macroeconomics, aid effectiveness, health economics and labour economics.

Dominique Anxo is professor of economics in the Department of Economics and Statistics, Linnaeus University, Sweden, and director of the Centre for Labour Market Policy Research (CAFO). His research interests fall broadly into the areas of labour economics, industrial relations and gender economics. He has been involved in labour market analysis at both the national and international level and has, during the last decade, actively participated in multidisciplinary large European research projects and a European network of excellence. Within this framework he has edited several books and scientific papers related to changing work patterns, labour market transitions, evaluation of labour market policy programmes and cross-country comparison of employment and welfare state regimes.

Beate Baldauf is a senior research fellow at the Institute for Employment Research (IER) at the University of Warwick, UK. She is a social scientist by background and her research has covered a range of areas, including projects on ageing and employment, health and social care labour markets and education and training. Prior to joining the IER she worked at other research institutes in both the UK and Germany.

Doris Bockermann finished her Master's degree in gerontology at the University of Vechta, Germany, in 2012, and worked as a student researcher at the Institute of Gerontology in Vechta. Her research interests are ageing and work, with a focus on civic commitment and non-profit organisations as well as the self-employment of older workers.

Carlos Chiatti holds a Master's degree in economics and a PhD in epidemiology. He is a research fellow at the Italian National Institute of Health and Science on Aging (INRCA), a visiting fellow at the University of Newcastle upon Tyne (UK) and post-doctoral researcher at Lund Universitet (Sweden). In addition, he teaches health economics at the University of Ancona (Italy). His doctoral thesis was specifically focused on social inequalities in health and healthcare, but he has also worked on several international projects in the field of active ageing. At INRCA he recently worked on the project FUTURAGE, aimed at defining the roadmap for future ageing research in Europe. He is now working on a large community trial (UP-TECH project), funded by the Italian Ministry of Health, which aims to improve the provision of health and social care for patients affected by Alzheimer's disease through a better integration of existing services and the use of new technologies.

Wieteke Conen works as a labour economist at Universiteit Utrecht, the Netherlands, where she completed a PhD study on older workers. Formerly she was the project manager of the European project Activating Senior Potential in Ageing Europe (ASPA).

Frerich Frerichs graduated in sociology and psychology and completed a PhD in sociology. He has been professor for ageing and work at the Institute of Gerontology, University of Vechta, Germany, since 2006. Until 2006 he was head of the Department of Demographic Change, Labour Market and Social Policy for older workers at the Institute of Gerontology, Dortmund. His current research activities encompass labour market/social policy for older workers and employment policies/human resource management for an ageing workforce.

Sheila Galloway is a principal research fellow in the Centre for Educational Development, Appraisal and Research, University of Warwick, UK. Her research is primarily qualitative. After a first degree and Master's in literature, her PhD in sociology was in professional development. She focuses on this and on researching people's working lives throughout the lifecycle, especially in the cultural sector in major national institutions and in the health sector.

Per H. Jensen is professor of social policy and director of the Centre for Comparative Welfare Studies, Denmark (www.ccws.dk). He has published widely in the fields of comparative welfare state analysis, formal and informal work, elder care, comparative labour market analysis, early exit/retirement, and the sociology of family and gender relations. He is coordinator of the 7th Framework Programme, Impact of Local Welfare Systems on Female Labour Force Participation and Social Cohesion (www.flows-eu.eu).

Giovanni Lamura is a social gerontologist with an international and interdisciplinary background, and has been working at the Italian National Institute of Health and Science on Aging (INRCA) since 1992. He graduated in economics in Italy in 1990; obtained a PhD in 'Life course and social policy' at Bremen University (Germany) in 1995; was a visiting fellow in 2006-07 at the University of Hamburg-Eppendorf (Germany); and was research director of the 'health and care' pillar of the European Centre for Social Welfare Policy and Research in Vienna (Austria) in 2010-11. He has gained experience in international research projects, mainly focusing on family and the long-term care of dependent older people, work–life balance, migrant care work, prevention of elder abuse and neglect, ICT-based initiatives to support informal carers, intergenerational solidarity, and interdisciplinary research on ageing in general.

Yuxin Li is a research fellow in the Institute for Employment Research at the University of Warwick, UK. She has a PhD in economics and holds an MSc in econometrics and finance from the University of York, UK. Her research interests are in labour market studies such as the impact of demographic change, supply of and demand for skills, employment transitions and other employment-related issues. She also has an interest in applied micro-econometrics and other quantitative techniques.

Robert Lindley is professor and founding director of the Institute for Employment Research, University of Warwick, UK. He is former pro-vice-chancellor for International Affairs and Chair of the Faculty of Social Sciences at Warwick. He initially graduated in physics and holds an MSc in operational research from the London School of

Economics and Political Science and a PhD in economics from the University of Warwick. His research interests include the labour market, its demographic context and relationships with the economy, social welfare and the education/training systems; and European socio-economies during the wider global transition.

Elena Mascova received her PhD in sociology from the Université Paris Descartes, France. A Laureate of Burgen scholarship, she worked as an assistant professor at the Institute of Political Studies in Rennes, France, and then held a postdoctoral research fellowship at Téléuniversité in Montreal, Canada. At present she is a research manager at the Association Française des Managers de la Diversité. Her research focuses on different aspects of ageing and the institutional dynamics of social inclusion.

Jolanta Perek-Białas graduated as a statistician and economist in 2001. She works at the Warsaw School of Economics and in the Institute of Sociology at Jagiellonian University in Kraków, Poland. She has been involved in international projects under the 5th, 6th and 7th Framework Programme of the European Union related to an active ageing policy and relevant topics (like Activating Senior Potential in an Ageing Europe – ASPA) and in projects for the Norwegian Research Council of Science, VW Foundation, OECD/LEED (Organisation for Economic Co-operation and Development/Local Economic and Employment Development) Programme. Her main scientific research interests include the socio-economic consequences of population ageing in Poland, and in selected Central and Eastern European countries, active ageing policy, age management, the social activity of older people, reconciliation of work and care, and the social exclusion/inclusion of older people.

Mélissa Petit has a PhD in sociology from the University Paris Descartes, France. She is a member of GEPECS (Groupe d'etudes pour l'Europe, de la culture et de la solidarité). Her thesis in 2012 was titled 'Ageing and social temporalities: a comparison of France-Quebec'. Her research is based on ageing, volunteering, work after retirement and social temporalities.

Marielle Poussou-Plesse is assistant professor of sociology and has been a member of the Center Georges Chevrier at the University of Burgundy, France, since 2009. Her research interests include social meanings related to retirement time and French social and employment policies promoting longer working lives.

Andrea Principi, sociologist, has been a researcher at the National Institute of Health and Science on Aging, Ancona, Italy, since 2000. His main research interests relate to active ageing, that is, work, volunteering and education in older age, working carers' reconciliation of work for the labour market with informal care of older family members, and informal caregiving to older family members. He has participated in several European projects, including: ASPA: Activating Senior Potential in Ageing Europe, funded by the European Commission in 2008-11; Carers@work, funded by the Volkswagen Foundation in 2009-10; Income from Work after Retirement – National Report Italy, funded by the European Foundation for the Improvement of Living and Working Conditions in 2012; and MOPACT: Mobilising the Potential of Active Ageing in Europe, funded by the European Commission in 2013-17.

Joop Schippers is professor of labour economics in the Department of Law, Economics and Governance at Universiteit Utrecht, the Netherlands. He has published a series of books and articles on male–female wage differences, human capital investments, labour market flexibility and organisational behaviour with respect to women and older workers.

Konrad Turek is a sociologist, labour market researcher and analyst working at Jagiellonian University, Poland, in the Institute of Sociology and in the Centre of Evaluation and Public Policy Analysis. He is co-coordinator of Human Capital Balance, one of the biggest research projects in Poland about the labour market (2010-14). In previous years he worked on the international project ASPA (Activating Senior Potential in Ageing Europe) within the 7th Framework Programme, and participated in several other international projects about population ageing. He specialises in the sociology of the economy, population ageing, the third sector, research methodology and statistics, especially in research and analysis of the labour market. He is the author of many scientific papers about the labour market, the ageing of society and the situation of older people, including articles in international journals and chapters in international books.

Acknowledgements

The research leading to these results has received funding from European Community's 7th Framework Programme (FP7/2007–2013) under grant agreement number 216289.

Foreword

This comprehensive book presents a unique and critical discussion of issues associated with older volunteers across eight different European countries. Its significance lies in its comparative analyses across diverse countries and contexts, and its attention to the contemporary challenges and changes faced by individuals, organisations and government policy in an era of population ageing. Fundamentally, this book asks the key and pertinent question, what can be done to enhance volunteering by older people in a diverse and changing world?

Volunteering is a complex social phenomenon, which has certainly been around for a long time. However, it has been described as an activity that has long been under-estimated, under-researched and under-valued. Studies on employment and the paid work context fill volumes of journals and whole libraries of books, but it is only much more recently that volunteering has been seen as a subject worthy of study.

The importance of volunteering and its relationship to other domains such as the state, the market and the family is increasingly being acknowledged. Volunteering has received some attention through the International Year of Volunteers in 2001 and the ensuing International Year of Volunteering +10 in 2011. Promotion by bodies such as the United Nations has encouraged many national governments to look at their approaches to volunteers and volunteering.

Within this context, the issue of older volunteers is particularly significant. Due to global population ageing, issues associated with a growing proportion of healthy older people are hitting the headlines. Older people are increasingly acknowledged as a segment of the population with much to offer, and volunteering is seen as a viable and positive option for many to keep them active and involved. Yet despite this, there is still a lack of good, comparative literature that investigates this phenomenon in depth and within its social, political and economic context.

This is the enormous value and contribution of this book. It focuses exclusively on older volunteers across different European countries with their diverse traditions and contexts, using active ageing, a key European Union (EU) policy approach, as an overarching theoretical frame. Furthermore, it does so using a conceptual framework that explores all levels of analysis: micro (individuals), meso (organisations), macro (policy and legal context) and structural (welfare regimes). It therefore contributes to knowledge in all of these areas, and as such provides a thoroughly comprehensive view of volunteering by older people.

Part II of the book focuses on each of the eight countries. It highlights the incredible diversity across EU countries, from those with low levels of volunteering, such as Poland and Italy, to those with high levels, such as Denmark and the Netherlands, with their strong volunteer traditions. Using experts in each country to present an analysis of volunteering, the nature of the non-profit sector, and the broader policy context, provide important insights into the topic. In each case, volunteering in later life is also discussed in relation to employment and caring activities, with gender differences explored. A common chapter framework enables a comparison across countries, and highlights the quite dramatic differences between them despite their geographical proximity.

While the diverse scenarios provide fascinating insights into volunteering at the micro level, it is perhaps at the meso level where the contribution of this book is most profound. As the authors acknowledge, there is a growing body of knowledge about individual volunteers, their profiles and motives. However, far less is known about the attitudes of organisations. For example, this book has an excellent discussion of which strategies and approaches work, with organisational perspectives on *age management*, a useful concept from the paid work literature.

This rich collection helps to answer questions such as: What is being done to include more older volunteers? Is their contribution recognised? What works? By being fundamentally research-driven and future-oriented, this volume should attract a broad audience of researchers, policy makers, non-profit managers, volunteer coordinators and volunteers. It offers insights into this topic well beyond Europe, and I believe it will make a great contribution to the emerging evidence base on older volunteers.

Professor Jeni Warburton
Chair, John Richards Initiative,
La Trobe University, Australia
May 2013

Part I

REALISING VOLUNTEERING BY OLDER PEOPLE IN EUROPE

An overarching approach

ONE

Introduction: enhancing volunteering in later life in Europe

Per H. Jensen and Andrea Principi

Introduction

'Active ageing' is a relatively new concept formulated in the 1990s on the basis of work carried out by the World Health Organization (WHO) and subsequently adopted by the European Union (EU) (Walker and Maltby, 2012). Use of this concept has become pervasive, especially in the EU, as a response to the ageing of the population, and to some degree as a result of shifts in the economic and demographic prospects for the future. The idea and concept of active ageing bears some resemblance to the concept of 'active society', that is, a society in which participation in paid employment is the norm for most social groups (Walters, 1997; Jensen and Pfau-Effinger, 2005). The emergence of such ideas and concepts represents a shift from a more passive to a more active citizenship, where paid work is the main route to social inclusion, and where individuals are expected to be autonomous, self-reliant, self-responsible, flexible and able to create their biography individually, continuously adapting to changing external conditions with the consequent individualisation of social risks (Beck, 1986; Sennett, 1998; Esping-Andersen et al, 2002).

The concepts of active ageing and active society, however, are not synonymous. Thus, from the perspective of an active society, the focus in relation to demographic change would be on increasing the employment rates of older workers through pension reforms that promote *late exit* from the labour market (cf Ebbinghaus, 2006, 2011; Immergut et al, 2007; Hofäcker, 2010; Palier, 2010). By contrast, active ageing is a broader concept, referring to a society where older adults are expected to be active beyond their participation in the labour market (Walker, 2002, 2006). In this sense, it is not solely about making older people work longer in paid employment, but also about a society with active older adults. The meaning of active ageing, as a concept that somehow extends beyond the labour market, is clear from the comprehensive definition of active ageing suggested by WHO, according to which it can be defined as a process 'of optimising opportunities for health, participation and security in order to enhance quality of life as people age' (WHO, 2002, p 12). This definition emphasises good health, participation and inclusion of older people in the social, economic, cultural, spiritual and civic areas of life. Similarly, the EU defines active ageing efforts as measures that help older people to 'keep playing an active role in society and live as healthy, independent and fulfilling lives as possible' (2011/413/EU). As such, active ageing is an umbrella concept encompassing various paid and unpaid activities, including volunteering and community work.

International organisations and policy makers are not the only ones to consider voluntary work important; it also appeals broadly to European citizens, among whom about 60 per cent consider volunteering an important activity in their life (Eurobarometer, 2005), and over 20 per cent of whom participate in voluntary and charitable activities (McCloughan et al, 2011). As to volunteering in older age, nearly 80 per cent of European citizens 'strongly' or 'somewhat' recognise that older people make a major contribution to society as volunteers (Eurobarometer, 2009). It has actually been argued that older inactive adults hold considerable volunteer potential, as volunteering 'is one of the possible ways for people to remain active as they age' (Walker, 2011, p 45), while at the same time the activation of older adults in the voluntary sector supposedly benefits both society and the individual (Leopoldina, 2010). On the one hand, voluntary work allows older adults to remain active, enjoying social recognition and integration which contributes to their physical, social and mental well-being throughout their lives, while on the other, the engagement of older adults in voluntary activities such as social care, recreational and local community work, would meet social needs and thus be beneficial to society (Walker, 2002, p 133).

The need to encourage older people to take an active role in the voluntary sector has been extensively debated for decades in the US. In Europe, the issue has been less discussed and practised, however, and coherent strategies aimed at activating older adults in the voluntary sector hardly exist (Principi et al, 2012a). In recent years, however, the interest in active involvement of older people in volunteering has grown, and this is demonstrated by the establishment of the 2012 European Year of Active Ageing and Intergenerational Solidarity that followed the 2011 EU Year of Volunteering. Moreover, the European

Older People's Platform (AGE) is striving to promote volunteering of older people to the largest possible extent (AGE, 2007). In summary, the activation of older adults in voluntary work, brought about by both a shift in the age structure of the population and a stronger awareness of the increasing potentialities of later life, is gaining prominence in European political and scientific discourses.

Aim of this book

As with most new ideas, active ageing in relation to formal voluntary activities presents both new promises and demands. On the one hand, it is expected that voluntary organisations will offer new participatory opportunities for older adults. That is, active ageing holds the promise that older adults can participate in voluntary organisations for as long as they are able to and wish to do so. On the other hand, it is expected (or demanded) from older retired adults that they actively engage themselves in civil society activities. Volunteering may thus be seen as the antidote to retirement being perceived as an exit from roles and relationships, as propagated by earlier theories of 'disengagement' (Cumming and Henry, 1961). Rather, it may tie in with the idea of active citizenship, in which activity is conceived as being the most important medium for bringing people into contact with one another, and as one of the main sources of human identity. In other words, it is expected that the formation of active ageing opportunities may contribute to the creation of new identities, new dispositions and new practices among senior citizens (Sennett, 1998; Bauman, 2003; Honneth, 2003).

It is not self-evident, however, that all of the promises emerging from the active ageing debate will be fulfilled, as many expectations may be highly unrealistic. There is often a considerable distance between ideas and actions, and recommendations seldom have a direct and immediate impact on social behaviour. We don't know, for instance, whether voluntary organisations are actually attractive to older adults, or whether they are willing to recruit older volunteers. It is thus unsure whether a greater supply of older volunteers will be met by a greater demand, which will certainly not be the case in as much as voluntary organisations are structured according to entrenched notions of chronological age.

Even if empirical findings on this issue are now increasing, mainly thanks to the Survey of Health, Ageing and Retirement in Europe (SHARE) (see, for example, Erlinghagen and Hank, 2006) and to other recent large-scale projects funded by the European Commission (for instance, the Activating Senior Potential in Ageing Europe, ASPA project, see www.aspa-eu.com), there are hardly any in-depth studies about volunteering in old age in Europe, in contrast to the vast amount of information on this topic from the US, Canada and Australia in particular (see Fischer and Schaffer, 1993; Morrow-Howell et al, 2001; Gottlieb, 2002; Warburton and Cordingley, 2004). These studies demonstrate some basic differences between the European and US context with regard to volunteering in older age, such as the fact that older US citizens usually volunteer through institutional (that is, federal and/or state-based) programmes, so that US organisations normally have less 'decisional power' on volunteers' ages, while European organisations habitually 'exist' regardless of such programmes, and are therefore freer to decide on their own about (age) recruitment/retainment/management strategies (Principi et al, 2012b). It must also be noted that US studies on volunteering seem to focus mainly on concepts such as 'successful ageing' (Walker and Maltby, 2012) and 'productive ageing' (Fischer and Schaffer, 1993, p 6; Morrow-Howell et al, 2001), rather than on the WHO approach based on active ageing.

However, the available studies do not provide detailed analytical information on whether and how new ideas and concepts such as active aging have an impact on Europe's national welfare systems, voluntary organisations, policies as well as on older citizens' orientations. That is, we don't know how the recent discourse about active ageing has had an influence on different societal levels such as the individual, voluntary organisations, policies and cultural values and belief systems. We therefore urgently need European-wide information in this area in order to be able to assess the factors that promote and inhibit volunteering in older age.

Using the international discourse about active ageing as an overall frame of reference, the purpose of this book is therefore to contribute to a deeper understanding of the inclusion/exclusion of older people in the formal voluntary sector in different European countries, through an analysis of the factors that condition their formal voluntary activities at the micro, meso, macro and structural levels.

At the *micro* or individual level, active ageing is associated with the idea that the roles that the growing number of older adults assume in society are changing. Older people's civic commitment is supposedly increasing, and it is expected that older people will take advantage of voluntary work opportunities, as this in turn has a positive impact on their well-being and personal growth. Active ageing thus represents a departure from notions about inactivity in old age as the norm, epitomised in earlier disengagement theories arguing that older people inevitably withdraw from society and experience a loss of role and social exclusion, often described as the 'pension shock' (Cumming and Henry, 1961; Daatland and Solem, 2011). Rather, active ageing is more in line with activity and continuity theories (Havighurst, 1961; Atchley, 1989), arguing that older adults will strive to the greatest possible extent (that is, in the face of health and physical limitations) to maintain or improve their previous lifestyle and status after retirement. In other words, it is hypothesised that older people themselves wish to remain active for as long as possible. Like the rest of the population, however, older adults do not form a homogeneous group, and the probability of working as a volunteer in older age may be associated with educational background, class position, income level and health conditions (Walker, 2011, p 45). Furthermore, we can expect that the character of voluntary engagement will vary among different age groups, due to diverse dispositions and motivations. With regard to the latter, it is possible, for instance, to distinguish between philanthropic voluntary work, such as contributing to the classical welfare provision against social risks (for example, poverty, homelessness, sickness and so on), and more self-oriented or self-expressive voluntary work, targeted towards cultural, recreational and other activities that do not necessarily address the needs of others (Barker, 1993, p 28; Sivesind et al, 2002). Contrary to what usually happens among younger people, it may be expected that older adults will be more inclined to enrol in philanthropic, rather than self-oriented or self-expressive, kinds of voluntary work, since they participate in particular in humanitarian and religious activities (Daatland and Solem, 2011, p 216). While a considerable body of US studies focusing on this micro level is available, much less is known about the actual pattern and preferences of older Europeans with regard to voluntary work.

At the *meso* level, the level of voluntary organisations, active ageing is associated with the idea that older people in the future will play a key role in many voluntary organisations. Whether this will actually be true or not may depend on whether the prevailing approaches of voluntary organisations will match the abilities, wishes and dispositions of older adults, and several factors may determine the inclusivity of voluntary organisations towards older people. First, some types of voluntary work might suit older people better than others. Organisations engaged in philanthropic voluntary work seem to be better able to meet older adults' individual needs and aspirations compared to organisations engaged in more self-centred or self-expressive kinds of voluntary work. For the prospects and potential of current older workers' future enrolment in voluntary organisations, it is worth mentioning that voluntary work most probably is on the verge of changing from being mainly based on philanthropy to moving towards a kind of work based more on citizens' wish for self-expression (Jensen et al, 2009, p 9). Second, the composition of and the atmosphere in a voluntary organisation may prevent older adults from being or remaining active. Older adults may feel uncomfortable if a voluntary organisation is primarily composed of younger people, as prejudices and/or indirect or direct discrimination towards older people, which is the antithesis of active ageing, may occur. Since a voluntary organisation may prefer younger rather than older volunteers, the character of voluntary organisations may thus be closed or open. Open organisations 'do not deny participation to anyone who wishes to join and is actually in a position to do so', while closed organisations are organisations in which 'participation of certain persons is excluded, limited, or subjected to conditions' (Weber, 1978, p 43). In other words, older adults may experience social exclusion due to the attribution of specific characteristics to older age. Third, the enrolment of older people into voluntary organisations may depend on the organisation's awareness and active appreciation of older volunteers, which in turn may call for the organisations to engage in pro-active age management strategies and measures. Parallel to commercial organisations, age management may be important for recruiting and retaining older adults in voluntary organisations, encompassing the traditional pillars in labour market praxis such as recruitment, training and flexible working practices (Walker, 1998, 2005; Walker and Taylor, 1999). At the meso level, however, very little is known about the strategies of voluntary organisation and their attitudes towards older adults.

At the *macro* level, that is, at the institutional and policy level, active ageing is closely related to a change in the perception of voluntary work. With regards to the altruistic type of volunteering, in the heyday of welfare capitalism, voluntary work was often portrayed as an amateurish and insufficient way of meeting social needs (Salamon, 1995). Permanent austerity and demographic change has, however, led to a change in the institutional perception of voluntary organisations. As a welfare-producing entity, voluntary work has increasingly been seen as a possible solution to economic and demographic challenges in several European countries (Beck, 2000). Ideas about voluntary organisations as a new kind of safety net towards social risks have led to a new definition of the role of the welfare state and of welfare policies. To pursue active ageing strategies, the welfare state is supposed to assume a new role as enabler and facilitator in the formation of new public–private partnerships (Walker, 2006, p 86), downplaying ideology and class as constitutive elements in social policy (Henriksen et al, 2012). Of course, these new visions imply a revision of policies and practices, that new approaches to governance are developed, and that voluntary organisations develop into a so-called 'social enterprise model'.

In connection to this, national governments are increasingly expected to change their perception of older people becoming more aware of their potentially relevant societal contribution, and thus considering them an important resource for society rather than only as a group of vulnerable and sick people to be protected. In light of this, active ageing calls for policy makers to encourage volunteering among older adults as well as encouraging voluntary organisations to recruit and retain older people. Despite the growing awareness that important changes in policies are needed to achieve changes in the behaviour of organisations and older adults *if* active ageing as a political slogan is to be turned into practice, very little is known about how national policies really stimulate the supply of and demand for older volunteers, or what factors may be responsible for the enrolment of older adults into voluntary work.

Ideas about active ageing have been developed at an international level and call for an integrated approach across European countries. It is more or less expected that it is transferable across different *social structures and welfare systems*. We cannot, however, a priori presume that identical policies are accorded the same meaning and will produce the same outcomes in different welfare systems. Welfare policies are embedded in a national context of cultural values, ideals and belief systems which mark the extent to which state intervention is most adequate, how welfare should ideally be provided and so on (Pfau-Effinger, 1999). The welfare regime approach originally suggested by Esping-Andersen (1990, 1996), and later integrated by the contribution of several scholars (Lewis, 1992; Anttonen and Sipilä, 1996; Ferrera, 1996; Pfau-Effinger, 1999; Manning, 2004), argues that the differences between welfare regimes (that is, between social democratic, conservative, liberal, Mediterranean and post-Communist welfare regimes) are based on variations in the 'basic principles' on which welfare state policies are founded, for example, in relation to solidarity, equality, the role of the state versus the market, of the family within the care system and the related (un)willingness of populations to engage in voluntary work. Accordingly, the extent and nature of voluntary work differ from one national welfare system to another. In some countries, charitable help to people in need predominates, whereas it is self-expressive kinds of voluntary work that outweighs in other countries, all this being related to different interactive processes and linkages between the state, the family, the labour market and the voluntary sector. This type of interaction is common knowledge. It has been argued, for instance, that comprehensive public social services tend to destroy intermediate institutions and crowd out voluntary work opportunities (Rostow, 1960; Fukuyama, 1995), while a lack of public service provision might foster non-profit organisations to replace the lack of public services (Weisbrod, 1977), but at the same time also reduce the probability of volunteering at the individual level, as care obligations lessen the time available for voluntary work (Marks, 1977).

While some empirical evidence on the characteristics of the third sector and the involvement of older people in volunteering already exists (Salamon and Anheier, 1998; Warburton and Jeppsson Grassman, 2011), in-depth comparative knowledge as to how institutions, policies and processes influence the involvement of older adults in voluntary organisations remains rather rudimentary, and promising practices that can be transferred from one national welfare system to another are far from being clearly identified.

Research questions

As volunteering by older adults is a highly complex phenomenon, no single causal factor can explain the patterns of voluntary work among older people. This book therefore seeks to account for the interaction and complexity of factors that condition the involvement of older adults in voluntary organisations, to identify the current characteristics and future prospects of volunteering by older people, and to search for answers to the following main research questions at four distinct levels:

- *Micro or individual level:* what are older adults' motivations for and preferences towards voluntary work?
- *Meso or organisational level:* what are the opportunities and restrictions for older people's volunteering? In this respect, how do interactions take place between major institutions in society (family, public, private and voluntary organisations)?
- *Macro or policy level:* what policies have been established to strengthen the role of older people in society through volunteering and to improve the match between the 'supply' of older volunteers and the 'demand' of voluntary organisations?

- *Structural level:* how do welfare regimes, including cultural values, condition volunteering by older people?

Cutting across these four levels of research questions, the aim of this volume is to analyse the complex and probably contradictory interrelations between national welfare models/mixes, welfare policies, voluntary organisations and individual factors. This will lead to policy considerations based on insights as to what kind of policy mixes and promising practices best serve the enrolment of older people in voluntary work. Similarly, which cultures, institutions, processes and actors support or constrain the transferability of promising practices from one country to another will also be assessed. The overall question on which this volume is based is the following: under what circumstances can volunteering function as a real basis for self-fulfilment and social integration of older adults in Europe?

Definitions

In light of the complexity of voluntary work, it is no surprise that it has been defined differently in various studies. With regard to our investigation, the following are the basic definitions adopted concerning what we consider to be 'volunteering' and 'voluntary organisations'.

As for the first, in some cases 'volunteering' has been considered to include paid work (Pfau-Effinger et al, 2009), or has been defined ignoring the issue of remuneration (for example, Hank and Stuck, 2008). In general, however, volunteering is considered as embracing a large range of activities undertaken by a person of their own free will, without concern for financial gain (Naegele and Schnabel, 2010; McCloughan et al, 2011), or for reimbursement of expenses (often partial) that cannot, however, be considered as actual remuneration (ILO, 2011). The work of the International Labour Organization (ILO) is particularly helpful in this respect as it reviews previous attempts to define volunteer work. All of the reviewed definitions underline that this activity is provided 'unpaid', or 'without pay', 'without being paid' or with 'no monetary or in-kind payment' (ILO, 2011, p 12).

Another point concerns what kind of activity should be considered as volunteering. A first specification is that volunteer work may be intended as the charitable and altruistic provision of help to people in need, thus involving a relationship between a volunteer helping a recipient and a recipient benefiting from this help (Haski-Leventhal et al, 2009, p 149). However, some observers underline that volunteering activities may include those that benefit the wider community or society, which may also be self-expressive in their intrinsic nature (for example, cultural, environmental, in sports organisations), while still having an indirect benefit for individuals in the community (Barker, 1993, p 28; Sivesind et al, 2002). Furthermore, volunteering may be formal or informal. Formal volunteering takes place in an organisational framework, whereas informal voluntary work is provided, for example, as unstructured self-help or assistance to neighbours (Naegele and Schnabel, 2010). In general, however, care to immediate family members is not considered volunteer work (ILO, 2011).

In light of the above, and being aware that some blurred situations may occur in different national contexts (one of the aims of this study is to analyse national differences), for the purposes of this book we consider volunteering as an *activity having either an altruistic or self-expressive nature carried out in voluntary organisations, freely chosen and unpaid*.

This means that we should also define what we mean by 'voluntary organisation'. Voluntary organisations as legal entities seldom exist in the European scenario, and furthermore they might not cover all of the activities included in our definition of volunteering (see, for example, the Italian case described in Chapter Three, this volume). Most often, voluntary work takes place in non-profit organisations that can sometimes be strongly dependent on paid employees. Some non-profit organisations resemble commercial organisations in that they sell goods and services although without the goal of making a profit, even though they may wish to make money for charitable reasons such as maintaining a museum or a sports club. For the aims of this book, we use an umbrella definition of voluntary organisation as any organisation in which people formally volunteer, in order to try to cover the phenomenon in its entirety. According to this perspective, voluntary organisations are assumed to be, to a large extent, non-profit and third sector organisations (including trade unions, housing organisations, and so on), excluding, however, those employing exclusively paid staff. In this perspective, voluntary organisations may also be private (for example, a private museum) or organised by public bodies (for example, user organisations in hospitals and schools). In light of these specifications and the heterogeneity of voluntary organisations, we use (depending on data availability in the different countries included in the study) the terms 'voluntary', 'civil society' and 'non profit' organisations/associations as synonymous in this volume.

Methodology

As active ageing is a multidisciplinary theme, the research questions highlighted above are answered by means of a comprehensive, interdisciplinary and comparative approach, analysing factors favouring volunteering among older people. Eight countries are included in the analysis, representing different kinds of welfare regimes: Denmark, England (data are shown for the UK, when unavailable for England), France, Germany, Italy, the Netherlands, Poland and Sweden.

Literature on volunteering by older adults has so far primarily been occupied with analysing micro-level factors. Very little research has been done on the meso or organisational level, whereas research on the macro and structural level hardly exists. This has influenced our research strategy. Two types of studies form the basis of this volume: country studies through national profile descriptions, on the one hand, and case studies in voluntary organisations, on the other. Both approaches have been used to analyse each of the eight countries included in this investigation. The country studies analyse how discourses about active ageing promoted at the international level have been translated and transferred into national efforts to promote and sustain volunteering by older people, as well as how structural, policy, organisational and individual features interact in different countries relative to volunteering by older people. The organisational case studies aim instead to analyse how European voluntary organisations conceive of and manage older people as volunteers. The national profile descriptions constitute Part II of this book, while the results from the case studies are presented in Part III.

National profile descriptions (Part II)

National profile descriptions (Chapters Three to Ten) include all of the aspects considered in the conceptual framework presented in detail in Chapter Two. They analyse volunteering in older age at the micro, meso and macro level, and consider its relationship with the labour market and care system within the specific country's welfare regime. Based on the qualitative and/or quantitative data available in the literature, the eight country chapters have been drawn up following the same structure to facilitate comparison. After a short introduction describing the characteristics of the country welfare regime and specific rules governing the voluntary sector, a more comprehensive illustration of voluntary work is presented, including data on volunteers by sector, gender and age, as well as a more specific focus on older volunteers in relation to several individual and organisational dimensions. A third section analyses in more depth the opportunities for and restrictions on older volunteers at the individual, organisational and policy level, by also examining possible conflicts between volunteering and labour market participation, as well as between volunteering and family care. Specific attention is dedicated to the organisational and policy level, analysing whether and how organisational and welfare policies are able to improve the match between the supply of older candidates and the demands of civil society organisations. Each chapter concludes with a summary of main findings and reflections as to what can be learned from the experience of the specific country.

Case studies (Part III)

To fill the lack of information at the meso level on this topic, we have analysed the under-investigated perspective of voluntary organisations by carrying out case studies in several European voluntary organisations. The first of the three chapters composing Part III of the book (Chapter Eleven) is dedicated to the results emerging from these case studies, describing the organisations involved and their strategies in managing older volunteers. In the second chapter (Chapter Twelve), the organisational perspective is adopted to analyse the societal framework and in particular the role of work for the labour market and that of family care of older relatives, in order to understand its impact on the volunteering of older people and its consequences for voluntary organisations. The third and last chapter (Chapter Thirteen) points to the future, and concerns organisational intentions about their older volunteer workforce in terms of (age) management, to respond to major expected future developments in society at the micro, meso as well as macro level. The three chapters consist of a cross-case analysis on cross-case issues (Yin, 2009).

The activity sector and age structure of the volunteer workforce were adopted as the main criteria for the selection of voluntary organisations in each country. In each country we focused on the three main sectors of voluntary activity based on the International Classification of Non-profit Organisations (ICNPO) that was chosen as a common criterion of classification among the European countries involved in the study (through a re-classification of national data when needed). With regard to the volunteers' age structure, the organisations were selected according to the share of older volunteers among all volunteers employed, and divided into two main groups: those with a rather high share (or above average) and those with a rather low share (or below average). This step allowed us to achieve a better insight into whether organisations adopt different policies/behaviours or have different attitudes according to the age composition of their volunteer workforce. The intention was not so much to establish an exact number of organisations to be investigated according to their stratification in terms of volunteers' age composition, but rather to have a sufficient number of them in both groups (at least 25 per cent of the whole sample) in order to identify the mechanisms affecting organisational behaviours and attitudes in relation to the age composition of the volunteers.

From spring 2009 to spring 2011, 73 case studies in voluntary organisations were carried out across Europe in the eight countries involved in the study: nine case studies were carried out each in Germany, Italy, the Netherlands, Poland and Sweden, eight in England and ten each in Denmark and France. The case study method was chosen because it allows the investigation of a phenomenon within its real-life context with limited resources, providing results that can be considered theoretically enriching even though it does not give the possibility of generalising results to populations or universes (Yin, 1994, 2009).

To select the voluntary organisations according to the sampling criteria, the following recruitment channels were used: available national data; suggestions from national experts in the field; and other channels (including the internet). Pre-interview information on the main sectors of activity and on the share of older volunteers was requested from the organisations in order to check criteria for inclusion.

Despite the quite broad range of recruitment channels, for several reasons the study for some countries includes data for organisations in different sectors from the main ones. Among these reasons, which are explained in detail in Principi and Lamura (2011), we should mention the need to obtain information on the activities of older volunteers (in Sweden and in Poland) and to have a clearer picture of gender-specific features (Denmark); in the Netherlands one case study in the health sector was based on two previous studies, since it was found to be a very profitable way of describing the volunteering of older people in this sector.

The final sample is presented in Chapter Eleven. Table 11.1 provides the following information for each organisation: country; name; main sector of activity; main services provided; number of volunteers; share of older volunteers in the organisation; and percentage of female volunteers. Both national/umbrella and local voluntary organisations were included in the study, while voluntary organisations exclusively targeting younger volunteers were excluded. In-text references to organisations through the three chapters are provided to show exemplary results, and are identified by writing part or all of the organisation's name (see Table 11.1, note a, for details).

Directors, leaders of the organisations, human resources managers and/or coordinators of volunteers and activities were interviewed in a replication design (Yin, 2009), and common guidelines were adopted in all countries to investigate opportunities and restrictions for older volunteers according to the same framework. The guidelines, conceived as a relatively open and flexible instrument for the compilation of the relevant information, were made up of five main sections: case study background; organisational views and policies; specific initiatives for older volunteers; external aspects; and future prospects on volunteers' age management.

Book structure

As anticipated in the previous section, Chapter Two proposes a conceptual framework for the understanding and discussion of volunteering of older people. This conceptual framework will function as a point of reference in the subsequent chapters and the whole book. It provides an integrated synopsis of the different dimensions of analysis, and also presents the state-of-the-art literature concerning the dimensions identified. According to this main framework, Chapters Three to Ten include national overviews on the state of volunteering by older people in the eight countries included in the study, the analysis constituting Part II of the book. In Part III, Chapters Eleven to Thirteen, we present the results of the 73 case studies carried out in voluntary organisations across Europe. The main content of these chapters has been described above. Here it is worthwhile underlining that the three chapters address the volunteering of older people from an organisational perspective by dealing with the internal management of older volunteers (Chapter Eleven); interactions with the welfare mix (Chapter Twelve); and future perspectives (Chapter Thirteen). Finally, Chapter Fourteen analyses the findings illustrated in the previous chapters in a cross-national perspective in order to then identify the main challenges to enhancing formal volunteering among older people on a European-wide scale.

References

2011/413/EU: Recommendation on the research joint programming initiative 'More years, better lives — the potential and challenges of demographic change'. *Official Journal of the European Union* L183 of 13.7.2011 p. 28

AGE (2007) *Healthy ageing: Good practice examples, recommendations, policy actions*, Brussels: The European Older People's Platform.

Anttonen, A. and Sipilä, J. (1996) 'European social care services: is it possible to identify models?', *Journal of European Social Policy*, vol 6, no 2, pp 87-100.

Atchley, R. (1989) 'A continuity theory of normal ageing', *The Gerontologist*, vol 29, no 2, pp 183-90.

Barker, D.G. (1993) 'Values and volunteering', in J.D. Smith (ed) *Volunteering in Europe*, Volunteering Action Research, No 2, London: The Volunteer Centre, pp 10-31.

Bauman, Z. (2003) *Liquid love*, Cambridge: Polity Press.

Beck, U. (1986) *Risikogesellschaft. Auf dem weg in eine andere moderne (Risk society: Towards a new modernity)*, Frankfurt am Main: Suhrkamp.

Beck, U. (2000) *The brave new world of work*, Cambridge: Polity Press.

Cumming, E. and Henry, W.E. (1961) *Growing old*, New York: Basic Books.

Daatland, S.O. and Solem, P.E. (2011) *Aldring og samfunn (Ageing and society)*, Oslo: Fagbokforlaget.

Ebbinghaus, B. (2006) *Reforming early retirement in Europe, Japan and the USA*, Oxford: Oxford University Press.

Ebbinghaus, B. (ed.) (2011) *The varieties of pension governance: Pension privatization in Europe*, Oxford: Oxford University Press.

Erlinghagen, M. and Hank, K. (2006) 'The participation of older European in volunteer work', *Ageing & Society*, vol 26, no 4, pp 567-84.

Esping-Andersen, G. (1990) *The three worlds of welfare capitalism*, Oxford: Polity Press.

Esping-Andersen, G. (1996) *Welfare states in transition: National adaptations in global economies*, London: Sage Publications.

Esping-Andersen, G., Gallie, D., Hemerijck, A. and Myles, J. (2002) *Why we need a new welfare state*, Oxford: Oxford University Press.

Eurobarometer (2005) *Social capital*, Special 223/Wave 62.2.

Eurobarometer (2009) *Intergenerational solidarity*, Flash 269.

Ferrera, M. (1996) 'The "southern model" of welfare in social Europe', *Journal of European Social Policy*, vol 6, no 1, pp 17-36.

Fischer, L.R. and Schaffer, K.B. (1993) *Older volunteers: A guide to research and practice*, Newbury Park, CA: Sage Publications.

Fukuyama, F. (1995) *Trust: The social virtues and the creation of prosperity*, New York: Free Press.

Gottlieb, B.H. (2002) 'Older volunteers: a precious resource under pressure', *Canadian Journal of Aging*, vol 21, no 1, pp 5-9.

Hank, K. and Stuck, S. (2008) 'Volunteer work, informal help, and care among the 50+ in Europe: further evidence for "linked" productive activities at older ages', *Social Science Research*, vol 37, no 4, pp 1280-91.

Haski-Leventhal, D., Meijs, L.C.P.M. and Hustinx, L. (2009) 'The third-party model: enhancing volunteering through governments, corporations and educational institutions', *Journal of Social Policy*, vol 39, no 1, pp 139-58.

Havighurst, R.J. (1961) 'Successful aging', *The Gerontologist*, vol 1, no 1, pp 8-13.

Henriksen, L.S., Smith, S.R. and Zimmer, A. (2012) 'At the eve of convergence? Transformations of social service provision in Denmark, Germany and the United States', *Voluntas*, vol 23, no 2, pp 458-501.

Hofäcker, D. (2010) *Older workers in a globalizing world: An international comparison of retirement and late-career patterns in Western industrialised countries*, Cheltenham: Edward Elgar.

Honneth, A. (2003) *Kampf um Anerkennung. Zur moralischen grammatik sozialer konflikte (The struggle for recognition: The moral grammar of social conflicts)*, Frankfurt am Main: Suhrkampf.

ILO (International Labour Organization) (2011) *Manual on the measurement of volunteer work*, Geneva: ILO.

Immergut, E.M., Anderson, K.M. and Schulze, I. (eds) (2007) *The handbook of West European pension politics*, Oxford: Oxford University Press.

Jensen, P.H. and Pfau-Effinger, B. (2005) '"Active" citizenship: The changing face of welfare', in J.G. Andersen, A.M. Guillemard, P.H. Jensen and B. Pfau-Effinger (eds) *The changing face of welfare: Consequences and outcomes from a citizenship perspective*, Bristol: Policy Press, pp 1-14.

Jensen, P.H., Pfau-Effinger, B. and Flaquer, L. (2009) 'The development of informal work in the work-welfare arrangements of European societies', in B. Pfau-Effinger, L. Flaquer and P.H. Jensen (eds) *Formal and informal work: The hidden work regime in Europe*, New York and London: Routledge, pp 3-20.

Leopoldina (2010) *More years, more life – Recommendations of the Joint Academy Initiative on Aging*, Halle: Deutsche Akademie der Naturforscher Leopoldina eV – Nationale Akademie der Wissenschaften.

Lewis, J. (1992) 'Gender and the development of welfare regimes', *Journal of European Social Policy*, vol 2, no 3, pp 159-73.

Manning, N. (2004) 'Diversity and change in pre-accession Central and Eastern Europe since 1989', *Journal of European Social Policy*, vol 14, no 3, pp 211-32.

Marks, S.R. (1977) 'Multiple roles and role strain: some notes on human energy, time and commitment', *American Sociological Review*, vol 42, no 6, pp 921-36.

McCloughan, P., Batt, W.H., Costine M. and Scully, D. (2011) *Participation in volunteering and unpaid work. Second European Quality of Life Survey*, Dublin: European Foundation for the Improvement of Living and Working Conditions.

Morrow-Howell, N., Hinterlong, J. and Sherraden, M. (eds) (2001) *Productive ageing: Concepts and challenges*, Baltimore, MD: The Johns Hopkins University Press.

Naegele, G. and Schnabel, E. (2010) *Measures for social inclusion of the elderly: The case of volunteering*, Dublin: European Foundation for the Improvement of Living and Working Conditions.

Palier, B. (ed) (2010) *A long goodbye to Bismarck? The politics of welfare reform in Continental Europe*, Amsterdam: Amsterdam University Press.

Pfau-Effinger, B. (1999) 'The modernization of family and motherhood in Western Europe', in R. Crompton (ed) *Restructuring gender relations and employment. The decline of the male breadwinner*, Oxford: Oxford University Press, pp 60-79.

Pfau-Effinger, B., Flaquer, L. and Jensen, P.H. (2009) *Formal and informal work. The hidden work regime in Europe*, New York and London: Routledge.

Principi, A. and Lamura, G. (2011) *Opportunities for older people in the civil society. International report*, ASPA Project, Deliverable D.5.2, Ancona: National Institute of Health and Science on Aging (INRCA).

Principi, A., Chiatti, C., Frerichs, F. and Lamura, G. (2012a) 'The engagement of older people in civil society organisations', *Educational Gerontology*, vol 38, no 2, pp 83-106.

Principi, A., Lindley, R., Perek-Bialas, J. and Turek, K. (2012b) 'Volunteering in older age: an organizational perspective', *International Journal of Manpower*, vol 33, no 6, pp 685-703.

Rostow, W.W. (1960) *The stages of economic growth*, London: Cambridge University Press.

Salamon, L.M. (1995) *Partners in public service*, Baltimore, MD: The Johns Hopkins University Press.

Salamon, L.M. and Anheier, H.K. (1998) 'Social origins of civil society. Explaining the non-profit sector cross-nationally', *Voluntas*, vol 9, no 3, pp 213-48.

Sennett, R. (1998) *The corrosion of character: Personal consequences of work in the new capitalism*, New York, NY: W.W. Norton.

Sivesind, K.H., Lorentzen, H., Selle, P. and Wollebæk, D. (2002) *The voluntary sector in Norway. Compositions, changes, and causes*, Oslo: Institutt for Samfunnsforskning.

Walker, A. (1998) *Managing an ageing workforce: A guide to good practice*, Dublin: European Foundation.

Walker, A. (2002) 'A strategy for active ageing', *International Social Security Review*, vol 55, no 1, pp 121-39.

Walker, A. (2005) 'The emergence of age management in Europe', *International Journal of Organisational Behaviour*, vol 10, no 1, pp 685-97.

Walker, A. (2006) 'Active ageing in employment: its meaning and potential', *Asia-Pacific Review*, vol 13, no 1, pp 78-93.

Walker A. (ed) (2011) *The future of ageing research in Europe: A road map*, Sheffield: University of Sheffield.

Walker, A. and Maltby, T. (2012) 'Active ageing: a strategic policy solution to demographic ageing in the European Union', *International Journal of Social Welfare*.

Walker, A. and Taylor, P. (1999) 'Good practice in the employment of older workers in Europe', *Ageing International*, vol 25, no 3, pp 62-79.

Walters, W. (1997) 'The "active society": new designs for social policy', *Policy & Politics*, vol 25, no 3, pp 221-34.

Warburton, J. and Cordingley, S. (2004) 'The contemporary challenges of volunteering in an ageing Australia', *Australian Journal on Volunteering*, vol 9, no 2, pp 67-74.

Warburton, J. and Jeppsson-Grassman, E. (2011) 'Variations in voluntary association involvement by seniors across different social welfare regimes', *International Journal of Social Welfare*, vol 20, no 2, pp 180-91.

Weber, M. (1978) *Economy and society*, Berkeley and Los Angeles, CA: University of California Press.

Weisbrod, B. (1977) *The voluntary nonprofit sector*, Lexington, MA: Lexington Books.

WHO (World Health Organization) (2002) *Active ageing: A policy framework*, Geneva: WHO.

Yin, R. (1994) *Case study research: Design and methods* (2nd edn), Beverly Hills, CA: Sage Publications.

Yin, R. (2009) *Case study research: Design and methods* (4th edn), Thousand Oaks, CA: Sage Publications.

TWO

Volunteering in older age: a conceptual and analytical framework

Per H. Jensen, Giovanni Lamura and Andrea Principi

Introduction

In this chapter we present the general conceptual and analytical framework adopted in this volume to explore the issues associated with volunteering in older age. The proposed framework, which draws on existing literature, represents an attempt to integrate the relevant dimensions identified in Chapter One and is used as a reference throughout the book. A starting point for our considerations is, as anticipated in the previous chapter, that voluntary work has lately gained in prominence and importance across the world. Since the United Nations (UN) declared 2001 the International Year of Volunteers, awareness campaigns encouraging voluntary work have primarily been addressed at the general public, while more recent attempts to encourage volunteering have targeted older adults. In Europe, older adults are increasingly considered to be a resource that can be drawn on by the voluntary sector, and the establishment of the European Year of Active Ageing and Intergenerational Solidarity in 2012, following the Year of Volunteering in 2011, clearly shows how efforts in this respect have been growing. Moreover, organisations such as the European Older People's Platform (AGE) have been promoting volunteering among older people as a tool to enable them to continue to participate in society and to better cope with daily life (AGE, 2007).

Volunteering has thus become a mantra for active and healthy ageing, although it is not always clear what it is all about. As anticipated in the previous chapter, basically, volunteering expresses itself as a relationship between two actors: a *volunteer*, who, as a provider gives his/her time freely to help or support others, and a client or *recipient*, who accepts the services provided by the volunteer (Haski-Leventhal et al, 2009, p 149). Accordingly, voluntary work may be defined as unpaid help or support given to another person who is not a member of one's family. This gift relation between the volunteer and recipient is freely chosen rather than being based on coercion, subordination or dominance, and both partners are expected to gain from the relationship. The recipient gets an unfulfilled need fulfilled, while the benefits from volunteering are numerous and include: strengthening of the social inclusion of the helper/provider, reduced loneliness and improved physical and psychological well-being (Wilson, 2000; Haski-Leventhal et al, 2009, p 140; Tang et al, 2010).

Volunteering in older age is affected by a variety of different and complex factors. This volume, however, is based on the assumption that five major factors condition the propensity of older people to engage in voluntary work: (1) at the *micro* (or individual) level motivations and predispositions among older people towards voluntary work presuppose voluntary practices; (2) at the *meso* level (that of voluntary organisations) the demand for older volunteers structures the opportunities for voluntary work for older people; (3) voluntary organisations interact with other welfare-producing institutions such as the labour market, care systems, family and so on, to constitute the specific *welfare mix* of a given country, which is an important determinant for voluntary work opportunities for older people; (4) at the *macro* level government policies may encourage or impede growth in voluntary work opportunity for older people; just as (5) the specific *welfare regime* and the set of cultural values and beliefs that characterise it may determine volunteering among older people. Table 2.1 represents an attempt to visualise these different dimensions.

This conceptual framework is used in the following discussion in which the different dimensions will be scrutinised. It is worthwhile underlining again that the focus of this volume is not so much on the needs of recipients or on the relationship between volunteers and recipients; rather, the focus at the *micro* level is on how the choice of becoming an older volunteer is socially structured. To this end, we examine a prototypical older volunteer in terms of social resources, socio-economic position and individual characteristics, and analyse the subjective dispositions and factors that motivate older adults to engage in voluntary work, identifying the type of voluntary work that older adults are inclined to do, and distinguishing between altruistic and self-expressive forms of voluntary work from a supply-side perspective.

At the *meso* level, voluntary or non-profit organisations represent the 'place' in which most voluntary work is carried out and 'transformed' from an informal to a formal activity. As already seen in Chapter One,

Table 2.1: Structuring mechanisms behind the extent and character of voluntary work among older adults

Structural or welfare regime level, including cultural values and belief systems	Social democratic, liberal, conservative, Mediterranean, post-Communist
Macro level	Specific policies conditioning voluntary work at the meso and micro level
Meso or the welfare mix level	Interactions between voluntary organisations, labour markets, public and private care systems, and the family
Micro or individual level	Characteristics, motivations and predispositions among older people towards voluntary work

voluntary organisations are a highly heterogeneous phenomenon. Sometimes they depend on the use of formal paid employees or resemble commercial organisations selling goods and services (although without the goal of making a profit), while in other cases they are anchored in local communities or have national or even international scope, and may be organised by public sector organisations or represent the interests of particular organisations such as trade unions. In this volume, we use the terms 'voluntary', 'civil society' and 'non-profit organisations' and 'associations' synonymously to refer to an organisation engaging in non-profit activities for the benefit of the wider society. As such, voluntary organisations orchestrate and structure the demand for older volunteers by defining the extent and quality of activities that they are expected to do. It would therefore make sense to investigate whether voluntary organisations perceive older adults as relevant and attractive volunteers or, if this is not the case, identify what the organisational barriers to volunteering by older people are, and what voluntary organisations actually do to recruit and retain them. At this *meso* level relevant research questions would therefore be: what type of organisations are especially targeting and recruiting older volunteers? Do voluntary organisations employ special measures in order to recruit older volunteers? Are voluntary organisations adjusting work tasks to meet the preferences and dispositions of older volunteers? From the point of view of retention, relevant questions are: how do voluntary organisations support older volunteers to enable them to continue to work as volunteers? What is actually offered to older volunteers by organisations (for instance, education or financial benefits)?

Voluntary organisations compete, complement or cooperate with other social institutions such as the family, the labour market and public welfare providers. Thus, a variety of welfare providers exist within the system of welfare production as a whole, and the division of labour among the different parts of this global system is often described as the *welfare mix*. The welfare mix in a given country at a given point in time is not an outcome of deliberated decision-making or strategic choices. The different welfare-producing entities, however, are interlinked, as decision-making in one sector has repercussions on the functioning of the other sectors (cf institutional choice theories), although the different welfare-producing entities cannot fully substitute for each other. Relevant questions thus become: what are the consequences of an increasingly older workforce, that is, the effects of increased participation of older people in the labour force, on their contribution to voluntary activities? Are there opportunities for collaboration between companies and voluntary organisations? Does it matter for volunteering in older age whether elder care is undertaken informally by older people? What is the relationship between the predominant type of elder care, family forms and the inclination to volunteer in older age?

At the *macro* level, governments can employ policies favouring volunteering among older people. As public policies frame the legal and practical conditions of voluntary organisations, they may stimulate the formation of certain organisations while stalling others, thereby improving or undermining the opportunities for older adults to participate. The legal framework of volunteering, including social policies such as tax policies, is conducive for the formation and trajectory of development of voluntary organisations and their staff (Goss, 2010). Major questions therefore become: what is the legal framework of volunteering? Does it push voluntary work in certain directions? Are these directions old or young-friendly? Does the legal framework support altruistic or self-expressive forms of voluntary work? Do special programmes exist for the inclusion of older adults in the voluntary sector? And how does the volunteering of older people figure on the political agenda? These questions are important because public policy helps to structure the orientation of voluntary organisations as well as the participatory energies of older people.

The *structural* level refers to the properties of identities and institutions within a social system as a whole, and it is often conceptualised as welfare regimes embedded in distinct cultural and ideological frameworks. In this volume, a distinction is made between five welfare regimes: social democratic, conservative, liberal, Mediterranean and post-Communist. This welfare regime approach presupposes that there is an organic interconnection between the structural characteristics of the institutions and identities in the system. In this volume we seek to analyse the interconnections between, on the one hand, the structural level epitomised by welfare regimes, and on the other, identities and cultural orientations of individual actors at the *micro* level; how the character of voluntary organisations at the *meso* level are coloured by the social context; how different policy frameworks at the *macro* level are shaped and develop in different welfare regimes; and how central welfare-producing institutions are mixed in different ways to produce different *welfare mixes* in different societies. Regarding this latter point, for instance, we examine the links between volunteering and the participation of older workers in the labour force, as well as the association of volunteering in older age with family forms and the provision of formal/informal elder care in different countries.

In the following, the general theoretical framework presented above is scrutinised in more detail to provide an overview of the empirical evidence emerging from the literature. This is done in order to integrate the relevant dimensions for older people's volunteering that will be used as a guide for the organisation of the following chapters in this volume.

The *micro* level: older volunteers

For decades, two opposing theories have dominated debates as to what drives the activities and behaviour of individuals in older age. On the one hand, disengagement theories argue that older people inevitably tend to grow more fragile, less social and less active, leading to voluntary retirement, which frees them from societal roles and allows for vegetative activities and self-reflection (Cumming and Henry, 1961; Daatland and Solem, 2011). Disengagement theories predict a decrease in the interaction between the ageing person and society; thus it can be assumed that older people are unlikely recruits for voluntary activities, according to these theories. In contrast, activity and continuity theories argue that satisfaction in old age is preconditioned by remaining active and continuing earlier lifestyles (Havighurst, 1961; Maddox, 1968; Atchley, 1989), making voluntary work an obvious choice for older people in maintaining a positive self-image, good health and longevity (Gottlieb and Gillespie, 2008). Neither disengagement theories nor activity and continuity theories have an all-encompassing explanatory power, as older adults are not a homogeneous group: some remain active, while others become more disengaged as they age. This therefore raises the following question: what makes some older adults more willing and able to volunteer than others?

Existing literature asserts that volunteering in older age is to a large extent a matter of having strong personal resources (Wilson and Musick, 1997; Tang, 2006; Cattan et al, 2011). Factors such as good health, which makes older people capable of volunteering (Li and Ferraro, 2005), community attachment and strong family, friends and social networks in general (Warburton et al, 2001; Kochera et al, 2005; Morrow-Howell, 2007; Wilson, 2012, p 182), as well as, perhaps most importantly, a high educational attainment (Fischer and Schaffer, 1993; Erlinghagen and Hank, 2006), are all strong predictors of volunteering in old age. The individual's income and socio-economic position are also significant factors behind voluntary activism in later life, as several studies have revealed that a high economic status encourages volunteering, while low-income earners are less likely to volunteer (see Warburton et al, 2001, for an overview).

Employment status, that is, job and work position, is normally considered to be important for the availability of older people for voluntary work (Haski-Leventhal et al, 2009), because participation in the labour market has, with some exceptions, a positive effect on the decision to participate in voluntary activities. The exceptions include the so-called *scarcity* theory (Marks, 1977), which holds that time spent on market work or family responsibilities, including informal family caregiving, usually reduces the time available for voluntary work, provoking a crowding-out effect. This effect may be softened by part-time work, as part-time workers are more inclined than full-time workers to engage in voluntary activities (cf Wilson, 2012, p 186). A second exception is represented by the observation that retirement or labour market exclusion may increase the propensity to volunteer, as volunteering may compensate for the loss of the work role and reduce the stigma attached to being inactive, although evidence seems to indicate that retirement in itself does not cause older people to take up volunteering, as those who do it in older age were most probably volunteers before retirement too (cf Wilson, 2012, p 190).

Individual characteristics such as gender, age, personal traits and subjective disposition can help to explain a propensity towards volunteering. As empirical evidence shows, the role of gender in this respect is not unequivocal, leading some authors to be cautious about generalising gender effects on volunteering (Cutler and Hendriks, 2000). However, it is quite clear that the frequency of volunteering decreases with age (Ehlers et al, 2011), although the availability of time after retirement may explain why older people are engaged in voluntary work for more hours than younger people (Morrow-Howell, 2007). Self-confidence, self-assurance, religious beliefs, church membership as well as individual values, for instance, the notion that one should help those in need, may also stimulate civic engagement and the willingness of older people to volunteer (Wymer, 1999).

Volunteering, however, may also be driven by motivations such as the desire to have more social contacts, to be active, to cultivate personal interests and goals, or for personal growth (Fischer and Schaffer, 1993; Steinberg and Cain, 2004). Following this line of argument, economists have claimed that volunteering is based on utility-based decision-making, that is, that individual choices to minimise expected costs and maximise benefits may have an impact on the decision to enter the voluntary sector (Butrica et al, 2009). Such benefits also depend on the degree of fulfilment of older volunteers' main motivational drivers. The latter are often associated with a need for emotional gratification (to feel good, to maintain a sense of self or to deepen intimacy in social contacts) rather than increasing one's knowledge, as younger people more frequently aim to (Fung et al, 2001). Thus, older people's decisions to volunteer may be more commonly linked either directly or indirectly to benefits such as improved social inclusion, reduced loneliness and increased physical and psychological well-being (Wilson, 2000; Haski-Leventhal et al, 2009, p 140; Tang et al, 2010).

These observations suggest that, in the end, despite its many different forms, voluntary engagement can be classified as philanthropic or self-centred/self-expressive (Barker 1993, p 28; Sivesind et al, 2002). As mentioned above, even if the motivations for volunteering represent a set of multidimensional and complex factors (Clary et al, 1998), older volunteers are most often found to be motivated by altruistic and philanthropic ideals such as the desire to help others, to serve the needs of society, or by feeling obligations for future generations (Putnam, 2000; Morrow-Howell, 2007). Although older people might prefer to carry out philanthropic activities, their availability to the voluntary sector might, however, depend to a high degree on its composition, and on how the demand for voluntary work is structured. Thus, if older people take up volunteering for altruistic reasons, the availability and extent of involvement of older volunteers may depend on whether the societal demand for voluntary work actually mirrors older people's dispositions towards the voluntary sector. Non-participation may thus not be a totally free choice, unless it is expected from older people that they participate in voluntary work independently of individual preferences.

The *meso* level: voluntary organisations

How attractive older adults are to voluntary organisations may depend on what the older adults have to offer. In this regard, expectations may be rather low, as images of old age are often associated with cognitive and physical decline. Perceptions of older adults, however, are often biased and based on prejudices, and social-gerontological studies have found that both younger and older people have different strengths and weaknesses. Among the strengths of older people are their life experience, stability, maturity, independence and professionalism, and that they radiate a sense of calmness, perspective and social understanding. Conversely, they are frequently described as being slower at learning new things, less flexible and physically weaker than younger people, and also more anxious when it comes to the development of new skills and competencies (Skirbekk, 2003; Henkens, 2005; Casey, 2007; Griffiths, 2007; Friis et al, 2008). As such, older people should not, a priori, be considered 'better or worse' volunteers compared to younger segments of the population. However, they are likely to be more effective in voluntary activities requiring a direct and strong personal relationship with clients (Endres and Holmes, 2006), thus benefiting voluntary organisations thanks to their social skills, commitment and experience (Steinberg and Cain, 2004; Warburton and Cordingley; 2004; Warburton and McDonald, 2009).

The crucial question therefore becomes whether voluntary organisations recognise and appreciate the specific strengths of older volunteers. As will be clear from the empirical evidence reported in Part III of this book, which analyses in more depth 73 case studies from eight European countries for which only preliminary findings could be previously disseminated (Principi et al, 2012b), voluntary organisations perceive the performance of older people as both positive and negative, in similar terms to what happens in the labour market in employers' assessment of older workers. Perceived advantages of older volunteers are: considerable knowledge, skills and experience; high levels of social skills and reliability; and lower turnover and recruitment costs, as they (supposedly) require less extensive training. Disadvantages of engaging older volunteers are reported to be: difficulties in terminating the relationship when capacities decline; lower ability to work well under pressure and generally lower productivity; and lower ability to cope with some physical tasks and greater health problems. These perceived advantages and disadvantages can certainly not be used to carry out assessments aimed at proving that the benefits of recruiting older seniors outweigh the shortcomings, or vice versa, but they do say something about the potential of older volunteers in terms of qualities that can be actively and meaningfully used in/by voluntary organisations.

Given the perceived qualities of older volunteers, it is hardly surprising that existing studies show that organisations involving the largest number of older volunteers are religious in nature (Burr Bradley, 1999; Warburton et al, 2001; Gottlieb, 2002; Gonyea and Googins, 2006), demand being especially high in religious organisations operating in the social and healthcare sectors (Thompson and Wilson, 2001; Gottlieb, 2002; Achenbaum, 2006) where older volunteers carry out activities targeted towards individuals in need. For example, this can involve transporting people, making friendly visits and carrying out other care activities associated with ageing and death in contexts such as hospices, hospitals, nursing homes and other senior settings and community welfare organisations (Kovacs and Black, 1999; Omoto et al, 2000; Warburton et al, 2001; Narushima, 2005; Morrow-Howell, 2006).

The educational area is another volunteering sector with a high demand for older volunteers (Narushima, 2005; Achenbaum, 2006). Here older volunteers are often enrolled in activities and roles such as mentoring, tutoring, teaching, coaching and counselling (Baldock, 1999; Warburton et al, 2001; Narushima, 2005; Morrow-Howell, 2006), but are also appreciated in unskilled activities such as preparing and serving food, working in charity shops and carrying out maintenance (Warburton et al, 2001; Warburton and Cordingley, 2004). There is also a demand for older volunteers in the cultural and recreational sector in activities such as being museum guides, amateur players in nursing homes and storytellers (Baldock, 1999; Warburton et al, 2001; Gottlieb, 2002; Narushima, 2005). It is also not uncommon to see a demand for them in high-ranking positions, such as the recruitment of new volunteers and public relations activities (Narushima, 2005), for which organisations benefit from the skills and knowledge that volunteers have obtained during their working life (Omoto et al, 2000; Warburton et al, 2001).

Once a voluntary organisation decides to make use of older volunteers, it is important that it develops good practice to support the recruitment, employability and retention of older volunteers throughout the whole volunteer cycle, in the form of appropriate volunteering programmes and (professional) management of volunteers (Haski-Leventhal et al, 2009, p 142). Often, however, voluntary organisations are not suited to the challenge of recruiting and maintaining older volunteers, a situation which, to a large extent, can be ascribed to organisational matters. Large organisations usually have adequate organisational resources and will tend to be well defined in their use of volunteers, whereas smaller organisations, which dominate the voluntary landscape, can be characterised by their 'from hand to mouth' practices and are typically less well defined in their use of volunteers. As in the case of for-profit companies (Naegele and Walker, 2006), in an ideal scenario, organisational policies supporting the growth and quality of an older volunteer workforce should therefore systematically address issues such as recruitment, retention and eventual termination of the relationship.

In terms of *recruitment*, the existing literature indicates that voluntary organisations need to create a meaningful image of volunteering and employ marketing strategies such as mail and newspaper advertisements as well as word-of-mouth communication to inform potential volunteers that they are needed (Kovacs and Black, 1999; Thompson and Wilson, 2001; Gottlieb, 2002; Smith, 2004; McBride, 2006; O'Neill, 2006), not least because many older people do not volunteer due to the fact that no one has asked them to do so (Rozario, 2006). In this respect voluntary organisations should have an eye for potential new segments in the older population, as they tend to draw their membership primarily from those who are well educated (Field, 2012, p 17). Furthermore, the literature emphasises that it is important that organisations are physically and geographically accessible. This could be achieved by opening new branches or allowing seniors to volunteer from their own homes, such as, for instance, giving telephone assistance to other older people (O'Neill, 2006). It is equally important that voluntary organisations help individuals to adjust to the tasks they perform by providing training and education to new recruits (Hendricks and Cutler, 2004; Steinberg and Cain, 2004; Warburton et al, 2007). For example, it is essential that hospice volunteers are instructed in patients' medical conditions and treatment (Mellow, 2007) to help them feel that they are capable and to master the assigned tasks. Moreover, voluntary organisations must be aware of what attracts older volunteers, and design work tasks so that they suit them, bearing in mind that older volunteers, as already mentioned, are especially interested in activities that allow them to build a direct and strong relationship with clients.

The literature on *retention* programmes is sparse; however, what there is shows that some organisationally relevant support measures may be crucial in enabling older volunteers to continue to perform. For example, the commitment of older volunteers increases when they receive adequate training and can choose the activities to be carried out (Morrow-Howell et al, 2009; Tang et al, 2009, 2010). Positive effects are also achieved when their role is unambiguously described, while a lack of a clear role specification can be stressful (Wilson, 2012, p 195). For the same reason, older volunteers should be less exposed to demanding clients (Gottlieb, 2002). At the same time, older volunteers are in need of autonomy and work flexibility. If it is not possible to alter work schedules, voluntary work may be perceived as a straitjacket, limiting opportunities for competing demands such as visiting sick grandchildren and other informal activities.

It is therefore hardly surprising that good management practices in the form of adequate supervision, recognition, review and appraisal have an evident impact on the commitment and retention of older volunteers (Principi et al, 2012b). As part of good management practices, it is particularly important to establish a clear division of labour between volunteers and paid employees, as the two groups may have opposite interests leading to conflicts, and volunteers quitting the organisation (Wilson, 2012). Incentives such as social events and minor economic remuneration (for example, reimbursement of transportation costs for volunteers using their own vehicle) may help to retain older volunteers (O'Neill, 2006). Most probably, however, continued training and retraining is the single most import retention instrument (Freedman, 2002; Wilson and Simson, 2003). Training of volunteers not only develops and improves organisational efficiency; learning has an impact on life satisfaction and well-being (Field, 2012), which in turn encourages older volunteers to continue volunteering.

Programmes focusing on older volunteers, however, should not be carried to extremes. Evidence from the for-profit sector shows that in some cases, focusing too much on older employees may be counter-productive (Friis et al, 2008) as younger employees may find it unfair if management discriminates in favour of older colleagues. In other cases, older employees might perceive that they are treated differently, pigeonholed or even stigmatised. In both situations, conflicts between different age groups within the organisation might be the unintended consequence. In addition, studies have shown that older volunteers can be quite costly for organisations because of high turnover rates, a decrease in productivity due to deterioration in health and sudden drop-out from voluntary activity. These problems call for the organisation to reflect on how to *conclude* the relationship with older volunteers at a certain point. Literature is scarce, and Part III of this book tries to shed more light on this delicate subject in order to better understand how a holistic view can be adopted in the 'recruitment–engagement cycle' (Principi et al, 2012b, p 696).

The welfare mix

As they are an integrated part of and directly linked to civil society, voluntary organisations assume certain roles and functions that contribute to the reproduction of society as a whole. For example, they may take the role of service provider or they may function to deal with social problems. Voluntary organisations, however, cannot be fully understood in isolation from the political, social and institutional environments in which they operate, as welfare-producing institutions such as the welfare state, the market and the family influence the scale and character of the voluntary sector. This has been conceptualised as the welfare mix (Evers and Wintersberger, 1990; Evers, 1995) or the welfare triangle (Pestoff, 1992, 1998), indicating that some sort of interaction and division of labour exists between the market, the state, the family and voluntary associations.

This division of tasks between major welfare institutions in society is not a natural given, nor is it once and for all. The welfare mix is continuously changing as welfare institutions such as the roles of the family, markets, state and third sector are in a continuous process of change. To understand what shapes the welfare mix, existing literature draws heavily on functional arguments and institutional choice theories, arguing that the choice between different institutional providers of welfare is the outcome of complex interrelationships between institutional actors (Badelt, 1990). The institutional choice theory ties in with interdependence theory, according to which the voluntary sector is a by-product of the state (Salamon and Anheier, 1998, p 225), predicting that welfare state growth will substitute or crowd out civil society and voluntary organised services (Rostow, 1960; Wolfe, 1989; Fukuyama, 1995; Henriksen et al, 2012). More recently, however, the crowding-out hypothesis has been questioned. In part, because it may be very difficult to identify clear demarcation lines between one institution and another, and also because it has been convincingly argued that different institutional actors actually cooperate and complement each other, and that this type of cooperation has been made topical by the challenges of 'market failure/government failure' (Pestoff, 2009).

Existing literature seems to support the idea, at least with regard to older volunteers, that interactions between institutional actors are highly complex, and that the work–volunteering nexus is, to a large extent, still unclear. Some studies have found that there is a negative association between work for the labour market and volunteering by older people, whereas other studies show that paid work and high employment rates are compatible with or have a positive impact on volunteering among older adults, especially among part-time workers (Erlinghagen and Hank, 2006; Gonyea and Googins, 2006; Hank and Stuck, 2008; Haski-Leventhal et al, 2009; Erlinghagen, 2010; Hank and Erlinghagen, 2010; Warburton and Jeppsson-Grassman, 2011). As it will become clearer from the evidence provided in the following chapters, participation in the labour market might even function as a trampoline for volunteering, since labour market participants have on average more social and economic resources than retirees. This finding suggests that the perception of volunteering as part of an ideal retirement lifestyle may be quite wrong (Smith, 2004; Gonyea and Googins, 2006; O'Neill, 2006).

In the same way, contradictory evidence exists when it comes to the relationship between the size and scope of the voluntary sector and informal caregiving of older family members, primarily carried out by women (Lamura et al, 2008). Some studies show that informal caregiving tends to discourage voluntary work, while other studies have found that older caregivers are more often volunteers than non-caregivers (for an overview, see Burr et al, 2005). That no conclusive evidence can be found is probably due to the complexity of the issue. Eldercare may take place in the family or be provided by public institutions as a right of the citizen. It seems as though the probability of volunteering is positively associated with the degree of eldercare formalisation, that is, that voluntary work among older adults is encouraged if the welfare state takes a major responsibility for eldercare provision (Warburton and Jeppsson-Grassman, 2011). It is thus necessary to reflect on whether older adults are involved in informal (not regulated), semi-formal (cash-for-care) or formal (home help/institutional care) forms of care (Geissler and Pfau-Effinger, 2005) as the different forms of care are associated differently with volunteering in older age (Burr et al, 2005).

Voluntary work and informal care responsibilities may likewise be associated with different family forms (Pfau-Effinger et al, 2009). Interactions between the voluntary sector and the family may thus differ depending on whether the predominant family form is: (1) the male breadwinner/female housewife (full-time carer) model; (2) the male breadwinner/women working part time/female part-time carer model; or (3) the dual breadwinner/external carer model. For instance, it seems that part-time workers are more involved in voluntary work than full-time workers.

The *macro* level: policies supporting volunteering

Even if the US can count on deeper roots in terms of the history of programmes and policies supporting volunteering in older age (Principi et al, 2012a), over the last decades European policy makers have increasingly shown an interest in voluntary work, and called for it to become a more vibrant part of civil society. Volunteering has been put high on the political agenda, and been promoted by international organisations (for example, the UN and the EU), national governments and local municipalities. In some countries, voluntary work has even become a cornerstone in the building of a new society, as, for instance, when in 2011 Prime Minister David Cameron declared voluntary work as a major building block in his vision for the 'Big Society'. It has been argued that this growing interest in voluntary work is a response to new societal needs, generated by the combined effect of 'market failure' which gave rise to the welfare state in industrial societies, and 'government failure' in which the welfare state has gone too far and become a co-producer of social problems (Weisbrod, 1977; Murray, 1984; Gilbert, 2002; Pestoff, 2009). The 'market failure/government failure' hypothesis points towards the voluntary sector as a key instrument in satisfying unsatisfied demands for public goods (Salamon and Anheier, 1998, p 221). In effect, new governance structures have emerged that assign the role of partners to voluntary organisations working in cooperation with governments and for-profit private organisations in the provision of welfare.

Policies shape identities, preferences, the nature of social participation and organisational capacities (Skocpol, 1985; Skocpol and Amenta, 1986; Pierson, 2000). Thus, in as much as governments and policy makers wish to enhance volunteering in older age, policies should be designed so that they stimulate voluntary activities in this segment of the population. Two factors are important if governments want to shape voluntary organisations in an elder-friendly direction: the legal framework and financial incentives (or funding).

First, the legal framework in the form of laws of association, administration and regulations defines the criteria for the official recognition of voluntary organisations and volunteers. It lays down the fundamental set of rights and obligations under which voluntary organisations can operate, as well as the basic principles and requirements for partnerships between the state and the third/non-profit sector. The legal framework can structure, frame and condition the internal life and accounting policies of voluntary organisations, and is very much present if public resources or subsidies are involved. Basically, the legal framework represents the essential values of the state and the status in society ascribed to a voluntary organisation, which may strengthen or weaken the societal role and prestige of such organisations and influence the normative ideals and orientation of citizens towards voluntary work. The legal framework therefore helps to favour certain types of organisational properties while constraining others (Goss, 2010). For instance, high levels of formal requirements for third sector organisations support bureaucratisation and paid work, while low levels of formal requirements allow for more anarchical and looser organisational structures, including the types of volunteering most favourable to older volunteers.

Second, social policies may stimulate the supply and demand for voluntary work by offering financial resources to promote it. A distinction is often made between distributive, regulative and redistributive policies (Lowi, 1964). A common feature of these policies is that they contain incentives that affect the propensity and willingness of *rational* actors to volunteer. In recent years, however, new forms of steering have emerged, for example, culture steering/governance (Bang, 2004). This is an interactive practice where governments and central political actors signal the importance of voluntary work and appeal to citizens to volunteer. Culture steering is about top–down communication of an all–inclusive vision (for instance, the visions of active ageing or the 'Big Society') often advanced in the form of codes of good conduct, benchmarking and best practices, thus allowing *self-reflexive* individuals or groups to connect and develop new local practices that fit into a larger societal project. As such, culture steering indicates that discourses and ideas rather than incentives help to mobilise and direct reflexive and responsible citizens towards the voluntary sector.

Social policies may enhance volunteering at both the individual and organisational level as they structure participatory opportunities (Haski-Leventhal et al, 2009; Goss, 2010). At the *organisational* level, social policies may privilege certain types of organisations over others. As argued by Goss (2010, p 122), income tax deductions for donations to voluntary organisations provide systematic incentives to create charity organisations rather than advocacy organisations, and as older volunteers prefer philanthropic organisations, policies helping to create or reinforce these organisations will most probably increase older people's availability for voluntary work. At the *individual* level, tax deductions for people who volunteer as well as publicly organised training and learning opportunities are expected to have an impact on the inclination of older adults to volunteer (Thompson and Wilson, 2001; Henkin and Zapf, 2006; O'Neill, 2006).

Besides creating social policy incentives for voluntary work, public policy may also create volunteer centres both locally and nationally by encouraging collaboration and networking between organisations. Such centres can improve chances for older people to learn about volunteer opportunities (Haski-Leventhal et al, 2009, p 145) and the prospects for them to become involved in voluntary work (Henkin and Zapf, 2006).

Welfare regime

The *structural* or *welfare regimes* level encompasses at least two dimensions. First, institutions and the welfare mix represent a functional division of responsibility for the production of welfare, and the division of labour between the state, market, family and voluntary sector has been measured as the degree of de-commodification. Second, culture, values, belief systems and ideology (social democratic, liberal, conservative, and so on) are the basic organising principles behind choices made by individuals and institutions (Esping-Andersen, 1990). Culture, values and belief systems, which can be fully understood only from a historical perspective, mark societal ideas and notions about the 'right' relation between the different welfare-producing institutions, that is, the 'just' order between the market, state, family and voluntary organisations, just as culture, values and belief systems define expectations and roles (for example, the role of older people) ascribed to social actors. Thereby, welfare regimes help to construct and frame identities and guide individual behaviour (Pierson, 1993), including older people's attitudes and decisions towards the voluntary sector.

Most probably, different welfare regimes have created different configurations in their third sectors, but very few studies have actually documented the relationship between welfare regimes and the scope and character of voluntary work. One exception is the study carried out by Salamon and Anheier (1998) that argues that the voluntary sector is embedded in broader social, political and economic relationships. Salamon and Anheier make use of the regime theory developed by Esping-Andersen, although with some minor modifications such as the reference to four (instead of three) regime types: the liberal, the social democratic, the corporatist and the statist, to find out how volunteer rates are affected by differences in regime as measured by indicators such as government social welfare spending and the non-profit scale.

The study of Salamon and Anheier is a commendable initiative as this type of cross-national study is rare, but it is far from being fully convincing, as the same authors recognise (Salamon and Anheier, 1998, p 245). It is difficult to understand, for instance, why in this study the non-profit scale has been based only on paid employment in this sector rather than on volunteer work, and why Italy (together with Sweden) is characterised as a social democratic non-profit regime.

In light of the above, it is not surprising that studies analysing older people's volunteering from a welfare regime perspective are even rarer. Recently, however, Warburton and Jeppsson-Grassman (2011) have analysed the involvement of older people in voluntary associations using a six-regime model. They distinguished between organisational membership in terms of active and inactive membership and the type of organisations in which older people volunteer, such as charitable, religious, sports and other types of organisations, and found that differences between countries can be explained by variations in the overall welfare context.

Final remarks

The theoretical and conceptual framework developed in this chapter will be used as a frame of reference in the country studies presented in Part II as well as the organisational studies presented in Part III. This main framework, which is based on the available literature on volunteering in older age, also guides the cross-national analysis in the conclusion of this volume.

A main consideration behind our decision to adopt such a comprehensive approach was that the most recent contributions on this issue, from an active ageing perspective, suggest that there is still a large gap in our understanding of the complex mechanisms underlying volunteering in older age. Volunteering in older age is explained by the interplay of different dimensions that we considered as the micro, meso, macro, welfare mix and welfare regime, while these dimensions have hardly ever been considered all together in a single study so far.

Another major goal of this book is to attempt to at least partially fill the endemic gap in terms of empirical studies on the organisational (*meso*) level of volunteering in later life. This has been pursued through a major effort of comparing the situation of over 73 voluntary organisations operating in eight selected European countries and almost as many different welfare regimes. Part III of this book allows us to verify whether the results emerging from this in-depth analysis have met the initial goal of the study in providing clear evidence of how and to what extent voluntary organisations across Europe are currently able to knowingly deal with older volunteers.

Moreover, the comparative nature of our analysis will hopefully also help us understand why the empirical evidence reported in the existing literature is sometimes contradictory. These contrasting findings could depend on the particular sample or the different methodology employed, suggesting that more in-depth analyses should be employed in light of the particular context under investigation to better understand and thus explain why differing results emerge from different studies on apparently the same topic. To this purpose, this volume applies the same conceptual framework to the analysis of the national contexts of the eight different European countries involved in the study.

References

Achenbaum, W.A. (2006) 'A history of civic engagement of older people', *Generations*, vol 30, no 4, pp 18-23.

AGE (2007) *Healthy ageing: Good practice examples, recommendations, policy actions*, Brussels: The European Older People's Platform.

Atchley, R. (1989) 'A continuity theory of normal ageing', *The Gerontologist*, vol 29, no 2, pp 183-90.

Badelt, C. (1990) 'Institutional choice and the nonprofit sector', in H.K. Anheier and W. Seibel (eds) *The third sector: Comparative studies of nonprofit organizations*, Berlin /New York: De Gruyter, pp 53-63.

Baldock, C.V. (1999) 'Seniors as volunteers: an international perspective on policy', *Ageing & Society*, vol 19, no 5, pp 581-602.

Bang, H.P. (2004) 'Culture governance: governing reflexive modernity', *Public Administration*, vol 82, no 1, pp 159-90.

Barker, D.G. (1993) 'Values and volunteering', in J.D. Smith (ed) *Volunteering in Europe*, Volunteering Action Research, Second Series, Number 2, London: The Volunteer Centre.

Burr, J.A., Choi, N.G., Mutchler, J.E. and Caro, F.G. (2005) 'Caregiving and volunteering: are private and public helping behaviors linked?', *Journal of Gerontology: Social Sciences*, vol 60B, no 5, pp 247-56.

Burr Bradley, D. (1999) 'A reason to rise each morning: the meaning of volunteering in the lives of older adults', *Generations*, vol 23, no 4, pp 45-50.

Butrica, B.A., Johnson, R.W. and Zedlewski, S.R. (2009) 'Volunteer dynamics of older Americans', *Journal of Gerontology: Social Sciences*, vol 64B, no 5, pp 644-55.

Casey, B. (2007) 'The employment of older people: can we learn from Japan?', in W. Loretto, S. Vickerstaff and P. White (eds) *The future for older workers: New perspectives*, Bristol: Policy Press, pp 43-63.

Cattan, M., Hogg, E. and Hardill, I. (2011) 'Improving quality of life in ageing populations: what can volunteering do?', *Maturitas*, vol 70, no 4, pp 328-32.

Clary, E.G., Snyder, M., Ridge, R.D., Copeland, J., Stukas, A.A., Haugen, J. and Miene, P. (1998) 'Understanding and assessing the motivations of volunteers: a functional approach', *Journal of Personality and Social Psychology*, vol 74, no 6, pp 1516-30.

Cumming, E. and Henry, W.E. (1961) *Growing old*, New York: Basic Books.

Cutler, S. J. and Hendricks, J. (2000) 'Age differences in voluntary association memberships: fact or artifacts', *Journal of Gerontology: Social Sciences*, vol 55B, no 2, pp 98-107.

Daatland, S.O. and Solem, P.E. (2011) *Aldring og samfunn (Ageing and society)*, Oslo: Fagbokforlaget.

Ehlers, A., Naegele, G., and Reichert, M. (2011) *Volunteering by older people in the EU*, Dublin: European Foundation for the Improvement of Living and Working Conditions.

Endres, T. and Holmes, C.A. (2006) 'RespectAbility in America: guiding principles for civic engagement among adults 55-plus', *Generations*, vol 30, no 4, pp 101-8.

Erlinghagen, M. (2010) 'Volunteering after retirement', *European Societies*, vol 12, no 5, pp 603-25.

Erlinghagen, M. and Hank, K. (2006) 'The participation of older European in volunteer work', *Ageing & Society*, vol 26, no 4, pp 567-84.

Esping-Andersen, G. (1990) *The three worlds of welfare capitalism*, Cambridge: Polity Press.

Evers, A. (1995) 'Part of the welfare mix: the third sector as an intermediate area', *Voluntas*, vol 6, no 2, pp 159-82.

Evers, A. and Wintersberger, H. (eds) (1990) *Shifts in the welfare mix. Their impact on work, social services and welfare policies*, Frankfurt am Main: Campus.

Field, J. (2012) 'Lifelong learning, welfare and mental well-being into older age: trends and policies in Europe', *Education in the Asia-Pacific Region: Issues, Concerns and Prospects*, vol 15, no 1, pp 11-20.

Fischer, L.R. and Schaffer, K.B. (1993) *Older volunteers: A guide to research and practice*, Newbury Park, CA: Sage Publications.

Freedman, M. (2002) 'Civic windfall? Realizing the promise in an ageing America', *Generations*, vol 26, no 2, pp 86-9.

Friis, K., Jensen, P.H. and Wégens, J. (2008) *Seniorpraksis på danske arbejdspladser – baggrund, indhold og effecter* (*Age management in Danish companies – Background, content and effects*), København: Frydenlund.

Fukuyama, F. (1995) *Trust: The social virtues and the creation of prosperity*, New York: The Free Press.

Fung, H.H., Carstensen, L.L. and Lang, F.R. (2001) 'Age-related patterns in social networks among European Americans and African Americans: implications for socioemotional selectivity across the life span', *International Journal of Aging and Human Development*, vol 52, no 3, pp 185-206.

Geissler, B. and Pfau-Effinger, B. (2005) 'Change of European care arrangements', in B. Pfau-Effinger and B. Geissler (eds) *Care arrangements in Europe: Variations and change*, Bristol: Policy Press, pp 3-17.

Gilbert, N. (2002) *Transformation of the welfare state: The silent surrender of public responsibility*, Oxford: Oxford University Press.

Gonyea, J.G. and Googins, B.K. (2006) 'Expanding the boundaries of corporate volunteerism: tapping the skills, talent and energy of retirees', *Generations*, vol 30, no 4, pp 78-84.

Goss, K.A. (2010) 'Civil society and civic engagement: towards a multi-level theory of policy feedbacks', *Journal of Civil Society*, vol 6, no 2, pp 119-43.

Gottlieb, B.H. (2002) 'Older volunteers: a precious resource under pressure', *Canadian Journal of Aging*, vol 21, no 1, pp 5-9.

Gottlieb, B.H. and Gillespie, A.A. (2008) 'Voluntarism, health, and civic engagement among older adults', *Canadian Journal of Ageing*, vol 27, no 4, pp 399-406.

Griffiths, A. (2007) 'Healthy work for older workers: work design and management factors', in W. Loretto, S. Vickerstaff and P. White (eds) *The future for older workers: New perspectives*, Bristol: Policy Press, pp 121-37.

Hank, K. and Erlinghagen, M. (2010) 'Volunteering in "old" Europe: patterns, potentials, limitations', *Journal of Applied Gerontology*, vol 29, no 1, pp 3-20.

Hank, K. and Stuck, S. (2008) 'Volunteer work, informal help, and care among the 50+ in Europe: further evidence for "linked" productive activities at older ages', *Social Science Research*, vol 37, no 4, pp 1280-91.

Haski-Leventhal, D., Meijs, L.C.P.M. and Hustinx, L. (2009) 'The third-party model: enhancing volunteering through governments, corporations and educational institutions', *Journal of Social Policy*, vol 39, no 1, pp 139-58.

Havighurst, R.J. (1961) 'Successful aging', *The Gerontologist*, vol 1, no 1, 8-13.

Hendricks, J. and Cutler, S.J. (2004) 'Volunteerism and socioemotional selectivity in later life', *Journal of Gerontology: Social Sciences*, vol 59B, no 5, pp 251-7.

Henkens, K. (2005) 'Stereotyping older workers and retirement: the managers' point of view', *Canadian Journal of Aging*, vol 24, no 4, pp 353-66.

Henkin, N. And Zapf, J. (2006) 'How communities can promote civic engagement of people age 50-plus', *Generations*, vol 30, no 4, pp 72-7.

Henriksen, L.S., Smith, S.R. and Zimmer, A. (2012) 'At the eve of convergence? Transformations of social service provision in Denmark, Germany and the United States', *Voluntas*, vol 23, no 2, pp 458-501.

Kochera, A., Straight, A. and Guterbock, T. (2005) *Beyond 50.05: A report to the nation on liveable communities*, Washington, DC: AARP.

Kovacs, P. J. and Black, B. (1999) 'Volunteerism and older adults: implications for social work practice', *Journal of Gerontological Social Work*, vol 32, no 4, pp 25-37.

Lamura, G., Mnich, E., Nolan, M., Wojszel, B., Krevers, B., Mestheneos, L. and Döhner, H. (2008) 'Family carers' experiences in using support services in Europe: empirical evidence from the EUROFAMCARE study', *The Gerontologist*, vol 48, no 6, pp 752-71.

Li, Y.Q. and Ferraro, K.F. (2005) 'Volunteering and depression in later life: social benefit or selection processes?', *Journal of Health and Social Behavior*, vol 46, no 1, pp 68-84.

Lowi, T.J. (1964) 'American business, public policy, case-studies, and political theory', *World Politics*, vol 16, no 4, pp 677-715.

McBride, A.M. (2006) 'Civic engagement, older adults and inclusion', *Generations*, vol 30, no 4, pp 66-71.

Maddox, G.L. (1968) 'Persistence of life style among the elderly: a longitudinal study of patterns of social activity in relation to life satisfaction', in B.L. Neugarten (ed) *Middle age and aging: A reader in social psychology*, Chicago, IL: University of Chicago Press, pp 181-3.

Marks, S.R. (1977) 'Multiple roles and role strain: some notes on human energy, time and commitment', *American Sociological Review*, vol 42, pp 921-36.

Mellow, M. (2007) 'Hospital volunteers and carework', *Canadian Review of Sociology*, vol 44, no 4, pp 451-67.

Morrow-Howell, N. (2006) 'Civic service across the life course', *Generations*, vol 30, no 4, pp 37-42.

Morrow-Howell, N. (2007) 'A longer worklife: the new road to volunteering', *Generations*, vol 31, no 1, pp 63-7.

Morrow-Howell, N., Hong, S.L. and Tang, F. (2009) 'Who benefits from volunteering?Variations in perceived benefits', *The Gerontologist*, vol 49, no 1, pp 91-102.

Murray, C. (1984) *Losing ground:American social policy, 1950-1980*, New York: Basic Books.

Naegele, G. and Walker, A. (2006) *A guide to good practice in age management*, Dublin: European Foundation for the Improvement of Living and Working Conditions.

Narushima, M. (2005) '"Payback time": community volunteering among older adults as a transformative mechanism', *Ageing & Society*, vol 25, no 4, pp 567-84.

Omoto,A.M., Snyder, M. and Martino, S.C. (2000) 'Volunteerism and the life course: investigating age-related agendas for actions', *Basic and Applied Social Psychology*, vol 22, no 3, pp 181-97.

O'Neill, G. (2006) 'Civic engagement on the agenda at the 2005 White House Conference on aging', *Generations*, vol 30, no 4, pp 95-100.

Pestoff, V.A. (1992) 'Third sector and co-operative services: An alternative to privatization', *Journal of Consumer Policy*, vol 15, no 1, pp 21-45

Pestoff, V. (1998) *Beyond the market and state: Social entreprises and civil democracy in a welfare society*, Aldershot: Ashgate.

Pestoff, V.A. (2009) *A democratic architecture for the welfare state*, London and New York: Routledge.

Pfau-Effinger, B., Flaquer, L. and Jensen, P.H. (eds) (2009) *Formal and informal work:The hidden work regime in Europe*, New York and London: Routledge.

Pierson, P. (1993) 'Policy feedback and political change', *World Politics*, vol 45, no 4, pp 595-628.

Pierson, P. (2000) 'Increasing returns, path dependences, and the study of politics', *American Political Science Review*, vol 94, no 2, pp 251-67.

Principi A., Chiatti C., Lamura G. and Frerichs F. (2012a) 'The engagement of older people in civil society organisations', *Educational Gerontology*, vol 38, no 2, pp 83-106.

Principi, A., Lindley, R., Perek-Bialas, J. and Turek, K. (2012b) 'Volunteering in older age: an organizational perspective', *International Journal of Manpower*, vol 33, no 6, pp 685-703.

Putnam, R.D. (2000) *Bowling alone. The collapse and revival of American community*, New York: Simon & Schuster.

Rostow, W.W. (1960) *The stages of economic growth*, London: Cambridge University Press.

Rozario, P.A. (2006) 'Volunteering among current cohorts of older adults and baby boomers', *Generations*, vol 30, no 4, pp 31-6.

Salamon, L.M. and Anheier, H.K. (1998) 'Social origins of civil society: explaining the nonprofit sector cross-nationally', *Voluntas*, vol 9, no 3, pp 213-48.

Sivesind, K.H., Lorentzen, H., Selle, P. and Wollebæk, D. (2002) *The voluntary sector in Norway. Compositions, changes and causes*, Oslo: Institutt for Samfunnsforskning.

Skirbekk, V. (2003) *Age and individual productivity: A literature survey*, MPIDR Working Paper WP 2003-028, Rostock: Max-Planck-Institut für demografische Forschung.

Skocpol, T. (1985) 'Bringing the state back in: strategies of analysis in current research', in P.B. Evans, D. Rueschemeyer and T. Skocpol (eds) *Bringing the state back in*, New York: Cambridge University Press, pp 3-43.

Skocpol, T. and Amenta, E. (1986) 'States and social policies', *Annual Review of Sociology*, vol 12, pp 131-57.

Smith, D.B (2004) 'Volunteering in retirement: perceptions of midlife workers', *Nonprofit and Voluntary Sector Quarterly*, vol 33, no 1, pp 55-73.

Steinberg, M. And Cain, L. (2004) 'Managing an ageing third sector workforce: international and local perspectives', *Third Sector Review*, vol 10, no 1, pp 7-26.

Tang, F. (2006) 'What resources are needed for volunteerism? A life course perspective', *Journal of Applied Gerontology*, vol 25, no 5, pp 375-90.

Tang, F., Choi, E.H. and Morrow-Howell, N. (2010) 'Organizational support and volunteering benefits for older adults', *The Gerontologist*, vol 50, no 5, pp 603-12.

Tang, F., Morrow-Howell, N. and Hong, S.L. (2009) 'Institutional facilitation in sustained volunteering among older adult volunteers', *Social Network Research*, vol 33, no 3, pp 172-82.

Thompson, E. and Wilson, L. (2001) 'The potential of older volunteers in long-term care', *Generations*, vol 25, no 1, pp 58-63.

Warburton, J. and Cordingley, S. (2004) 'The contemporary challenges of volunteering in an ageing Australia', *Australian Journal on Volunteering*, vol 9, no 2, pp 67-74.

Warburton, J. and Jeppsson-Grassman, E. (2011) 'Variations in older people's social and productive ageing activities across different social welfare regimes', *International Journal of Social Welfare*, vol 20, no 2, pp 180-91.

Warburton, J. and McDonald, C. (2009) 'The challenges of the new institutional environment: an Australian case study of older volunteers in the contemporary non-profit sector', *Ageing & Society*, vol 29, no 5, pp 823-40.

Warburton, J., Paynter, J. and Petriwksyj, A. (2007) 'Volunteering as a productive aging activity: incentives and barriers to volunteering by Australian seniors', *Journal of Applied Gerontology*, vol 26, no 4, pp 333-54.

Warburton, J., Terry, D.J., Rosenman, L.S. and Shapiro, M. (2001) 'Differences between older volunteers and nonvolunteers: attitudinal, normative, and control beliefs', *Research on Aging*, vol 23, no 5, pp 586-605.

Weisbrod, B. (1977) *The voluntary nonprofit sector*, Lexington, MA: Lexington Books.

Wilson, J. (2000) 'Volunteering', *Annual Review of Sociology*, vol 26, pp 215-40.

Wilson, J. (2012) 'Volunteerism research: a review essay', *Nonprofit and Voluntary Sector Quarterly*, vol 41, no 2, pp 176-212.

Wilson, J. and Musick, M. (1997) 'Who cares? Towards an integrated theory of volunteer work', *American Sociological Review*, vol 62, no 5, pp 694-713.

Wilson, L.B. and Simson, S.P. (2003) 'Combining lifelong learning with civic engagement: a university-based model', *Gerontology and Geriatrics Education*, vol 24, no 1, pp 47-61.

Wolfe, A. (1989) *Whose keeper? Social science and moral obligation*, Berkeley, CA: University of California Press.

Wymer, W.W. (1999) 'Understanding volunteer markets: the case of senior volunteers', *Journal of Nonprofit & Public Sector Marketing*, vol 6, no 2/3, pp 1-23.

Part II

OPPORTUNITIES AND RESTRICTIONS FOR OLDER VOLUNTEERS

National experiences

THREE

Older volunteers in Italy: an underestimated phenomenon?

Andrea Principi, Carlos Chiatti and Giovanni Lamura

Introduction

Despite recent changes, the familistic Mediterranean Italian welfare state (Esping-Andersen, 1996; Ferrara, 1996) is still largely anchored in the male breadwinner/female carer family model (Lewis, 1992; Pfau-Effinger, 2005). According to this model and its cultural context, women are expected to have the main responsibility for carrying out homemaking and caring tasks, often on a full-time basis, and particularly in the Central-Southern regions. This explains why female labour force participation rates – as for older workers – are still very low in most Italian regions (although a trend towards higher participation rates can be observed in recent years), whereas the state's role is mainly that of providing not so much in-kind services, but rather care allowances (Bettio and Plantenga, 2004), financial support that is frequently used by households to privately hire migrant care workers (Di Rosa et al, 2012).

The limited extent of state-run or funded care services helps explain why voluntary work in Italy is concentrated in this field. On the whole, however, the voluntary sector in Italy appears to be underdeveloped when compared to other European countries, especially those in the North. This may be explained by the fact that, on the one hand, volunteering in Italy is not felt as a 'social norm' (Ascoli and Cnaan, 1997), while on the other, actual volunteering-like activities, particularly in the culture and recreation fields, may not be perceived as such in the eyes of many Italians. Indeed, the dominant profile of volunteering in Italy has often been described as mainly 'altruistic' and 'service-oriented' (ISTAT, 2006a; Fondazione Roma Terzo Settore, 2010). However, the amount of 'self-expressive' volunteering may be underestimated by some of the existing surveys, due to sample biases and cultural social norms, as this form of volunteering is, to some extent, not perceived as such by the common Italian mentality. As a consequence, only about 10 per cent of the population describes itself as being actively engaged in voluntary activities (ISTAT, 2011), which are performed in about 220,000 non-profit institutions, mainly registered as associations, 81 per cent of whose workforce is made of volunteers (ISTAT, 2001a). The total contribution produced by voluntary work has been estimated to reach 0.7 per cent of GDP (gross domestic product), while the whole non-profit sector adds up to over 4 per cent of GDP (CNEL–ISTAT, 2011).

In light of this situation, the Italian voluntary sector does not seem to fit any of the models envisaged by Salamon and Anheier (1998) in their social origin theory (see Chapter Two, this volume). Indeed, even if for some structural aspects it looks rather similar to the social democratic pattern, the existence of many substantial differences from this model suggests that the Italian model might represent an original form of volunteering, with a focus on social services. Moreover, in contrast to what was found by Salamon and Anheier, government social welfare spending is rather low in Italy compared to that of most Northern and Western European countries (Eurispes, 2006).

The emphasis of the Italian voluntary sector on social services seems to be in accordance with the interests and preferences of older Italians, who prefer to carry out intragenerational activities (Frisanco, 2006). However, they are also often engaged in culture and recreation activities, to an extent that is probably underestimated by existing research, as already observed. In 2010, about 9 per cent of people aged 65-74, and 4 per cent of those aged 75 or older, were found to participate in voluntary activities.

This chapter aims to describe the main opportunities and restrictions for volunteering by older people in Italy. After a brief introduction to the traditional features, current situation and legal framework characterising volunteering, the next section provides a quantitative overview of the organisations, sectors and volunteers, including older volunteers. The third section addresses the main individual, organisational and institutional opportunities existing in Italy for volunteering in older age, and also considers the impact of paid employment and family care of older people. The fourth section deals with future perspectives, before concluding with some reflections on what can be learned from the Italian situation.

The Italian tradition of voluntary action

Historically, in Italy 'volunteering' is meant as an activity that is 'carried out for free', but it is not particularly supported by social norms, as there is no social expectation that volunteering should be part of an average citizen's everyday life (Ascoli and Cnaan, 1997). Nevertheless, voluntary work in Italy has deep historical roots. It mushroomed in the 18th century, when voluntary organisations and charities were promoted by the Catholic Church and Socialist movements, mainly in the field of social work, healthcare, alms housing and education (Borzaga and Santuari, 2000). During the 19th century and up to the 1970s, the voluntary sector was scaled down, in parallel to the birth of the modern welfare state, which assumed some of the responsibilities previously provided to the community by voluntary organisations (Borzaga, 2004). Between the 1970s and 1990s, as a consequence of the financial constraints affecting the Italian welfare state after the first oil crisis, there was a slow re-emergence of the voluntary sector. In this period, while the state remained responsible for public services, the voluntary sector experienced progressive growth (Barbetta and Maggio, 2002; Borzaga, 2004), and became increasingly recognised as a crucial actor in public policy, which culminated with the establishment of a permanent platform called the Third Sector Forum. After the 1990s, however, there was a renewed phase of retrenchment at the institutional level, coinciding with the centre-right government coming to power. In this period, the role of the third sector was significantly downgraded, and protocols and documents produced in the earlier period were neglected (Ranci et al, 2009). In 1999 public subsidies to non-profit organisations were 36 per cent of total earnings of the sector, while only 13 per cent of organisations were 'mainly' publicly funded (ISTAT, 2001a). Public funding represents the main source of financial support only for 10 per cent of organisations in the culture, sports and recreation sector (compared to 40 per cent of those in health care, 26 per cent in social care and 26 per cent in economic development and social cohesion). This shows that, albeit they represent the great majority (almost 50 per cent) of all organisations relying mainly on public funding, public support is not central for volunteer activity in this sector. On the other hand, in 2003, 50 per cent of voluntary organisations stated that they received some kind of public funds (ISTAT, 2006a). Recently, however, as will be discussed later in this chapter, there has been a renewed institutional interest around volunteering, particularly the volunteering of older people. While in the 1980s governmental policies only considered older people as recipients of health and social services, starting from the 1990s attention shifted, albeit slowly, to the 'free time' of older people who are increasingly considered as a valuable resource for society (Frisanco, 2006).

The legal framework

Italian legislation concerning the voluntary sector (and the third sector in general) is highly fragmented (Ranci et al, 2009). Several laws mention volunteers and volunteering; however, the most relevant national laws that focus mainly on the regulation of organisations, their activities, infrastructure and access to public funds are as follows:

- *Law 266-1991:* the law on volunteering which established the 'Register of voluntary organisations'. A basic principle stated by this law is that voluntary activities must be provided spontaneously and for free for reasons of solidarity (that is, mainly to people outside, not belonging to, the organisation itself), even if costs sustained by volunteers may be reimbursed. Paid staff can only be employed to a very limited extent by voluntary organisations. Registers of voluntary organisations are established at a regional level, that is, the regions manage enrolment. To be enrolled it is necessary to register the founding charter and the statute at the tax office, where a tax code is given to the organisation. The main benefits of being registered are that organisations can access public funds, tax benefits and stipulate agreements with public bodies. Furthermore, at the local level the law established service centres for voluntary work (CSV), to provide technical and professional assistance to voluntary organisations.

- *Law 383-2000:* regarding social promotion associations. The main objective of this law is to define the legal framework for those organisations carrying out, without profit, 'socially useful activities' in favour of both their members and non-members, although the law excludes organisations aiming at defending people's economic interests (for example, political parties, unions, employers' organisations, private clubs, and so on). These organisations mainly promote social rights, solidarity, equal opportunities, the arts, sport and research, so this law fits well mainly with the self-expressive type of volunteering. It envisages the possibility – in exceptional cases – of hiring paid staff (even among members of the organisation) to carry out their activities. The registration process is similar to the one described for voluntary organisations, but it takes place in a different 'list'. Registered associations can access public funds, stipulate agreements with public bodies and are able to benefit from other economic advantages.

In recent years, particularly at the local level, some normative measures specifically aimed at encouraging the participation of older people in volunteering have been employed, even if the positive effect of these measures has not yet been captured in available data. The national Law 133/2008 introduced (until 2014) the remarkable possibility of public employees close to retirement age being able to retire earlier from their work and to receive 70 per cent of their wages, under the condition that they documented their regular volunteering. However, this was abrogated by Law 214/2011. On the one hand, it has not been very successful in terms of application, since most entitled people preferred to carry on working, and more importantly, it was the victim of one of the decisions taken by the Monti government to reduce public expenditure within the so-called 'Save Italy' manoeuvre. Apart from this national policy, which is no longer available, some regional initiatives focusing on the social participation of older people have also recently been enacted. For example, the regional Veneto Law 9/2010 extended Voluntary Service (that is, *servizio civile*, a specific Italian system that allows people aged 18-28 to work in different non-profit organisations, receiving a payment of around 400 per month from the state) to older people, in order to promote them as a resource for the community. Similarly, in 2004 the Piedmont region established Voluntary Service for people over 65 years of age (regional Law 1/2004). A similar example comes from the Emilia Romagna region, where Law 20/2003 established that Voluntary Service could also be performed by adults and older people. In 2009, the Liguria region enacted a law on the 'promotion and valorisation of active ageing' (Law 48/2009), with the aim of planning and implementing, within a broad regional triennial social plan, activities carried out by people over 60 that are gratifying, socially dignified and useful to older people themselves and to the community, in the fields of education, work, volunteering, culture, tourism, free time and so on.

The dimension of volunteer work

Participation in voluntary activities by the Italian population has been slightly but steadily increasing in the last decade (see Table 3.1), a period in which the share of the population stating that it was engaged in formal volunteering grew from 7.5 per cent in 1999 to

10 per cent in 2010. As stressed in more depth later, there has been a remarkable increase in formal volunteering, particularly in the older age groups (55 year old and over).

Voluntary organisations

The increasingly positive attitude to volunteering reported by Italians is reflected in the fact that voluntary organisations are experiencing an expansion in numbers. During the period 1995-2003, the number of organisations registered according to Law 266/1991 increased from 8,343 to 21,021, 40.6 per cent of them being formed after 1995 (ISTAT, 2000a, 2006a). Nevertheless, the most detailed picture regarding organisations in the Italian voluntary sector is provided by the ISTAT (Istituto Nazionale di Statistica, National Institute for Statistics) survey of voluntary organisations from 2003, which is rather dated, however, and refers more to service-oriented organisations as specified by Law 266/91 (ISTAT, 2006a). In 1999 ISTAT investigated for the first time the heterogeneous mix of organisations constituting the non-profit sector as a whole, finding that there was a total of 221,412 active organisations in this sector, of which, in terms of legal form, the most relevant group (202,061) was represented by associations (ISTAT, 2011a - preliminary data from a second survey in 2011 suggesting that the total number of active organisations has

Table 3.1: Population volunteering in an organisation in the last 12 months, 1999-2010 (%)

Age group	1999	2003	2007	2010	Δ% (1999-2010)
14-17	6.3	6.9	9.1	7.3	+15.9
18-19	8.4	10.0	11.9	11.8	+40.5
20-24	8.8	10.7	10.9	11.2	+27.3
25-34	8.3	9.5	9.4	10.1	+21.7
35-44	9.1	8.0	9.6	9.6	+5.5
45-54	9.5	11.4	10.7	11.7	+23.2
55-59	8.6	11.0	11.6	13.8	+60.5
60-64	6.8	8.9	10.2	12.9	+89.7
65-74	4.1	6.2	7.9	9.3	+126.8
75+	2.1	2.4	3.4	4.0	+90.5
Total population	7.5	8.5	9.2	10.0	+33.3

Notes: People answering 'Yes' to the question: 'In the last 12 months, have you worked for free in voluntary associations or groups?'

Rates per 100 people of the same age group.

Source: Authors' elaboration on ISTAT (2000b, 2005, 2008, 2011)

grown to over 300,000; ISTAT, 2013). This underlines a clear bias in the survey that is exclusively based on 'voluntary organisations', as much information in the culture and recreation sector, including that regarding volunteers, was not surveyed, since most of the activities performed in it were not legally considered as volunteering.

Regarding the size of the organisations in terms of numbers of volunteers, the majority enrol less than 20 volunteers (53 per cent), while large organisations (with more than 60 volunteers) represent 13 per cent of the total. The distribution of voluntary organisations across the country is not uniform, with more in the Northern and Central regions (ISTAT, 2006a).

According to ISTAT (2001a), most Italian non-profit organisations operate in the culture and recreation sector (63.4 per cent), the second area by total number of organisations being social care (8.7 per cent). When only taking into consideration recognised voluntary organisations (ISTAT, 2006a), most are reported to be active in health and social services (65 per cent).

Paid staff represent a very limited component of human resources (HR) in voluntary organisations. Only 12 per cent of all voluntary organisations can count on the presence of employees, the latter being reported in particular by large organisations and by those operating in the health and social care sectors. In 2003 employees reached a total of 11,900. Another HR category, which, as mentioned earlier, can be considered a hybrid between employees and volunteers, is that represented by young volunteers doing Voluntary Service, who, in the same year were 9,389 (ISTAT, 2006a). When we consider non-profit organisations as a whole, in 1999 there were 531,926 employees and 27,788 young volunteers in Voluntary Service (ISTAT, 2001a).

Volunteers by sector, gender and age

Surveys have revealed that there were 825,955 unpaid volunteers in voluntary organisations and 3,221,185 working in 80 per cent of non-profit organisations as a whole (ISTAT, 2001a, 2006a). Recent preliminary data show that the latter number grew by 2011 to more than 4,700,000 (ISTAT, 2013).

Table 3.2 shows that the health and social services sectors are the main areas in which volunteers operate in Italy, and they are hosting a growing number of volunteers. A different scenario is described by the more comprehensive census of all non-profit organisations that shows that most volunteers are in the culture and recreation sector (52 per cent – recent data showing that their share is further increasing; ISTAT,

2013), with 15 per cent and 10 per cent in the health and social care services, respectively.

The increase in volunteering is also confirmed by a survey on the 'daily life activities' of individuals, which reported a growth from 7.5 to 10 per cent between 1999 and 2010 in the share of the population 14 years and older who declared having spent time in non-paid activities for a voluntary organisation (see Table 3.1 above). This 10 per cent may be estimated to be the equivalent of about 5,000,000 individuals. This survey shows (see Table 3.3) that the gender composition of volunteers is rather similar, even if men are slightly more represented (10.5 per cent against 9.5 per cent of women). A stronger male representation is reported in the census of non-profit organisations, which indicates that 65 per cent of all volunteers are men (ISTAT, 2001a). According to this source, both men and women are more present in the culture and recreation sector, social services and health, but in different proportions: while men volunteer more frequently in the former sector (55 per cent), women are more concentrated in social services (55 per cent) and health (60 per cent). A different picture is provided by data collected on a sample of voluntary organisations by Fondazione Roma Terzo Settore (2010), which found that in 2008, 52 per cent of volunteers were women and 48 per cent were men.

Considering the total population, people in 2010 volunteered more in the age group 55-64, whereas in 2007 the most active age groups were represented by people aged 18-24 and 45-59 (ISTAT, 2008, 2011). Overall, volunteering patterns are changing, especially among

Table 3.2: Number of volunteers by main sector of activity, 1995-2003

Area of activity	Voluntary organisations			All third sector
	1995	1999	2003	1999
Social services	150,860	189,099	256,250	492,875
Health	194,237	231,702	235,543	318,894
Culture and recreation	66,995	107,972	111,170	1,677,936
Civil protection	37,113	64,997	83,937	a
Environment	11,568	36,380	35,800	85,274
Sport	7,230	14,445	24,205	b
Education and research	8,676	9,779	19,351	114,447
Human rights	5,302	7,186	13,652	208,347
Other sectors	–	9,266	46,047	323,412
Total	481,981	670,826	825,955	3,221,185

Notes: [a] Included in social services; [b] Included in culture and recreation.
Source: ISTAT (2001a, 2006a)

Table 3.3: Activity in voluntary organisations at least once a year, 2010

Age group	Male	Female	Total
14-17	5.9	8.8	7.3
18-19	9.3	14.5	11.8
20-24	9.3	13.0	11.2
25-34	10.2	10.0	10.1
35-44	10.5	8.7	9.6
45-54	12.0	11.4	11.7
55-59	14.4	13.3	13.8
60-64	15.0	10.9	12.9
65-74	10.7	8.2	9.3
75+	4.2	3.9	4.0
Total	10.5	9.5	10.0

Note: Rates per 100 people of the same gender and age group.
Source: ISTAT (2011)

men. Whereas in the past the volunteering peak was reached for both genders in younger age ranges, in 2010 engagement in voluntary activities among men increased up to the age of 64 (ISTAT, 2005, 2008, 2011).

When we analyse participation in voluntary organisations by age group and activity sector (see Table 3.4), volunteers aged 55 and over constitute about 50 per cent of all those collaborating in the social services sector, about one third of those volunteering in the health sector and more than one third of those engaged in the culture and recreation sector.

Figure 3.1 shows that in 2008-09 volunteers aged 65 and over spent on average the same time as adult and younger people in voluntary activities (1.35 hours, 1.41 and 1.28 hours per day, respectively; ISTAT, 2012). So the Italian case seems to differ somewhat from what is generally reported in the literature, that is, that older volunteers devote more time than younger ones to voluntary activities (see, for example, Warburton and Cordingley, 2004).

The literature suggests that a higher educational level is correlated with higher participation in voluntary activities. The ISTAT survey (see Figure 3.2) confirms this positive correlation in all age groups, both for men and women (the latter having a higher education than men in both younger and older age groups). As well as being more highly educated, volunteers are also more highly qualified compared to non-volunteers (ISTAT, 2011).

Table 3.4: Number of volunteers by main sector of activity and age group, 2003

Main sector of activity	Up to 29	30-54	55-64	65+	Total	55+	% 55+
Social services	36,832	90,034	77,420	51,964	256,250	129,384	50.5
Health	60,978	103,035	49,827	21,703	235,543	71,530	30.4
Culture and recreation	27,002	41,172	24,078	18,918	111,170	42,996	38.7
Civil protection	24,860	43,047	12,159	3,871	83,937	16,030	19.1
Environment	8,970	16,454	7,131	3,245	35,800	10,376	29.0
Sport	8,814	10,465	3,253	1,673	24,205	4,926	20.3
Education and research	4,481	8,684	3,911	2,275	19,351	6,186	32.0
Human rights	2,041	6,541	3,405	1,665	13,652	5,070	37.1
Other sectors	8,545	19,645	11,718	6,139	46,047	17,857	38.8
Total	182,523	339,077	192,902	111,453	825,955	304,355	36.8

Source: ISTAT (2003)

Figure 3.1: Average time spent in voluntary activities in an average weekly day, by age group, 2008-09 (hours and minutes per day)

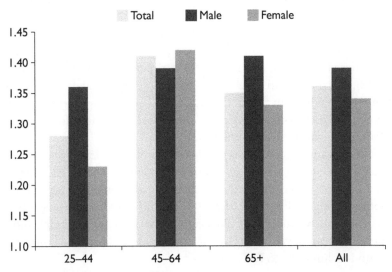

Source: Authors' elaboration on ISTAT (2012)

In light of the information mentioned earlier, we can conclude that the 'prototypical' Italian volunteer is male, aged 55-64, operates in the culture and recreation sector, is highly educated and qualified, and dedicates about 1.30 hours per day to voluntary activities. The female prototype is slightly different, being younger (aged 45-59), and while operating mostly in the culture and recreation sector, does so to a lesser extent than men, is more represented in the social services and health sectors, is more educated in both younger and older age groups, dedicates more time than her male counterpart in middle age.

Participation of older volunteers

While volunteer activity rates by age and sector are not available for the non-profit sector as a whole, according to the survey on voluntary organisations, older volunteers are mostly present in social services, as shown in Table 3.4. In general, male participation starts decreasing after the age of 64. Older males dedicate weekly about 10 minutes more than older females to volunteering and are less educated than middle-aged male volunteers. The typical older female volunteer is likely to give up after the age of 59, is more educated than older male volunteers, but less so than younger volunteers.

Figure 3.2: Activity in voluntary organisations among males and females, by age group and educational level, 2010 (%)

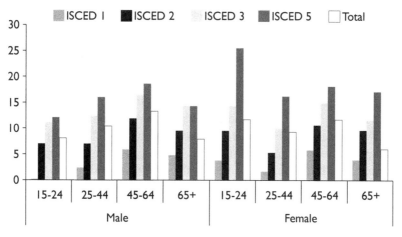

Notes: International Standard Classification of Education (ISCED): 1 = primary; 2 = lower secondary; 3 = upper secondary; 5 = tertiary.
Source: Authors' elaboration on ISTAT (2011)

Older volunteers seem to be mainly motivated by altruistic reasons and ideals of solidarity, whereas younger volunteers are more involved in different sectors (including the environment, sports and education), and are more likely to be driven by self-fulfilment reasons and by goals of social utility and human growth (Fondazione Roma Terzo Settore, 2010). This may be explained by the greater older volunteers' desire to maintain a sense of self and to deepen intimacy in social contacts through altruistic activities (that is, emotional gratification) against younger volunteers' greater preferences for pursuing knowledge through volunteering (Carstensen et al, 1999; Fung et al, 2001).

Looking at the trends in volunteering in older age, the proportion of volunteers aged 65 years and over in organisations grew between 1997 and 2003, from 8.9 to 13.5 per cent. In the same period, the share of mature volunteers (aged 55-64) also grew, from 18.3 to 23.3 per cent (ISTAT, 2000a, 2006a). On the other hand, Table 3.1 shows remarkable increases in the activity in voluntary organisations of all of the older age groups 65-74 (+126.8 per cent), 75+ (+90.5 per cent), 60-64 (+89.7 per cent) and 55-59 (+60.5 per cent), compared to the younger groups.

As already observed (see p 47), volunteering among older people in Italy may be a largely underestimated phenomenon, since part of its self-expressive component is probably not well captured by surveys. Indeed, Frisanco (2006) estimated that the number of older people carrying out unpaid social activities in these organisations in 2001 was almost twice as high as those who had officially been considered volunteers. According to Frisanco, the reason for this is that older Italians tend to prefer to organise themselves in autonomous intragenerational social and recreational centres. So an additional 'unofficial' profile of older volunteer emerges from these reflections, which is that of someone who prefers self-expressive cultural and recreational activities among peers.

Regarding the organisational dimension, and partly linked to what has just been mentioned, there are different kinds of organisations in Italy in which older people volunteer exclusively: (trade) unions of older people, voluntary and social associations to promote social events (including those linked to the unions), universities of the third age, and so on. There are also organisations for volunteers of all ages but with a prevalence of older volunteers, particularly in the social services and health sectors. Nevertheless, using data from two non-representative surveys on voluntary organisations, Frisanco (2006) found that between 1997 and 2001, the share of voluntary organisations composed totally or mainly of volunteers aged 65 or over decreased from 6.5 to 5.5 per cent of all voluntary organisations. In contrast, in investigating the universe of registered voluntary organisations, ISTAT underlined that in 2003 these kinds of organisations were much more numerous, and constituted about one third of all voluntary organisations (De Sario et al, 2010).

Frisanco (2006) identified the main characteristics of organisations composed of older volunteers as follows: longstanding history; female overrepresentation; provision of (light) care, support and socialisation services to a higher extent (more so than in other age-profiled organisations); and very limited involvement in emergency assistance, transportation of sick people and environmental protection. They represent intragenerational organisations, and the main beneficiaries of these organisations are older people themselves and poor people, as they are often strongly linked to the Catholic Church. Furthermore, they are characterised by a certain degree of isolation, as they are less linked to other kinds of institutions or organisations. In addition, they can count on lower levels of funding compared to other organisations, are less engaged in recruiting new volunteers and the volunteers of these organisations also receive less training.

Older people's participation in voluntary organisations: opportunities and restrictions

Despite the recent increase in the number of older Italians participating in voluntary activities, recent societal and demographic changes as well as some unfavourable transformations affecting voluntary organisations may have hampered current volunteer opportunities for older people. This section analyses the current opportunities and restrictions for volunteering in older age in Italy from three different perspectives: individual, organisational and political/institutional, also taking into consideration connections with other roles such as those of (paid) worker and (unpaid) family carer.

Opportunities and restrictions for volunteering for older people

Looking at the *individual level*, it is well known that a high level of education, good health and high socio-economic status represent factors that facilitate volunteering in later life (Principi et al, 2012b), and that older people generally have fewer resources in these areas compared to younger people. Indeed, as Caltabiano (2006) observed, despite the general volunteers' ideal of 'activism for solidarity', Italian older citizens do not fit so well with this profile of volunteer, as they are described mainly as passive people who are distant from social and political engagement because of their particular social conditions (for example, their low educational level and retired occupational status), rather than due to a real individual choice. In this context, the strongest intentions to volunteer are expressed by older adults who view volunteering as a useful, interesting and pleasant activity (Grano et al, 2008). Nevertheless, they seldom take the decision to volunteer by themselves. Indeed, the social participation of older Italians seems to increasingly depend on their positive answer to a request, for example, by a friend, or by an organisational representative, to get involved. They tend to answer this request positively, mainly for reasons of togetherness, to maintain social relationships and to count more in society as an older person (Mastropietro, 2009). This stronger need for social relations in older volunteers compared to younger people was also found by Capanna et al (2002), who explored the main motivations of Italian volunteers. However, motivation in older volunteers is a multidimensional phenomenon going beyond just social reasons, as underlined, for example, by Principi et al (2012c), who found that important drivers for older Italian volunteers are altruistic motivations and the desire to protect their ego from negative feelings through volunteering.

With respect to the *organisational level*, there is a substantial lack of Italian studies on what is offered to older volunteers in terms of measures and initiatives. In addition to what was discussed earlier (see p 59), Frisanco (2006) underlines that voluntary organisations composed mainly of older people are likely to be linked mainly to the local area (for example, the parish or municipality), and are less likely to be involved in carrying out research or other kinds of studies. Also, they have less funds and do less fundraising in general, have less developed communication and promotion strategies and are less active in networking. Thus, there seem to be several negative organisational aspects linked to volunteering in older age. Focusing on the positive aspects, organisations composed mainly of older volunteers seem to offer themselves mainly for recognition and intragenerational support in the mutualistic and recreational context (Frisanco, 2006).

At the *political/institutional level*, until recently there has been no specific overarching national policy addressing active ageing or even volunteering among older age groups, as reflected by the few and disconnected initiatives that are available. This does not seem purely an age-related problem, since in Italy the support of the third sector in general has never been an overarching public policy goal (Ranci et al, 2009). However, as described earlier, the institutional support of the social participation of older people has recently increased. A further driving force in this has surely been the European designation of 2012 as the Year of Active Ageing and Intergenerational Solidarity, which led the Ministry of Labour and Social Policies to promote specific initiatives aimed at increasing the social participation of older people and initiatives for intergenerational solidarity. For example, through ministerial directives, the funding of experimental projects on active ageing and intergenerational solidarity has been considered a priority, and both voluntary organisations and social promotion associations have been invited to present project proposals. Specific funds have also been envisaged for projects on this issue by municipalities, in partnership with third sector organisations and research bodies, to further promote active ageing at the local level (Presidenza del Consiglio dei Ministri, 2012). It will be interesting to see the extent to which the latter activities can realistically be implemented in the near future, given the state spending review currently underway in a climate characterised by budget cuts, which already seem to have caused some limitations on volunteer opportunities for older people (see p 51).

Older people between employment and volunteering

There seems to be no evidence that in Italy working for the labour market may hamper participation in voluntary activities in older age groups. On the contrary, since both volunteer and paid work activities are experiencing an increase, as reported by several studies (see, for example, Haski-Leventhal, 2009), working for the labour market seems to have a phasing-in effect on volunteering by increasing personal social relations and opportunities for social engagement.

Even in a context of low rates compared to most European countries, the employment rate of older workers, both men and women, is increasing in Italy mainly due to a gradual rise in the statutory retirement age in the latest pension reforms. From January 2012 the retirement age limit in Italy has been increased to 66 years for both men and women employed in the public sector, and to 62 years for women employed in the private sector. The same level (that is, 66 years) for workers of all sectors and genders will be reached by 2018. Between 2004 and 2011 the employment rate of people aged 55-64 increased from 42.2 to 48.4 per cent for men and from 19.6 to 28.1 per cent for women. In 2011, the employment rate of the population over 65 was 5.6 per cent for men and 1.3 per cent for women (Eurostat, 2012).

Despite governmental efforts to increase the retirement age in Italy, only 48 per cent of 50 to 65-years-olds declared that they "would enjoy having a paid job even if they did not need the money". This is a rather low value compared with most European countries (ISSP, 1997). However, apart from the Italian orientation to work, working in older age due to economic need may become an issue in the near future in Italy given the expected reduction of pension income as an effect of the pension reform. There is already some evidence that in the last few years people have increased their participation in the labour market after retirement, especially beyond the age of 70 (Principi et al, 2012a).

What may be the consequences of this changing scenario on volunteering by older Italians? According to SHARE data (Survey of Health, Ageing and Retirement in Europe), in 2004 Italian older adults in paid employment participated slightly less in voluntary activities (10.6 per cent) than retirees and other non-working older people (11.4 per cent), and relatively low rates of engagement were associated with being in paid work (Erlinghagen and Hank, 2006). The subsequent wave of SHARE data suggested a different interpretation: while the rate of volunteering by employed people stayed the same (that is, 10.6 per cent), the participation in volunteering of non-employed older people decreased to 6.6 per cent (Haski-Leventhal, 2009). This may suggest that retirement crowds out volunteering, which seems to be confirmed by the ISTAT data that show (see Table 3.3) that participation rates of both men and women decrease after they retire (in 2009 the effective average age was 61.1 years for men and 58.5 for women; see OECD, 2011). This positive relation may be further improved by planning and implementing programmes linking companies and voluntary organisations, for example, through employee volunteer programmes, as a useful way to respond to the need of promoting active ageing and thus facilitating engagement in the period between work and retirement (Mastropietro, 2009). These are not widespread in Italy, however.

Older people between family care and volunteering

The Italian informal care system has been changing in the last few years. Most of the in-house caring responsibilities have shifted to migrant care workers, and disabled older people are much more likely to live alone than in the past. Family carers, particularly women, continue to provide informal care, but increasingly in terms of the 'organisation of care' rather than care in itself. Keeping this in mind, it is possible to observe that older people's engagement in both volunteering and informal family care to non-cohabitant people is growing in Italy, so it can be assumed that a growth in the family help/care activities of older people does not necessarily mean a decline in the participation of older people in voluntary activities, even if a gender effect may be present.

Considering elder care, in Italy, as in most Mediterranean and Eastern European countries, a significant percentage of people (50 per cent) think that the best option for an old parent living alone in need of regular help is to live with their children, or one of the children should regularly visit the older person's home to adequately care for them (Eurobarometer, 2007). Thus in Italy care is considered a family matter – women are often culturally expected to assume the role of housewives and informal full-time carers (Anttonen and Sipilä, 1996), whereas the state traditionally provides care allowances rather than in-kind social services (Bettio and Plantenga, 2004). This is reflected in the use of long-term care services for people aged 65 years and over: about 9 per cent of older people receive a care allowance, less than 5 per cent some kind of home care and 3 per cent residential care (Gori and Lamura, 2009). So even if elder care in Italy is mainly informal, it should be considered that a cash-for-care scheme (the care allowance, that is, *indennità di accompagnamento*, which totalled about 470 monthly in 2009) is present, and the dependent person can freely use this benefit. However, this scheme is available not only to older people but also to disabled people of all ages, even if most of those who receive it are older people

Nonetheless, family ties are weakening (Naldini, 2002) due to factors such as a falling fertility rate, an increase in conjugal instability, decreasing intergenerational cohabitation and the greater employment rate of women in the labour market. Family solidarity has not disappeared, but has, rather, undergone a process of adaptation (Tomassini and Lamura, 2009). For example, the care allowance is likely to be used to employ migrant care workers to look after older people living alone (Lamura et al, 2010; Di Rosa et al, 2012). For this reason, today more than in the past, Italians aged 55 years and over are engaged, on the one hand, in providing help to non-cohabitant younger (children and grandchildren), while on the other, to non-cohabitant older (parents) family members (ISTAT, 2001b, 2006b). Can this trend of increasing but changing engagement in family care have consequences on participation in voluntary activities by older people? As already observed, despite these trends, a growth in volunteering in older age at aggregate level has been observed, so at first sight this may suggest a positive relation between the two activities. However, Italian voluntary organisations generally perceive family caregiving as a significant barrier to older people volunteering (Principi et al, 2010) and, given the female care family model that is widespread in the country, women may be especially penalised in this game. As a consequence it may be no coincidence that women are less involved in volunteering than men in adult and older age groups (see Table 3.3).

Improving the match between supply of older candidates with the demand of voluntary organisations: future perspectives

Increasing the participation rate of older European people in voluntary activities represents a key challenge for the future, and Italy is no exception in this, as demonstrated by national and local policy efforts on the matter. The voluntary sector represents a field in which older Italians can find new meaning and experiences that may compensate for the loss of engagement following retirement from the labour market, and hence they are no longer considered solely as recipients of services and care (Frisanco, 2006). If a higher commitment among older Italians is to be pursued, future actions to improve the match between supply of older candidates and the demands of civil society organisations must be undertaken, both by organisations themselves and by institutions. The literature does not tell us much on organisational efforts undertaken to improve this match in Italy. Frisanco (2006) underlined that older volunteers are often excluded by voluntary organisations with more resources, and some Italian studies have indicated what actions should be undertaken by organisations. Grano et al (2008), for example, underlined that to attract older volunteers, voluntary organisations should arrange policy programmes providing salient and accessible information on the importance of volunteering, and highlight the advantages of volunteering, thus encouraging older people to identify their own reasons for volunteering. Furthermore, they should create age-targeted recruitment programmes, provide more training opportunities and consider the motivation behind volunteering.

As for the institutional level, despite the stronger interest in promoting active ageing shown recently that is likely to determine a further increase in volunteering by older people in the near future, Mirabile (2009) comments that more focused and effective thinking and actions by policy makers at various levels are needed as ageing is still often addressed mainly in terms of prevention of health risk factors and retention in the labour market, completely neglecting the social engagement of older people. De Sario (2009), on the other hand, highlights that more specialised tools and conditions are needed, such as, for example, targeted volunteer programmes.

Conclusions

In Italy about 10 per cent of the overall population volunteers, with participation rates peaking for those aged 45-64 years (about 12-14 per cent), and decreasing in older age groups. However, a sharp increase in voluntary participation is observed in the age bracket 65-74, which means that older people are increasingly involved in community life. Official sources depict older volunteers as those mainly involved in the social services and healthcare sectors, but their participation in self-expressive activities may be underestimated. Despite the increase in participation at the individual level, voluntary organisations do not seem to be ready to fully exploit older volunteers' potential. There are several organisations where older volunteers might actually contribute, but they seem to be those characterised by a lower availability of resources.

At the institutional level, efforts to involve an increased number of older citizens in voluntary activities have recently mushroomed, and are likely to help voluntary organisations remove the main barriers for older volunteers in the future, for example, by providing older volunteers with more opportunities for training and qualifications to carry out activities. At the moment these are only intentions, and it will be interesting to observe if they will turn into concrete facts. The expectedly longer working life deriving from the recent pension reforms does not seem to represent a threat, but rather an incentive to volunteering in older age. It is no coincidence that older men, while working more and longer, are more involved in volunteering than older women. On the other hand, informal family care of older relatives or grandchildren may be seen as a barrier to volunteering, especially for older women. Thus, even with the perspective of an overall positive scenario for the future volunteering of older Italians in the global framework, more effective thinking on how to overcome this dilemma is needed at both the institutional and organisational level, for example, through more gender-specific targeted programmes.

Speaking in terms of social origins theory, which relies mainly on the non-profit scale and the social welfare spending to categorise third sector regimes, Salamon and Anheir (1998) included Italy in the social democratic model (see Chapter Two, this volume). Nevertheless, we found evidence that Italy does not fit very well in this model. Indeed, Italy is characterised by a rather low social welfare spending, and a low scale of volunteering, since volunteering in Italy (as probably in other Mediterranean countries) may not really be perceived by (older) individuals as a social norm compared to other countries. It can therefore be concluded that more specific attention should be paid to this Mediterranean third sector pattern as a relevant variation of the other, more well-known, models.

Acknowledgements

The authors would like to thank Renato Frisanco for his useful comments.

References

Anttonen, A. and Sipilä, J. (1996) 'European social care services: is it possible to identify models?', *Journal of European Social Policy*, vol 6, no 2, pp 87-100.

Ascoli, U. and Cnaan, R.A. (1997) 'Volunteering for human service provisions: Lessons from Italy and the USA', *Social Indicators Research*, vol 40, no 3, pp 299-327.

Barbetta, G.P. and Maggio, F. (2002) *Nonprofit. Il nuovo volto della società civile* [*Non profit. The new face of civil society*], Bologna: Il Mulino.

Bettio, F. and Plantenga, J. (2004) 'Comparing care regimes in Europe', *Feminist Economics*, vol 10, no 1, pp 85-113.

Borzaga, C. (2004) 'From suffocation to re-emergence: the evolution of the Italian third sector', in A. Evers and J.L. Laville (eds) *The third sector in Europe*, Cheltenham: Edward Elgar, pp 139-53.

Borzaga, C. and Santuari, A. (2000) *Le imprese sociali nel contesto europeo* [*Social enterprises in the European context*], Working Paper no 13, Trento: Dipartimento di Economia dell'Università di Trento.

Caltabiano, C. (2006) *Gli anticorpi della società civile. Nono rapporto sull'associazionismo sociale* [*The antibodies of civil society. Ninth report on social associations*], Working Paper Iref-Acli, Roma: Pragma Srl.

Capanna, C., Steca, P. and Imbimbo, A. (2002) 'Una scala per la misura della motivazione al volontariato' ['A scale to measure the motivation to volunteer'], *Rassegna di Psicologia*, vol 19, no 1, pp 73-90.

Carstensen, L.L., Isaacowitz, D.M. and Charles, S.T. (1999) 'Taking time seriously. A theory of socioemotional selectivity', *American Psychologist*, vol 54, no 3, pp 165-81.

CNEL-ISTAT (2011) *La valorizzazione economica del lavoro volontario nel settore non profit* [*The economic value of volunteer work in the nonprofit sector*], Roma: Ministero del Lavoro e delle Politiche Sociali.

De Sario, B. (2009) 'Italia. L'associazionismo anziano emergente: orientamenti soggettivi, network e pratiche associative' ['Italy. The emerging associational trend of older people: subjective orientations, networks and associative practices'], in M.L. Mirabile (ed) *Vita attiva? I 'giovani anziani' fra insicurezza e partecipazione* [*Active life? The 'young-old' between insecurity and participation*], Roma: Ediesse, pp 215-43.

De Sario, B., Sabbatici, A. and Mirabile, M.L. (2010) *Il capitale sociale degli anziani. Stime sul valore dell'attività non retribuita* [*The social capital of older people. Forecasts of the value of unpaid activity*], Roma: IRES.

Di Rosa, M., Melchiorre, M.G., Lucchetti, M. and Lamura, G. (2012) 'The impact of migrant work in the elder care sector: recent trends and empirical evidence in Italy', *European Journal of Social Work*, vol 15, no 1, pp 9-27.

Esping-Andersen, G. (1996) 'After the golden age? Welfare state dilemmas in a global economy', in G. Esping-Andersen (ed) *Welfare states in transition: National adaptations in global economies*, London: Sage Publications, pp 1-30.

Erlinghagen, M. and Hank, K. (2006) 'The participation of older European in volunteer work', *Ageing & Society*, vol 26, no 5, pp 67-84.

Eurispes (2006) *Le politiche sociali in Italia, il confronto con gli stati europei* [*Social policies in Italy, comparison with European countries*], Roma: Istituto di Studi Politici Economici e Sociali.

Eurobarometer (2007) *Health and long-term care in the European Union*, Special Eurobarometer 283/Wave 67.3 – TNS Opinion & Social (ec.europa.eu/public_opinion/archives/ebs/ebs_283_en.pdf).

Eurostat (2012) 'Employment rate of older workers' (epp.eurostat.ec.europa.eu).

Ferrara, M. (1996) 'The "Southern model" of welfare in social Europe', *Journal of European Social Policy*, vol 6, no 1, pp 17-37.

Fondazione Roma Terzo Settore (2010) *Organizzazioni di volontariato tra identità e processi. Il fenomeno delle rilevazioni campionarie 2008* [*Voluntary organisations between identities and processes. The phenomenon of the 2008 sample surveys*], Roma: Fondazione Roma Terzo Settore.

Frisanco, R. (2006) 'Volontariato e anziani' ['Older people and volunteering'], in Osservatorio Nazionale per il Volontariato (ed) *Rapporto biennale sul volontariato 2005* [*2005 biennial report on volunteering*], Roma: Ministero della Solidarietà Sociale.

Fung, H.H., Carstensen, L.L. and Lang, F.R. (2001) 'Age-related patterns in social networks among European Americans and African Americans: implications for socioemotional selectivity across the life span', *International Journal of Aging and Human Development*, vol 52, no 3, pp 185-206.

Gori, C. and Lamura, G. (2009) 'Lo scenario complessivo' ['The global scenario'], in NNA (Network Non Autosufficienza) (ed) *L'assistenza agli anziani non autosufficienti in Italia. Rapporto 2009 [Care of dependent older people in Italy. 2009 report]*, Rimini: Maggioli, pp 17-34.

Grano, C., Lucidi, F., Zelli, A. and Violani, C. (2008) 'Motives and determinants of volunteering in older adults: an integrated model', *International Journal of Aging and Human Development*, vol 67, no 4, pp 305-26.

Haski-Leventhal, D. (2009) 'Elderly volunteering and wellbeing: a cross-European comparison based on SHARE data', *Voluntas*, vol 20, no 4, pp 388-404.

ISSP (International Social Survey Programme) (1997) 'Work Orientations II', Mannheim: ISSP (www.gesis.org/issp/issp-modules-profiles/work-orientations/1997).

ISTAT (Istituto Nazionale di Statistica) (2000a) *Le organizzazioni di volontariato in Italia. Anno 1997 [Voluntary organisations in Italy. Year 1997]*, Roma: ISTAT.

ISTAT (2000b) *Cultura, socialità e tempo libero. Anno 1999 [Culture, society and spare time. Year 1999]*, Roma: ISTAT.

ISTAT (2001a) *Istituzioni nonprofit in Italia. Anno 1999 [Non-profit institutions in Italy. Year 1999]*, Roma: ISTAT.

ISTAT (2001b) *Parentela e reti di solidarietà. Anno 1998 [Kinship and solidarity networks. Year 1998]*, Roma: ISTAT.

ISTAT (2003) *Rilevazione delle organizzazioni di volontariato. Anno 2003 [Survey on voluntary organisations. Year 2003]*, Roma: ISTAT.

ISTAT (2005) *Cultura, socialità e tempo libero. Anno 2003 [Culture, society and spare time. Year 2003]*, Roma: ISTAT.

ISTAT (2006a) *Le organizzazioni di volontariato in Italia. Anno 2003 [Voluntary organisations in Italy. Year 2003]*, Roma: ISTAT.

ISTAT (2006b) *Parentela e reti di solidarietà. Anno 2003 [Kinship and solidarity networks. Year 2003]*, Roma: ISTAT.

ISTAT (2008) *La vita quotidiana nel 2007 [Daily life in 2007]*, Roma: ISTAT.

ISTAT (2011) *La vita quotidiana nel 2010 [Daily life in 2010]*, Roma: ISTAT.

ISTAT (2012) *Uso del tempo. Anni 2008-2009 [Time use. Years 2008-2009]*, Roma: ISTAT.

ISTAT (2013) *9° Censimento dell'industria e dei servizi e Censimento delle istituzioni non profit. Primi risultati [9th Census of industry and services, and Census of non-profit institutions. First results]*, Roma: ISTAT

Lamura, G., Chiatti C., Di Rosa, M., Melchiorre, M.G., Barbabella, F., Greco, C., Principi, A. and Santini, S. (2010) 'Migrant workers in the long-term care sector: lessons from Italy', *Health and Ageing*, no 22, pp 8-12.

Lewis, J. (1992) 'Gender and the development of welfare regimes', *Journal of European Social Policy*, vol 2, no 3, pp 159-73.

Mastropietro, E. (2009) 'La partecipazione degli anziani al volontariato: spinte e motivazioni individuali' ['Participation of older people in voluntary activities: individual motivations and thrusts'], in M.L. Mirabile (ed) *Vita attiva? I 'giovani anziani' fra insicurezza e partecipazione* [*Active life? The 'young-old' between insecurity and participation*], Roma: Ediesse, pp 198-214.

Mirabile, M.L. (2009) *Vita attiva? I 'giovani anziani' fra insicurezza e partecipazione* [*Active life? The 'young-old' between insecurity and participation*], Roma: Ediesse.

Naldini, M. (2002) *The family in the Mediterranean welfare states*, London: Frank Cass.

OECD (Organisation for Economic Co-operation and Development) (2011) *Ageing and employment policies: Statistics on average effective age of retirement*, Paris: OECD (www.oecd.org).

Pfau-Effinger, B. (2005) 'Culture and welfare state policies: reflections on a complex interrelation', *Journal of Social Policy*, vol 34, no 1, pp 3-20.

Presidenza del Consiglio dei Ministri (2012) *Programma nazionale di lavoro. Per un invecchiamento attivo, vitale e dignitoso in una società solidale* [*National work-programme. For an active, vital and dignified aging in an inclusive society*], Roma: Dipartimento per le politiche della famiglia (www.invecchiamentoattivo.politicheperlafamiglia.it).

Principi, A., Checcucci, P. and di Rosa, M. (2012a) *Income from work after retirement in Italy*, Ancona: INRCA (www.inrca.it/inrca/files/focuson/Income from work after retirement in Italy.pdf).

Principi, A., Chiatti, C., Barbabella, F. and Lamura, G. (2010) *Opportunities for older people in the civil society. National report Italy*, Ancona: INRCA.

Principi, A., Chiatti, C., Frerichs, F. and Lamura, G. (2012b) 'The engagement of older people in civil society organisations', *Educational Gerontology*, vol 38, no 2, pp 83-106.

Principi, A., Chiatti, C. and Lamura, G. (2012c) 'Motivations of older volunteers in three European countries', *International Journal of Manpower*, vol 33, no 6, pp 704-22.

Ranci, C., Pellegrino, M. and Pavolini, E. (2009) 'The third sector and the policy progress in Italy: between mutual accommodations and new forms of (blurred) partnership', in J. Kendall (ed) *Handbook on third sector policy in Europe*, Cheltenham: Edward Elgar, pp 95-118.

Salamon, L.M. and Anheier, H.K. (1998) 'Social origins of civil society: explaining the nonprofit sector cross-nationally', *Voluntas*, vol 9, no 3, pp 213-48.

Tomassini, C. and Lamura, G. (2009) 'Population ageing in Italy and Southern Europe', in P. Uhlenberg (ed) *International handbook of population ageing*, New York/Heidelberg: Springer, pp 69-90.

Warburton, J. and Cordingley, S. (2004) 'The contemporary challenges of volunteering in an ageing Australia', *Australian Journal on Volunteering*, vol 9, no 2, pp 67-74.

FOUR

Older volunteers in Denmark: a large voluntary sector in a highly developed welfare state

Per H. Jensen

Introduction

It has sometimes been alleged that a voluminous welfare state as well as a heavy workload from formal employment reduces people's propensity to carry out voluntary work (Rostow, 1960; Wolfe, 1989; Fukuyama, 1995). One should therefore expect the level of voluntary work to be rather low in Denmark, in part because Denmark has a highly developed institutional welfare state, and because Danish labour force participation rates are rather high, reaching, in 2007, 81.8 per cent for men and 76.2 per cent for women. Furthermore, most women in employment work full time, which has been made possible by the provision of extensive and universal social services (child and elder care), financed by individual and progressive taxation. The Danish family model may thus be characterised as a dual breadwinner/external care model (Pfau-Effinger, 2004).

The welfare state–labour market–family–voluntary work nexus, however, is rather complex. In accordance with the findings of Williams and Windebank (1998, p 31), the Danish experience demonstrates that welfare state growth, increasing labour force participation rates and growth in civil society organisations can take place simultaneously. In 2007 the total number of voluntary organisations in Denmark was about 100,000. Out of a total population of 5.5 million, 38 per cent was engaged in voluntary work, and the economic value of voluntary work amounted to 9.6 per cent of GDP (gross domestic product) (Center for frivilligt socialt abejde, 2001). The voluntary sector has earnings totalling DKK 96.4 billion per year, equivalent to 12.9 billion. Of this, 50 per cent is from membership fees and production of goods, 37 per cent from public transfers, 7 per cent from gifts and sponsoring and 6 per cent from other sources such as interest rates.

Although the welfare state has not crowded out voluntary work in Denmark, it has certainly helped to structure (and is itself structured by) the voluntary sector. Voluntary work is a highly complex phenomenon, but it is possible to make a distinction between two major forms, according to the motives of the providers (Sivesind et al, 2002; Jensen et al, 2009): voluntary work may be philanthropic, that is, targeted at the production of classical welfare provision against social risks such as poverty, homelessness, sickness and so on; or it may be self-centred or self-expressive, that is, targeted towards leisure activities in the form of sport, culture and so on. In a highly advanced and de-commodifiying welfare state there is little room for philanthropic or charitable activities. Accordingly, voluntary work in countries such as Denmark is concentrated around sport, culture and leisure activities, rather than private charitable giving (Jensen and Rathlev, 2009).

In countries where voluntary work is extensive and/or increasing, one may expect that older people become more and more enrolled in the voluntary sector. This assumption ties in with a shift in the perception of older people. The first retirement studies, dating from the 1950s and 1960s, assumed that older people would lose the skills to function socially and would disengage from social life (Burgess, 1960; Cumming and Henry, 1961). By contrast, more recent theories have argued that the loss of role of the retiree as participant in the labour market would be compensated for by a more active role in other social fields (Atchley, 1989; Laslett, 1989; Richardson, 1999; Phillipson, 2002). As such, the role compensation theory allows for stable or even increased social integration, and continuity may be attained through volunteering (Richardson, 1999; Phillipson, 2002). In 2004, about 15 per cent of all volunteers in Denmark were aged 66-85, while 23 per cent of the total population in this age group was enrolled in voluntary work (Koch–Nielsen et al, 2005).

The aim of this chapter is to analyse the background, size, composition and enrolment of older people in the voluntary sector in Denmark. It then discusses factors that may facilitate or restrict the entry of older people into civil society organisations, and it examines discrepancies between the supply and demand for older people in the voluntary sector. It concludes with a brief discussion as to how older people are related to the voluntary sector in the Danish welfare state.

The Danish tradition of voluntary action

Voluntary work in the form of charity giving in Denmark can be traced back to the late 18th century, but it was not until the mid-19th century that voluntary work mushroomed (Lützen, 1998; Henriksen et al, 2012) and became an integrated part of civil society. As the welfare state matured in the 1960s and 1970s, however, philanthropic forms of voluntary work became somewhat marginalised. In particular, philanthropic voluntary work within the area of social policy gained a reputation as being something without any professional expertise, although well intentioned, and therefore not representing a serious contribution to solving social problems.

As of the 1980s, however, a new discourse emerged, propagating a positive view of philanthropic voluntary work and voluntary philanthropic organisations as active participants in Danish society. In 1983 the Minister for Social Affairs set up the Danish Committee on Volunteer Effort, a political committee made up of representatives from public authorities and voluntary organisations. The aim of this 'Committee on Volunteer Effort is to bolster the possibility for individuals, groups of citizens and private associations and organisations to participate in the solution of tasks in the social policy area' (Ministry of Social Affairs, 2001, p 14). Indeed, philanthropic voluntary work has gained a much higher status than previously, and has now become widely appreciated in Danish society, in the hope or belief that the voluntary sector could relieve economic pressure on the welfare state by preventing and solving social problems (Hegeland, 1994; Henriksen, 1995). To support this endeavour, philanthropic voluntary institutions have increasingly been subsidised by the state over the last 10-15 years. The aim has not been to replace public welfare services by voluntary organisations, but rather to stimulate the development of alternative initiatives that can reach those vulnerable groups (drug addicts, prostitutes and so on) who have turned their back on the public welfare system. Philanthropic voluntary work has, however, remained a marginal phenomenon within the Danish social policy area, in that it has remained a minor supplement to the public sector (Boje, 2006a). Voluntary organisations within the social policy area are often staffed with paid employees, that is, in some voluntary organisations work is paid for and carried out as ordinary full-time wage work.

Nevertheless, as already underlined, volunteering in Denmark is mainly self-centred or self-expressive – to some extent subsidised by the public sector, but mainly financed by users' fees, for example, in sports clubs – and this kind of volunteering is most often carried out as unpaid work. As self-centred or self-expressive forms of voluntary work predominates, it can be said that the development trajectories of the voluntary sector in Denmark is more young- than old-friendly, since young people in particular seem to prefer non-philanthropic volunteer work (Morrow-Howell, 2010).

The legal framework

Voluntary organisations in Denmark are regulated by civil law. Because there is no official register for such organisations, they do not register, either totally or within the different areas of their voluntary activities. Volunteer organisations are, however, obliged to register as a 'company' by public authorities, if they employ people and/or buy or sell goods, the aim being to avoid tax evasion or tax fraud in relation to income tax and/or value-added tax (VAT). About 45 per cent of all voluntary organisations are registered as a 'company' (Boje and Ibsen, 2006).

Hardly any legal framework regulates the voluntary sector in Denmark, with two exceptions: first, in 2005 the entry of teachers/ instructors into voluntary organisations was restricted in some ways. The aim of the legislation was to prevent people convicted of paedophilia from enrolling in voluntary organisations such as scout clubs, sports clubs, and so on, in which children below the age of 15 are active. The legislation implies an obligation for such organisations to obtain a so-called 'child certificate' for volunteers before recruiting them as instructors or teachers. This is issued by public authorities and contains information about convictions for paedophilia. This legislation mirrors the reality that a large share of voluntary work is targeted towards children and younger people within areas such as sports, culture and so on.

Second, in Denmark municipalities bear the major responsibility for providing welfare services (schools, child and elder care and so on), which are financed, to a large extent, by local taxes. The Law on Social Service, however, includes a paragraph (para 18) that concerns voluntary work within the social policy area. It stipulates that municipalities must cooperate with voluntary social organisations and annually earmark an amount of money for voluntary social work. This may, of course, increase local government expenditure. To soften the economic pressure on the municipalities, the Parliament has granted municipalities about DKK 130 million (about 17 million) per year in the form of extra conditional grants (from the state), to compensate for the costs of subsidising voluntary organisations.

The Law on Social Service (para 79) also allows municipalities to transfer prophylactic social policy schemes to pensioners' clubs or senior associations. In addition to encouraging seniors' own voluntary work, the Ministry of Welfare also supports voluntary work targeting older people. For instance, in 2006 and 2007 the Ministry of Welfare granted about DKK 4.5 million (equivalent to 0.6 million) to projects aimed at relieving older people's feelings of isolation (Rambøll, 2009).

The dimension of volunteer work

In Denmark, the number of people participating in voluntary work has increased substantially over the last 15 years. In the early 1990s about 25 per cent of the adult Danish population (aged 16-85) participated in unpaid voluntary work, while the number increased to 35 per cent[1] by 2004. On average, each volunteer performs about four hours of unpaid voluntary work per week (Koch-Nielsen et al, 2005; Fridberg et al, 2006).

Voluntary organisations

The total number of voluntary organisations in Denmark is 100,200: 83,000 associations, 8,000 independent institutions, 6,200 'funds for the common good' and 3,000 nationwide organisations (Boje and Ibsen, 2006). These voluntary organisations enrol, as already mentioned, about 35 per cent of the total population aged 16-85 (about 1.5 million people) into unpaid voluntary work. The non-profit sector furthermore employs about 200,000 people as wage earners, of which 70 per cent work full time (Boje, 2006b). A large share of these are employed in independent schools, non-profit kindergartens, trade unions and so on. Employees in the non-profit sector amount to about 5 per cent of total employment.

European data seem to indicate that there is a connection between volunteering and the degree of urbanisation (Gaskin and Smith, 1995). In accordance with these findings, volunteering in Denmark is slightly more predominant in the rural provinces compared to highly urbanised areas. Indeed, Koch-Nielsen et al (2005, p 32) have found that volunteering amounts to 36 per cent in rural districts and provinces and 31 per cent in the capital and its suburbs. And the creation of longstanding social networks seems to increase the propensity to volunteer, as data show that the longer a person has been living in the same municipality, the more they will be inclined to engage in voluntary work.

Volunteers by sector, gender and age

Table 4.1 shows the sectoral and gendered composition of voluntary activities in Denmark. As can be seen, 35 per cent of the population is engaged in voluntary work, although if the column 'All' is added up, it amounts to more than 35 per cent. This inconsistency is due to the fact that the same person may perform voluntary work in more than

Table 4.1: Proportions of the Danish population performing voluntary work during 2004, by sector and gender (%)

Sector	Men	Women	All
Sport (eg sports clubs, dancing, swimming)	14	9	11
Housing, local community (eg housing associations, cable services provision)	8	4	6
Other leisure activities (eg hobbies, genealogy, scouting)	5	4	5
Culture (eg museums, local historical archives, choirs)	3	3	3
Education, research (eg boards of directors, adult or spare-time education)	3	4	3
Health-related (eg blood donor, patients' associations, crisis counselling)	2	4	3
Social (eg drop-in centres, refugee support groups)	2	4	3
Organisational work, trade and branch organisations (eg trade unions, employers' associations)	3	2	3
International activities (eg humanitarian, peace and solidarity organisations)	1	2	2
Religion, church-related (eg parochial church council, Sunday School)	2	2	2
Politics, party associations (eg constituency associations, grass-roots organisations)	2	1	1
Environment (eg environmental preservation, protection of animals)	1	>1	>1
Counselling, legal aid (eg consumer, human rights, legal aid)	1	>1	>1
Other areas	2	3	3
Volunteer work in all	38	32	35
n	1,502	1,632	3,134

Note: Question asked to respondents: 'Here are some questions about voluntary unpaid work. Voluntary unpaid work can be performed in many different areas. Often voluntary work is done for voluntary organisations, but it can also be done for a public or private company. Unpaid voluntary work is conducted in many different areas of society and is related to many different activities: one can train a local football team; one can be a custodian in a museum, collect money for charity, be a board member for a homeowner's association or at a school, help out at a drop-in centre, etc. The term "voluntary work" does not, however, include help given to family members or close friends. Do you work as a volunteer within one or more of the following areas?'

Source: Fridberg et al (2006)

one voluntary sector. Of all volunteers in Denmark, 24 per cent are active in more than one voluntary sector (Fridberg et al, 2006, p 44).

The major part of voluntary work in Denmark is performed in sports, culture and similar activities, as about 45 per cent of all voluntary work in Denmark is done in these two sectors of societal life (Koch-Nielsen and Clausen, 2002). Sport is the primary sector of voluntary work, with 11 per cent of the total population – or 29 per cent of all volunteers –active in this sector. Activities such as 'housing, local community' (16 per cent of all volunteers) and 'other leisure activities' (13 per cent of all volunteers) subsequently follow. 'Social' and 'health-related' activities are not extensively performed, as altogether only about 16 per cent of all voluntary activities are carried out in these two 'traditional' welfare sectors of voluntary work.

Men seem to be slightly more likely to volunteer as compared with women, and tend also to commit more hours to voluntary work. They are also more inclined to volunteering even when having a full-time job, while women are more disposed to do voluntary work when they have only a part-time job (Jensen and Rathlev, 2009). Another gender-specific feature is that, while men are more active in sectors such as 'sport' and 'housing, local community', women are more inclined to do voluntary work in sectors associated with the care of people, such as in the 'health' and 'social' sectors. Gender differences, however, are generally not so conspicuous.

Table 4.2 shows how voluntary work is structured according to sector and age. In agreement with studies based on data from the US, Australia and the European Union (EU) (Warburton et al, 2001; Erlinghagen and Hank, 2006; Rozario, 2006), the frequency of volunteering peaks in middle age and declines in later life. In Denmark, only 23 per cent of the total population aged 66+ is enrolled in voluntary work. By contrast, Danish data also shows that

Table 4.2: Voluntary work by sector and age (%)

Age/ sector	Leisure	Social/ health	Politics	Educa- tion	Housing/ local commu- nity	Other	Total	n
16-29	18	4	4	3	1	5	32	622
30-49	23	6	6	6	8	5	41	1,240
50-65	15	7	7	1	8	6	35	805
66-	10	6	2	1	5	5	23	467
All	18	6	5	3	6	5	35	3,134

Source: Fridberg et al (2006, p 58)

the number of hours each individual spends on voluntary work tends to increase with age: while volunteers aged 30-49 spend on average 15 hours per month, people aged 66+ on average spend 18 hours per month (Anker and Koch-Nielsen, 1995; Koch-Nielsen et al, 2005). It furthermore seems that different age cohorts are attracted by different kinds of voluntary work. People aged 66+ are dispositioned towards voluntary work in sectors such as 'social/health', 'housing, local community' and 'other', and less so in areas such as 'leisure' and 'education'.

In general, voluntary work in Denmark is not primarily done by people who have the most leisure time, but by those who are already very active with their job and family. The 'typical' volunteer worker is male, aged 30-49, has a higher education, is full-time employed, has children and lives in a small town or rural area. A large part of voluntary work is performed by people in relation to their own children's leisure activities (Fridberg et al, 2006, p 52).

Participation of older volunteers

The prototypical older volunteer in Denmark is a 'younger' senior with relatively good health, relatively well educated and wealthy, and an ethnic Dane. Older males, however, are more active in regard to volunteer administrative work, whereas women and men are more or less equally active when it comes to practical kinds of work (Leeson, 2005). Still, women are more active in terms of practical voluntary work such as planning an excursion, a summer fête, transporting older people, providing counselling, volunteering as a visiting friend, helping in a second-hand shop or senior centre. Every eighth woman, or 13 per cent of the group of 60- to 74-year-olds, has volunteered in this kind of work – among the men, the share is only half this number. That is, voluntary work is linked to gender in the sense that older women primarily volunteer for practical work, while older men primarily volunteer in activities such as board work (Andersen and Appeldorn, 1995).

The main reason for older volunteers doing voluntary work is based on a combination of self-centred and altruistic motivations. As can be seen from Table 4.3, the predominant reason older adults engage in voluntary work is an inclination to do something for other people, which is especially the case for males aged 75+. But self-centred motives, such as an interest in meeting new people and to make one's life more meaningful, are also a main drive behind voluntary work.

Table 4.3: Motives reported for volunteering, according to age and gender, 2002 (%)

		75-79	65-69	55-59	45-49
My life becomes more meaningful	Males	44	62	56	68
	Females	44	60	54	53
I meet other people	Males	60	77	66	79
	Females	65	68	71	70
It gives me better self-esteem	Males	31	22	28	34
	Females	31	26	29	34
I get greater influence over something	Males	22	29	28	42
	Females	20	23	25	39
I do it to help others/to do something for others	Males	67	55	58	76
	Females	58	66	68	77
I do it because I am interested in the specific project or issue	Males	62	71	75	70
	Females	60	71	69	75
I learn new things	Males	29	52	48	57
	Females	26	52	44	60

Note: Question asked to respondents: 'People have different reasons for engaging in voluntary work. Have any of the circumstances we will now mention had importance for you?'
Source: Leeson (2005, p 54, Table 1.19)

There is also a difference between how older and younger people are recruited by the voluntary sector: younger people volunteer for 'self-expressive' reasons, that is, they are driven by pure interest, whereas older people often volunteer on being requested or persuaded to do so by other people (Koch-Nielsen et al, 2005).

Organisations of older volunteers are not widespread in Denmark; rather, few voluntary organisations target older people. The largest body organising older people in Denmark is the DaneAge Association, which is a mix of a special interest institution, non-governmental organisation (NGO) and voluntary organisation, although independent of party politics, religion and ethnic origins. It was founded in 1986, has 542,000 members and organises about 27 per cent of all Danes aged 50+ (see www.aeldresagen.dk/Medlemmer-/detgoervifordig/omos/english/Sider/Default.aspx). It is a nationwide organisation with 219 local committees across Denmark, whose purpose is to 'support a person's right to create an active and meaningful life on their own terms, and actively be able to participate in society, regardless of age'. DaneAge provides assistance, support and counselling to those who need or want to engage in volunteer work. Within its framework, about 5,500 volunteers are engaged in social humanitarian activities, such as strengthening the networks of older people living alone, escorting them to hospital and so on. Even if not expressly targeting only older volunteers, another large organisation that involves mostly the latter is the Danish Red Cross, organising 5,000 volunteers in a 'visiting friend' scheme, its aim being to break the isolation and loneliness of older people living alone.

Older people's participation in voluntary organisations: opportunities and restrictions

The numerous voluntary organisations in Denmark function as an 'opportunity structure' for older people to act as volunteers in civil society. Studies from the US, Australia and the Netherlands (Baldock, 1999; Warburton and Cordingley, 2004; Hinterlong and Williamson, 2006) have shown, however, that older people are sometimes faced with discriminatory practices and negative stereotypes held about older people, which might function as a barrier to actual participation. Therefore, the aim of this section is to (1) give an account of the opportunities for and restrictions on older people's participation in voluntary organisations in Denmark; (2) show how older people experience the tension between employment and volunteering; and (3) illustrate how older people are positioned in the relationship between care and volunteering. This endeavour is, however, somewhat constrained by the fact that Danish data seldom specifies older people's engagement in civil society organisations, whereas data on restrictions and opportunities for the population as a whole are more easily available.

Opportunities and restrictions for volunteering for older people

In general, volunteering is strongly associated with preferences as to how people wish to spend their leisure time. In Denmark, 65 per cent of all non-volunteers state that they don't have the time for or prefer to spend their time with something other than voluntary work. In later life, when leisure time increases, however, volunteering may be progressively more obstructed by physical limitations and mental health conditions. Thus, illness and disability as a barrier to participation might primarily well apply to older people. Indeed, in Denmark, 24 per cent of the population aged 66+ refers to health as a reason for not volunteering (Koch-Nielsen et al, 2005).

Socio-economically advantaged segments of the population are more disposed to participate in voluntary work than less advantaged groups. There is a particularly strong association between volunteering and higher education (Fridberg et al, 2006) – that is, higher education is a strong predictor for volunteering. This does not apply to the 'social' sector of voluntary work, however, where education does not influence participation. Another influential factor on volunteering is place of residence – volunteering is more widespread in the countryside or provincial towns than in Denmark's capital and its suburbs.

Church attendance and other forms of civic engagement, such as political participation, are positively associated with volunteering. Voluntary activities are systematically related to the frequency of church attendance and the degree to which people are interested in politics and political conditions (Fridberg et al, 2006, pp 55ff). The frequency of church attendance increases with age; while 16.8 per cent of people aged 30-39 attend church 2-11 times a year, the figure is 32 per cent for people aged 80-89. By contrast, interest in politics peaks at the ages of 50-59, as 30.5 per cent of the population in this age group report that they are strongly interested in politics. Still, an interest in politics is more pronounced among older than younger people: only 14.9 per cent of those aged 30-39 are strongly interested in politics, while the figure is 24.3 for those aged 80-89 (data from the 2005 Danish election survey).

The disposition to participate in voluntary work may not turn into actual practice, however, inasmuch as there is a mismatch between supply and demand for voluntary workers. As argued by Ibsen (2006), for instance, organisational characteristics of the voluntary sector are of vital importance for the degree of volunteering. Such characteristics are the size, structure, membership composition and the purpose of the voluntary organisations. As to the latter, 57 per cent of all activities are cultural, leisure and pastime activities, whereas only 9 per cent of all voluntary activities are made up of social and health-oriented services. As such, the characteristics of voluntary organisations only partially match the predispositions of older adults. The latter are mainly disposed towards activities that benefit the receiver of the service, and older volunteers are mainly engaged in social and humanitarian activities (Leeson, 2005), such as 'visiting friends', self-help groups, drop-in centres and so on. Hence, the share of people who volunteer in social and humanitarian activities increases from 13 per cent for men aged 45-49 to 20 per cent for men aged 75-79, and from 17 per cent for women aged 45-49 to 45 per cent for women aged 75-79.

Since the mid-1980s, the state has been implementing several social investment programmes supporting the development of the voluntary sector. Typically, these programmes support economically voluntary work with the aim of solving social problems, combating marginalisation and exclusion, and so on. Within these programmes nationwide voluntary organisations are also subsidised economically. Such organisations include organisations for people with disabilities, organisations for older people and similar bodies. The social investment programmes have, over the years, also supported research in to how to improve the functioning of the voluntary sector.

In 1998 the interaction between the welfare state and voluntary social work organisations was taken one step further, as the Social Service Act (para 18) imposed on municipalities the duty to support economically and cooperate with voluntary organisations. In effect, about 60-80 per cent of all municipalities in Denmark have a voluntary policy (Socialministeriet, 2010), and 55 per cent of all municipalities have established a voluntary council, which functions as a bridge between the municipality and the local voluntary organisations. Voluntary organisations are represented in the voluntary council, and the voluntary council recommends to the municipality what type of activity should be supported according to paragraph 18 of the Social Service Act. However, no programmes targeting older volunteers exist so far.

In 1992 a national Centre for Voluntary Social Work was established with financial support from the welfare state. Its aim is to collect and spread information about voluntary work and to encourage the setting up of public–private partnerships to combat social problems (Henriksen et al, 2012).

Older people between employment and volunteering

Employment rates for older workers, that is, those aged 55-64, are rather high in Denmark. According to Eurostat the employment rate of older males in 2011 was 63.8 and 55.3 among older females. The high participation rates tie in with a very strong work orientation in Denmark, as 71.6 per cent of people aged 50-65 'strongly agree' or 'agree' with the following statement: 'I *would* enjoy having a paid *job even if I did not need the money' (ISSP, 1997).*

In Denmark labour market participation clearly has an impact on the disposition to do voluntary work. Adults in paid employment volunteer more than those outside the labour market (Koch-Nielsen et al, 2005; Fridberg et al, 2006, p 55), the main reason most probably being that engagement with the corporate world increases the number of social contacts and opportunities for networking. It thus seems that integration into the labour market entails a form of social integration that is conducive to voluntary work. What adds to this picture is that employers in recent years have increasingly established formal employee volunteer programmes as an integrated part of their emerging social responsibility initiatives. In a voluntary work perspective, however, labour force participation is most probably less important for women than men as a bridge to the voluntary sector. At least gender differences in the frequency of voluntary work decrease with age (Leeson, 2005, Table 1.14).

Voluntary work decreases with age as people outside the labour market may not have the same opportunities for volunteering as those who are professionally active. This does not mean, however, that people outside the labour market are excluded from voluntary work. For instance, voluntary early retirees (that is, people retiring before the pensionable age of 65) are very active as volunteers in the 'social' sector.

Older people between family care and volunteering

Principi et al (2012; see also Chapter Two, this volume) have argued that there might be a relationship between family caregiving and formal volunteering, implying that older adults' involvement in care provision for grandchildren, a parent or partner might reduce their participation in civil society organisations. The question is, however, whether this hypotheses is valid for Denmark, since Denmark can be characterised as a 'public care' society, where informal care plays a minor role in comparison with other European countries.

The welfare state assumes responsibility for frail older people in the form of home help or residential care, and coverage of public elder care is high. Relative to the population aged 65+, 25 per cent received home help and 5 per cent institutional care in 2007 (Huber et al, 2009). In 2001 total public expenditure on old-age benefits in kind amounted to 1.75 per cent of GDP, and the elder care sector functions as a formal employment 'machine'. In 2005 about 100,000 people (about 3.7 per cent of total employment) were employed full time in this sector (Jensen and Rathlev, 2009). This high coverage of elder care in Denmark ties in with specific cultural orientations towards eldercare. A total of 75.4 per cent of the population think that a parent should move into an old people's home, or receive appropriate home help in the parent's own home, if the parent can no longer manage to live on his or her own, whereas only 8.9 per cent think that 'I or one of my brothers or sisters should invite my father or mother to live with one of us' (Eurobarometer, 1998).

The extent of informal or intergenerational childcare is also modest. In 2006, 63.2 per cent of all children aged 0-2 and 96 per cent of all children aged 3-5 were enrolled in daycare institutions (Danmarks Statistik, 2007). Opening hours in daycare institutions allow mothers to work on a full-time basis. In 1996, 75 per cent of all mothers with children aged 0-6 worked full time, that is, more than 36 hours a week (Christoffersen, 1997). So there is no need, as such, for grandparents to take care of their grandchildren. In effect, only a small fraction of child or elder care is provided in private households on an informal or unpaid basis, which seems to indicate that care does not constrain choice in relation to voluntary activities in Denmark; rather, the contrary may be true. As will be shown in the next section (see Table 4.4), an 'Interest in the situation of a relative' may actually help promote volunteering.

Improving the match between supply of older candidates with the demand of voluntary organisations: future perspectives

Most third sector organisations are highly dependent on volunteers, and about 20 per cent of all voluntary organisations in Denmark find it difficult to recruit volunteer workers (Ibsen, 2006, p 87), while at the individual level voluntary work is often considered something desirable, as it fosters personal identity, and leads to social integration and individual self-fulfilment (see, for example, Principi et al, 2012). It is therefore relevant to reflect on which measures and initiatives can be implemented by civil society organisations and policy makers to improve the match between supply and demand for older volunteers. Nevertheless, considerations as to how to improve this match are unfortunately lacking in Denmark, although such considerations may be on the verge of emerging. The government announced in its 'Denmark 2020' programme from 2010 that it intended to strengthen voluntary organisations, but so far no proposals have been initiated. Such reflections, however, may have their point of departure in questions such as: why do people provide voluntary work? How are volunteers recruited? Are the types of voluntary work in demand in accordance with older adults' wishes and aspirations? Is voluntary work considered meaningful?

Personal ideals and a wish to help others is the main driving force behind enrolment in the voluntary sector (Habermann, 2001), while time constraints are the major barrier to engagement (Fridberg et al, 2006, p 70). Therefore, it may not, as suggested by several authors (see, for example, Zedlewski and Schaner, 2005; Martinson and Minkler, 2006; O'Neill, 2006), help to introduce economic support for voluntary workers in order to increase their inclination to volunteer. Rather, the contrary effect may result – economic support for volunteers could encourage processes of professionalisation in voluntary organisations, which in turn may make it even harder to recruit new segments of older volunteers (cf Horch, 1994, p 223). In Denmark people are more willing to engage in voluntary work if they feel that they are needed.

Table 4.4 shows how older adults have actually been recruited into volunteer work. As can be seen, older adults are primarily recruited into volunteer work through personal requests or word-of-mouth recommendations: 69 per cent of all volunteers aged 66+ have volunteered for this reason. It would seem to indicate that the volume of voluntary work increases when those already volunteering function as active ambassadors in the promotion of voluntary work. It is, on the other hand, less likely, as posited by Thompson and Wilson (2001), that recruitment campaigns in the form of newspaper advertisements and the like will recruit many additional voluntary workers – only a very small fraction of older voluntary workers volunteered in response to advertisements for unpaid voluntary work.

Older adults are less educated than younger people, which may have an unavoidable structural impact on the propensity of older adults to volunteer. In addition, older adults orient themselves towards different types of voluntary work than younger people, as the former are disposed towards philanthropic or charity-like forms of voluntary work in the 'social/health' sector, that is, types of voluntary work that

Table 4.4: Factors that initiated older adults volunteering, 2004 (%)

	50-65	66+
Had a wish to engage in a social community	11	13
Had some extra spare time	6	14
Existing membership in the organisation concerned	18	17
Resulted from a job/profession/education	7	3
Interest in the situation of a relative	50	37
It was necessary – somebody had to do something	16	16
Had to react to unfairness	4	1
TV programme, newspaper article about voluntary work	1	3
Advertisements for unpaid voluntary work	2	6
Was personally requested/elected	62	69

Source: Leeson (2005)

tend to be crowded out by the welfare state. However, discrepancies between orientations and opportunities do not create a meaningless image of volunteering among older adults: 68 per cent of males and 65 per cent of females aged 75-79 disagree with the following statement: 'In Denmark it is not necessary to volunteer' (Leeson, 2005, p 62). Thus, the major challenge is to encourage more actively older adults to engage in voluntary work by word-of-mouth practices.

Conclusions

The Danish social democratic welfare regime, with its high social welfare spending, demonstrates that a highly developed welfare state does not necessarily crowd out civic engagement, mutual trust and voluntary work. The voluntary sector in Denmark is quite large and activity levels are high. One may actually speak of a specific Danish welfare mix composed of a strong welfare state and a strong civil society, in which the role of voluntary organisations is to organise all sorts of cultural and leisure activities. About 35 per cent of the Danish population is enrolled in unpaid voluntary work. Still, a relative small proportion of all volunteers are older people, as only about 15 per cent of all volunteers in Denmark are aged 66-85. This may be due to some discrepancies between the demand and supply of voluntary work.

At the micro level, the typical older volunteer is a 'younger' senior with good health and oriented towards traditional charity giving based on altruistic motivations; older volunteers are especially active in sectors such as 'social/health', 'housing, local community' and similar areas. Unfortunately, however, the demand for voluntary work at the organisational or meso level is primarily centred round sectors such as sport, culture and similar activities, where young people in particular with self-centred or self-expressive motivations are active. In the past, the welfare state at the macro level has done little to increase the demand for older volunteers. Over the last 30 years, however, social policy has taken on new directions. More emphasis has been put on the role of voluntary social work within the area of traditional social policy, primarily with the aim of helping the most marginalised groups that find it difficult to enrol in the formal welfare state apparatus. This may, in turn, increase the demand for older volunteers in sectors such as 'social/health' in the future. But this will not necessarily be the case, since work in 'social/health' organisations is, to a large extent, carried out as full-time paid work.

The enrolment of older people into voluntary work does not collide with labour market activity: the employment rate for older people aged 55-64 is relatively high, while it is very low for people aged 65+ when volunteering rates also decrease. Neither does voluntary work collide with care obligations towards grandchildren or frail elder parents or relatives, since coverage of child and elder care institutions in Denmark is very high, which ties in with cultural perceptions of care being a public issue. Major barriers to voluntary work for older people are that the demand for volunteer work is outside the domain of traditional charity giving, and that it often requires networking, as older volunteers are mainly recruited through word-of-mouth practices.

Note

[1] This figure originates form a survey carried out in 2004, and it shows that 35 per cent of the Danish population has carried out voluntary work within the last year, while only 26 per cent has carried out voluntary work within the last month.

References

Andersen, D. and Appeldorn, A. (1995) *Tiden efter tres − De 60-74-åriges deltagelse i foreninger, frivilligt arbejde og private netværk* [*After 60 years of age − Participation in associations, voluntary work and private networks by people 60-74 years of age*], København: Socialforskningsinstituttet.

Anker, J. and Koch-Nielsen, I. (1995) *Det frivillige arbejde* [*Voluntary work*], København: Socialforskningsinstituttet.

Atchley, R.C. (1989) 'A continuity theory of normal aging', *The Gerontologist*, vol 29, no 2, pp 183-90.

Baldock, C.V. (1999) 'Seniors as volunteers: an international perspective on policy', *Ageing & Society*, vol 19, no 5, pp 581-602.

Boje, T. (2006a) 'Nonprofitsektorens samfundsøkonomiske og beskæftigelsesmæssige betydning' ['The importance of the non-profit sector for the economy and employment pattern'], in T.P. Boje, T. Fridberg and B. Ibsen (eds) *Den frivillige sektor i Danmark − Omfang og betydning* [*The voluntary sector in Denmark − Extent and importance*], København: SFI-rapport 06:18, pp 119-42.

Boje, T. (2006b) 'Nonprofitsektorens beskæftigelsesmæssige størrelse og sammensætning på det danske arbejdsmarked' ['The importance of the non-profit sector for the size and composition of the labour force'], in T.P. Boje, T. Fridberg and B. Ibsen (eds) *Den frivillige sektor i Danmark − Omfang og betydning* [*The voluntary sector in Denmark − Extent and importance*], København: SFI-rapport 06:18, pp 199-215.

Boje, T.P. and Ibsen, B. (2006) *Frivillighed og non-profit i Danmark – omfang, organisation, økonomi og beskæftigelse* [*Voluntarity and non-profit in Denmark – Extent, organisation, economy and employment*], København: SFI-rapport 06:18.

Burgess, E. (1960) 'Aging in western culture', in E. Burgess (ed) *Aging in western societies*, Chicago, IL: University of Chicago Press, pp 3-28.

Center for frivilligt socialt arbejde (2001) *The voluntary social sector in Denmark*, Socialministeriet i samarbejde med Center for frivilligt socialt arbejde (www.frivillighed.dk).

Cumming, E. and Henry, W. (1961) *Growing old: The process of disengagement*, New York: Basic Books.

Christoffersen, M.N. (1997) *Spædbarnsfamilien* [*Families with babies*], København: SFI-rapport 97:25.

Danmarks Statistik (2007) *Statistisk Tiårsoversigt 2007* [*Statistical teen-years overview 2007*], København: Danmarks Statistik.

Erlinghagen, M. and Hank, K. (2006) 'The participation of older European in volunteer work', *Ageing & Society*, vol 26, no 4, pp 567-84.

Eurobarometer (1998) 50.1: *Information society services, food quality, the family, and aid to development*, November-December 1998 (www.icpsr. umich.edu/icpsrweb/ICPSR/studies/02831)

Fridberg, T., Koch-Nielsen, I. and Henriksen, L.S. (2006) 'Frivilligt arbejde' ['Voluntary work'], in T.P. Boje, T. Fridberg and B. Ibsen (eds) *Den frivillige sektor i Danmark – Omfang og betydning* [*The voluntary sector in Denmark – Extent and importance*], København: SFI-rapport 06:18, pp 41-77.

Fukuyama, F. (1995) *Trust: The social virtues and the creation of prosperity*, New York: The Free Press.

Gaskin, K. and J.D. Smith (1995) *A new civic Europe – A study of the extent and role of volunteering*, London: The Volunteer Centre.

Habermann, U. (2001) *En postmoderne helgen? Om motiver til frivillighed* [*A post-modern saint? About movites behind volunteering*], Lund: Lund Universitet.

Hegeland, T.J. (1994) *Fra de tusind blomster til en målrettet udvikling* [*From the thousand flowers to a targeted development*], Aalborg, Forlaget ALFUFF

Henriksen, L.S. (1995) *Frivillige organisationer i den decentrale velfærdsstat* [*Voluntary organisations in the decentralised welfare state*], Aalborg: Aalborg Universitet, Institut for Sociale Forhold og Organisation.

Henriksen, L.S., Smith, S.R. and Zimmer, A. (2012) 'At the eve of convergence? Transformations of social service provision in Denmark, Germany and the United States', *Voluntas*, vol. 23, no 2, pp 458-501.

Hinterlong, J.E. and Williamson, A. (2006) 'The effects of civic engagement of current and future cohorts of older adults', *Generations*, vol 30, no 4, pp 10-7.

Horch, H.-D. (1994) 'Does government financing have a detrimental effect on the autonomy of voluntary associations? Evidence from German sports clubs', *International Review for the Sociology of Sport*, vol 29, no 3, pp 269-85.

Huber, M., Rodrigues, R., Hoffmann, F., Gasior, K. and Marin, B. (2009) *Facts and figures on long-term care. Europe and North America*, Vienna: European Centre for Social Welfare Policy and Research.

Ibsen, B. (2006) 'Foreningerne og de frivillige organisationer' [Associations and voluntary organisations], in T.P. Boje, T. Fridberg and B. Ibsen (eds) *Den frivillige sektor i Danmark – Omfang og betydning* [*The voluntary sector in Denmark – Extent and importance*], København: SFI-rapport 06:18, pp 71-117.

ISSP (International Social Survey Programme) (1997) 'Work Orientations II', Mannheim: ISSP (www.gesis.org/issp/issp-modules-profiles/work-orientations/1997).

Jensen, P.H. and Rathlev, J. (2009) 'Formal and informal work in the Danish social democratic welfare state', in B. Pfau-Effinger, L. Flaquer and P.H. Jensen (eds) *Formal and informal work. The hidden work regime in Europe*, New York and London: Routledge, pp 39-61.

Jensen, P.H., Pfau-Effinger, B. and Flaquer, L. (2009) 'The development of informal work in the work-welfare arrangements of European societies', in B. Pfau-Effinger, L. Flaquer and P.H. Jensen (eds) *Formal and informal work. The hidden work regime in Europe*, New York and London: Routledge, pp 3-20.

Koch-Nielsen, I. and Clausen, J.D. (2002) 'Værdierne i det frivillige arbejde' ['Values in voluntary work'], in P. Gundelach (ed) *Danskernes værdier 1981-1999* [*The values among Danish citizens, 1981-1999*], København: Hans Reitzels Forlag.

Koch-Nielsen, I., Henriksen, L.S., Fridberg, T. and Rosdahl, D. (2005) *Frivilligt arbejde – den frivillige indsats i Danmark* [*Voluntary work – The voluntary effort in Denmark*], København: SFI-rapport 05:20.

Laslett, P. (1989) *A fresh map of life. The emergence of the Third Age*, London: Weidenfeld & Nicolson.

Leeson, G. (2005) *Fritid og frivilligt arbejde* [*Leisure time and voluntary work*], København: Ældre Sagens Fremtidsstudie: Rapport nr 5.

Lützen, K. (1998) *Byen tæmmes – Kernefamilie, sociale reformer og velgørenhed i 1800-tallets København* [*The city is tamed – The nuclear family, social reforms and charity in Copenhagen in the 19th century*], København: Hans Reitzels Forlag.

Martinson, M. and Minkler, M. (2006) 'Civic engagement and older adults: a critical perspective', *The Gerontologist*, vol 46, no 3, pp 318-24.

Ministry of Social Affairs (2001) *Voluntary social work in Denmark and public policy towards the voluntary social sector*, Copenhagen: Ministry of Social Affairs.

Morrow-Howell, N. (2010) 'Volunteering in later life: research frontiers', *Journal of Gerontology: Social Sciences*, vol 65B, no 4, pp 461-9.

O'Neill, G. (2006) 'Civic engagement on the agenda at the 2005 White House Conference on aging', *Generations*, vol 30, no 4, pp 95-100.

Pfau-Effinger, B. (2004) 'Historical paths of the male breadwinner family model – explanation for cross-national differences', *British Journal of Sociology*, vol 55, no 3, pp 177-99.

Phillipson, C. (2002) *Transitions from work to retirement. Developing a new social contract*, Bristol: Policy Press.

Principi, A., Chiatti, C., Lamura, G. and Frerichs, F. (2012) 'The engagement of older people in civil society organisations', *Educational Gerontology*, vol 38, no 2, pp 83-106.

Rambøll (2009) *Evaluering af frivillige tilbud til ufrivilligt ensomme ældre [An evaluation of voluntary schemes targeting lonely older people]*, København (www.ramboll-management.dk).

Richardson, V.E. (1999) 'Women and retirement', *Journal of Women and Aging*, vol 11, no 2/3, pp 49-66.

Rozario, P.A. (2006) 'Volunteering among current cohorts of older adults and baby boomers', *Generations*, vol 30, no 4, pp 31-6.

Rostow, W.W. (1960) *The stages of economic growth*, London: Cambridge University Press.

Sivesind, K.H., Lorentzen, H., Selle, P. and Wollebæk, D. (2002) *The voluntary sector in Norway. Compositions, changes, and causes*, Oslo: Institutt for Samfunnsforskning.

Socialministeriet (2010) *Den frivillige social indsats – Årsrapport 2010 [Voluntary social activities – Yearly report, 2010]*, Silkeborg: Center for frivilligt socialt arbejde.

Thompson, E. and Wilson, L. (2001) 'The potential of older volunteers in long-term care', *Generations*, vol 25, no 1, pp 58-63.

Warburton, J. and Cordingley, S. (2004) 'The contemporary challenges of volunteering in an ageing Australia', *Australian Journal on Volunteering*, vol 9, no 2, pp 67-74.

Warburton, J., Terry, D.J., Rosenman, L.S. and Shapiro, M. (2001) 'Differences between older volunteers and nonvolunteers: attitudinal, normative, and control beliefs', *Research on Aging*, vol 23, no 5, pp 586-605.

Williams, C.C. and Windebank, J. (1998) *Informal employment in the advanced economy. Implications of work and welfare*, London: Routledge.

Wolfe, A. (1989) *Whose keeper? Social science and moral obligation*, San Francisco, CA: University of California Press.

Zedlewski, S. and Schaner, S. (2005) 'Older adults' engagement should be recognized and encouraged', *Perspectives on Productive Aging*, no 1, pp 1-5.

FIVE

Older volunteers in Germany: opportunities and restrictions in the welfare mix

Paula Aleksandrowicz, Doris Bockermann and Frerich Frerichs

Introduction

Voluntary work in Germany is firmly rooted in a strong civil society, and particularly involved in the provision of social services through churches and large welfare organisations. However, volunteering in Germany is not only limited to the social sector – which includes elder care activities and care for people with disabilities (Gensicke, 2005a) – but is also strong in such fields as sport, culture and politics. Although no data is available on voluntary organisations as such and on the sector's contribution to GDP (gross domestic product), the number of volunteers (which is known) has increased substantially in recent decades, reaching nowadays about one third of the German population.

For a long time, voluntary work in Germany was related to the tradition of the male breadwinner model of the family and thus, the structures of volunteering were strongly gendered: men were usually active in voluntary work as well as having full-time employment, often in leadership roles that could also contribute to improving their professional reputation, whereas women were much more often not employed housewives performing voluntary activities in charity work and social services (Pfau-Effinger and Magdalenic, 2009). Since the 1990s, however, a shift has taken place towards a male breadwinner/ female part-time career model, in which the participation of women in gainful employment has become more important (Pfau-Effinger and Magalenic, 2009). Overall, the engagement level of men as volunteers is still slightly higher than that of women.

As mentioned before, civil society and volunteering play a big role in the provision of welfare beside the state and the market. Without the participation of volunteers, welfare institutions and organisations would be overburdened, so volunteers involvement is usually appreciated and taken into account (Thiel, 2006). This also reflects the fact that Germany is a relatively strong welfare state of a 'conservative' type (Esping-Andersen, 1990), where a large share of informal work can be assumed. Thus, the welfare mix in Germany is represented by state provision and services and profit-oriented enterprises, on the one hand, and by voluntary engagement in intermediate actors such as non-profit and self-help organisations, informal social initiatives, the family, kinship and neighbourhood, on the other (Thiel, 2006).

Faced with financial constraints and thus with high demands for 'social capital', the political debate has reacted by postulating civic commitment as an inevitable requirement for civil society's solidarity (Enquete Commission, 2002). In 1999, the Enquete Commission on 'The future of civic commitment' was assigned the task of compiling data and conveying recommendations for political strategies and actions to develop volunteering in Germany.

According to this approach, the policy calls for more civic commitment of older people in the form of an individual contribution to fulfil the intergenerational contract. It is argued that older people should show more social responsibility in coping with the societal consequences of demographic development (Bäcker et al, 2008). The theses on the civic participation and democratic involvement of older people are mirrored by a scholarly discussion about a re-bondage of the 'released' older generation (Backes and Höltge, 2008). Research has confirmed this change of values and motivations for voluntary work, from altruistic motives to motives of self-fulfilment, and an increased interest in co-decision- making (Künemund, 2007).

In the following, the development of volunteering in Germany in general, as well as the role of volunteering in older age, is analysed. This is embedded in a description of the specific tradition of voluntary action in Germany and its legal framework. However, the main purpose of this chapter is to investigate the main opportunities and restrictions for older people to participate in volunteering – highlighting features such as education, employment and care obligations. Derived from this, future perspectives to foster the civic engagement of older volunteers, both on the organisational and the institutional level, are shown.

The German tradition of voluntary action

Scholarly literature points out the importance of local relations for the evolution of volunteering in Germany. This was emphasised through the concept of the 'Elberfeld system' (1853), which was developed to relieve poor citizens. With this system, social volunteering was formally introduced and implemented in municipal social policy (Sachße, 2000). Particularly in urban communities, organised social life rose up in the form of cooperatives and associations (Schroeter, 2006). On the one hand, self-help was seen as a basic necessity for the new working class to improve their living conditions in the second half of the 19th century. On the other hand, the reformer Wilhelm Emmanuel Ketteler pointed out the complementary role of governmental protection and assistance as a pre-condition for successful self-help, especially for the working class (Sachße, 2003), as problems regarding the distinction and coordination between private and public welfare work arose with the expansion of the local public welfare system at the end of the 19th century (Sachße, 2000).

Thanks to Ketteler's concept, the regulatory idea of subsidiarity took shape and became one of the guiding principles of German welfare state arrangements. Subsidiarity, in the interpretation of Catholic social studies, serves a regulatory function with regard to the relation between individuals and communities in terms of individual responsibility and social assistance (Sachße, 2003). The coordination and linking of governmental and non-governmental welfare work was organised in Germany according to this principle.

From the end of the 19th century to the 1920s, non-governmental/non-profit organisations were established to operate countrywide, with highly institutionalised structures aiming at rationalisation and coordination. Due to the circumstances and needs emerging after the First World War, welfare organisations gained in importance through a nationwide alliance of umbrella and specialist associations, while the relevance of private civic commitment declined. With this development, volunteering was no longer locally motivated but guided by central values (Sachße, 2000). In other areas, for example, sports or culture, volunteering gradually gained in importance.

Today, the third sector is made up of a broad range of organisations located between the state with its services (first sector), the market with its profit-oriented companies (second sector) and the family system (informal sector). It consists of welfare organisations/charities, non-profit institutions in culture and recreation, environmental organisations, consumer and advocacy groups, civic associations, foundations and other non-governmental organisations (Birkhölzer et al, 2005). Voluntary work in the third sector is generally unpaid and informal, despite regulations for tax relief and expenses allowances. Nevertheless, voluntary work may be seen as indirectly subsidised, as large welfare organisations – where still the majority of volunteers are active and which assumes tasks in the public interest – are contracted and financed by the state. Accordingly, voluntary work in this sphere can be seen as traditionally encouraged and strengthened by the German welfare state (Pfau-Effinger and Magdalenic, 2009, p 92). In this respect, volunteers are 'drawn into' the social services sector, although no specific age preference is made here.

Since the 1990s a significant change in volunteering could be observed, in the form of an increase in the number of individually self-determined and autonomously acting volunteers (Kolland and Oberbauer, 2006). The motives for volunteering gradually changed from duty-guided 'old' activities for others (that is, driven by 'altruistic' motives) to a 'new' form of activities for oneself and for others (that is, fun-related or for self-fulfilling motives). Functional motives are also increasing, such as gaining in reputation or investing in one's future (Künemund, 2006a).

The legal framework

In general, there are no specific laws that regulate volunteering in Germany as such or for particular groups such as older people, and regulations for volunteering are usually embedded in tax, insurance or public law.

Legally recognised forms of non-profit organisations are associations, incorporated societies and foundations. The association is the most common legal form of voluntary activity in Germany (43 per cent) (Igl et al, 2002). From a legal point of view, changes in definitions and forms of voluntary activity in the 1990s became a problem. Legal regulations in tax laws referred to the old-termed 'honorary activity', which was linked to holding an office. Various new terms of volunteering applied to people, while the activity itself and their formal frame were not specified, and civic commitment, with its special legal problems, played no guiding role when these legal regulations were formulated (Igl et al, 2002). To strengthen the voluntary action of citizens, several tax laws were reformed and merged into an overarching law to promote civic engagement in 2007. Benefits were upgraded in the welfare sector considering tax breaks, tax benefits for donations and tax-exempted reimbursements for volunteers.

Various groups of volunteers (for example, those volunteering for certain institutions governed by public law or for the public good) are statutorily insured during their voluntary activities by statutory accident insurance (*Gesetzliche Unfallversicherung*). Organisations employing volunteers can contract public and association liability insurance, financial loss insurance or organiser liability insurance, as private liability insurance does not cover all kinds of voluntary activities (for example, those carried out for municipalities or in the form of a voluntary leading position within an organisation).

The dimension of volunteer work

On the whole, participation in voluntary activities, when the definition is not confined to holding a formal position, is quite frequent and involves one third of the German population, old and young alike. The development of a civil society in Germany benefited from a change in social norms and values that occurred between 1965 and 1975. In addition, an expansion in education together with a rising population has contributed to increasing involvement rates in volunteering over the last decades (European Foundation, 2011, p 15). Longitudinal data – which have only been available since 1999 through the Volunteer Survey – show that the proportion of volunteers slightly increased from 34 to 36 per cent between 1999 and 2009. Older people in Germany are increasingly participating in volunteering. Comparing 1999 and 2009 in the Volunteer Survey, the proportion of volunteers aged 65 and over grew from 23 to 28 per cent. However, older people are still participating below average compared with the whole population, with a marked decline after retirement.

Voluntary organisations

So far, no general overview on voluntary organisations can be found in Germany, partly because the voluntary sector is rather diverse and voluntary activities take place in rather different organisational forms. Thus, the following overview is restricted only to the volunteers participating in civic activities, as no data on number, dimensions, geographical location of voluntary organisations and people employed in them is available.

Volunteers by sector, gender and age

There is a rather divergent view on the scope of volunteering among older people in Germany, depending on the sources used. For example, the Socio-Economic Panel (SOEP) has a narrow understanding of 'civic engagement', as does the Ageing Survey, which limits the concept of volunteering to just holding an honorary position in an organisation (Rohleder and Bröscher, 2002). Volunteer Survey, one of the main sources, employs a broader concept, which also includes voluntary activities not connected to holding an honorary position, as does the Time Budget Survey and Prognos' *Commitment atlas*. If we compare figures from surveys with a narrow understanding of civic engagement with those from surveys with a broader concept (which are, in most cases, twice as high), it becomes clear that a large part of this difference is due to the underlying definition.

According to the Volunteer Survey, 36 per cent of the German population aged 16 and over was volunteering in 2004. Table 5.1 shows the difficulty of comparing data based on different concepts of 'voluntary work' and applying different methods of measurement. Moreover, no detailed aggregated data for all age groups is available in the literature.

According to the 2004 Volunteer Survey, the most popular areas of voluntary work provided by the German population of all ages were those described in Table 5.2.

As to gender, participation structures show that women are more often involved in voluntary social work, while men are rather occupied

Table 5.1: Share of population participating in volunteering (%)

Age ranges	Volunteer Survey (2004)	Ageing Survey (2002)	SOEP, 2005	SHARE, 2006-07	Commitment atlas, 2008
40-54		15.6			
45-55					40.4
46-65	40				
40-85		13.8			
50+			26-32% (East/West Germany)		
60+	30				
50-64				18	
55-65					36
55-69		16.1			
60-69	37				
65+					26.1
66+	26				
65-74				21	
Total (14+/16+)	36				34.3

Sources: Gensicke (2005b); Künemund (2006c); Erlinghagen and Hank (2009); Prognos and AMB Generali (2009)

with more prestigious political honorary work or in areas requiring craftsmanship and expert knowledge (Backes, 2006).

Men have slightly higher participation rates in volunteering than women, according to the Volunteer Survey (Gensicke, 2005b). This is particularly true for higher age groups (men: 36 per cent in the age group 14–30, 33 per cent among the over-65s; women: 33 and 21 per cent, respectively). The gender difference in older age is explained by the fact that the generation of women aged 65 years and older has a weak tradition of voluntary involvement in general (Picot and Gensicke, 2005, p 285). This is also consistent with latest international evidence that employment in the labour market fosters volunteering, whereas older women were more often not employed housewives.

For younger women, working full time and caring for children are inhibitors to voluntary work (Picot and Gensicke, 2005). Nevertheless, participation rates in civic engagement are higher among parents with children aged four years or older than among Germans of the same age without children. The opposite is true for parents with children below the age of four, for which there is an insufficient number of childcare facilities. Analyses show that, when childcare facilities for the latter group are available, the rate of volunteering among mothers rises from 27 to 44 per cent, while among fathers no effect is observed (Geiss and Picot, 2009).

Civic engagement rates among women with children are lower than among men in the same situation (Picot and Gensicke, 2005). This implies that the full-time employment of fathers and their civic engagement is only made possible by the mother working part time, and vice versa (Klenner et al, 2001). However, between 1999 and 2004, a significant change in family role models must have taken place, as the percentage of volunteering of women with children below the age of four increased, while that of men in the same situation decreased (Picot and Gensicke, 2005). Therefore, legislative activities of the state which shift the share of responsibilities for family work between the sexes, such as the so-called 'family time for fathers', may

Table 5.2: Top three areas of voluntary activity (by number of volunteers) provided by the German population, 2004

Area	% of total
Sports and exercise	11
School and kindergarten	7
Church and religion	6

Source: Authors' calculation based on Gensicke (2005a)

also contribute to a levelling off of volunteering rates for men and women. This is all the more important, as the formerly dominating family model of the husband as the main breadwinner is losing its importance.

On average, people in Germany spend 2.8 hours per week on volunteering and informal help (2001/02 Time Budget Survey). Among people with a higher education, the share of volunteers is higher by 13 percentage points above the average, confirming the positive role played by this factor in increasing participation in voluntary activities (Schmidt and Schnurr, 2009). People with a low or medium school qualification prefer 'social activities' as their main sector of voluntary engagement, while people with a high school leaving qualification are more often found in the cultural sectors in which they can pursue their own intellectual interests.

The prototypical volunteer in Germany is active in the 'sports and exercise' sector, is between 35-49 years old, male, employed, has a high school qualification and school-age children.

Participation of older volunteers

The main areas of involvement of people aged 46-65 and over 65, as recorded in the Volunteer Survey, do not deviate much from those of the whole population. Most of these people are active in 'sports and exercise', 'leisure and sociable activities', 'social affairs', 'culture and music' and 'Church and religion', which are among the top six categories (out of 14) for the whole population. Only the category 'school and kindergarten' (7 per cent of the whole population) loses in importance (between 1.5-5 per cent of older people are active in this area) (Gensicke, 2005b). Table 5.3 shows the top three categories of the volunteering activities of older people.

People aged 50-69 years made up 39 per cent of all Germans who were volunteering in 2004. A marked decline in participation rates is visible among people of retirement age (Gensicke, 2005b; Backes, 2006), especially in the case of women. However, this is not based on longitudinal data, and may be put down to different levels of engagement in subsequent cohorts.

Civic engagement rates of people aged 50 years and over have risen slightly in the last 10 years (Gensicke, 2005a; Erlinghagen, 2009), predominantly in traditional age-specific sectors of volunteering such as senior dancing and sports groups or senior recreation centres (Künemund, 2006b). The increase was higher than in other age groups. The percentage of people aged 40 years or older pursuing a voluntary

Table 5.3: Main areas of voluntary activity of older Germans, 2004

46-65 years	Over 65
1 Sports and exercise (11.5%)	Social affairs (7%)
2 Social affairs (7.5%)	Church and religion (6%)
3 Church and religion (same rank as above) (7.5%)	Sports and exercise (5.5%)

Source: Gensicke (2005b)

task or holding an honorary position in an organisation rose from 13 per cent in 1996 to 18 per cent in 2008 (Ageing Survey data at www.gerostat.de). According to the Volunteer Survey, the participation quotas among 60-year-olds and older people increased between 1999 and 2004, rising from 31 to 37 per cent in the age group 60-69 and from 10 to 14 per cent among those aged 80 and over.

Older people are especially active at the intersection of self-help activities and civic engagement on behalf of others (BMFSFJ, 2006). People covered by the Ageing Survey (aged 40-85) are seldom active in 'new' forms of civic commitment, for example, in self-help groups (Künemund, 2006b). As recorded in the SOEP, the share of 'sporadically active' people (as contrasted with those 'frequently active') rises with age (Rohleder and Bröscher, 2002). This may be somewhat surprising since older volunteers are supposed to have more time available.

The participation rates of women in voluntary work change markedly across the life span, while that of men is rather constant. One third of women aged 15-24 is engaged in voluntary activities. This level goes down to 27 per cent at the age of 25-34, reaches a peak at the age of 35-44 with 38 per cent, and falls to 18 per cent at the age of 65 years or older (Picot and Gensicke, 2005). Older women are more often volunteering in 'traditional' age-specific sectors and organisations than men (Künemund, 2006c). The prototypical older volunteer in Germany is either a 65- to 70-year-old or older retired male active in the 'sports and exercise' sector or a 65- to 70-year-old or older female former housewife active in the 'social affairs' sector.

Stressing the organisational level, there are examples in Germany of specific voluntary organisations that are targeting older volunteers, and these are mainly active on the local level. There are examples of organisations mainly oriented at providing an 'altruistic' type of volunteering, such as, for example, senior help seniors (in Minden the organisation carries out various activities aiming at preventing the need for the long-term care of very old people through mutual support), and also of organisations interested in self-expressive volunteering. For example, at ZWAR, between work and retirement (North Rhine-Westfalia), members become voluntarily active in a self-chosen field. The current trends of their commitment are in intergenerational and housing projects (European Foundation, 2011).

Older people's participation in voluntary organisations: opportunities and restrictions

In this section, factors that inhibit or foster the civic commitment of older people in Germany are analysed. At the micro level, individual preferences and level of education are taken into account and contrasted with possible beneficial structures on the meso and macro level. In this respect, employment and care responsibilities do not seem to represent, contrary to popular judgement, a hindrance for commitment.

Opportunities and restrictions for volunteering for older people

Civic commitment declines in older age, in particular after the age of 70. This phenomenon is confirmed by all data sources already quoted in this chapter, with Table 5.4 visualising, however, the data collected just by the Ageing Survey.

According to multivariate analysis, the decreasing voluntary activity rates in older age cannot be explained by age-specific effects such as a deteriorating health status (Künemund, 2006b), but rather by formal age thresholds or other individual factors. Also, cohort effects are possible, as the educational level has the largest impact on the probability of volunteering. However, all previous three effects on the decreasing participation rates of older people are suppositions and have not yet been tested.

An argument in favour of cohort effects is the stronger orientation of people aged 50-59, compared to older cohorts, towards self-fulfilment, the wish to change things and social and political commitment. This encourages the conclusion that future cohorts of seniors will be more

Table 5.4: Gender-specific rates of voluntary activity, 2002 (%)

Age group	Men	Women	Total
40-54	21.8	23.2	22.5
55-69	23.4	17.8	20.5
70-85	15.0	5.3	9.0

Source: Data from the 2002 Ageing Survey (www.gerostat.de)

interested in volunteering (Jakob, 2001; Brendgens and Braun, 2009). This is also relevant with regard to fostering the civic engagement of older people. A comparison based on the international SHARE data (Survey of Health, Ageing and Retirement in Europe) shows that in countries with high voluntary activity rates among older people, structures exist that support a positive experience of well-being in performing voluntary work (BMFSFJ and FFG, 2008).

As already mentioned, the probability of taking up or continuing voluntary work at any age rises with educational level (Gensicke, 2005b; Künemund, 2006b). Also, social integration (for example, expressed by the number of friends) and affiliation to a church have a high predictive power in this regard (Gensicke, 2005b). Older people (50+) are more prone to take up a voluntary activity or to continue it if they have had experience with volunteering in former life phases (Erlinghagen, 2009). Early 'inflow' into voluntary work is more typical of 'traditional' forms of volunteering. In the case of 'new' forms, ties with the volunteers' biography consist of taking up self-referential activities (for example, people whose relatives are in a nursing home are more prone to engage in such a facility; see Jakob, 2001).

People who have considered a reduction of their voluntary work experience report physical and/or psychical burdens and problems with work–life balance more often than people who have not had such thoughts (Süßlin, 2008). Financial incentives do not influence the consideration of a reduction of voluntary work, although one third of people who do not perform voluntary work gave 'I cannot afford it in financial terms' as a reason for non-commitment (Süßlin, 2008). A higher percentage of volunteers assess their financial situation as '(very) good' compared to those who are only interested in volunteering (Brendgens and Braun, 2009). Therefore, good material status is apparently an important resource, for both taking up and continuing voluntary work.

On the meso level, encouragement for engagement of older people is given by a variety of civil society organisations to different degrees, and support and impulses for organisations that are upheld by civic engagement are often provided by umbrella associations, as local resources in this respect are usually weak. Nevertheless, initiatives on the organisational level that target and support older people in particular are not very widespread (European Foundation, 2011). And although organisations can increasingly count on professional staff with expert knowledge on how to develop civic involvement in new fields with innovative methods, knowledge on the particular interests and needs of older volunteers is often lacking (Dienel, 2011). On the whole, organisations where older volunteers are active do not seem to be prepared for future cohorts of 'project-orientated' seniors (Karl and Kolland, 2010).

On the macro level, engagement policy for older people has only recently become a growing policy field. In 2002, the Enquete Commission into 'The future of civic commitment' reported a set of recommendations for political strategies and action to develop volunteering in Germany. Since then, the government has gradually taken the function of supporting the development of civic engagement and civil society. The report also emphasised the potential of 'younger seniors' to provide productive community work. Thus, the civic engagement of older volunteers has been encouraged by a wide range of initiatives and model programmes, mainly launched by the Federal Ministry of Family Affairs, Senior Citizens, Women and Youth (BMFSFJ). These measures are often supported by federal states, local authorities, non-profit organisations, associations and other initiatives serving the public good. However, all these initiatives were only valid for a limited time and have not been embedded into a sustainable and coherent engagement policy for older people.

Model programmes and initiatives promoted by the BMFSFJ for the older generation aim at opening up new engagement fields and at launching further incentives. This policy aimed to reach a new balance in responsibility between the state, market and citizens (BMFSFJ, 2008), through sponsored projects and networking measures such as voluntary agencies and various online platforms for volunteering.

The latest model programme, 'Voluntary services of all generations', ran in 2009-11 and was a continuation of the model programme, 'Intergenerational voluntary services' (2005-08). It was developed all over the country, through 46 'lighthouse projects', mobile teams to deliver an advisory service for target groups, the qualification of volunteers and instructors, building up linked local and nationwide internet platforms.

In October 2010, the German government approved a National Strategy for the Promotion of Volunteering, including the implementation of a National Volunteering Service for all Generations, which is to replace the mandatory civilian service for young men. So far, the recruitment of older volunteers has gained more importance at the federal level. However, in the first year of its existence, 70 per cent of participants were aged 27 or younger (BFD, 2012), thus demonstrating that this measure does not particularly appeal to older people.

Older people between employment and volunteering

Participation rates in volunteering among employed people aged 45 years and over are higher than among those who are unemployed or out of the labour force (Backes and Höltge, 2008), and in particular, the share of volunteers is lower among unemployed people of any age (Gensicke, 2005b). The trend of decreasing voluntary activity rates in older age (see Table 5.4) does not come into effect in the case of people who, although having reached retirement age, are still in employment (Brendgens and Braun, 2009). Employment seems therefore to activate resources that can be used for volunteering, both in the form of facilitated access to technical appliances (such as, for instance, a printer, computer and so on), qualifications and social contacts.

Some aspects of the employment relationship, however, do not play a univocal role in that respect, as shorter working hours, for instance, seem to stimulate the civic engagement of women (albeit not in Eastern Germany), while the opposite is true for men (Klenner and Pfahl, 2001).

The average retirement age in Germany and the employment rates of workers aged 55 years and over have both risen since 2000 (DRV, 2009), as has the employment rate of pensioners between 1996 and 2002 (Künemund, 2009). According to Eurostat data, in 2008 61.8 per cent of the male population aged 55-64 were employed (female: 46.1 per cent), and 9.9 per cent of the male population aged 65-69 (female: 5.6 per cent). Work orientation in the age group 50-65 compared to the total population in Germany is rather strong: 65.1 in the age group 50-65 strongly agree or agree with the statement 'I would enjoy having a paid job even if I did not need the money' (ISSP, 1997). Compared to other countries, the work orientation in the age group 50-65 is on an average level.

It is unclear whether the shifting time balance between employment and leisure time will bring about large changes in the participation rates of older people in voluntary work over the next decades. Empirical evidence seems to suggest that the timing of retirement is not a predictor of taking up voluntary work (Erlinghagen, 2009), and that time set free from work is not replaced with voluntary activities (Künemund, 2009). Moreover, civic engagement rates have risen between 1999 and 2004 in all age groups (with the exception of those younger than 30), irrespective of economic status (Gensicke, 2005b), although a reversal of the early exit trend was already visible at that time.

In the context of raising the legal retirement age to 67, not only the form of work (flexible or not) but also the duration of working life and the standard of living among people retiring early becomes relevant for the reconciliation of gainful employment and civic engagement. On the one hand, as already observed, a higher retirement age is in principle assumed to strengthen older people's participation in volunteering; on the other hand, it may worsen the position of the 'young-old' who have left work or who have lost a job but who are not yet eligible for old-age pension (Künemund, 2009). This may reduce their ability to volunteer, as they will have to maintain their living standards by taking up temporary jobs.

It is known that companies can have a role in supporting employees' volunteering, through, for example, specific volunteer programmes. Nevertheless, even if there is some evidence of this in Germany within corporate social responsibility programmes (see also Chapter Eleven, this volume), the role of these initiatives is assumed to be not so significant, so far. This holds true for older volunteers in particular.

Older people between family care and volunteering

In Germany, those in need of long-term care can opt for care provision from a commercial external provider of long-term care (benefits in kind), or be cared for by their own relatives, partners or friends (through benefits in cash). The latter option was established by the law as a 'semi-formal' form of care provided by relatives or friends, to be paid in relation to the degree of disability of the older person (Pfau-Effinger and Magdalenic, 2009, p 100). Care provided exclusively by family members is still the dominant form of long-term care in Germany, as its share reaches almost two thirds of all care given (Pfau-Effinger and Magdalenic, 2009).

The dominance of family care is also reflected in the predominant attitudes towards elder care. According to a Eurobarometer survey from 1998, almost 60 per cent of the population in West Germany and almost 50 per cent in East Germany would offer some kind of family support to their parents in need of care, and not rely on nursing homes or healthcare services.

According to data for Germany for 2002, 2.25 million people needed long-term care. Of these, more than two thirds (68.4 per cent) were cared for in private households, and the other 31.6 per cent in residential settings. Furthermore, of those care-dependent people living at home, another two thirds (67 per cent) relied wholly on informal care (BMG, 2010), revealing thus that formal home care reaches about 22.6 per cent of people in need of long-term care. Focusing on beneficiaries of long-term care aged 65+, in 2006 6.7 per cent received home care and 3.8 per cent institutional care (Huber et al, 2009).

European-based studies seem to suggest that informal care provided to close relatives and civic engagement reinforce each other (Hank and Stuck, 2008). However, there are only few studies in Germany examining the correlation between these two dimensions. A general finding is that over-50-year-old Germans living in multi-person households have a higher chance of being involved in eldercare (Alscher et al, 2009). However, the field in which people with family responsibilities volunteer tends to remain within the same care sector (Jakob, 2001).

The Time Use Survey (Menning, 2006) uses the concept of 'informal help (given to other households)' but does not distinguish between the support given to family members and that provided to other people (with the exception of eldercare and the care of children living in the same household, which is, however, recorded as a separate item). People aged 60 years and older report higher participation rates in informal help (11-12 per cent) than those belonging to younger cohorts. The Ageing Survey measures informal help to people living both in the same household and in other households. The share of people engaged in family and non-family care of sick and frail people declines slightly between the ages of 40 and 85 in the case of women, although the time spent for these activities increases (Künemund, 2009). A similar development can be seen with regard to (grand) children care, while in the case of men only, those living in Eastern Germany show declining care rates between the ages of 40 and 85. This implies that care activities could have a crowding-out effect on the voluntary work of women in older age, but the study of possible interrelations has not been pursued further in this direction in the quoted study.

More information on the correlations between the domain of (family) care and volunteering performed by the over-50-year-old can be gained from the European SHARE survey, which distinguishes between 'informal help for family members, friends and neighbours' and 'care'. The results point out a significant correlation between these three activity domains, in Germany (Alscher et al, 2009). In sum, the correlation between elder care and volunteering is still not so clear, in Germany, due to some contrasting results.

Improving the match between supply of older candidates with the demand of voluntary organisations: future perspectives

As good material security and educational status are important resources for both taking up and continuing voluntary work in older age (Gensicke, 2005b; Künemund, 2006b; Süßlin, 2008; Brendgens and Braun, 2009), how to activate other categories of older people should be taken into account, if the hidden reserve of potential volunteers is to be activated.

At the organisational level, targeted qualification measures are needed, in order to alleviate social inequalities in accessing specific forms of voluntary work for older women (political work) and older men (social work) (Backes and Höltge, 2008; Brendgens and Braun, 2009). Not only should older volunteers be included to a larger extent in qualification programmes, but also salaried staff in organisations of voluntary work and in senior agencies, in order to facilitate the coordination of volunteers and concerted work of staff and volunteers (Kühnlein and Böhle, 2002).

Groups of older people with lower educational resources should also be recruited to a larger extent by voluntary organisations. In Germany, this could be fostered by means of low-threshold measures, such as small projects with a defined beginning and end, or through the opportunity to inquire about civic engagement opportunities via a telephone hotline or online consultancy number (Menke, 2007). These ways of recruitment have been applied successfully by the Catholic charity Caritas within the governmental programme 'Intergenerational Volunteer Services' and beyond (Lencz and Plichta, 2009).

Measures targeted at the meso level and at improving voluntary organisations' capacities to engage more older volunteers should also aim at building a more professional volunteer administration and management (Hank and Erlinghagen, 2010). For the successful recruitment and retention of older volunteers, it seems necessary to extend qualification opportunities and to encourage volunteers to participate in the design and further development of their volunteering activities. Companies might encourage the civic engagement of people approaching retirement age by fostering the reconciliation of voluntary and paid work. Civic engagement could also be integrated into programmes for preparation to the transition into retirement, as an option for post-productive life. All this would require flexible infrastructures, especially in the big welfare organisations in Germany, and a sound qualification of the professional staff in charge of older volunteers.

At the federal state level, a better and more sustainable policy of coordination and promotion is needed. The *Report on the situation and perspectives of civic commitment in Germany* (Alscher et al, 2009) recommends the coordination of engagement policy by a new ministry for civic engagement and civil society, in order to develop a cross-sectional policy. However, such an exposed governmental position could give rise to objections, as a dominant state-governing civil society might possibly restrain non-profit organisations. There are further recommendations that could also be realised independently: (1) a coordination authority within the government should link responsibilities of various ministries; (2) a special link between government and parliament is necessary and could be realised in the form of a subcommittee on 'civic engagement'; and (3) coordination should be improved between the German state and the federal states as well as between voluntary organisations, in order to stimulate infrastructural development for civic engagement (Alscher et al, 2009).

Furthermore, as problems with work–life balance are considered as risk factors for giving up volunteering (Süßlin, 2008), policy should support the infrastructure that makes it possible to combine family care and civic engagement. The German social security system has already adopted measures to grant security contributions benefiting people caring for an older adult; similar steps could be taken for supporting voluntary work in the field of care of older, sick or disabled people, as well as in other areas (Backhaus-Maul and Brandhorst, 2001).

Both at the organisational and institutional level, increased voluntary activity rates in older age groups might also be achieved by establishing an 'appreciation culture' (Zeman, 2008). A representative survey of volunteers in the Catholic charity Caritas revealed that people who are prone to expand their voluntary activity experience, to a larger extent, joy, appreciation, freedom of decision and a positive challenge (Süßlin, 2008). However, the form of appreciation must fit in with the social expectations of the older volunteers concerned: volunteers who are less well-off might, for instance, favour lump-sum payments or benefits in kind, while others may prefer an award ceremony hosted by a high-ranking official.

Conclusions

The main areas of involvement of older people do not deviate much from those of the whole population, and show a growing need for self-fulfilment in voluntary engagement. This fact may encourage the conclusion that future cohorts of seniors might be even more interested in voluntary work. However, this conclusion only holds true if the material and economic situation of older people will not worsen further, if voluntary organisations react accordingly and state authorities support voluntary initiatives on a more continuous basis.

Although senior potential for volunteering is of prominent interest in public, political and scientific discussions in Germany, several criticalities have still to be properly addressed:

- individual preferences of future cohorts of older people have to be investigated further and be analysed, especially at the organisational level;
- disadvantages affecting older people due to a so far lower educational level or to health problems in very old age should also be overcome in recruiting, training and health promotion in the workplace;
- sizeable initiatives and programmes to promote older people's voluntary engagement are rather recent in Germany, and both the effects and sustainability of these measures are not clearly proven, yet. Thus, there is a need for in-depth evaluation and for a longstanding programmatic approach.

Direct measures in the German welfare mix need to reflect the different levels of possible interventions. Initiatives targeted at the micro-individual level – adding to what has been said already – need to consider that people who have had experience with volunteering in former life phases are more prone to volunteer in older age. This poses important conclusions for policy makers: people should be encouraged to take up voluntary work in earlier life phases, so this should be made more compatible with family or gainful work, as well as through appropriate investment in educational resources. The introduction of social security credits for voluntary work, and the equal treatment of 'time credits' and monetary donations in taxation, could also contribute to promote civic engagement among younger and middle-aged people.

On the background of the described development of volunteering in Germany, the support of municipalities at the local level plays an increasingly important role for civic engagement, as shown in the growing number of voluntary agencies/centres. While senior agencies are contact centres, especially for older people, voluntary agencies offer a service to all age groups. This is embedded in a general shift currently taking place in Germany, from 'senior' to 'intergenerational' programmes, and to primarily establish forms of service open for people of all generations. This opened concept of civic engagement might enhance intergenerational relationships and understanding, and at the same time provide more room to take into account the different motivations and interests of volunteers themselves.

Besides direct measures to promote the voluntary engagement of older people, the German welfare mix has indirect effects on older adults' unpaid productive engagement and its role in society (Hank and Erlinghagen, 2010). Germany's traditional male breadwinner family model is transforming towards a male breadwinner/female part-time career model. Concerning the care sector, for example, this results in a semi-formal type of elder care. On the one hand, this may result in increasing conflict between the social expectations concerning the amount of older people's engagement in voluntary tasks and their own feeling of being (re-)obligated too much. On the other hand, if their role is strengthened, this may offer additional opportunities for satisfying older people's motivations to volunteer.

References

Alscher, M., Dathe, D., Priller, E. and Speth, R. (2009) *Bericht zur Lage und zu den Perspektiven des bürgerschaftlichen Engagements in Deutschland* [*Report on the situation and the perspectives of civil commitment in Germany*], Berlin: Wissenschaftszentrum Berlin für Sozialforschung.

Backes, G.M. (2006) 'Widersprüche und Ambivalenzen ehrenamtlicher und freiwilliger Arbeit im Alter' ['Contradictions and ambivalences of honorary office and voluntary work in old age'], in K. Schroeter and P. Zängl (eds) *Altern und bürgerschaftliches Engagement – Aspekte der Vergemeinschaftung und Vergesellschaftung in der Lebensphase Alter* [*Ageing and civic engagement – Aspects of communal relationship and socialization of life in old age*], Wiesbaden: VS Verlag, pp 63-94.

Backes, G.M. and Höltge, J. (2008) 'Überlegungen zur Bedeutung ehrenamtlichen Engagements im Alter' ['Considerations on the importance of voluntary engagement in old age'], in M. Erlinghagen and K. Hank (eds) *Produktives Altern und informelle Arbeit in modernen Gesellschaften – Theoretische Perspektiven und empirische Befunde. Band 16: Altern und Gesellschaft* [*Productive ageing and informal work in modern societies – Theoretical perspectives and empirical findings, Volume 16. Ageing and society*], Wiesbaden: VS Verlag, pp 277-99.

Bäcker, G., Naegele, G., Bispinck, R., Hofemann, K. and Neubauer, J. (2008) *Sozialpolitik und soziale Lage in Deutschland. Band 2: Gesundheit, Familie, Alter und Soziale Dienste* [*Social policy and social situation in Germany. Volume 2: Health, family, age and social services*], Wiesbaden: VS Verlag.

Backhaus-Maul, H. and Brandhorst, A. (2001) 'Mit Sicherheit Gutes tun – Über den Zusammenhang von sozialem Engagement und sozialer Sicherung' ['Definitely do good – about the relationship between social engagement and social security'], in R.G. Heinze and T. Olk (eds) *Bürgerengagement in Deutschland: Bestandsaufnahmen und Perspektiven* [*Civic engagement in Germany: Review and perspectives*], Opladen: Leske/Budrich, pp 189-208.

BFD (2012) 'Der Bundesfreiwilligendienst feiert Geburtstag' ['The federal Volunteering Service celebrates its birthday'], Pressemeldung des BFD vom 01, July.

Birkhölzer, K., Klein, A., Priller, E. and Zimmer, A. (2005) *Dritter Sektor/Drittes System – Theorie, Funktionswandel und zivilgesellschaftliche Perspektiven* [*Third sector/third system: Theory, functional change and civil society perspectives*], Wiesbaden: VS Verlag.

BMFSFJ (2006) *Fünfter Bericht zur Lage der älteren Generation in der Bundesrepublik Deutschland. Potentiale des Alters in Wirtschaft und Gesellschaft – Der Beitrag älterer Menschen zum Zusammenhalt der Generationen* [*Fifth report on the situation of the older generation in the Federal Republic of Germany. Potentials of age in economy and society – The contribution of older people to the cohesion of generations*], Berlin: Deutscher Bundestag.

BMFSFJ (2008) *Engagementpolitik wirksam gestalten. Neue Impulse für die Bürgergesellschaft – Ein Jahr Initiative Zivil Engagement* [*Creating an effective policy of commitment. New impulses for the civil society – One year of civil commitment initiative*], Berlin: Bundesregierung.

BMFSFJ and FFG (2008) *Strategien zur Stärkung des bürgerschaftlichen Engagements älterer Menschen in Deutschland und den Niederlanden* [*Strategies to strengthen the civic engagement of older people in Germany and the Netherlands*], Dortmund: FFG.

BMG (2010) *Pflegestatistik 2009* [*Care statistics 2009*], BMG: Berlin.

Brendgens, U. and Braun, J. (2009) 'Freiwilliges Engagement älterer Menschen' ['Voluntary engagement of older people'], in S. Picot (ed) *Freiwilliges Engagement in Deutschland: Freiwilligensurvey 1999. Band 3: Frauen und Männer, Jugend, Senioren, Sport* [*Volunteering in Germany. Volunteer Survey 1999. Volume 3: Women and men, youth, seniors, sports*], Wiesbaden: VS Verlag, pp 109-302.

Dienel, C. (2011) 'Demografischer Wandel und Bürgerengagement – ein Traumpaar?' ['Demographic change and volunteering – a dream couple?'], *Informationsdienst Altersfragen*, vol 5, no 38, Jahrgang, pp 5-11.

DRV (2009) *Rentenversicherung in Zeitreihen* [*Pension insurance in Time Series*], Berlin: DRV.

Enquete Commission (2002) *Bürgerschaftliches Engagement: auf dem Weg in eine zukunftsfähige Bürgergesellschaft* [*Civic engagement: Towards a sustainable civil society*], Opladen: Leske/Budrich.

Erlinghagen, M. (2009) 'Soziales Engagement im Ruhestand: Erfahrung wichtiger als frei verfügbare Zeit' ['Social engagement in retirement: Experience is more important than free disposable time'], in J. Kocka, M. Kohli, W. Streeck et al (eds) *Altern: Familie, Zivilgesellschaft, Politik* [*Ageing: Family, civil society, politics*], Halle: Deutsche Akademie der Naturforscher Leopoldina, pp 211-20.

Erlinghagen, M. and Hank, K. (2009) 'Ehrenamtliches Engagement und produktives Altern' ['Volunteering and productive ageing'], *Nova Acta Leopoldina*, vol 102, no 366, pp 143-57.

Esping-Andersen, G. (1990) *The three worlds of welfare capitalism*, Oxford: Polity Press.

European Foundation (2011) *Volunteering by older people in the EU*, Dublin: European Foundation for the Improvement of Living and Working Conditions.

Geiss, S. and Picot, S. (2009) 'Familien und Zeit für freiwilliges Engagement' ['Families and time for voluntary engagement'], in M. Heitkötter, K. Jurczyk, A. Lange and U. Meier-Gräwe (eds) *Zeit für Beziehungen? Zeit in und Zeitpolitik für Familie* [*Time for relationships? Time in and time policy for families*], Leverkusen: Budrich, pp 291-317.

Gensicke, T. (2005a) 'Freiwilliges Engagement älterer Menschen im Zeitvergleich 1999-2004' ['Voluntary engagement of older people in time comparison 1999-2004'], in BMFSFJ (ed) *Freiwilliges engagement in Deutschland* [*Voluntary engagement in Germany*], Munich: TNS Infratest, pp 303-46.

Gensicke, T. (2005b) 'Hauptbericht des Freiwilligensurveys 2004' ['Main report of Volunteering Survey 2004'], in BMFSFJ (ed) *Freiwilliges engagement in Deutschland* [*Voluntary engagement in Germany*], Munich: TNS Infratest, pp 1-201.

Hank, K. and Erlinghagen, M. (2010) 'Volunteering in "old" Europe: Patterns, potentials, limitations', *Journal of Applied Gerontology*, vol 29, no 3, pp 3-20.

Hank, K. and Stuck, S. (2008) 'Ehrenamt, Pflege und Netzwerke in Europa: Komplementäre oder konkurrierende Dimensionen produktiven Alters?' ['Honorary office, nursing and networks in Europe: complementary of competing dimensions of productive age?'], in M. Erlinghagen and K. Hank (eds) *Produktives Altern und informelle Arbeit in modernen Gesellschaften: Theoretische Perspektiven und empirische Befunde* [*Productive ageing and informal work in modern societies: Theoretical perspectives and empirical findings*], Wiesbaden: VS Verlag, pp 27-50.

Huber, M., Rodrigues, R., Hoffmann, F., Gasior, K. and Marin, B. (2009) *Facts and figures on long-term care. Europe and North America*, Vienna: European Centre for Social Welfare Policy and Research.

Igl, G., Jachmann, M. and Eichenhofer, E. (2002) *Ehrenamt und Bürgerschaftliches Engagement im Recht – ein Ratgeber* [*Honorary office and civic engagement in law – A guide*], Opladen: Leske/Budrich.

ISSP (International Social Survey Programme) (1997) 'Work Orientations II', Mannheim: ISSP (www.gesis.org/issp/issp-modules-profiles/work-orientations/1997).

Jakob, G. (2001) 'Wenn Engagement zur "Arbeit" wird... Zur aktuellen Diskussion um freiwilliges Engagement im Wandel der Arbeitsgesellschaft' ['If volunteering turns to "work"... On the current discussion of voluntary engagement in a changing labour society'], in R.G. Heinze and T. Olk (eds) *Bürgerengagement in Deutschland: Bestandsaufnahmen und Perspektiven* [*Civic engagement in Germany: Review and perspectives*], Opladen: Leske/Budrich, pp 141-66.

Karl, U. and Kolland, F. (2010) 'Freizeitorientierte Soziale Arbeit mit älteren und alten Menschen' ['Social work with older people in leisure time'], in K. Aner and U. Karl (eds) *Handbuch Soziale Arbeit und Alter* [*Handbook of social work and old age*], Wiesbaden: VS Verlag, pp 77-87.

Klenner, C. and Pfahl, S. (2001) '(Keine) Zeit für's Ehrenamt? Vereinbarkeit von Erwerbsarbeit und ehrenamtlicher Tätigkeit' ['(No) Time for honorary office? Compatibility of paid work and voluntary activity'], *WSI Mitteilungen*, no 3, pp 179-87.

Klenner, C., Pfahl, S. and Seifert, H. (2001) *Ehrenamt und Erwerbsarbeit – Zeitbalance oder Zeitkonkurrenz?* [*Voluntary and paid work – Time balance or time competition?*], Düsseldorf: Schäfer Graphics.

Kolland, F. and Oberbauer, M. (2006) 'Vermarktlichung bürgerschaftlichen Engagements im Alter' ['Marketisation of civic engagement in old age'], in K.R. Schroeter and P. Zängl (eds) *Altern und bürgerschaftliches Engagement, Aspekte der Vergemeinschaftung und Vergesellschaftung in der Lebensphase Alter [Ageing and civic engagement: Aspects of communal relationship and socialisation of life in old age]*, Wiesbaden: VS Verlag, pp 153-74.

Kühnlein, I. and Böhle, F. (2002) 'Das Verhältnis von Erwerbsarbeit und bürgerschaftlichem Engagement: Ersatz – Ergänzung – Konkurrenz?' ['The relationship between paid work and civic engagement: replacement – supplement – competition?'], in Enquete Commission (ed) *Bürgerschaftliches engagement und erwerbsarbeit [Civic engagement and paid work]*, Opladen: Leske/Budrich, pp 87-110.

Künemund, H. (2006a) 'Tätigkeiten und Engagement im Ruhestand' ['Activities and engagement in retirement'], in C. Tesch-Römer, H. Engstler and S. Wurm (eds) *Altwerden in Deutschland. Sozialer Wandel und individuelle Entwicklung in der zweiten lebenshälfte [Ageing in Germany. Social change and individual development in the second half of life]*, Wiesbaden: VS Verlag, pp 289-323.

Künemund, H. (2006b) 'Partizipation und Engagement älterer Menschen' ['Participation and engagement of older people'], in Deutsches Zentrum für Altersfragen (ed) *Gesellschaftliches und familiäres Engagement älterer Menschen als Potenzial [Social and informal engagement of older people as a potential]*, Münster: LIT, pp 283-432.

Künemund, H. (2006c) 'Methodenkritische Anmerkungen zur Empirie ehrenamtlichen Engagements' ['Critical remarks on the methods of empiricism regarding voluntary engagement'], in K.R. Schroeter and P. Zängl (eds) *Altern und bürgerschaftliches Engagement: Aspekte der Vergemeinschaftung und Vergesellschaftung in der Lebensphase Alter [Ageing and civic engagement: Aspects of communal relationship and socialisation of life in old age]*, Wiesbaden: VS Verlag, pp 111-34.

Künemund, H. (2007) 'Vom "Ehrenamt" zum "bürgerschaftlichen Engagement" – Individuelle, organisationelle und gesellschaftliche Perspektiven' ['From "honorary office" to "civic engagement" – Individual, organisational and social perspectives'], in B. Menke and T. Länge (eds) *Aus freien Stücken! Motivation und Qualifikation von älteren Erwachsenen für das bürgerschaftliche Engagement [On your own accord! Motivation and qualification of older adults for civic engagement]*, Recklinghausen: Forschungsinstitut Arbeit, Bildung Partizipation, pp 127-42.

Künemund, H. (2009) 'Erwerbsarbeit, Familie und Engagement in Deutschland' ['Paid work, family and engagement in Germany'], *Nova Acta Leopoldina*, vol 106, no 370, pp 19-39.

Lencz, M. and Plichta, A. (2009) 'Online-Beratung im Generationsübergreifenden Freiwilligendienst' ['Online counselling in intergenerational volunteer service'], in E. Baldas, R.A. Roth and H. Schwalb (eds) *Talente einsetzen – Solidarität stiften: Modellprogramm Generationsübergreifende Freiwilligendienste [Use talents – Create solidarity: Model programme in intergenerational volunteer services]*, Freiburg im Breisgau: Lambertus, pp 301-9.

Menke, B. (2007) '"Aus freien Stücken": Motivation und Qualifikation für das bürgerschaftliche Engagement' ['"On your own accord": motivation and qualification for civic engagement'], in B. Menke and T.W. Länge (eds) *Aus freien Stücken! Motivation und Qualifikation von älteren Erwachsenen für das bürgerschaftliche Engagement [On your own accord! Motivation and qualification of older adults for civic engagement]*, Recklinghausen: Forschungsinstitut Arbeit, Bildung Partizipation, pp 9-24.

Menning, S. (2006) 'Die Zeitverwendung älterer Menschen und die Nutzung von Zeitpotenzialen für informelle Hilfeleistungen und bürgerschaftliches Engagement' ['The use of time by older people and the potential of time for informal help and civic engagement'], in Deutsches Zentrum für Altersfragen (ed) *Gesellschaftliches und familiäres Engagement älterer Menschen als Potenzial [Social and informal engagement of older people as a potential]*, Münster: LIT, pp 433-525.

Pfau-Effinger, B. and Magdalenic, S.S. (2009) 'Formal and informal work in the work-welfare arrangement of Germany', in B. Pfau-Effinger, L. Flaquer and Per H. Jensen (eds) *Formal and informal work: The hidden work regime in Europe*, New York, London: Routledge, pp 89-116.

Picot, S. and Gensicke, T. (2005) 'Freiwilliges Engagement von Männern und Frauen im Zeitvergleich 1999-2004' ['Voluntary engagement of men and women in time comparison 1999-2004'], in BMFSFJ (ed) *Freiwilliges engagement in Deutschland [Voluntary engagement in Germany]*, Munich: TNS Infratest, pp 258-302.

Prognos and AMB Generali (2009) *Engagementatlas 2009. Daten. Hintergründe. Wirtschaftlicher Nutzen [Engagement atlas 2009 (Commitment atlas). Data. Background. Economic benefits]*, Berlin/Aachen.

Rohleder, C. and Bröscher, P. (2002) *Freiwilliges Engagement älterer Menschen. Band 1: Ausmaß, Strukturen und sozial- räumliche Voraussetzungen [Voluntary engagement of older people, Vol 1: Proportions, structures and socio-spatial preconditions]*, Düsseldorf: MFJFG.

Sachße, C. (2000) 'Freiwilligenarbeit und private Wohlfahrtskultur in historischer Perspektive' ['Voluntary work and private welfare culture in historical perspective'], in A. Zimmer and S. Nährlich (eds) *Engagierte Bürgerschaft, Traditionen und Perspektiven* [*Engaged citizenship, traditions and perspectives*], Opladen: Leske/Budrich, pp 75-88.

Sachße, C. (2003) 'Subsidiarität: Leitmaxime deutscher Wohlfahrtsstaatlichkeit' ['Subsidiarity: guiding maxim of the German welfare state'], in S. Lessenich (ed) *Wohlfahrtsstaatliche Grundbegriffe, Historische und aktuelle Diskurse* [*Basic ideas of welfare state, historical and current discourses*], Frankfurt: Campus-Verlag, pp 191-212.

Schmidt, B. and Schnurr, S. (2009) 'Freiwilliges Engagement' ['Volunteering'], in R. Tippelt, B. Schmidt, S. Schnurr, S. Sinner and K. Theisen (eds) *Bildung Älterer: Chancen im demografischen Wandel* [*Education of older people: Prospects in demographic change*], Bielefeld: Bertelsman, pp 113-24.

Schroeter, K.R. (2006) 'Einleitung: Vom "alten Ehrenamt" zum "bürgerschaftlichen Engagement im Alter"' ['Introduction: from "old honorary office" to "civic engagement in old age"'], in K.R. Schroeter and P. Zängl (eds) *Altern und bürgerschaftliches Engagement, Aspekte der Vergemeinschaftung und Vergesellschaftung in der Lebensphase Alter* [*Ageing and civic engagement: Aspects of communal relationship and socialization of life in old age*], Wiesbaden: VS Verlag, pp 7-25.

Süßlin, W. (2008) 'Allensbacher Ehrenamtsbefragung 2006 – Ergebnisse einer repräsentativen Befragung von Ehrenamtlichen im Bereich der Caritas' ['Allensbacher volunteering survey 2006 – Results of a representative survey of volunteers in the field of charity Caritas'], in E. Baldas and C. Bangert (eds) *Ehrenamt in der Caritas: Allensbacher Repräsentativbefragung. Qualitative Befragung. Ergebnisse – Perspektiven* [*Volunteering in the charity Caritas: Allensbacher representative survey. Qualitative survey. Results – Perspectives*], Freiburg: Lambertus, pp 17-86.

Thiel, W. (2006) 'Bürgerschaftliches Engagement, Selbsthilfe und Welfare Mix. Institutionelle und infrastrukturelle Voraussetzungen, gesellschaftliche Rollen und Förderperspektiven. Eckpunkte für eine Diskussion' ['Civic engagement, self-help and welfare mix. Institutional and infrastructural preconditions, social roles and promotion perspectives. Key points for a discussion'], in DAG SHG (ed) *Selbsthilfegruppenjahrbuch 2007* [*Self-help group yearbook 2007*], Gießen: DAG, pp 143-51.

Zeman, P. (2008) 'Rahmenbedingungen für das Engagement im Alter' ['Framework conditions for engagement in old age'], *Informationsdienst Altersfragen*, no 2, pp 2-7.

SIX

Older volunteers in England: towards greater flexibility and inclusiveness?

Robert Lindley, Beate Baldauf, Sheila Galloway and Yuxin Li

Introduction

The UK voluntary sector comprises over 160,000 *registered* organisations, contributing roughly £12 billion (14 billion) or 0.8 per cent of UK gross value added (GVA) (Clark et al, 2012).[1] However, measuring the size of the sector in official terms (that is, according to rules followed by national accounts statisticians) fails to capture the value of the 'unmeasured output' contributed by volunteers. Often described as the 'lifeblood' of the charitable sector, about 20 million people in the UK volunteer formally at least once a year, amounting to about 40 per cent of the adult population (DCLG, 2011a). Taking just those volunteering at least once a month, this represents an economic value of £23 billion (28 billion) if volunteers were to be replaced by paid staff (Clark et al, 2012). Although most volunteers provide unpaid help to voluntary sector organisations, volunteering also takes place in the public and private sectors. And some volunteers participate in employer-supported volunteering schemes.

The range of activities of these organisations and the motives of volunteers behind engaging in them are varied. Rochester et al (2010) observe that the 'conceptual map' of volunteering is broader than the type of activity that dominates public discussion, namely, volunteering in the area of social care, presumed to be driven by altruistic motives. The map also includes 'activism' (mutual aid, self-help or campaigning for changes in provision concerning a wide range of public policy areas) and 'serious leisure' (typically in areas such as the arts, culture, sport and recreation) where self-expressive or intrinsic motives prevail. Indeed, whereas by far the largest group of *registered voluntary organisations* is engaged in social services, followed by culture and recreation, and religion, survey data indicate that the highest levels of *volunteering* can be found in sports, hobbies and the arts (DCLG, 2011b), which are mainly associated with 'serious leisure'.

The voluntary sector has grown substantially over the last decade, both in terms of financial turnover and employment, but the rate of participation in volunteering changed only slightly overall, increasing during the first half of the decade and then falling back. The growth of the sector has been particularly fuelled by the increase in public contracting-out of services to private profit-making and non-profit organisations. Relationships between the three groups have become complex, and there has been an accompanying research interest into the identities of and values underpinning the voluntary sector during this transition (Alcock, 2010).

However, while much has happened to the voluntary sector, our focus here is on volunteering, particularly by older people. Their experiences have been given far less attention than those of the organisations themselves; the same is true of the rest of Europe, in contrast to the US (Principi et al, 2012). Thus, this chapter does not offer a general treatment of developments in the English voluntary sector or in volunteering. Nor does it cover the journey taken by the policy discourse from 'voluntary sector' to 'third sector' to 'civil society' (HM Treasury and the Cabinet Office, 2007; Office for Civil Society, 2010; Milbourne and Cushman, 2012; Taylor et al, 2012). These changing orientations of policy and in the relationships between 'the sector' and governments have had implications for older volunteers, but these are best handled in terms of their more direct effects. This means that significant parts of policy and research in the voluntary field lie outside the scope of this chapter, as do the theoretical perspectives.

While the voluntary sector goes well beyond the provision of support for those in need, the fostering of social well-being is a core element of its activities. This then brings it into interaction with the public welfare system. The welfare regime in England has been described as 'liberal' because of its supposedly 'residual' nature due to the predominance of means-tested, modest levels of benefit, and the encouragement of market solutions to welfare provision. This is in contrast to approaches that offer greater rights to welfare or 'degrees of decommodification' for those who cannot afford what the market would otherwise supply (Esping-Andersen, 1990).

It is often assumed that low degrees of de-commodification leave unmet needs among disadvantaged people that encourage the formation of voluntary organisations aiming to address them. Moreover, when governments cease or reduce their provision of some such services, debate often ensues both about the extent to which the voluntary sector has the capacity to step in and about whether or not it should in fact do so.

Alongside the liberal welfare regime lies the labour market. Although in a European Union (EU) context the UK is seen to have a relatively deregulated, flexible labour market, there is a substantial floor of common EU regulation co-existing with a high employment rate among older workers and relatively high labour force participation among women. Anti-age discrimination has been brought within the comprehensive treatment of the Equality Act 2010.

Caring responsibilities can affect participation both in the labour market and in voluntary work, constricting, or, in some respects, stimulating the latter, depending on the nature and scope of the caring responsibilities. The predominant family care model in England is still that of the male breadwinner with women working part time and undertaking the main carer role. Mothers with a dependent child often take up a part-time job, yet the percentage of mothers working full time has increased since the late 1990s (ONS, 2011).

The voluntary sector's wide range of activities already includes older volunteers in many areas (DCLG, 2011b). How far participation from older people can be enhanced so as to reap the benefits they bring to both others and themselves is considered later in this chapter. Two key ingredients to achieving this, however, seem to be the promotion of 'flexibility' and 'inclusiveness' in developing the older volunteer force. The interpretations of these concepts and reasons for identifying them as being important are also developed in this chapter.

Volunteering is one of the areas of public policy responsibility devolved to the constituent four nations that form the UK. This chapter focuses on volunteering by older people in England (about 84 per cent of the UK population). However, some data are available/ published only for the UK or Great Britain (England, Wales and Scotland). The remainder of this section summarises very briefly the tradition of the voluntary sector and the legal framework currently affecting it. The next section expands on the nature and scope of volunteering, looking at participation in volunteering generally and that of older people in particular. The third section investigates opportunities for and barriers to volunteering in later life. The fourth section explores how the preferences of older people and volunteering opportunities could be better aligned. The chapter ends with some concluding reflections.

The English tradition of voluntary action

Looking for the roots of modern *voluntary* activity devoted to the relief of poverty and the broader promotion of social welfare leads back to the late Middle Ages (indeed, earlier; see Davis Smith, 1995), and the emergence of charitable practices and ways of organising mutual aid associated with monasteries, guilds, brotherhoods and hospitals for the infirm. Yet while these were undoubtedly concerned with alleviating social distress, the extent of both *corruption* of intended purposes and *compulsion* of 'voluntary commitment' was quite extensive within the structures of both church and state.

The two centuries up to the formation of the post-war welfare state in the late 1940s (Beveridge, 1948) displayed most of the attitudes towards the disadvantaged, the dilemmas in designing policy and the shakiness of its implementation that are associated with present-day experience. During this period, the voluntary sector acted in partnership with the state but, from the late 19th century, experienced major changes in its role and in the framework within which it operated. The state began to regulate parts of the sector, notably the charities and friendly societies, at the same time as drawing on the sector to administer parts of the emerging state welfare provision (Harris, 2010). Different elements of the latter took over some of the functions that had hitherto been carried out by the voluntary sector on a partial basis: notably, unemployment insurance, schooling, health and social care, and pensions. Eventually, the so-called 'mixed economy of welfare' was progressively colonised by the state in the interests of consistency of access to and quality of provision.

Coming to the present day, the Charity Commission (2008, p 8) recognises specific areas as being for charitable purposes, including the 'prevention or relief of poverty' and the advancement of 'education', 'religion'; 'health or the saving of lives'; 'citizenship or community development'; 'the arts, culture, heritage or science'; and 'amateur sport'.

Only about a quarter of all voluntary sector organisations receive funding from statutory sources (contracts or grants). Moreover, the amount of funding the charitable sector attracts from statutory sources varies widely by sub-sector, with social services attracting one of the highest shares. Furthermore, there has been an important shift within statutory funding, with an absolute and relative increase of funding from statutory contracts for public service delivery during 2003/04 to 2009/10 at the expense of grant funding as voluntary organisations chose to bid for specific funding opportunities (Clark et al, 2012).

However, in the aftermath of the financial crisis of 2008, both streams of UK public spending were subject to major reductions in planned levels that began to come into effect particularly with the formation of the 2010 Coalition government.

The legal framework

The main areas of the law that affect volunteering are those that deal with (1) the legal basis of the organisation for tax and public liability purposes (according to its status as a public body or agency, private company or partnership, charity, etc); (2) employment law as it applies to employees; (3) employment law as it is extended to volunteers; (4) the social security rights of voluntary workers; (5) the regulation of certain areas of activity, notably, to working in a paid or voluntary capacity with vulnerable groups (for example, children in general and vulnerable adults such as those with learning difficulties); and (6) equality legislation governing the provision of goods and services (see Restall, 2005, in relation to items 2-5).

However, whereas there is in law an *organisation* devoted to mobilising volunteers, there is no such *legal person* as a volunteer. For an organisation, although the position is quite complex, the main tax advantages of acquiring charitable status relate to zero liability to pay corporate income tax and the benefits they derive from personal tax incentives in favour of charitable giving. Unlike a private or public sector organisation, however, they suffer from an irrecoverable value-added tax (VAT) burden since they can neither offset the tax via their suppliers as in the private sector nor take advantage of special tax recovery arrangements available to the public sector.

For individuals, when acting as volunteers, they are subject to the same legal provisions applicable to any citizen or non-citizen resident within the territory. These include the right to a duty of care from their employer if they are volunteering (whether on or off site) as part of their employer's scheme to assist the non-profit sector. Moreover, in respect of health and safety regulations, the volunteer organisation has a similar duty of care towards volunteers as to their paid employees. The main difference between employing employees and volunteers is that the former have an employment contract that brings with it protection against unfair dismissal and of minimum wage legislation and other negotiated agreements, together with the full extent of employment law dealing with anti-discrimination regarding gender, ethnicity, disability, age and sexual orientation. Thus no special legal provisions depending on age apply to volunteers, whereas there are now protections against age discrimination relating to employed people.

Moreover, employers are now advised to follow certain practices that ensure that volunteers are not inadvertently given employment status in the eyes of the law and to ensure, especially, that the laws of unfair dismissal do not apply. This means (Directory of Social Change, 2011):

- emphasising a non-contractual relationship in behaviour and language
- avoiding employee-related policies and terms
- reimbursing actual expenses only
- only offering training which is necessary to the volunteer role itself.

Organisations recruiting volunteers are thus encouraged to stress that there are no legal rights or obligations constraining the roles of their volunteers, and that these roles are not therefore protected by UK legislation but lie rather at the centre of a set of hopes and light expectations shared by the individual and the organisation.

The dimension of volunteer work

The UK voluntary sector has expanded during the first decade of the 21st century, both in terms of the number of organisations and its employee workforce (Clark et al, 2011, 2012), but experienced a sharp drop (8.7 per cent) in paid staff between the third quarters of 2010-11 following public sector spending cuts (Weakley, 2012). Participation in formal volunteering increased somewhat between 2000 and 2005 but, by the end of the decade, it had more or less returned to the levels recorded at the start (see Figure 6.1). Despite anecdotal evidence that volunteering enquiries increased following the onset of the recession, this has not, to date, resulted in higher levels of volunteering (Clark et al, 2012).

Voluntary organisations

More than half of the 160,000 registered organisations that the National Council for Voluntary Organisations (NCVO) includes in its UK voluntary sector overview were small organisations with an annual income below £10,000 (12,000), and relatively few (2.8 per cent) were large with an annual income of £1 million (1.2 million)

Figure 6.1: Participation in formal volunteering among the population aged 16 and over, England, 2001-2010/11

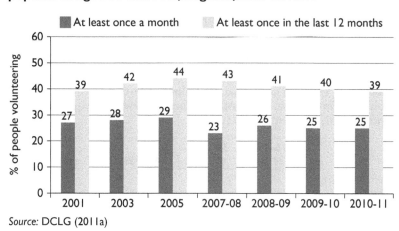

Source: DCLG (2011a)

or more (Clark et al, 2012). The latter include well-known charities that operate nationally and at a local level through branches or local charity retail outlets.

The voluntary sector is estimated to employ around 765,000 paid staff, representing 2.7 per cent of the UK workforce (Clark et al, 2011). Most of the employees work in social work without accommodation (37 per cent) and residential care activities (15 per cent), followed by, for example, education and activities of membership organisations.

Volunteers by sector, gender and age

Formal volunteering in the Citizenship Survey[2] has been defined as 'giving unpaid help as part of a group, club or organisation to benefit others or the environment', and is recorded according to level of intensity (DCLG, 2011a, p 27). In the 2010-11 Survey, 39 per cent of the adult population in England participated in formal volunteering at least once within the last 12 months (16.6 million people), and 25 per cent at least once a month (10.6 million volunteers, providing hours of work roughly equivalent to those of 1.1 million full-time employees) – henceforth referred to as 'regular' volunteering (DCLG, 2011a). Those who participated via employer-supported volunteering amounted to 5 percentage points of those volunteering at least once a year and 2 percentage points of the regular volunteers.

Volunteering takes place across a wide range of sectors and activities, often with multiple volunteering where the same individual contributes to more than one sector (Low et al, 2007). The highest incidence of regular formal volunteering involves (see Table 6.1) sport/exercise, where over half of volunteers are engaged; about a third or more are involved in hobbies, recreation/arts/social clubs; religion; children's education/schools; and youth/children's activities (outside school). A fifth of volunteers mentioned health, disability and social

Table 6.1: Types of organisation helped through regular formal volunteering in the 12 months before interview, by age group and gender, England, 2009-10 (%)

	16-24	25-34	35-49	50-64	65-74	75+	Male	Female	All
Sport/exercise (taking part, coaching or going to watch)	67	58	65	50	34	32	60	49	54
Hobbies, recreation/arts/social clubs	45	40	38	47	42	37	46	38	42
Religion	25	34	34	36	41	53	30	40	36
Children's education/schools	36	35	52	27	15	13	26	42	34
Youth/children's activities (outside school)	37	32	43	25	11	6	31	29	30
Health, disability and social welfare	14	15	21	25	19	16	14	24	19
Local community or neighbourhood groups	7	10	18	24	29	29	19	19	19
Supporting older people	10	11	11	25	28	32	15	20	18
The environment, animals	14	9	19	25	21	17	19	18	18
Education for adults	16	21	17	19	16	12	16	18	17
Safety, first aid	19	12	13	12	6	4	11	12	12
Other	13	10	7	10	13	10	10	9	10
Trade union activity	3	8	11	12	4	2	9	8	8
Citizens' groups	3	4	5	10	17	14	7	9	8
Justice and human rights	6	8	5	9	5	4	6	7	7
Politics	6	3	4	5	9	5	7	3	5
Respondents[a]	*161*	*266*	*653*	*541*	*344*	*219*	*936*	*1.248*	*2.184*

Notes: [a] Core sample, only includes those listed in the table headings.
Multiple responses, hence percentages sum to more than 100.

Source: DCLG (2011b)

welfare; supporting older people; or community/neighbourhood groups.

Turning to the types of activity undertaken (see Table 6.2), regardless of the voluntary field concerned, about half of volunteers cited assisting with the running of activities or events and raising or handling money. These were followed by leading a group or committee membership and offering other practical help. Other activities reported by about a quarter of the volunteers included offering information, advice or counselling; visiting people; befriending and mentoring; and providing transport.

Gender differences in volunteering were very small in 2009-10 with about 40 per cent of both men and women volunteering in the last 12 months and about 25 per cent volunteering regularly; the same was more or less true a decade earlier. However, whereas women's participation was about 1 percentage point above that of men in these years, this gap rose to about 4 or 5 points in the middle of the decade

Table 6.2: Types of formal volunteering activities undertaken by regular formal volunteers in the 12 months before interview, by age group, England, 2010-11 (%)

	16-24	25-34	35-49	50-64	65-74	75+	All
Organising or helping to run an activity or event	55	45	56	51	52	42	52
Raising or handling money	43	48	58	53	50	45	51
Leading the group/ member of committee	33	26	40	41	43	32	37
Other practical help	40	36	41	31	26	25	35
Giving information/ advice/counselling	29	31	27	31	25	16	27
Providing transport/ driving	14	22	30	30	27	19	26
Visiting people	17	24	17	30	36	32	24
Befriending or mentoring people	28	24	20	23	24	20	23
Secretarial, clerical or admin work	12	11	18	25	25	15	18
Representing	22	14	15	17	14	11	16
Any other activities	12	11	13	16	15	16	14
Campaigning	8	4	8	13	12	6	9
Respondents[a]	*161*	*266*	*653*	*541*	*344*	*219*	*2,184*

Notes: [a] Core sample, only includes those listed in the table heading.
Multiple responses, hence percentages sum to more than 100.

Source: DCLG (2011b)

before declining. Women are more likely to be engaged in children's education/schools, religion, and health, disability and social welfare. Men are more likely to volunteer in sport/exercise and hobbies/arts/ social clubs (DCLG, 2011b).

Volunteering, as a percentage of the population age group concerned, whether at least once a year or regularly, is lowest for 25- to 34-year-olds (the family formation phase), peaks at ages 35-49 and then tails off before increasing again at the onset of and during the main post-retirement phase of 65-74, declining thereafter for those aged 75+, for reasons relating to health or disability (see Figure 6.2). However, the average number of hours of volunteering is actually at a minimum for the 35- to 49-year-olds. Taking this into account, the extent of regular volunteering is characterised more simply by the low point among those aged 25-34 and a peak among 64- to 74-year-olds; for the wider definition of volunteering, the (modest) peak shifts to the 50- to 64-year-olds.

Figure 6.2: Formal volunteering: percentage who volunteered and average number of hours volunteered during the last four weeks prior to the interview, by age group, England, 2009-10

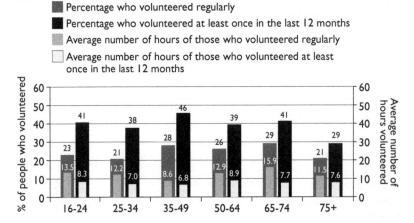

Source: Figures based on DCLG (2011b)

Participation in volunteering is affected by the level of education of volunteers, with degree holders volunteering more often than those with a GCSE (General Certificate of Secondary Education) or no qualifications (see Figure 6.3). Similarly, those in higher socio-economic groups (higher/lower managerial and professional occupations) participate more often in volunteering than those in less

Figure 6.3: Participation in formal volunteering by highest qualification level, England, 2009/10

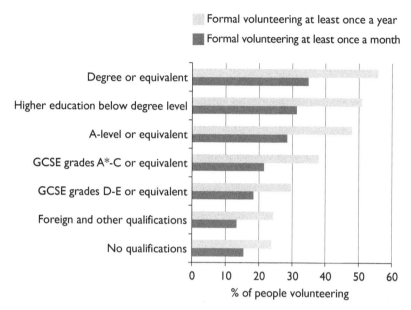

Notes: A-level = advanced level after secondary education; GCSE = General Certificate of Secondary Education.
Source: Figures based on DCLG (2011b)

skilled occupations. Volunteering at least once a year is markedly more common among the employed (44 per cent) than the unemployed or economically inactive (35 per cent), but only slightly more when considering regular volunteering (27 versus 23 per cent, respectively). Other groups with higher rates of regular volunteering include those who are White (26 per cent), Black (25 per cent), have a religious affiliation (26 per cent) or live in a rural area (31 per cent) (DCLG, 2011b).

The above differences in patterns of volunteering when hours are taken into account rather defy attempts to identify a *prototypical* volunteer any more specifically than being someone aged between 35 and 64, who is well educated and, if employed, holds a skilled or highly skilled job.

Participation of older volunteers

Bearing in mind the difficulties of comparing surveys over time, regular volunteering among the older age groups (50-64 and 65-74) appears to have fallen more gradually between the years 2005 and 2009 than that among the younger age groups (DCLG, different years).

A *prototypical* older regular volunteer may be described as someone in the early/middle stage of retirement (64–74). He or she could be described as someone raising or handling money, helping to run an event or engaging in committee work/leading a group in an organisation running recreational activities, a sports organisation (volunteering rate declining with age) or a religious organisation (volunteering rate increasing with age). However, compared to other age groups, older volunteers are more likely to be committee members/lead a group, visit people (likely to include or even focus on older people), engage with religious organisations, provide support to other older people or local community groups – and are less likely to engage in organisations concerned with sports, children/youth activities outside school or young people or to provide practical help (see Tables 6.1 and 6.2).

In general, men are more likely to provide transport and advice, and women are more likely to provide 'other practical support' and, while there is no survey information on the form of voluntary help given, by age group and gender, there is some anecdotal information that this may also apply to older volunteers.

There appears to be little information on volunteer age structures at an organisational level, an exception being the study undertaken by Rochester and Thomas (2006). Their non-representative survey of 400 largely voluntary sector organisations found that the percentage of volunteers aged 50+ was highest in areas relating to social services (75 per cent) and health (73 per cent), and lowest in culture and recreation (43 per cent). These results largely mirror the findings of the Citizenship Survey. Older volunteers were reported to have taken up a wide range of roles, with the most frequent ones reported to include 'reception, administration and clerical' (30 per cent), 'befriending and mentoring' (25 per cent) and 'provision of specialist expertise' (25 per cent).

While organisations providing services for older people (for example, WRVS or Age UK) tend to attract predominantly older volunteers, there appear to be few examples of organisations targeting mature volunteers, as such. Virtually unique in the UK is the Retired Senior Volunteer Programme (RSVP). Set up in 1988 as a free-standing programme within Community Service Volunteers (CSV), it offers volunteering opportunities to the over-50s. RSVP continues to expand, and currently has more than 16,000 volunteers in the UK (CSV, 2011), working on volunteer-led and volunteer-managed projects in a range of areas, including education, environment, health and social care, heritage and, for example, knitting items to support good causes.

Older people's participation in voluntary organisations: opportunities and restrictions

Promotion of active ageing through extending working lives and engagement in volunteering is a key policy response to an ageing society in which people are living healthier lives for longer. Moreover, research shows that older people, like other age groups participating in volunteering, derive benefits from it, such as intrinsic satisfaction, enjoyment and social contacts (DCLG, 2010; see also Age UK, 2011). While there is, in principle, an opportunity to engage growing numbers of older people in volunteering, there may also be barriers to volunteering that relate to (1) individual perceptions and preferences; (2) civil society organisations' approaches to deploying volunteers; and (3) public policy. This section explores the available evidence and briefly looks at how older volunteering interacts with labour market participation and caring responsibilities.

Opportunities and restrictions for volunteering for older people

Studies exploring the motivation to volunteer usually find that volunteers give more than one reason (see, for example, Davis Smith and Gay, 2005). Rochester and Hutchinson (2002, p 47) report that volunteering enables older people 'to meet personal needs and interests and provides them with opportunities for personal development.' More specifically, motivations include being valued, 'putting something back' into the community, filling a void following retirement or bereavement or for some, helping other older people.

At the same time, older people's own perceptions can act as a barrier, as they may be unaware of the range of volunteering opportunities, have stereotypical views about who volunteers, or lack confidence in their abilities because they may not recognise the experience and skills they are able to offer (Rochester and Hutchinson, 2002).

Moreover, survey evidence on the barriers to regular formal volunteering shows that 50- to 64-year-olds mostly cite other commitments, notably work and looking after children/the home, and other interests. The 65- to 75-year-olds reported barriers less frequently and referred to a wider range of reasons (including health issues and work commitments); those aged 75+ indicated that illness or disability and feeling too old were the most prevalent barriers (DCLG, 2011b).

With regard to opportunities at an organisational level, Rochester and Hutchinson (2002) tentatively concluded that organisations promoting the well-being of older people tended to be more successful in attracting older volunteers (mirrored in Table 6.1) as were those organisations where volunteering was a 'recognised and central feature' (p 44), since these organisations were more predisposed towards understanding, mobilising and supporting them. The study also identified areas where older volunteers in particular could make a valuable contribution, such as offering frail and isolated older people education and recreational activities, helping people with long-term health problems to manage their condition and intergenerational activities (Rochester and Hutchinson, 2002). Besides that, there is a wider range of organisational volunteering opportunities older people enjoy, for example, in culture and recreation, where people can take on public-facing or back office roles in museums in which they take a keen interest (see Lindley et al, 2011).

Organisations acknowledge that older volunteers have a lot to offer, such as maturity, skills, loyalty, greater availability of time and ability to engage with (older and younger) service users. However, certain policies and practices have been identified as presenting barriers to effective older volunteering (Dingle, 2001; Rochester and Hutchinson, 2002). These include the overtly ageist policy of imposing an upper age limit for volunteers (partly blamed on difficulties in insuring older volunteers and partly used as a blanket approach to retire older volunteers). More recently, Rochester and Thomas (2006, p 3) have concluded that there is 'some evidence of [age] limits being removed or eased.' More nuanced are a bias towards younger volunteers and allocations of tasks to older volunteers that tend to be somewhat limited and less interesting than those that older volunteers actually want (Rochester and Hutchison, 2002).

Turning to the institutional level, a number of initiatives to support volunteering were put in place during the New Labour governments (1997-2010), notably (a) activities that created a positive environment for volunteering, including targets for volunteering in public service agreements with central and local governments; (b) various volunteering initiatives, targeting all or particular groups, such as young people, the unemployed or older people; and (c) activities that supported the volunteering infrastructure and improved the capacity of the voluntary sector (Zimmeck, 2010).

Between 1999 and 2006, three government-led initiatives focused specifically on older volunteers:

- The Home Office Older Volunteer Initiative (1999-2003) aimed to raise the number and quality of opportunities for people aged 50+ to volunteer and to engage with their community. The £1.5 million (1.8 million) initiative funded 26 projects, nearly all led by voluntary organisations, and attracted volunteers aged 50-80. The final evaluation report acknowledged the many achievements of the programme but noted that its design and implementation had limitations that affected the achievement of its overall aims; one of these was sustaining activities beyond the funding period (Rochester and Hutchinson, 2002).
- An initiative aimed at recruiting exclusively older volunteers has had limited success. Funded by a grant from the Home Office, a new non-profit company, named Experience Corps, was set up in 2002 in order to help recruit 250,000 volunteers aged 50-65 by 2004, but funding was withdrawn in 2003 because the actual recruitment (130,000 at the time) was below target (Shifrin, 2003).
- The two-year programme, Volunteering in the Third Age (VITA, 2004-06), was designed to support volunteering by people aged 65+, aiming at improving the volunteering experience, tackling barriers to volunteering, promoting the value and impact of volunteering and attracting more older volunteers (Price, 2007).

As part of its overall support for volunteering, the Coalition government (which was formed in May 2010) funded a small project on the volunteering of older people in health and social care as part of the activities that marked the 2011 EU Year of Volunteering, culminating in two Age UK-led events on older volunteering and reports (Age UK, 2011, 2012).

From a somewhat different perspective, promoting volunteering in later life has, to different degrees, also been part of government initiatives to promote the well-being of older citizens. These include, especially, programmes such as LinkAge Plus (2006-08), Partnerships for Older People Projects (2005-09), the Ageing Well Programme (2010-12) and the Active at 60 Community Agent Programme (2011). The last of these, for example, tested a new role for older people willing to take the lead in developing the activities of an existing community group and encouraging more older people to participate. An assessment by Hatamian et al (2012) suggests that the role was valuable, sustainable beyond the end of the programme (through the majority of community agents wanting to continue), and helped to increase volunteering opportunities for other older people in support of the group's activities.

Overall, these two overlapping aims of promoting older volunteering and older people's well-being come together as just part of the Coalition government's strategy to create what it has called the 'Big Society' by (a) giving local authorities and other local players more power to make decisions; (b) engaging the voluntary, community and private sectors more in the delivery of public services; and (c) encouraging people to take on a more active role in society (Office for Civil Society, 2010). A key initiative currently under way is to train 5,000 community organisers by 2015, the large majority being unpaid volunteers. However, the launch of the 'Big Society' coincided with a period of significant public spending cuts. While new funding streams were set up to support this ambition, funding cuts elsewhere are likely to hamper the realisation of the wider goals (Slocock, 2012). A contrast can be seen in the idea of greater autonomy alongside reduced resources offered by the Coalition as opposed to strong central government control with greater resource growth offered under Labour.

Older people between employment and volunteering

In 2011, the UK's employment rate was above the EU27 average, both for the 50- to 64-year-olds (65.0 versus 57.6 per cent) and the 65+ (8.9 versus 4.8 per cent). The UK employment rates for women aged 50-64 and for those aged 65+ stood at 59.2 and 6.3 per cent, respectively, with comparable figures for men being 71.1 and 11.9 per cent, respectively (Eurostat, April-June 2011). Given the gradual rise of the UK state pension age for women from 60 to 65 planned for 2010-18, to equalise that for men, women's employment rates are likely to grow further.

As to future intention, 66 per cent of the age group 50-64 in Great Britain agree that they would like to continue working after they reach the age when they are entitled to a pension (Eurobarometer, 2012). Another source records that 53 per cent of this age group agree/strongly agree that they would enjoy having a paid job even if they did not need the money (ISSP, 2005), suggesting that non-financial motives play a role in the preference for a possible extension of working lives. However, both survey samples concerned are very small once broken down to country and age group.

Some volunteer before retirement (intermittently or fairly continuously) and some begin to volunteer in retirement (Davis Smith and Gay, 2005; Baines et al, 2006), often because work commitments precluded participation in volunteering during their working lives (Baines et al, 2006).

Some quantitative evidence is beginning to emerge, however, that those who participated in volunteering before retirement are more likely to engage in volunteering after retirement than those who had no prior volunteering experience (Erlinghagen, 2010; Jivraj and Nazroo, 2012).

This reinforces the importance of promoting volunteering throughout the life cycle. Some authors (see, for example, Davis Smith and Gay, 2005; Hatton-Yeo, 2006; Commission for the Future of Volunteering, 2008) have argued that more could be done to increase volunteering *before* retirement; this would mean going beyond delivering pre-retirement courses to consider schemes to foster more employer-supported volunteering as part of phased retirement.

Employer-supported volunteering has been adopted mainly by private corporations companies and public sector organisations as part of their corporate social responsibility activities (Rochester et al, 2010). Volunteering opportunities may be offered by the company itself or as a result of the employer's collaboration with a charity or an intermediary, and schemes vary as to whether volunteering takes place in the employee's own time or within working hours (Low et al, 2007). However, while some see employer-supported volunteering as a growth area (as reported in Rochester et al, 2010), survey data have yet to show an increase in participation in this form of volunteering.

Without adequate data on volunteering over time, it is not possible to do the necessary econometric modelling so as to ascertain the likelihood of a negative or positive impact of an extension of working lives on the propensity to volunteer (in terms of the time given or the participation rate). Nevertheless, the overall number of older volunteers is likely to rise through the scale of increases in the size of older populations cohorts. Yet the increasing role of part-time work during later life may allow more flexibility, unless other roles or aims gain more prominence, and retirement in itself may not be *the* decisive factor for taking up volunteering in later life.

Older people between family care and volunteering

Care services for older people in England are delivered by a range of public, private and voluntary providers following assessment by local authorities, yet most care is provided by unpaid informal carers.

Should the need for care arise, public opinion is divided as to how this should be arranged, with most either expecting the children to get involved with the care of an older parent living on his or her own, either by inviting the parent to live with one of the children (20 per cent) or one of them regularly visiting their parent (23 per cent) or expecting care providers to provide the appropriate care at home (34 per cent) (Eurobarometer, 2007, UK figures).

In 2010/11 more than 1 million people aged 65 and over received (one or more) services from local authorities, mainly community-based services, including home care (over 400,000 people) and direct payments (over 300,000 people) intended to enable them to purchase the types of service that best met their needs. In addition 167,000 received residential care and 79,000 nursing care (NHS Information Centre, 2012). However, the number of service users has declined over time, as local authorities have tightened eligibility criteria (CSCI, 2008).

In England, caring for an ill, disabled or older person peaks at the age of 45-64, and nearly half of the overall 12 per cent of people aged 16 or over providing care for this group dedicate about 20 or more hours per week to unpaid caring (NHS Information Centre, 2010). Older women, in particular the 50- to 59-year-olds, are more often caring for someone than men, and a substantial proportion of women care for more than one person (an older relative, a child/grandchild, spouse/partner or someone else) (Vlachantoni, 2010).

Given the time demands of caring and related logistical issues, this is likely to affect the capacity to volunteer. This is borne out by survey data which identify those who see 'looking after someone elderly or ill' as a barrier to regular formal volunteering: this applies to between 13 and 16 per cent of the over-50s age groups compared to 8 per cent overall (DCLG, 2010).

While there is also some evidence from voluntary organisations that people reduce their volunteering hours or drop out while they are caring for someone older or looking after a grandchild, it has also been reported that some may return to volunteer with the same organisation at a later stage, particularly if their volunteering experience has been positive. Moreover, a large organisation providing support for older people observed that 'quite a few' people whose parent had received services from the organisation volunteered with them after the parent had passed away as they wanted 'to give something back' (Lindley et al, 2011).

Improving the match between supply of older candidates with the demands of voluntary organisations: future perspectives

There is widespread recognition that the demand for certain kinds of voluntary activity, notably in health and social care, will rise significantly as a result of population ageing. A recent study has explored roles for volunteers in health and social care, with a particular view to promoting active ageing. These roles are concerned with, for example, exercise and activity, traditional one-to-one assistance and practical help, or provision of transport (Age UK, 2012). They offer opportunities in areas where older people have a strong interest, such as in supporting the elderly or 'giving something back to the community'.

From an organisational point of view, important key *potential barriers* arise throughout the volunteer cycle. If these were to be addressed, recruitment and retention of (older) volunteers could be improved. Voluntary organisations may argue that an increase in volunteering opportunities needs to be accompanied by additional resources to support volunteers throughout the volunteer cycle, which, in the current climate of budget cuts, would be difficult to achieve.

Moreover, some commentators/researchers point to changing attitudes towards volunteering in later life due to a significant generational change. Looking specifically at older volunteers, Evans and Saxton (2005) argue that those born in the aftermath of the Second World War, the so-called 'baby-boomers', have lived through different economic and political times, resulting in changes in attitudes and motivations compared to previous generations, with some commentators stressing that they are more demanding, more non-conformist or 'wish to pursue their dreams in later life'. These motivations and expectations, maintains the report, will need to be addressed by the voluntary sector when targeting this group. Mirroring this, organisations with a large number of older volunteers may argue that the key to attracting additional volunteers can be getting the package of volunteering opportunities right and preparing the organisation to 'ride that wave' (Lindley et al, 2011).

Overall, a central plank would be to aim for a more flexible and inclusive environment that aligns with the skills and interests of the volunteer while offering meaningful tasks that enable effective deployment from an organisational point of view. Taking stock of the research findings reported in this chapter suggests that voluntary organisations may consider the following strategies in their efforts to increase the supply of older volunteers in line with their demands for them:

- Formulate organisational demands in terms that help to foster an underlying long-term commitment among a population of potential future volunteers, while making it as convenient as possible for them to volunteer in packages of time that suit the pattern of their lives, and enable them to make positive contributions.
- Work to convey an accurate image of what volunteering is like nowadays, stressing the benefits that volunteering brings to people and the benefits people themselves can get from volunteering (Commission for the Future of Volunteering, 2008; Age UK, 2011).
- Reach out to older people and offer them a wider range of volunteering opportunities while, at the same time, deploying the skills and interests of older volunteers to the advantage of the organisation (Rochester and Hutchison, 2002).
- Anticipate the welfare implications of an ageing society, and encourage 'younger-older' people to help to create services for 'older-older' people that they themselves may want to take advantage of later in their own lives.
- Promote volunteering across the life cycle as there is some evidence that people are more likely to re-engage in volunteering than to participate for the first time in retirement.
- Support older volunteers in adapting their roles in line with their changing interests and capabilities and offer training that supports a career in volunteering (see, for example, Davis Smith and Gay, 2005; Commission for the Future of Volunteering, 2008).
- Introduce more human resources-style professional management practice with respect to volunteers while retaining a balance between the formal and informal so as to preserve key elements of the culture of the organisation.
- More generally, monitor volunteers' age structure and seek out intergenerational activities that help to strengthen social cohesion at the same time as benefiting the organisation in the short and long term (on the side of the older person, for example, foster opportunities to bring to bear their capabilities and life experience, learn new skills from younger people, and keep in touch with the younger generation).

While there have been some government-led older volunteer initiatives during the last decade or so, less attention is apparently being paid currently to older volunteering, partly because there is more emphasis on integrating young people into the labour market through the stepping-stone of youth volunteering opportunities. Baines and Hardill (2008) argue that putting too much emphasis on promoting volunteering as a way of enhancing employability may discourage older people not in paid work from volunteering, hence their more intrinsic motives need to continue to resonate in recruitment strategies.

Focusing on how public policy could support voluntary sector organisations in better matching volunteer supply and demand, the following areas of intervention can be identified:

- (older) volunteers who are unemployed should be clearer that this does not jeopardise their right to benefits (currently being addressed; see Office for Civil Society, 2012);
- tax relief systems should be better designed to increase the volume and stability of charitable giving so as to produce income streams that are independent of income derived from supplying services;
- there should be a much clearer public policy strategy to underpin the terms under which service contracts are offered by the public sector to the third sector;
- the training and development activities of the third sector should be the subject of more substantial state financial support;
- there should be greater recognition, supported by further research, of the benefits of volunteering to the health and well-being of older volunteers and service users, and this should be properly taken into account in assessing public financial and in-kind resources given to the voluntary sector;
- institutional capabilities for collaboration among voluntary organisations at local, regional and national level need reinforcing – public funding to support this should be further considered.

Conclusions

Currently in the UK, around 40 per cent of the age groups 50-64 and 65-74 volunteer at least once a year, with participation levels dropping after the age of 74. Demographic changes mean that there is an increasing pool of people aged 50+, many approaching retirement, who could be attracted into volunteering for the benefit of the individuals whose activities they support, society at large and themselves. The current generation of older people differs in some respects from previous generations as they are, on average, expected to lead healthier lives for longer, work for longer, and may have different aspirations for their retirement as better health and increased income and wealth extend their range of choice. However, 'older people' are a very diverse group with many facing much less benign situations that voluntary organisations need to recognise in dealing with them as potential volunteers as much as potential clients for the services or associational activities they provide.

In particular, voluntary organisations are faced with some evidence that older people are changing their preferences. The currently retiring generation, including the first generation of women having participated in the labour market for a major part of their adult life, may be more demanding – less willing to commit to regular volunteering and more inclined to seek specific opportunities that meet their own goals. They are also extending or planning to extend their working lives either out of necessity or choice or a mixture of both. Thus, short-term strategies that simply rely on the presumed leeway offered by rising cohorts of retirees may come unstuck. Moreover, evaluation findings have shown that more can be done to attract older volunteers by reaching out to people and offering a wider spectrum of volunteering opportunities, taking into account their skills, interests and changing capacities as well as the organisation's needs.

Concern over the supply of volunteers is often expressed, at least implicitly, in terms of the *viability of multiple activities* – at its most testing, can people work, care for family members and volunteer at the same time? If extending working life also coincides with greater family care responsibilities, where does that leave volunteering? A conclusion of this chapter is that this is too simplistic a formulation of the volunteer–supply nexus. This is because it fails to recognise the *multiple time horizons* over which practical dilemmas face individuals and families and the choices they make.

For example, there is evidence suggesting that experience of volunteering over the early-to-mid stage of the life cycle has an important bearing on volunteering in later life; retirement as such may not be the crucial factor, although it does (eventually) often trigger volunteering for a range of reasons. Moreover, caring can lead to volunteering in the longer run, even if it obstructs commitment in the short run.

Nevertheless, more flexible opportunities for working in later life and more flexible volunteering opportunities may offer positive mutual reinforcement on older volunteer supply if allowance is made for their aggregate overall effects over the future rather than concentrating on the fates of individual strategies to cope with multiple activities largely in the present. In the latter context, however, the role of employer-supported volunteering programmes, which are still on a modest overall scale, could become increasingly important in helping employees to reconcile in particular part-time working and volunteering for those approaching retirement.

While pursuing more 'flexibility' in both the workplace and in volunteering should increase the supply of volunteers, it may do so within those groups that already have relatively high participation rates. Paying more attention to the extent to which less well represented groups might be supported can largely be seen as a 'volunteer supply strategy' but, in fact, also introduces another possible part of the voluntary organisation's mission – promoting *equality and diversity* in the process of volunteering, not just in the access to services that volunteers help to supply.

The notion of 'diversity' has gradually been replacing 'equality' in the lexicon of British human resources policy and practice as it shifts from 'asserting rights and meeting them' to 'celebrating diversity', although the 'business case rationale' still stalks the equality debate. In the context of volunteering, a better term would probably be *inclusiveness* as it sets a context in which the interests of service users are considered together with the opportunities made available to potential older volunteers. This falls short of asserting the right to make a voluntary contribution alongside the right to work. But it moves the volunteer supply debate onto more positive ground in which social well-being is understood to be generated not only by accessing services but also volunteering to support them. Aiming for more inclusiveness as well as flexibility in approaching the volunteering environment may seem to set yet another challenge for voluntary organisations to surmount. However, together they offer the prospect of a richer conceptual framework within which to consider the future of older volunteering than one tied primarily to demographic opportunism and the retirement bubble.

Finally, it must be recognised that government-led initiatives on volunteering in later life, run by New Labour between 1999 and 2006, had some success but only a limited impact beyond the duration of the programme. The incoming Coalition government's new *Big Society* programme represented a challenging set of attitudes towards and expectations of the whole voluntary and community sector. Creating the 'Big Society' implies harnessing the capacity of the voluntary sector so as to 'produce' more well-being. But the launch of this policy in 2010 alongside an austerity-driven economic strategy failed to recognise the importance of the public funding that underlies many of the sector's activities. It also failed to acknowledge that the treatment of both welfare benefits for older age groups and state/occupational pensions are key parts of the environment in which relationships between older volunteers, organisations and the state develop. Given the likely economic climate, the future of the 'non-market force of older volunteering' will probably be determined more by innovations explored by voluntary organisations than anything that UK governments are willing to do well into the medium term.

Notes

[1] As yet there are no officially produced GDP (gross domestic product) figures for the registered voluntary organisations of the third sector, hence the use of GVA estimates. Moreover, there are about 110,000 unregistered charities that lie entirely outside the boundary of official financial statistics. See Westhall (2009) for perspectives on the measurement and measurability of the third sector.

[2] See Staetsky and Mohan (2011) for a review of statistical sources on UK volunteering. Long-term volunteering participation rates have been relatively stable regardless of the source and whether or not restricted or inclusive definitions of volunteering are used.

Acknowledgements

The authors are grateful to Giovanni Lamura and Andrea Principi for their leadership of the ASPA (Activating Senior Potential in Ageing Europe) research dealing with voluntary organisations and in particular, to Andrea Principi, for his very helpful comments on earlier drafts of this chapter.

References

Age UK (2011) *Older people as volunteers. Evidence review*, London: Age UK (www.ageuk.org.uk/Documents/EN-GB/For-professionals/Research/OlderPeopleAsVolunteers.pdf?dtrk=true)

Age UK (2012) *Ideas for volunteering roles in health and social care. Supporting older people through volunteering*, London: Age UK (www.ageuk.org.uk/Documents/EN-GB/For-professionals/ID200430%20Getting%20Ideas%20For%20Volunteering%20Roles.pdf?dtrk=true)

Alcock, P. (2010) 'A strategic unity: defining the third sector in the UK', *Voluntary Sector Review*, vol 1, no 1, pp 5-24.

Baines, S. and Hardill, I. (2008) '"At least I can do something": the work of volunteering in a community beset by worklessness', *Social Policy and Society*, vol 7, no 3, pp 307-17.

Baines, S., Mabel, L. and Wheelock, J. (2006) *Volunteering, self-help and citizenship in later life*, Newcastle: Age Concern Newcastle and University of Newcastle (www.worldvolunteerweb.org/fileadmin/docdb/pdf/2006/newcastle_senior_volunteer.pdf)

Beveridge, W. (1948) *Voluntary action: A report on methods of social advance*, London: Allen & Unwin.

Charity Commission (2008) *Charities and public benefit: The Charity Commission's general guidance on public benefit*, Liverpool: Charity Commission (www.charity-commission.gov.uk/Charity_requirements_guidance/Charity_essentials/Public_benefit/default.aspx).

Clark, J., McHugh, J. and McKay, S. (2011) *The UK voluntary sector workforce almanac 2011* London: Skills-Third Sector in partnership with NCVO and the Third Sector Research Centre. (http://data.ncvo.org.uk/previous-editions/)

Clark, J., Kane, D., Bass, P. and Wilding, K. (2012) *NCVO UK civil society almanac*, London: National Council for Voluntary Organisations. (www.ncvo.org.uk/component/redshop/1-publications/P17-uk-civil-society-almanac-2012).

Commission for the Future of Volunteering (2008) *Manifesto for change*, London: Volunteering England.

CSCI (Commission for Social Care Inspection) (2008) *The state of social care in England 2006-07*, London: CSCI.

CSV (Community Service Volunteers) (2011) *Annual review 2010/2011*, London. CSV (www.csv.org.uk/about-us).

Davis Smith, J. (1995) 'The voluntary sector tradition: philanthropy and self-help in Britain 1500-1945', in J. Davis Smith, C. Rochester and R. Hedley (eds) *An introduction to the voluntary sector*, London: Routledge, pp 9-39.

Davis Smith, J. and Gay, P. (2005) *Active ageing in active communities. Volunteering and the transition to retirement*, Bristol: Policy Press.

DCLG (Department for Communities and Local Government) (2010) *2008-09 citizenship survey. Volunteering and charitable giving topic report*, London: DCLG (http://webarchive.nationalarchives.gov.uk/20120919132719/http://www.communities.gov.uk/publications/corporate/statistics/citizenshipsurvey200809equality).

DCLG (2011a) *Citizenship survey: 2010-11 (April 2010 – March 2011), England*, London: DCLG (http://webarchive.nationalarchives.gov. uk/20120919132719/http:/www.communities.gov.uk/publications/ corporate/statistics/citizenshipsurveyq4201011).

DCLG (2011b) *Community action in England: A report on the 2009-10 Citizenship Survey*, London: DCLG (http://webarchive.nationalarchives. gov.uk/20120919132719/http://www.communities.gov.uk/ publications/corporate/statistics/citizenshipsurvey200910action).

Dingle, A. (2001) *Involving older volunteers: A good practice guide*, London: Institute for Volunteering Research.

Directory of Social Change (2011) *Legal eyes: Volunteers and the law – An update*, (www.dsc.org.uk/PolicyandResearch/news/ legaleyesvolunteersandthelawanupdate).

Erlinghagen, M. (2010) 'Volunteering after retirement', *European Societies*, vol 12, no 5, pp 603-25.

Esping-Andersen, G. (1990) *The three worlds of welfare capitalism*, Cambridge: Polity Press.

Eurobarometer (2007) *Health and long-term care in the European Union*, Special Eurobarometer 283 (www.gesis.org/eurobarometer/data-access).

Eurobarometer (2012) *Active ageing*, Special Eurobarometer 378 (www. gesis.org/eurobarometer/data-access).

Eurostat (2011) Labour Force Survey online data (http://epp.eurostat. ec.europa.eu/portal/page/portal/employment_unemployment_lfs/ data/database).

Evans, E. and Saxton, J. (2005) *The 21st century volunteer. A report on the changing face of volunteering in the 21st century*, London: nfpSynergy.

Harris, B. (2010) 'Voluntary action and the state in historical perspective', *Voluntary Sector Review*, vol 1, no 1, pp 25-40.

Hatamian, A., Pearmain, D. and Golden, S. (2012) *Outcomes of the Active at 60 Community Agent Programme*, Sheffield: Department for Work and Pensions. (www.gov.uk/government/publications/outcomes-of-the-active-at-60-community-agent-programme-rr808).

Hatton-Yeo, A. (2006) *Ageing and social policy. A report for volunteering in the third age*, Beth Johnson Foundation (www.volunteering.org.uk/ images/stories/Volunteering-England/Documents/VE-Info/R_ Ageing-and-Social-Policy.pdf).

HM Treasury and the Cabinet Office (2007) *The future role of the third sector in social and economic regeneration: Final report*, Cm 7189, London: The Stationery Office.

ISSP (International Social Survey Programme) (2005) 'Work orientations', Mannheim: ISSP (www.gesis.org/issp/issp-modules-profiles/work-orientations/2005).

Jivraj, S. and Nazroo, J. (2012) 'Social domain tables', in J. Banks, J. Nazroo and A. Steptoe (eds) *The dynamics of ageing. Evidence from the English Longitudinal Study of Ageing 2002-10. Wave 5*, London: Institute for Fiscal Studies, pp 259-93 (www.ifs.org.uk/ELSA/publicationDetails/id/6367).

Lindley, R.M., Baldauf, B. Galloway, S. and Li, Y. (2011) *Opportunities for older people in the civil society. National report: United Kingdom*, ASPA Project, Deliverable 5.1, Coventry: Institute for Employment Research, University of Warwick.

Low, N., Butt, S., Ellis Paine, A. and Davis Smith, J. (2007) *Helping out. A national survey of volunteering and charitable giving* (http://webarchive.nationalarchives.gov.uk/+/http:/www.cabinetoffice.gov.uk/media/cabinetoffice/third_sector/assets/helping_out_national_survey_2007.pdf).

Milbourne, L. and Cushman, M. (2012) 'From the third sector to the big society: How changing UK government policies have eroded third sector trust', *Voluntas: International Journal of Voluntary and Nonprofit Organisations*, vol 24, no 2, pp 485-508.

NHS Information Centre, Social Care Team (2010) *Survey of carers in households 2009/10*, Leeds: Health and Social Care Information Centre (www.hscic.gov.uk/catalogue/PUB02200).

NHS Information Centre, Social Care Team (2012) *Community care statistics 2010-11: Social services activity report, England*, Leeds: Health and Social Care Information Centre (www.hscic.gov.uk/catalogue/PUB10291).

Office for Civil Society (2010) *Building a stronger civil society*, London: Cabinet Office (www.gov.uk/government/uploads/system/uploads/attachment_data/file/78927/building-stronger-civil-society.pdf).

Office for Civil Society (2012) *Unshackling good neighbours: Report and one year on. Implementing the recommendations of the Civil Society Red Tape Task Force*, London: Cabinet Office (www.gov.uk/government/uploads/system/uploads/attachment_data/file/62645/201205-Report-to-Lord-Hodgson-Formatted-1_P1-7-5.pdf).

ONS (Office for National Statistics) (2011) *Mothers in the labour market – 2011* (www.ons.gov.uk/ons/dcp171776_234036.pdf).

Price, S. (2007) *Volunteering in the third age. Findings and conclusions from the VITA programme and looking to the future of older volunteering*, VITA Report.

Principi, A., Lindley, R., Perek-Bialas, J. and Turek, K. (2012) 'Volunteering in older age: an organizational perspective', *International Journal of Manpower*, vol 33, no 6, pp 685-703.

Restall, M. (2005) *Volunteers and the law*, London: NCVO Volunteering and Development (www.volunteering.org.uk/resources/publications/volunteersandthelaw).

Rochester, C. and Hutchison, R., with Harris, M. and Keely, L. (2002) *A review of the home office older volunteers initiative*, Home Office Research Study 248, London: Home Office (http://webarchive.nationalarchives.gov.uk/20110220105210/http://rds.homeoffice.gov.uk/rds/pdfs2/hors248.pdf).

Rochester, C. and Thomas, B. (2006) *The indispensable backbone of voluntary action: Measuring and valuing the contribution of older volunteers*, London: VITA and Volunteering England (www.volunteering.org.uk/images/stories/Volunteering-England/Documents/VE-Info/R_The-indispensible-backbone-of-voluntary-action_.pdf).

Rochester, C., Ellis Paine, A. and Howlett, S. with Zimmeck, M. (2010) *Volunteering and society in the 21st century*, Houndmills, Basingstoke: Palgrave Macmillan.

Shifrin, T. (2003) 'Volunteer army faces funding axe', *The Guardian*, 4 August (www.guardian.co.uk/society/2003/aug/04/politics.volunteering).

Slocock, C. (2012) *The big society audit 2012*, Civil Exchange (www.civilexchange.org.uk/the-big-society-audit).

Staetsky, L. and Mohan, J. (2011) *Individual voluntary participation in the United Kingdom: An overview of survey information*, TSRC Working Paper 06, Birmingham: Third Sector Research Centre, University of Birmingham.

Taylor, R., Parry, J. and Alcock, P. (2012) *From crisis to mixed picture to phoney war: Tracing third sector discourse in the 2008/9 recession*, TSRC Research Report 78, Birmingham: Third Sector Research Centre, University of Birmingham.

Vlachantoni, A. (2010) 'The demographic characteristics and economic activity patterns of carers over 50: evidence from the English Longitudinal Study of Ageing', *Population Trends*, no 141, pp 84-73.

Weakley, K. (2012) 'Voluntary sector workforce has fallen by 70,000', *Civil Society Media*, 9 January (www.civilsociety.co.uk/governance/news/content/11273/further_decline_in_sector_workforce).

Westhall, A. (2009) *Economic analysis and the third sector: Overview of economic analysis in relation to the third sector*, TSRC Working Paper 14, Birmingham: Third Sector Research Centre, University of Birmingham.

Zimmeck, M. (2010) 'Government and volunteering. Towards a history of policy and practice', in C. Rochester, A. Ellis Paine, and Howlett, S. with Zimmeck, M. (eds) *Volunteering and society in the 21st century*, Houndmills, Basingstoke: Palgrave Macmillan, pp 84-102.

SEVEN

Older volunteers in France: recognising their social utility in a less and less corporatist welfare state

Marielle Poussou-Plesse, Elena Mascova and Mélissa Petit

Introduction

In international comparisons, the French welfare state is usually classified as continental and 'corporatist': generous welfare benefits are funded by contributions related to occupational status and managed jointly by representatives of employer and trade union organisations (Esping Andersen, 1990). However, the welfare state has become more heterogeneous given changes over the past 30 years; it has now taken on characteristics of other welfare 'models' depending on the type of risk covered (Barbier and Théret, 2009). The French welfare state, as in other European countries, is seeking to redefine itself as a social investment state, where the prevention of social risks is as important, if not more important, than compensation for them. The characteristics of the French welfare state and its evolution have created certain relations between public authorities and the non-profit sector.

The non-profit sector in France is characterised by a high level of social expenditure financed by public authorities, and the relatively large size of this sector, with a historical core of big associations, both financed and overseen by the public administration and a Bismarckian type social security system (CPCA, 2008). The Johns Hopkins programme for comparing non-profit sectors in several countries thus qualified the relations of French public authorities with voluntary organisations as 'corporatist' (Salamon and Anheier, 1998). However, nowadays this model in France reproduces the main features of the liberal model as far as cooperation between non-profit organisations and public authorities has evolved from institutional oversight towards a contractual partnership based on a shared responsibility for social investment (Archambault, 2002, 2012).

The heterogeneous nature of the French 'third sector' – which comprises cooperatives, mutual aid societies and foundations as well as the non-profit organisations (or associations) at the centre of this chapter – can largely be put down to its regulation based on the principle of social utility. This principle underlies the standards for cooperation between non-profit organisations and public authorities. Recognising the social utility of volunteering is an official priority of associative public policy but, as argued later, the situation is different regarding senior volunteers.

With its 14 million volunteers giving their time to more than a million active associations (with more than 60,000 associations created each year since 2003), the French non-profit sector is relatively dynamic. Employment in associations has grown steadily (equivalent to 5 per cent of all employment), notably in health, education and social work, partly as a result of the decentralisation of public policy starting in the 1980s and of the modernising reforms of public administration. It is also interesting to link the labour market situation to the evolution of the non-profit sector: in the context of mass unemployment with restricted access to jobs for young and old, voluntary organisations have often been seen as offering significant employment opportunities. They have therefore been targeted by public policies through subsidised jobs and civic engagement service (after a symbolic allowance) for the young. The high employment rate of French women, in what has been called a 'dual breadwinner/ external care' model, has been another factor in the growth of wage earning in non-profit organisations.

Although the associations with employees account for more than 80 per cent of the total budget of all associations (70 billion, 3.5 per cent of gross domestic product, GDP), they make up only 15 per cent of the country's 1.3 million associations and represent less than 25 per cent of the volunteer work done in France (Tchernonog, 2007). In other words, most volunteer work is performed in associations that do not have any employees. Associations whose members practice an activity (sports, recreation and culture) represent 60 per cent of all associations and nearly half the time devoted to volunteer work. Volunteering in France is both self-centred and altruistic.

Over the past decades, the percentage of volunteers in the population over the age of 15 has been stable, hovering at around 25 per cent. The participation rate of 60- to 70-year-olds in volunteer work equals the national average, thus placing France in the middle ranks of the European Union (EU) in this group as in the younger group (Erlinghagen and Hank, 2006). Apparently, public policies aiming at promoting active ageing have not led more baby-boomers to become involved in volunteer work.

This chapter describes the principal barriers to, and opportunities for, volunteer work by seniors in France. After a brief introduction to the traditional features, current situation and legal framework characterising volunteering, the second section offers a statistical panorama of senior volunteering from national data. The third section draws attention to the individual, organisational and institutional factors underlying senior volunteering. The fourth section discusses the possible prospects to improve the match between the 'demand' from associations for older volunteers and the 'supply' of senior applicants. The conclusion explains why these prospects amount, in the main, to words and not deeds.

The French tradition of voluntary action

Voluntary associations in their modern form received recognition under an Act passed by French Parliament in 1901 which still provides the general legal framework for French associations, but 'volunteer work' as an idea with a similar meaning to the phrase in English emerged much later, along with the strong increase in number of associations during the 1970s. Before this period volunteer work had little distinction from charitable activities and political militantism. It can therefore be seen as the outcome, on the one hand, of a secularisation of 19th-century paternalism and charities, and, on the other, of a de-politicisation of worker mutual aid societies (Demoustier, 2002).

The strong development of voluntary organisations in the second half of the 20th century in France could be considered as characteristic of the historic evolution of the social state (Hély, 2009), in which three main periods can be distinguished. The first, the post-Second World War period of growth, when the social, centralised and protective state was built, was characterised by the strong development of voluntary associations in the health and social care sector. The regulation of the associative sector by the public authority could be seen as directly supervised by the administrations.

The development of volunteering has also been based on a sociological trend in activism that sees voluntary organisations as a laboratory for participatory democracy. Following the events of May 1968, the social demands of the middle class for a better quality of community life favoured the development of volunteering (Demoustier, 2002). Volunteering was encouraged as a concrete citizenship exercise and even as a way of integrating the underprivileged through the associations that carry out social work or run educational programmes: this blurred the distinction between beneficiaries and volunteers. The cleavage has become a rift between, on the one hand, the volunteer managerial work of staff members (especially in the more professionalised organisations) and, on the other, a spontaneous volunteer work oriented towards democratic participation. However, the boom of associations in 1970-80 also benefited self-expressive voluntarism with the creation of senior citizens' clubs and universities.

During the second period in the 1980s, along with decentralisation and the consequent cuts in public funding, the legal and financial relations between voluntary associations and public authorities moved from a role of supervision to that of partnership, in which associations were encouraged to contract with local governments directly at the regional, departmental and municipal level. The urban policy, with its neighbourhood-based associations aiming at recreating social ties and combating social exclusion locally, represents a symbolic area of this new public action.

The third mode of regulation arises during the 1990s in the form of a partnership between for-profit firms and non-profit associations. Driven by the social responsibility movement, big corporations has subsidised associations and has developed volunteer programs for employees encouraging their commitment to educational, social and cultural associations.

These evolutions underlie major changes in the public funding system and as a consequence, a growing professionalisation of voluntary organisations. The incremental process of the professionalisation of associations has led to the division of labour inside associations: once certain tasks became 'professional', others were deemed 'voluntary'. Volunteers started to be seen as a source of 'extra' labour that, although necessary, was still suspected of being amateurish by the swelling ranks of permanent staff members comprising voluntary heads of associations and wage earners.

Accounting for half the income of associations in France, public funding now comes mainly from communes, departments and regions (28 per cent of the total budget of associations), more than twice the amount paid by central government. If central government finances actions in the social, health, educational and cultural field, regions favour education and culture while departments subsidise more social actions. Funding has become more selective, based on projects and performance evaluation, and more dependent on local priorities (Archambault, 2010, 2012). Thus, current debates focus on the recognition of social utility produced by associations: the statistical measure of their productive contribution and recognition of the various statuses of workers within the voluntary sector (CNIS, 2010).

The legal framework

Legislation concerning the voluntary sector in France is highly complicated. From within the broad, supple framework established in 1901, public authorities have extended recognition to several types of associations as a function of their general interest and field of action (Morange, 2008). Nevertheless, the most relevant laws – as far as recognition of social utility of associations and volunteers is concerned – are the following:

- *Tax rule 170-1998:* measuring the social utility of associations so as to justify the funds served to them has become the issue shaping state policy towards associations. From a strictly legal viewpoint, social utility has not been defined save by the tax rule in 1998 that exonerated certain associations from taxes. This text defines a series of steps and criteria (services rendered, the public targeted, the price of services, advertisement, etc) for attributing case by case the qualification of 'social utility' to associations. This tax rule also allowed associations to pay volunteers in positions of responsibility.[1] The Socialist government adopted these measures in response to the diagnosis of a leadership crisis in the non-profit sector.
- *Law 73-2002 on social modernisation:* this allows people to obtain diplomas based on accreditation of previous work experience, and recognises the skills acquired not only during occupational careers, but also through volunteer work in associations. More and more universities are providing volunteering students with European Credit Transfer and Accumulation System (ECTS) credits to their academic curricula.
- *Law 240-2010 on civic service:* this law creates specific civic engagement service contracts allowing for 16- to 25-year-olds to have a 6- to 12-month assignment with social security coverage and an allowance from the government (422 net per month in 2012). In 2011, 15,000 civic service contracts were signed, and the objective for 2012 was 25,000. Given all this, and that there are no specific rules to support the volunteering of older people,

it can be said that government subsidies to associations have been youth-friendly.

A national conference on the non-profit sector held in 2006 underlined the importance of better recognising and accompanying volunteering as a priority of associative life in France. However, how this is to be recognised is still under question. The recent creation of a specific civic service contract for younger volunteers questions the very meaning of volunteering as a voluntary, disinterested activity done for free (*bénévolat*, in French). The definition of an official status and advantages for volunteers is still at stake.

The dimension of volunteer work

The rate of 'formal' volunteering among the French over 15 years old increased significantly, from about 15 per cent in the mid-1980s to 25 per cent 10 years later. Estimates since then agree that it has remained steady at this level. The rate of volunteering among people at least 50 years old stands at the national average and, like the figure for those over 15, has been stable. However, major differences exist between 50- to 69-year-olds, whose volunteering rate is above average (around 30 per cent) and people 70 years old or older, whose rate is lower, at 17 per cent. Specialists in this field have drawn attention to the discrepancy between the membership rates in associations – the senior rate is the highest – and the degree of volunteering among seniors, given the free time available to them (Prouteau and Wolff, 2007).

Voluntary organisations

Between 2000 and 2010, the number of associations rose from less than a million to approximately 1.3 million, a 20 per cent increase if the focus is on 'active' organisations. The structural split, between associations with and without employees, runs through Tchernonog's (2007) typology of French associations:

- Associations with missions that are linked to interventions by public authorities represent 15 per cent of all associations, and 83 per cent of total budgets. The large majority of association employees fall in this group. Among these organisations, which often manage considerable budgets and benefit from special recognition by public authorities, are healthcare and social work establishments as well as cultural and sports organisations.

- Associations that are often advocacy groups, with strongly activist and humanitarian objectives (29 per cent of all associations, 5 per cent of total budgets). Most are all-volunteer organisations.
- Associations with members who practice an activity (sports, culture, leisure): 56 per cent of all associations, 12 per cent of total budgets. These associations account for half of all volunteers: organising activities for members implies a lot of voluntary work.

This typology must be related to public funding: it barely flows into very small associations, but accounts for more than 60 per cent of income in associations with employees (especially in social work and health). The geographical distribution of associations is not uniform. Historically, they have been strongest in southern and northern France. The third sector is more solidly established there for reasons having to do with politics, history, the influence of the Catholic Church and the rural environment (ONESS, 2009).

Associations employ 1,800,000 wage earners, whose work has been estimated to be equivalent to the volunteer work done by non-wage earners in associations. The average association has around 15 volunteers, four on their staff roll.

Volunteers by sector, gender and age

The last update of statistics on volunteering in 2010 paints a picture in three concentric circles: 23 per cent of the French are involved if we just take into account volunteers in associations (strictly speaking), 28 per cent if we include other organisations (religious organisations, labour unions, etc) and 36 per cent if we also bring into this picture 'informal volunteering', that is, services for people other than family members performed outside any organisational setting (Recherches & Solidarités, 2011).

During the first decade of the new century, the increase in the number of volunteers in associations – more than 14 million people at present – roughly equals the increase in the French population: 10 per cent. It is far from the percentage increase in the number of active associations during this same period: 20 per cent. Talk about a 'volunteering crisis', often by association staff members, can mainly be understood as an increasing demand for volunteers. Older associations find it difficult to attract new volunteers; the latter surge, sometimes in fits and starts, towards new associations and causes, and volunteer in more than one organisation (Recherches & Solidarités, 2011). The only reliable, detailed description of volunteering is, unfortunately, not very recent: the Associative Life Survey conducted by the French National Institute of Statistics (INSEE) in 2002. It can, however, be partly updated from other sources. In 2002, the principal fields for volunteering were cultural and recreational activities (32.6 per cent of volunteers), sports (26.2 per cent) and advocacy groups (18.5 per cent).

Volunteering is higher among men than women: 35 versus 28 per cent of people over the age of 18, according to the most recent figures (Archambault and Tchernonog, 2012). Men tend to volunteer in associations related to sports or their jobs, whereas women tend towards social work, healthcare and education. Proportionately more women volunteer in small associations. A gender-based distribution of tasks to volunteers can be detected. Women are in a majority in tasks that call for lending a sympathetic ear or providing support or care to individuals. However, they hold only 31 per cent of positions as president of an association (Tchernonog, 2007).

Volunteering is definitely correlated, except in sports clubs and religious organisations, to a higher occupational status, household income and education. The volunteering rate rises from 16 per cent for people without a secondary school diploma to 44 per cent for those with two or more years of higher education (Archambault and Tchernonog, 2012). Another positive correlation is with residence in a rural commune or small town. As much can be said about the family environment: people whose parents or spouse have been volunteers more often become volunteer themselves.

What do the statistics tell about the relation between volunteering and age? It varies by age group. According to the 2002 survey, the volunteering rate varied little – between 25 and 29 per cent – for those aged 15-29, 30-39, 40-49, 50-59 and 60-69; but there was a drop to 17 per cent after the age of 70. Refining these figures with other variables, a bell-shaped age profile emerges with a peak toward the age of 45. Analysis comparing people over and under 60 brings to light differences between the two groups regarding the rate of volunteering and its orientation by sector (see Table 7.1).

This difference turns out to be noticeable only in the case of occasional volunteer activities, but to be much less consequential for regular volunteer work.

Were the profile of the French volunteer to be sketched, it would be of a man in his forties or fifties with a higher education and a higher income, living as part of a couple in a small town, and devoting

Table 7.1: Volunteering rate by age group, volunteering frequency and sector, 2002

	Age group				
	15-60		60+		
	All	50-59	All	60-69	70+
Volunteering	**29.2**	**30.0**	**22.8**	**31.2**	**16.5**
Regular volunteering	12.4	14.6	11.3	15.5	8.1
Occasional volunteering	20.2	19.2	13.9	18.9	10.2
Volunteering sector					
Sport	29.3	25.7	14.5	18.1	9.4
Culture and recreation	30.3	28.6	41.5	38.4	45.9
Education	16.3	7.0	4.6	5.8	2.9
Social and health services	14.1	19.5	20.9	23.5	17.1
Advocacy	18.6	28.4	18.3	20.0	15.9
Religious	5.9	5.9	13.8	10.3	18.7
Other	6.8	9.3	8.1	7.8	8.6

Source: Survey Associative Life Survey, INSEE, 2002 (Prouteau and Wolff, 2007)

2.5 hours of work per week to an association related to sports, recreation or his work. His counterpart is a woman, who volunteers more in organisations in social work, religion or education, but is less active, and her volunteering is more occasional.

Participation of older volunteers

Attention in France has been drawn to the difference between the membership rate of seniors in associations and their degree of involvement. People over 60 are 'joiners', 51.3 per cent, as compared with 42.2 per cent of the rest of the population over the age of 15. For them, however, joining an association less often entails active participation: in the group of under-60s four members from ten volunteer, while it is three per ten members over 60. However, the group over 60 is not homogeneous, as Table 7.2 clearly shows. The rate of volunteering for 60- to 70-year-olds is not lower than for younger age groups, and the sharp drop in volunteering occurs after 70.

Why is the rate of volunteering by young retirees, who have more time available and the highest membership rate, not significantly higher than that of people in their fifties? Although the next section answers this question in more detail, a combination of two effects might be mentioned here. First, the number of people for whom retirement is the right time to discover volunteering might have as a counterpart the number who, when they retire, stop doing volunteer work because it was related to their life at their former workplace. Second, volunteer work right after retirement might be an extension of participation that started much earlier. Despite the regrettable absence of data from longitudinal surveys, available estimates show that a clear-cut majority – from 60 to 75 per cent – of retiree volunteers were already volunteers before retiring (Prouteau and Wolff, 2007). This high percentage of volunteers 'who have just grown older' and step up their participation once they retire might explain two noteworthy characteristics of senior volunteering: it is steadier, more regular (Table 7.2), and seniors are overrepresented in positions of responsibility inside voluntary organisations.

On average, volunteers over 60 put in five hours of work per week in an association – one hour more than those under 60. Their share in total volunteer work is equivalent to their percentage in the population over 15 years old. Their contribution has been estimated to amount to 212,000 full-time jobs, in other words, 26 per cent of all volunteer work. In charities and social work, it rises to more than 40 per cent.

What stands out in the landscape of French associations is the predominance of seniors in leadership positions: 57 per cent of the presidents of associations are at least 55 years old, and a third are over 65. Specifically, 46 per cent of the presidents are retirees. In four out of ten cases, the president is the founder of the organisation. Among people between 60 and 70 years old who belong to an association,

Table 7.2: Number of hours per year of voluntary work, 2002

	Age group				
	15-60		60+		
	All	**50-59**	**All**	**60-69**	**70+**
Volunteering	93.8	112.0	122.8	137.1	102.8
Regular volunteering	166.7	183.0	205.9	233.0	167.4
Occasional volunteering	32.6	34.6	34.7	35.3	33.9
Volunteering sector					
Sport	78.6	109.9	80.1	87.0	ns
Culture and recreation	88.3	55.5	79.6	96.2	60.5
Education	44.6	68.5	63.8	ns	ns
Social and health services	91.6	93.9	156.2	197.8	76.1
Advocacy	73.1	78.8	104.8	64.3	174.8
Religious	113.7	ns	104.9	105.8	104.2
Other	60.1	42.1	121.5	142.4	ns

Source: Survey Associative Life Survey, INSEE, 2002 (Prouteau and Wolff, 2007)

10 per cent of the women hold a position of responsibility; by comparison, the rate nearly doubles for men. According to recent data, which are yet to be confirmed from longitudinal surveys, the gender gap in volunteering has narrowed considerably among young retirees (Recherches & Solidarités, 2011).

Six out of ten retirees active in associations say they use the skills acquired while they were still working. These skills are more often relational than technical (Malet and Bazin, 2011). This can be related to the motivation for doing volunteer work mentioned more often by those over 60 (21.5 per cent) than under that age (12.9 per cent), namely, 'meet people, make friends'. In their quest for sociability, young retirees definitely try to find an intergenerational setting; they do not feel at home in senior citizen organisations, where most members belong to the 80-85 age group.

From these data, given the reserves due to gaps in the statistics, a profile can be drawn of the typical senior volunteer, even though it might not represent the majority of volunteers in this age group: a man who used to work in a white-collar job in the private sector, is president of an advocacy group in which he has participated for a long time. His volunteer work taps into the skills and knowhow acquired during his life at work: managerial qualifications, consultancy, law, etc. His feminine counterpart tends to be a former civil servant, very likely a teacher, who is often a widow or single, and who has been involved for a long time in an association in education or social work (for example, literacy, tutoring).

The types of organisations that try to recruit seniors are, of course, but not only, senior citizen clubs. Volunteers over 60 have a lower rate than those under 60 in sports and education, but a higher rate in social work, charity, cultural and leisure activities and religion – people over 70 are more typically involved in the last two fields (see Table 7.1). In the leisure activities sector, it is worth mentioning that the associations oriented toward seniors (senior citizen clubs, retiree associations, veteran and alumni organisations) accounted for 23.2 per cent of volunteers over the age of 60 in 2002 (Prouteau and Wolff, 2007).

As mentioned previously, federations of retiree associations, some of them linked to labour unions, have been recognised as representing senior citizens and sit, therefore, on the advisory committees at various levels in the public administration that deals with old-age policy. Although these federations officially represent this category of the population and defend their interests, their role – even their existence – is not widely known, not even by retirees. Few national networks propose to retirees volunteer assignments that require professional qualifications (in consultancy, for example), use 'coaches' over the age of 50 for developing sports adapted to people over that age, or have a clear intergenerational orientation by helping children learn to read. Since no study has followed up on the age pyramid of volunteers by association, it is impossible to describe the associations that mainly recruit senior volunteers. However, regular surveys of the leaders of associations have drawn attention to the degree of retiree involvement in neighbourhood activities (theatres, museums, libraries, friendly societies, and so on) or in operations related to national solidarity.

Older people's participation in voluntary organisations: opportunities and restrictions

The discrepancy between the rate at which seniors join an association as members and at which they do volunteer work – along with the fact that a large majority of retiree volunteers (60-75 per cent) and, in particular, the ones who regularly volunteer, were already active members before they retired – lead to an examination of the individual, organisational and institutional factors underlying the decisions made by seniors to volunteer. Analysing them entails studying how volunteer work comes into competition with professional commitments and (unpaid) family care.

Opportunities and restrictions for volunteering for older people

The two statistically most important factors at the *individual level* are education and the state of health rather than age itself (Sirven and Debrand, 2013). A qualitative analysis of the transitions between work and retirement brings to light the opportunities and limitations of three individual motivations for volunteering (France Bénévolat, 2010). These three types are likely to respond differently to institutional incentives and give rise to different problems for the associations where they volunteer:

• Retirees who are used to being involved in causes or who volunteered during their youth or work life. Admission to retirement is an easy way for them to increase involvement by taking on new responsibilities in associations with which they are already familiar. This group represents a minority of retirees but the majority of retiree volunteers.

- Retirees who try to make up for their loss of status by volunteering. These new volunteers tend to maintain the same pace of activity and exercise of authority as in the firm where they used to work. They are often former white-collar workers, men who risk experiencing tensions in relations with wage earners in the association and who risk being disappointed since they fail to understand how associations differ from private companies.
- Retirees who experience the shift towards retirement as a paradox. This group feel both a need to be socially involved and reluctance about doing volunteer work. They are seldom familiar with associations and do not know how to proceed, and fear being overbooked or lacking competence.

What does it mean at the *organisational level*? The first type forms the pillar of associations owing to its size and seniority in office holding. Two major risks for organisations can be detected in this case: the clearly perceived risk of a lack of turnover with, as a consequence, an ageing leadership; and the feeling of wear-and-tear, lassitude, which volunteers over 60 clearly express more often than those under 60. To cope with this two-fold risk, some associations have started appointing 'pairs' to positions of responsibility in order to share the workload and to be prepared in case of defection, ill health or death.

Quite different opportunities and difficulties for associations arise in relation to the second type of retiree volunteers. These volunteers, unlike those in the first type, tend to feel uneasy with the sense of activism that marks volunteer work in some associations. They are looking for activities that tap into their skills and qualifications in order to realise a project that, normally limited in time, will let them directly appreciate the results. A perception of the effectiveness of the volunteer work performed – although often invisible in the complicated operations of some associations – is the reason volunteers often mention. Three national organisations (France Bénévolat, Passerelles et Compétences, Espace Bénévolat) serve as 'middlemen' between applicants and associations; they ask the former for their profiles and the latter to define their needs. This sort of volunteer work is not yet widespread, however, because the heads of associations are not familiar with it.

Retiree volunteers of the third type more deeply challenge associations, since they hesitate to become involved, at least on a regular basis. Some associations, now aware of the limits of attracting these retirees through forums or mass media campaigns, have turned to recruiting through personal contacts, which, as all statistical surveys show, is by far the major channel towards volunteering. Some associations have developed programmes whereby current members sponsor or tutor new recruits. Even though this third type wants to exercise control over its time budget, no association has tried to propose volunteer work that would be compatible with both the aspiration to experience retirement as a time of leisure and with the obligations of grandparents.

Although ageist practices cannot be detected in voluntary organisations, the increasing professionalisation of associations (in particular those that mainly depend on wage earners) should also be mentioned as an obstacle not only for retirees with a low level of qualifications (correlated statistically with less volunteering) but also for better-educated retirees. The latter might, after retirement, soon lose confidence in their skills, which often need updated, in new technology, for instance (Malet and Bazin, 2011).

At the *political/institutional level* – and unlike for young people – France has never had programmes that targeted seniors for volunteer work. Leaving aside the representation of retiree associations in public institutions, senior volunteering has recently had a place on the policy-making agenda on three occasions. First of all, the *National plan on successful ageing* (*Bien vieillir*) adopted in 2007 depicted the increased social participation of seniors in volunteer work as a way to boost their well-being and to prevent isolation. Since then, a handbook (*Passport for active retirement*) has been given to new retirees to inform them of the possibilities and procedures for volunteering, and to orient them. It urges retirees to volunteer in four fields: youth work, care for the aged, work with the 'excluded' and the environment. Second, an official report on senior citizens in 2009, detailed later (see p 166), has discussed the prospects of volunteering of older people. At the same time, few agreements signed as part of the obligation imposed on firms to open negotiations about senior employment before 1 January 2010 (with a fine amounting to 1 per cent of the total wage bill if the firm failed to do so) provide for allowing older employees to do civic service. But these practices have hardly been developed. Finally, 2012 was declared the EU Year of Active Ageing and Intergenerational Solidarity, with many local initiatives undertaken in France (often as trivial as, for example, a regional prize for retiree volunteers). These three occasions have mainly amounted to communication stunts.

Older people between employment and volunteering

Current trends in regard to the employment of older people are ambivalent. Given the prevailing idea that work is to be 'shared' among generations and resulting public policies favouring early exits, the French are not inclined to work beyond the age of retirement with a full pension. Only 48 per cent of 50- to 65-year-olds said they were in favour of working when there was no economic need to do so – a lower percentage than in other countries (ISSP, 1997). Thus, the French, after the Spanish, hold the strongest opinions against work for pay after retirement (European Commission, 2000). However, recent pension reforms and vulnerability of careers might leave no choice, thus making working for pay an economic necessity for many older people.

By gradually raising the retirement age from 60 to 62, along with the extension of the contribution period, successive pension reforms (1993, 2003, 2010) have set off an increase in the number of seniors in the labour market. Since 2000, all age groups, men as well as women, have been affected. Although the French employment rate of 55- to 64-year-olds (41.5 per cent) is still 8 percentage points lower than that in the EU15, it rose from 41.5 to 44.1 per cent for men and from 35.7 to 39.1 per cent for women between 2005 and 2011 (DARES, 2012). The employment rate in 2011 was more than 80 per cent for 50- to 54-year-olds, only 64 per cent for 55- to 59-year-olds, but then fell to 18.9 per cent for 60- to 64-year-olds. Thus two age thresholds still mark older employees' careers: 55 and 60, the latter deeply rooted in public opinion. The economic meltdown since 2008 has made it even harder to keep older wage earners on the workforce, and seniors are still overrepresented among the long-term unemployed. Moreover, despite public disincentives for pre-retirement schemes, some companies are still financing early exit arrangements.

Another reform adopted in 2009 loosened restrictions on combining a pension with wages. It is still too early to assess the impact, but available estimates suggest that more retirees will be drawing wages: 6.6 per cent of those who retired in 2004 cumulated wages with a pension during at least one of the four years following retirement (DARES, 2012). Seniors who work on retirement have contrasting motivations. Some of them – in particular former white-collar workers or those with qualifications that are in high demand – are strongly attracted towards doing consultancy for pay instead of as volunteer work. Furthermore, those in their fifties who have been unemployed for a long time and will soon be unable to draw unemployment benefits 'retire with pay': they retire since they have no choice, do not draw a full pension, but hope to find work that pays enough to round their budgets. In this regard, it is possible to make a hypothesis of the time-competition effect played by recent reforms.

At the same time, the perception of the social utility of the volunteer work done by retirees in associations has broadened. It has been separated from the 'feelings of lack of social utility' among young (pre) retirees whom employers have pushed out of the workforce. Social utility came to be associated with the aspiration of some (pre)retirees to find in volunteer work a prolongation of the occupations that they used to have but that will now be done for free.[2] Owing to the impact of EU studies and discussions that have emphasised the benefits on the individual's mental and physical well-being, the issue has taken a turn towards active ageing. A few larger firms in France have adopted employee volunteer programmes[3] with two main aims: to manage the end of employees' careers and, more broadly, to improve their organisation's corporate social responsibility.

There is a dire need for a longitudinal study in France of the effects of making the work life longer on senior volunteering. As Table 7.1 shows, the volunteering rate of older age groups, most of whose members are still working (50- to 59-year-olds), is roughly the same as that of young retirees (60- to 69-year-olds), and is higher than the national average. However, the available data does not allow us to distinguish the age effect from the generational one.

Older people between family care and volunteering

No studies have been made in France to test the hypothesis of a conflict between the involvement of seniors in family care and their participation in volunteer work. The main question that has been officially raised concerns the compatibility of family care with participation in the labour market, especially for women (CAS, 2010). According to the SHARE survey (Survey of Health, Ageing and Retirement in Europe), France is among the countries where more grandmothers both work and look after grandchildren (usually on a regular basis). Thanks to the well-developed system of daycare centres, French grandmothers are more easily able to do both (Attias-Donfut, 2008). In like manner, a combination of public and private aid provides support for aged parents. France's long-term care policy has, since 1993, taken the form of cash-for-care with the goal of easing the burden on families. Only 36 per cent of the French think that an old parent who lives alone and needs regular care would be better off if he/she lived with children (18 per cent), or if one of the children provided the necessary help at the parent's home (18 per cent) (Eurobarometer, 2007). The older people who need support receive a monthly allocation from departmental authorities. The amount depends on the beneficiary's state of health, income and housing (at home or in a residential setting). In 2010, allowances were provided to 1,117,000 people over the age of 60: 60 per cent at home, 40 per cent in institutions.

While home-based care (4.9 per cent) and institutional care (3.1 per cent) are not widespread in France among people aged 65 years or more (Huber et al, 2009), the majority (85 per cent) of people aged 80 and over live at home. When they have a disability or health problems, they receive the cash-for-care allowances; and in addition, 80 per cent of them receive support from their families, mostly from daughters or granddaughters. France has adopted a semi-formal 'family carer' policy: the cash-for-care allowance can be used to pay someone close (but not the spouse). Furthermore, since 2007 a leave of absence for family care allows family members who hold a job to take up to three months per year during their careers to tend to an aged parent. Although the number of family carers is increasing as the population grows older, it is not easy to foresee the impact on senior volunteer work. According to a few surveys (Le Bihan-Youinou and Martin, 2006), French senior women try to balance all their commitments (occupational, family or civic) by budgeting their time. This explains why the gender gap in volunteering has narrowed instead of widening. According to the heads of associations, the care that older volunteers provide to a spouse is one reason for interrupting or decreasing volunteer work (Poussou-Plesse et al, 2010).

Improving the match between supply of older candidates with the demand of voluntary organisations: future perspectives

According to regular surveys and studies, the heads of associations have a hard time recruiting new volunteers and finding skills according to their needs. One association out of three lacks volunteers. In France, the match between the 'demand' from associations for volunteers and the 'supply' of senior applicants raises the question of transitions between work and retirement. In this perspective, the successful development of the voluntary work of seniors is conditioned by its recognition by all the stakeholders (non-profit sector, private companies, public authorities and seniors) as a way to prolong working lives.

Concluding the report *Seniors and citizenship* (CESE, 2009), the Social and Economic Council underlines the win–win advantages of such a partnership. Its proposals address both organisations (non-profit organisations or companies) and public authorities. It depicts the idea of the social utility of volunteer work in a context where the state carries responsibility for social investment:

- Voluntary associations are advised to bring more transparency to their activities and to respect volunteers in regard to their timely investment. The first contact of new volunteers with the non-profit organisations makes them face their stereotypes on 'real voluntary work' and their fear of not being able to control their time investment. A charter on relations between employees and volunteers could help to better define voluntary work conditions and time investment. Developing training and mentoring programmes could contribute to better value volunteers' skills, but also to retain them in organisations.
- Through collaboration with voluntary associations, private firms could promote longer working lives and improve their corporate image. For older workers participating in employees' volunteer programmes it could be the occasion to set up a new life project.
- Public authorities could create territorial poles dedicated to the development of up-to-date solutions to face demographic ageing. While designing new programmes that enhance volunteering, municipalities should also pay attention to the diversity within the group of older people.
- At a national level, pension funds could promote the advantages of volunteering more actively and much earlier. Given the fact that senior volunteers have often been volunteering long before retirement, it is important to encourage volunteering as early as possible. Pension agencies and social centres could thus help older people evaluate their skills as well as perform a health check, and help them setting their life goals.

The key question that marked public debates during the EU Year of Volunteering in 2011 was related to the lifelong training of volunteers, including retirement. Further professionalisation of associations requires more regular training of people involved in volunteering. Last but not least, budget restrictions that associations face, along with the insufficiency of public policies aiming at recognising voluntary activities, appear as major obstacles to the development of training programmes.

Conclusions

Since 2000, the participation rate of 60- to 70-year-olds in volunteer work has not increased substantially and is equal to the national average: approximately 25 per cent. This phenomenon has two explanations. First, in France as in other countries, older volunteers are mainly those who already have experience with and who are committed to the activity. Second, retiring newcomers replace those who abandon volunteering. 'Volunteers who have aged', according to Gallagher's expression (1994), thus play an important role in the French non-profit sector. They are overrepresented in positions of responsibility and spend long hours volunteering. However, this model of strong commitment does not fit the majority of retirees who look for a better control of time spent on different activities.

In a context of an evolving welfare state and a non-profit sector characterised by increasing cooperation between different actors (as, for example, voluntary organisations, institutions and companies), the situation in France could be described in terms of a gap between public policies aimed at encouraging senior volunteering as part of work–life activities, and the real nature of volunteers' commitment to non-profit organisations enhanced by their sense of civic responsibility. Public policies and organisations that seek to encourage senior volunteering do not succeed in taking into account the diversity within the retirees' population. This implies a better understanding of the mechanisms of volunteer commitment, for example, of the importance of word-of-mouth volunteer recruitment underlined by many empirical studies, or of the role of informal family care, especially for women. For many retirees, volunteering is directly linked to the possibility of taking part in the life of the local community and creating new interpersonal relations. Nevertheless, the social utility of senior volunteering still suffers from poor public recognition. The historical roots of this phenomenon are related to employment policies and retirement system reforms that had an impact on work–retirement transitions. Since the explosion of early-exit schemes in the 1980s, a 'reserve army of volunteers' was meant to join the non-profit sector, bringing their skills and enthusiasm. However, their contribution was only praised when related to specific forms of volunteering such as those where their professional skills were used.

Active ageing is promoted as a positive way to envisage the end of working lives and retirement. Companies are given an important role in bridging work to retirement. Pension agencies and social centres are other key actors in informing future and present retirees about the societal benefits of seniors' volunteering and the individual benefits for older volunteers. The arguments used to build the recognition of the social utility of senior volunteering focus mainly on the possibilities of lifelong training, the importance of productive contribution and a substitution status. Will this rhetoric, with its focus on a productive utility of volunteering, have a positive impact on volunteering among older people? The answer is not quite that simple. On the one hand, the feeling of being useful does not appear to be an important factor of motivation for French senior volunteers. On the other hand, the processes of professionalisation of non-profit organisations and new requirements contribute to the development of new forms of management coming from the productive sector and applying equally to volunteers. This could have a negative impact on the capacity of associations to attract volunteers given that the idea of a free commitment that characterises the act of volunteering is questioned. The end of working lives in France continues to be a concern: they are often abrupt because of lay-offs, they are poorly prepared and there is rarely a transition between full-time work and total inactivity. That is why, in order to respond to a double aspiration – both self-expressive and service-oriented – of retirees, progressive retirement schemes should be encouraged and developed. This solution has been promoted by a few policy makers and social scientists (Taddei, 2000) as allowing a better balance of social times and activities, but remains underdeveloped.

Notes

[1] For 'small' associations, pay for a staff member may not exceed three fourths of the official minimum wage. 'Big' associations may not pay more than three staff members within a limit of three times an amount set by social security; in addition, these people benefit from a leave of absence to fill their duties of representation, from a training fund and from social security coverage.

[2] Three networks were set up that focused exclusively on mobilising (pre) retires, pioneer associations addressing mainly former white-collar workers, and proposing volunteer work as consultants in the service of economic development in France or abroad: ECTI (Échanges et Consultations Techniques Internationaux), AGIR (Association Générale des Intervenants Retraités) and EGEE (Entente des Générations pour l'Emploi et l'Entreprise).

[3] The *mécénat de compétences* (skills' sponsorship) targets wage earners who devote time at work to projects sponsored by the firm. It refers to the work done for free by wage earners or retirees as consultants on short assignments.

Acknowledgements

The authors would like to thank the Centre d'Etudes des Mouvements Sociaux in Paris for its support.

References

Archambault, E. (2002) 'Le bénévolat en France et en Europe' ['Volunteering in France and in Europe'], *Revue française des affaires sociales*, no 2, pp 13-36.

Archambault, E. (2010) 'Les institutions sans but lucratif en France et aux États-Unis. Comparaison, évolution récente et réaction face à la crise' ['Non-profit institutions in France and the United States. Comparison and responses to crisis'], *Cahiers du Cirtes*, no 5, pp 393-410.

Archambault, E. (2012) 'Diversité et fragilité des associations en Europe' ['Diversity and weakness of associations in Europe'], *Informations sociales*, no 172, pp 20-8.

Archambault, E. and Tchernonog, V. (2012) *Repères sur les associations en France* [*Insight into associations in France*], Paris: Conférence Permanente des Coordinations Associatives (CPCA).

Attias-Donfut, C. (2008) 'Les grands-parents en Europe: de nouveaux soutiens de famille' ['Grandparents in Europe: New support for families'], *Informations sociales*, no 149, pp 54-67.

Barbier, J.C. and Théret, B. (2009) *Le système français de protection sociale* [*French social protection system*], Paris: La Découverte.

Le Bihan-Youinou, B. and Martin, C. (2006) 'Travailler et prendre soin d'un parent âgé dépendant' ['Working and caring for a frail aged parent'], *Travail, genre et sociétés*, no 16, pp 77-96.

CAS (Centre d'analyse stratégique) (2010) *La 'grand-parentalité active': un triple enjeu de solidarité, de conciliation travail/hors travail et d'emploi des seniors* [Active grand parenting: A triple matter of solidarity, work/ family articulation and older workers' employment], Paris: La Note d'analyse, no 199.

CESE (Conseil economique, social et environnemental) (2009) *Seniors et cité* [*Seniors and citizenship*], Report by Monique Boutrand, Paris: CESE.

CNIS (Conseil national de l'information statistique) (2010) *Connaissance des associations* [*How to improve knowledge about associations*], Paris: CNIS.

CPCA (Conférence Permanente des Coordinations Associatives) (2008) *Les secteurs associatifs et leurs relations avec l'Etat dans l'Europe des 27* [*Associative sectors and their relationship to the state in Europe of the 27. A comparative analysis*], Etudes et Documents, no 4.

DARES (Direction de l'Animation de la Recherche, des Etudes et des Statistiques) (2012) *Emploi des seniors: synthèse des principales données* [*Data synthesis on seniors' employment in France*], Document d'études, no 64, Ministère du travail.

Demoustier, D. (2002) 'Le bénévolat, du militantisme au volontariat' ['Volunteering: from militantism to volunteer work'], *Revue française des affaires sociales*, no 4, pp 97-116.

Erlinghagen, M. and Hank, K. (2006) 'The participation of older European in volunteer work', *Ageing & Society*, vol 26, no 5, pp 67-84.

Esping-Andersen, G. (1990) *The three worlds of welfare capitalism*, Oxford: Polity Press.

Eurobarometer (2007) *Health and long-term care in the European Union*, Special Eurobarometer 283, Wave 67.3, TNS Opinion & Social (ec. europa.eu/public_opinion/archives/ebs/ebs_283_en.pdf).

European Commission (2000) *Social situation in EU 2000*, Brussels: Directorate General of Employment, Social Affairs & Equal Opportunities and EUROSTAT.

France Bénévolat (2010) *Bénévolat et retraités, une implication réfléchie* [*Volunteering and retired people, a thoughtful commitment*], Paris: France Bénévolat (www.francebenevolat.org).

Gallagher, S.K. (1994) 'Doing their share: Comparing patterns of help given by older and younger adults', *Journal of Marriage and the Family*, vol 56, no 3, pp 567-78.

Hély, M. (2009) *Les métamorphoses du monde associatif* [The metamorphosis of the voluntary sector], Paris: Presses Universitaires de France.

Huber, M., Rodrigues, R., Hoffmann, F., Gasior, K. and Marin, B. (2009) *Facts and figures on long-term care. Europe and North America*, Vienna: European Centre for Social Welfare Policy and Research.

ISSP (International Social Survey Programme) (1997) 'Work Orientations II', Mannheim: ISSP (www.gesis.org/issp/issp-modules-profiles/work-orientations/1997).

Malet, J. and Bazin, C. (2011) 'Donner du temps pour les autres mais aussi pour soi' ['Giving one's time to others but also to oneself'], *Gérontologie et société*, no 138, pp 165-80.

Morange, P. (2008) *Rapport parlementaire sur la gouvernance et le financement des associations* [*Parliamentary report on governance in associations*], Paris: National Assembly.

Observatoire National de l'Economie Sociale et Solidaire (2009) *Atlas de l'économie sociale et solidaire en France et dans les régions* [*Panorama of the social economy in France and its regions*], Montreuil: Le *Conseil National des Chambres Régionales de l'Economie Sociale* et Solidaire (CNCRES).

Poussou-Plesse, M., Petit, M. and Mascova, E. (2010) *Opportunities for older people in the civil society. National report (France), Part 2 – Case studies,* ASPA Project, Deliverable 5.1, Paris: École des hautes études en science sociales.

Prouteau, L. and Wolff, F.C. (2007) 'La participation associative et le bénévolat des seniors' ['Participation in voluntary organisations and volunteering in old age'], *Retraite et société*, no 50, pp 157-89.

Recherches & Solidarités (2011) *Les différents visages de la solidarité en France: importance de l'adhésion aux associations* [*Different faces of solidarity in France: The importance of the associative membership*], Recherches & Solidarités (www.recherches-solidarites.org).

Salamon, L. and Anheier, H. (1998) 'Social origins of civil society', *Voluntas*, vol 9, no 3, pp 213-48.

Sirven, N. and Debrand, T. (2013) 'La participation sociale des personnes âgées en Europe. Instrument du "bien vieillir" ou facteur d'inégalités sociales de santé?' [Social participation of elderly people in Europe. An instrument of "healthy ageing" or a factor in the social inequality of health?], *Retraite et société*, no 65, pp 59-80.

Taddei, D. (ed) (2000) *Retraites choisies et progressives* [*Progressive and decided retirement*], Paris: La documentation française.

Tchernonog, V. (2007) *Le paysage associatif français. Mesures et évolutions* [*Portraying the French associative sector. Measures and evolutions*], Paris: Dalloz.

EIGHT

Older volunteers in Poland: the heritage of a Socialist regime

Konrad Turek and Jolanta Perek-Białas

Introduction

After 1989, Poland transitioned from a centrally planned economy (controlled and monitored by the state) to an economy with a substantial share of the private sector, before eventually becoming a member of the European Union (EU) in 2004. In line with other post-Socialist welfare states, Poland aimed its welfare regime system in the direction of a liberal-residual regime type, even though a clear type of welfare regime had not been fully developed (Ferge, 2001). As with other post-transitional European states, Poland is characterised by a mix of various social insurances, social assistance and privatisation and, more importantly, has experienced stronger economic development over the last few years, which has led to a higher level of social well-being than in the former countries of the USSR (Fenger, 2007).

Before the collapse of the Socialist regime in Poland, the dominant family model was the dual earner/female double burden model, characterised by high female employment and women taking full responsibility for house and care duties. This dual breadwinner household is still quite common today. New forms of households have since emerged, such as cohabitation and single young households or single parents (Slany, 2002). During the last two decades, Poland has grappled with the challenges of inflation, privatisation, unemployment and major system reforms. An ageing population and low activity rates among the older generations have presented minor problems for policy makers. Until recently, the pension system and extensive early retirement options, along with an eligible retirement age for women at 60 and for men at 65, have favoured early exit from the labour market. As a result, the employment rates for older generations are among the lowest in Europe. The same applies to participation by seniors in voluntary activity. And the fact that this generation grew up and for most of their lives lived under a Socialist system is not to be overlooked.

The 1990s were a time of rebuilding civil society in Poland, both in the social self-consciousness and in the system regulations. Non-governmental organisations (NGOs) offered support in areas where governmental policy and public institutions were ineffective. Since the 2000s it has been a time of professionalisation and stabilisation of the third sector. Nevertheless, the participation rates of Poles in voluntary activity are well below the European average. Depending on the definition of 'voluntary activity', it ranges from 6 per cent (ESS, 2008) to 12 per cent (Eurobarometer, 2011) to 16 per cent (Przewłocka, 2011) of the population. In 2010, there were about 60,000-65,000 active non-profit organisations. The total revenues reported in 2008 by all active associations, similar social organisations and foundations amounted to PLN 12.7 billion (about 3.1 billion), accounting for 1 per cent of Poland's gross domestic product (GDP) (GUS, 2010). Although there are legal regulations for voluntary work, it is still often provided in an informal way (without a contract with the non-governmental organisation [NGO] concerned or membership), particularly in smaller organisations or for short periods of time. Most voluntary work in Poland takes place in the areas of charity, religion, sport and education, making it difficult to recognise if an altruistic or self-centred type of volunteering prevails.

In this chapter we focus on the voluntary activity of the Polish 50+ generation, its conditions, limitations and opportunities. First, we present the country-specific tradition of the voluntary sector. Then we describe the dimensions of volunteering by providing some relevant facts and figures. We also identify the main opportunities and limitations for participation in the Polish voluntary sector by older people, before concluding with an analysis of how the supply of older candidates and the demands of civil society could be better matched.

The Polish tradition of voluntary action

The roots of modern Polish civil society institutions and voluntary activity can be found in the 19th century, when, under annexations by Prussia, Austria and Russia, voluntary associations substituted for non-existent national institutions, cultivating the Polish culture, tradition and identity (Bartkowski, 2003). After Poland gained independence in 1918, voluntary associations continued to develop, but the Second World War brought a halt to this process. After the war, the Soviets established a Communist government in Poland, and the following decades were dominated by Socialist ideology. Most voluntary organisations were totally eliminated from social life or replaced by mass organisations (in practice, obligatory and under state control) that more often served political goals. Social activity became a tool of political control, and for half a century it was restricted and depreciated to the effect that it lost its meaning, becoming an opportunistic and *façade* routine. On the other hand, another kind of voluntary activity at that time operated primarily against the system, its rules and indoctrination. It was run unofficially, often in an illegal manner (for example, underground press, education, cultural activity, help for victims of repression, and illegal political organisations). The peak of this process was a mass social movement: the independent self-governing trade union Solidarity (1980-81), which quickly assembled 10 million members (more than 80 per cent of the workforce in Poland at the time) to become the biggest voluntary organisation in history.

At the beginning of its transformation from a Socialist to a democratic system in 1989-90, a 'boom' in citizens' initiatives occurred in Poland. The 1990s were a period of development in the third sector, as well as gradual change(s) in people's mentality. New voluntary organisations took care of areas where public institutions were helpless or ineffective. The early 2000s were characterised by professionalisation of the third sector, during which legal acts and adjustments laid the grounds for formalisation of the third sector and the foundations of intersectorial cooperation. A fundamental step was Polish accession to the EU in 2004, as EU priorities emphasised the role of the non-governmental sector and structural funds contributed to developing new opportunities for organisation and stabilisation in this area.

Compared to the other countries of Central and Eastern Europe, the Polish third sector is currently considered to be strong. Nevertheless, some structural barriers remain, including very low voluntary activity among Poles, weak and limited social dialogue, insufficient collaboration between actors within the sector, and organisational inefficiency with ineffective and non-transparent management and financial unviability (Klon/Jawor, 2008; USAID, 2009).

Voluntary organisations use various sources for financing their activities. For many of them, a major source of funding is the European Structural Fund and international foundations. The NGO sector is also subsidised by the state through the Civil Initiatives Fund (*Fundusz Inicjatyw Obywatelskich*) that was established in 2005. Another source of funding is 1 per cent of the citizens' personal income tax, which citizens can decide to assign to any public benefit organisation. Fundraising, sponsors, private donors and membership fees play a minor role. Experts emphasise the economic weakness of the whole sector due to limited access to public funds and hence poor financial stability (Rymsza, 2008; Schimanek, 2011). Furthermore, sometimes decisions related to organisations depend on a single decision-maker, as local representatives who are responsible for meting out public funds for social activity (the financing system is still being improved in Poland). Due to all these factors, many organisations are normally unable to predict how their financial situation will look like in the next year or months, and whether they will get the necessary funding to run their projects. This makes it very difficult to draw up any development plan for the organisation over a longer time frame.

There is no clear perception of the role of volunteers among Polish NGOs (PTS, 2008; Turek and Perek-Białas, 2011). Even if the law provides a definition of 'volunteer' (see p 177), the distinction between paid staff, members, voluntary workers, other participants or activists engaged in the activity of an organisation is often unclear, particularly in younger and smaller organisations or those functioning on a small scale (that is, at a neighbourhood or local level). One of the reasons is the informal character of the relationships in NGOs and the reluctance towards unnecessary bureaucracy in order to emphasise that everyone may join the organisation. Older and bigger organisations more often employ regular paid staff, offering better and more stable working conditions, and mostly signing voluntary agreements with volunteers. Forms of voluntary cooperation are also very diverse. It is common that a person who has a paid contract with an NGO in one project or in the form of part-time work (it can even be a small remuneration) could additionally provide voluntary work in other activities (Herbst and Przewłocka, 2011). In 2008, according to some studies, 78 per cent of organisations used voluntary work, and about 56 per cent fully relied on voluntary work (Gumkowska and Herbst, 2008; Herbst and Przewłocka, 2011).

The legal framework

The legal regulations for volunteering and civil society organisations were implemented very late in Poland. During the 1990s, the NGOs' legal framework was complex and confusing, and the introduction of Poland's new constitution in 1997 did not regulate the sphere sufficiently and clearly, setting up only the general framework for non-profit activity. The first comprehensive general bill was enacted in 2003: the Law on Public Benefit Activity and Volunteerism. Among other things, this defined the term 'volunteer', regulated the procedures for voluntary work, defined the status and principles for the functioning of NGOs, and provided new opportunities for the non-profit sector. It introduced the mechanism of the 1 per cent tax return to organisations mentioned above, and regulated relationships between the public sector and the third sector (Makowski, 2008). At the Polish government level, the third sector is represented by the Council of Public Benefit Activities (*Rada Działalnosci Pozżytku Publicznego*), created in 2004.

According to the Law, a volunteer is an individual who provides his or her services voluntarily and without remuneration. Volunteers provide services based on an agreement with the institution that engages them. If the services provided by the volunteer are implemented over a period exceeding 30 days, a written volunteer agreement is required. For periods of less than 30 days, the volunteer can request a written agreement or written confirmation of the services provided. A volunteer with a formal arrangement is automatically covered by the general national healthcare insurance. If a volunteer provides work for a period of less than 30 days, the organisation is obliged to provide accident insurance.

So far, there are no specific legal regulations concerning older people's participation in voluntary activity.

The dimension of volunteer work

Until 2005-06, participation in voluntary activity in Poland has constantly increased, along with the development of the third sector. The following years (2007-09) brought, however, a drop in the number of volunteers (even though the number of organisations continued to increase). This was mainly a result of two linked processes: improvement in the labour market situation (employment rates significantly rose and unemployment fell), which helped people focus on their professional carriers, and second, mass emigration of young Poles, who constituted a significant group of volunteers, to EU countries that opened up their labour markets. Nevertheless, in 2010 there was a slight increase of volunteering among the population (see also Figure 8.2 below).

Voluntary organisations

From 1989, the number of new third sector organisations formally registered in the official census (REGON) systematically increased each year, reaching 6,000 in 2000. It then stabilised at a level of about 4,000-5,000 new foundations and associations being established every year. Between 2005 and 2010, the number of third sector organisations increased by 22 per cent. Experts emphasise that in recent years the third sector in Poland has been stabilising, as evidenced by the increasing number of organisations that have been established for more than five years (Herbst and Przewłocka, 2011; GUS, 2012b).

In 2010, about 12,000 foundations and 71,000 associations were formally registered in Poland (excluding 16,000 Volunteer Fire Brigades, which possess the legal form of association but in practice operate on a different basis). However, recent studies have shown that about 25 per cent of these organisations are not functional (Herbst and Przewłocka, 2011). Therefore, the number of active organisations should be estimated at a level of about 60,000-65,000.

The most often declared fields of activity, as indicated by 53 per cent of the investigated organisations (Figure 8.1), were sport, tourism, recreation and hobbies. Next in line were education (47 per cent), culture and art (31 per cent), health services (19 per cent), and social services and social help (17 per cent).

The majority comprise small and medium-size organisations in terms of people being employed or involved in the organisation. Half of all associations have fewer than 35 members and only 16 per cent have more than 100 (Herbst and Przewłocka, 2011). However, only half of the formal members are considered to be fully active, and about 30 per cent of members are fully inactive (Gumkowska and Herbst, 2008). There is also significant inequality in the distribution of resources within this sector: 10 per cent of the biggest organisations accumulated 88 per cent of the total financial resources of the sector. The majority of NGOs are located in cities (64 per cent), particularly in Warsaw and other major cities (GUS, 2010).

Almost half of organisations employed a paid staff, 24 per cent had regular employees and 20 per cent had occasional employees hired through short-term contracts. The proportion of employees increases with the organisation's age and scope of activity. More than 60 per cent of the youngest NGOs, functioning for less than five years, do not employ any paid staff. The same applies to more than two thirds of organisations functioning in the local area, while among regional

Figure 8.1: Main fields of organisation's activity in 2010 (excluding fire brigades and religious organisations)

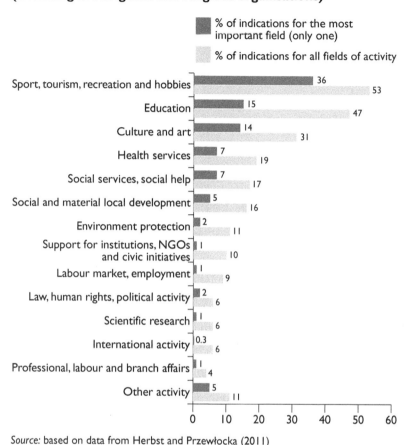

Source: based on data from Herbst and Przewłocka (2011)

or countrywide NGOs, half could afford to hire their own employees (Herbst and Przewłocka, 2011).

Volunteers by sector, gender and age

According to the European Social Survey (ESS) (2008), only 6 per cent of the Polish population aged 18-59/64 volunteered (in the last month), which was far below the European average (11 per cent). The more recent national research by Klon/Jawor (Baczko and Ogrodzka, 2008; Przewłocka, 2011) estimated that 16 per cent of Poles aged 15+ were engaged in voluntary activity in 2010 (that is, in carrying out social work for free in an NGO, social or religious movement; see Figure 8.2). This represents a significant increase compared to the

Figure 8.2: Volunteers in the third sector (population aged 15+) and employment rate (population aged 15-64) (%)

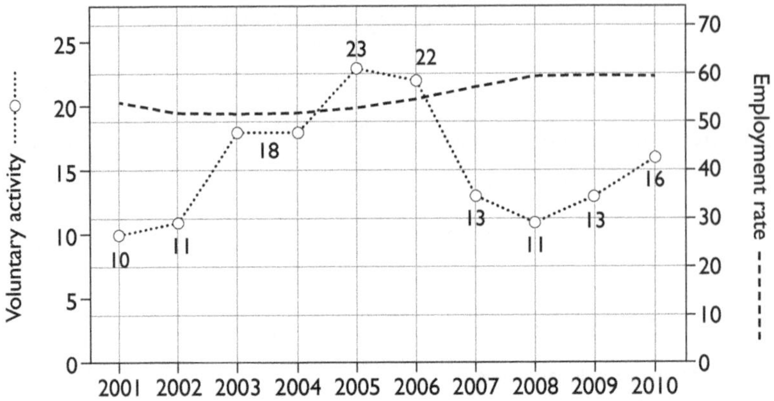

Source: Baczko and Ogrodzka (2008); Eurostat (2010); Przewłocka (2011)

previous three years, although it remains lower compared to the peak reached between 2003 and 2006.

For the last few years, the highest participation rates (of volunteers and members) have occurred in charitable, religious, sport and educational organisations (Baczko and Ogrodzka, 2008). In 2011, 60 per cent of NGOs members were men; however, women accounted for 59 per cent of volunteers and 60 per cent of NGO employees. The highest share of women volunteers (74-80 per cent) was observed in organisations operating in the fields of health, social services and education, with the lowest in sport and tourism (GUS, 2010).

In the under-25-year-old group, 22 per cent were volunteers (among pupils and students it was 29 per cent), and in the group aged 36 to 45, about 19 per cent (see Table 8.1). The lowest share was among older people (10 per cent for the group aged 55+) and pensioners (7 per cent). People with a higher education were involved in NGOs much more often (28 per cent) than other education-level groups (13-14 per cent).

Out of the 16 per cent who were involved in volunteering in 2010, only a small proportion did it on a regular basis, while the majority participated occasionally or even only once (Przewłocka, 2011). This is reflected in the time devoted to volunteering in the previous 12 months: only 5 per cent volunteered more than 150 hours yearly in total (on average three hours per week), while more than half provided less than 15 hours during the whole year.

Table 8.1: Proportion of volunteers by level of education, age and work status

	Characteristics	Share of volunteers (%)
Education	Lower	13
	Lower vocational	13
	Secondary	14
	Higher	28
Age	25 and less	22
	26-35	14
	36-45	19
	46-55	17
	55 and more	10
Work status	Employed	18
	Unemployed	13
	Retired/disabled	7
	Student/pupil	29
	Inactive/taking care of home	11

Source: Przewłocka (2011)

Based on the above statistics, in Poland volunteering is more popular among younger people (particularly pupils and students), and among working middle-aged people with a higher education (Przewłocka, 2011). Non-profit engagement is often considered an important part of career paths, and highly valued by employers. It is an especially important experience for younger people, who are in the first steps of their professional career (Makowski and Schimanek, 2008). Additionally, students and pupils have more time for participation. More often than other groups, they engage in broad nationwide initiatives, as well as in activity aimed at the ecology, environment and animal protection (Przewłocka, 2011). Young and middle-aged men also dominate sporting and tourist organisations.

Participation of older volunteers

With the exception of volunteers in the care sector, it is hard to sketch the profile of a 'prototypical' Polish older volunteer, as there are not many of them. Statistical data are not very helpful in this case. Based on qualitative studies, however, we may specify the main and most common types of activities among older volunteers in Poland (Leszczyńska-Rejchert, 2005; Rosochacka-Gmitrzak, 2011; Turek and Perek-Białas, 2011; Pazderski and Sobieszak-Penszko, 2012). Older volunteers are active in and for local communities, participate in educational projects aimed at improving their skills and competences, take part in health and recreational activities, as well as in integrative (cultural) projects in which they work with younger generations or share their knowledge, experiences and memories.

At the *individual level*, the third sector presents itself poorly when it comes to older Poles. Poland has one of the lowest voluntary activity rates among the 50+ in Europe. According to SHARE data (Survey of Health, Ageing and Retirement in Europe), in 2006–07 (see Figure 8.3), only 2 per cent of the Polish 50+ 'formally' volunteered (that is, did voluntary or charity work in the last month), and 5 per cent 'informally' volunteered (provided help to family, friends or neighbours in the last month).[1]

Table 8.2 shows the level of participation among older Poles in volunteering according to different sources. In 2010, almost 10 per cent of the 55+ could be classified as being active in voluntary organisations (including religious ones) during the previous year (Przewłocka, 2011), while in the 46–55 age group, 17 per cent of

Figure 8.3: Voluntary or charity work (formal volunteering) and providing help to family, friends or neighbours (informal volunteering) in the last month (% of adults 50+)

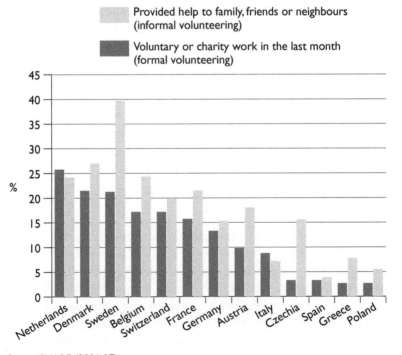

Source: SHARE (2006-07)

Table 8.2: Voluntary activity of seniors in Poland by data sources

Type of activity	%	Age group	Year of research	Source
Voluntary work for organisation (currently)	12.0	55+	2011	Eurobarometer
Voluntary activity in non-profit (including religious) organisation last year	17.0	46-55	2010	Klon/Jawor
Voluntary activity in non-profit (including religious) organisation last year	10.0	55+	2010	Klon/Jawor
Voluntary work last month	5.2	50+	2008	ESS
Active voluntary involvement in work of social or political organisation last year	7.0	60+	2007	CBOS
Voluntary or charity work last month (formal volunteering)	2.0	50+	2006-07	SHARE
Help to family, friends or neighbours last month (informal volunteering)	4.7	50+	2006-07	SHARE
Involvement in religious organisation last month	9.8	50+	2006-07	SHARE
Involvement in political organisation last month	1.8	50+	2006-07	SHARE

Sources: SHARE (2006-07); ESS (2008); CBOS (2010); Eurobarometer (2011); Przewłocka (2011)

Poles were active. A similar picture is presented in the Eurobarometer data for 2011 (12 per cent of volunteers aged 55+).

The ESS (2008) shows that about 5 per cent of the 50+ population volunteered (in the last month), which is consistent with SHARE results and places Poland well below the European average. It should be underlined, however, that despite the generally high sense of being religious, 90 per cent of 50+ Poles did not declare any activity in religious organisations (SHARE, 2006-07).

The national representative survey of CBOS (2010) reports that as many as 86 per cent of people aged 60 or older were not interested in any activity within their own close environment, municipality or parish. At the same time, only 7 per cent admitted to having been actively involved in voluntary work for a social or political organisation in 2007.

According to the SHARE study for Poland (2006-07), the reasons for voluntary activity among Poles aged 50+ are mostly related to the need to do something useful (for 81 per cent of respondents) and the opportunity to meet other people (47 per cent). For almost one in ten, it was an almost daily activity, whereas more than 60 per cent worked voluntarily or charitably less than once a week. Older Polish volunteers were usually those who had been active in the social domain throughout their lives (Turek and Perek-Białas, 2011). They also differ in their motivation from younger people, who tend to treat volunteering as an initial period of their career and a source of work experience. For seniors, volunteering is a way of being active and filling their time, an opportunity to work for and with people. In many cases, it is a form of repayment to others and to society. Senior volunteering is an expression of maturity when the roles of parent, grandparent and spouse have been fulfilled, making it possible for free time to be spent on social activity (Bogacz-Wojtanowska and Rymsza, 2009).

At the *organisational level*, the situation for older volunteers in the third sector has improved in recent years, mainly due to legal regulations and accession to the EU. Organisations have finally been given clear guidelines for operating and financing, as well as a significant inflow of funds from the EU. These processes have fostered the progress of the sector and promoted new activities, including those aimed at seniors.

It is difficult to estimate the number of Polish NGOs aimed at older volunteers. There are many organisations – about 1,300 (Dudkiewicz and Sobiesiak-Penszo, 2011) – that provide help and support to older people, mitigating the results of unemployment and exclusion, even though they do not address the activation of people aged 50+ directly. The involvement of seniors in the third sector has actually begun to develop in the last decade, although some isolated organisations aimed at activating older people have been operating for 20 years or longer. One of the first platforms for assembling non-profit organisations for seniors was established in 2004: *Forum 50+ Seniors of the 21st Century*. It is comprised of 22 organisations, mostly small or medium-sized, operating mainly in the fields of social services, education, health and recreation. Another example is a programme supporting and financing initiatives for the activation of the older generations, *Seniors in Action*, that until 2011 awarded 133 projects for activating people aged 50+ (it is run by the Association of Creative Initiatives 'ę', thanks to funding from the Polish-American Freedom Foundation). Despite the large number, the awarded projects were mainly small and could not contribute to the fast and significant development of volunteering in older age in Poland.

A particularly successful example of organisations engaging older people in recent years has been Third Age Universities (Halicka and Kramkowska, 2011), which provide a place for spending leisure time rather than just a place for developing and improving professional skills. There are currently about 385 universities of this kind in Poland, bringing together more than 100,000 participants (data from the Congress of Third Age Universities in 2012). It is worth mentioning that the biggest and oldest seniors' organisation in Poland, with a 70-year-long tradition and almost one million formal members, is the Polish Association of Retired Persons, Pensioners and the Disabled, which acts for the improvement of life conditions for older and disabled people and represents them at governmental level.

The most active senior organisations are mainly established in Poland's major cities, with small towns and the countryside being areas where voluntary activity is still rare. The gap is partly filled by traditional forms of activities, such as country Housewives' Circles, Voluntary Fire Brigades and religious organisations, but the level of involvement of older people in these organisations is hard to estimate (Kamiński, 2008).

Older people's participation in voluntary organisations: opportunities and restrictions

Although a third sector focusing on seniors is slowly developing in Poland, participation of older volunteers remains very low. Let us now consider the opportunities and restrictions in terms of their activation, as well as the impact of an increasingly older workforce and of family care duties, on the contribution of older people to civil society.

Opportunities and restrictions for volunteering for older people

The low participation of Poland's older people in volunteering can be explained by a few factors. At the individual level, we may recognise a *problem of mentality* and *of life situation*. At the organisational and institutional levels, we observe a *problem of limited possibilities* for their involvement in civil society.

The first *problem of mentality* is a subjective barrier that can only be resolved with the help of seniors themselves. The Socialist period had a significant impact on the awareness of older generations. The degeneration of the public sphere and imposition of ideological definitions of 'volunteering', 'common wealth' and 'social activity' have increased their reluctance to belong to any association or organisation (Synak, 2000). The dominant image of older age contradicts active attitudes, as it is perceived as the time of retirement, inflexibility and aversion towards updating or changing skills (Bogacz-Wojtanowska and Rymsza, 2009). The willingness to be active and the awareness of one's own capabilities are fundamental and necessary elements in the process of active ageing. Activity is still not widely seen as necessary for maintaining a good physical and mental condition, and retirement is treated as a moment of 'deserved rest' or a safe solution amidst unstable labour market conditions with limited possibilities for finding a new job (MPiPS, 2008).

The second problem at the individual level is related to the *life situation* of Polish seniors, primarily in financial and health terms. The dysfunctions in the health and social care systems are considered to be relevant obstacles for activation (Turek and Perek-Białas, 2011). Many older Poles have too many everyday life obligations (also within the family) and worries to find the time and energy for voluntary activity. Pension benefits are often fairly low (the average retirement pension was about 380 per month in 2010, with the minimum wage at 315; GUS, 2012a). Nevertheless, the financial situation of older Poles is very differentiated and generally not as bad as it is often perceived by the media and public opinion (the poverty rate – below 60 per cent of the median equivalent income after social transfers – for people aged 65 or more in Poland was lower than the European average; Eurostat, 2012). Additionally, working in NGOs sometimes offers the possibility of additional earning. This is actually moving away from the strict concept of volunteering as an activity that is provided for free, but is sometimes what happens de facto in Poland.

At the organisational level, the third sector is a unique area that may provide many opportunities for the activation of older people in different ways from the profit sector, and there have already been some steps in this direction (see pp 184–185). Certainly, its significant strengths are flexible patterns of employment and voluntary engagement (Bogacz-Wojtanowska and Rymsza, 2009). We should remember that NGOs may well be a place of paid work for seniors. Although this is no longer a voluntary activity, it is particularly important from the perspective of activating older people, and it is often impossible to separate these two dimensions. In the Polish third sector, paid workers would also usually involve themselves in voluntary activity. NGOs may provide better working conditions compared to companies (except for the pay), for example, a friendly atmosphere, the possibility of reconciling work and private life (including care responsibilities), help in difficult life situations, as well as an opportunity to provide useful and important work. For seniors, being active in NGOs is a way of living, spending leisure time, self-development through work, as well as having the chance for small additional earnings (Bogacz–Wojtanowska and Rymsza, 2009).

On the other hand, both at the organisational and institutional level, it has been recognised that one of the most important barriers is the *problem of limited possibilities* for activation in older age. There are still not many NGOs that are able to meet the needs and aspirations of older volunteers, and most of them are focused on big cities. Even more generally, seniors in Poland are often considered as passive objects of help and care, rather than as active participants (Szatur–Jaworska, 2000; Błędowski, 2002). Another problem is the lack of knowledge about volunteering among older generations and the possibilities of staying active after retirement (Turek and Perek-Białas, 2011). Nevertheless, much has changed during the last two decades since the transition. During the 1990s, the third sector actually had nothing to offer to older volunteers. But a growing awareness of the challenges posed by an ageing society has resulted in increasing concerns about the activation of older generations. The media are now more frequently showing older people being active and full of energy. After accession to the EU and the European Years of Volunteering (2011) and Active Ageing and Intergenerational Solidarity (2012), seniors are today recognised as a large group of potential participants in civil society by NGOs and, as already mentioned, more visible and real possibilities of participation and NGO initiatives are becoming available to them.

On the other hand, the activity of the third sector in this field has still not gained any institutional or systematic support from national government. There is no real public policy towards older volunteers or support for NGOs focusing on older people in Poland, although some recent strategic documents have considered this issue (Pazderski and Sobieszak-Penszko, 2012). Public policy addressing the challenges of an ageing society in Poland during the last two decades has focused on the financial aspects of demographic change, pension system reform, limitation of early retirement and increasing eligible retirement age. The main programme from 2008 on the challenges of ageing, 'Solidarity across Generations', was also focused on productivity and employment rather than on a more broad approach to active ageing.

Older people between employment and volunteering

The employment rates of older people in Poland are among the lowest in the EU, reaching in 2011 in the group aged 50-64 57 per cent for men and 41 per cent for women. In the 65+ age group, it was 8 and 3 per cent respectively (Eurostat, 2011). The effective average age of people who for the first time received pension benefits in 2010 was 59.0 years for women and 60.2 years for men (ZUS, 2011).

Poland may be described as a 'medium' work-oriented country from a comparative perspective. The proportion of people aged 50–65 who would have decided to work, even if they did not need the money, amounted to 68 per cent in 1997, while the average for the countries covered in this study was 61 per cent (ISSP, 1997). In 2008, about 66 per cent of people in the same age range would have chosen to work even if they were quite affluent (PGSS, 2008).

Low employment rates combined with low voluntary activity rates among seniors make the analytical attempt at reconciling professional and voluntary work very limited and not so clear. According to the ESS (2008), the percentage of people aged 50-60 who are volunteers but who also work totalled 4.5 per cent, decreasing to less than 1 per cent after the age of 60. According to the SHARE 2006-07 data, among Polish volunteers aged 50+ (*n*=46), more than one third are employed or self-employed, 43 per cent are retired, 9 per cent are looking for work and 9 per cent declare themselves to be permanently sick or disabled (the low number of cases limits the analysis, however, and any interpretations must be used with caution). The relatively frequent conjunction of profit and non-profit work is, however, not really related to employee volunteer programmes provided by companies, as such initiatives are still very rare in Poland (Centrum Wolontariatu, 2008).

There is currently almost no discussion about the impacts of an increasingly older workforce on the contribution of older people to civil society. The marginal share of older volunteers means that the third sector is still not considered an important field of activity in older age by policy makers and civil society in general.

Older people between family care and volunteering

It is often stressed that the traditional model of family, where the care of older relatives is considered an obligation, is strongly embedded in Polish mentality and reality (Kotowska and Wóycicka, 2008). Family in Poland is seen as the main care supplier – about 60 per cent of Poles consider that older people requiring care or support should live with one of their children (Eurobarometer 2007). Institutionalised care is usually valued negatively and not readily available (Synak, 2000; Racław, 2011). In comparison to the rest of Europe, Poland has one of the lowest levels of formal care provisions: residential care covers only 1 per cent of the population aged 65+ and formal home care 1.7 per cent; it is, however, compensated for by a high informal involvement of family caregivers (Bettio and Verashchagina, 2012).

In 2008 (Kotowska and Wóycicka, 2008), 31 per cent of women aged 50-65 and 20 per cent of men aged 55-70 were caregivers (providing regular and free care to adults or children). The Central Statistical Office (GUS) data for 2005 showed that the percentage of people providing care to a person aged 60 or more increased significantly among older generations, reaching, in the 55-64 age group, about 10 per cent for men and almost 20 per cent for women.

According to SHARE (2006-07), however, the numbers are much lower. Only 3.7 per cent (n=101) of the 50+ population cared for a sick or disabled adult in the previous month (the second lowest result among the 13 European countries in the SHARE project). This can partly be explained by a possibly slightly narrower definition of caregiver by the SHARE study, and the time restriction to within the last month. A marginal number (26 per cent) of caregivers provided additional help to family, friends and neighbours, as well as voluntary or charitable work. For the 50+, care responsibilities implied significant limitations in everyday life, causing tiredness, sadness or helplessness, a situation certainly not conducive to voluntary activity (Principi and Perek-Białas, 2011).

The lack of appropriate data prevents a more precise analysis of the relation between family care and volunteering; however, caregiving itself can be considered in two ways. On the one hand, care duties seem to be an obstacle and limitation to voluntary activation. On the other hand, care for family members can be considered a kind of voluntary and unpaid work, provided on the basis of a personal (and not institutional) relationship.

Improving the match between supply of older candidates with the demand of voluntary organisations: future perspectives

Despite the current low volunteering rate among older people, after two decades of transition, the third sector in Poland is increasingly offering a relatively broad range of opportunities for activity among seniors. Recent organisational initiatives show that there is room for older volunteers and an interest in their work. Volunteering can serve as a tool for the activation of retired people. As emphasised by Schimanek (2006), there are no legal or formal restrictions limiting the access of older people to the third sector.

Therefore, the fundamental elements are ambition and willingness among seniors themselves, even though they need to meet a responsive environment for activity in terms of public policy, institutions and

NGOs. The success of senior initiatives is usually related to the determination, hard work and vision of single individuals – local leaders – who are able to assemble a team and motivate them to work. Still, there are not enough systematic solutions aimed at activating older volunteers so as to make them a significant and solid element of the third sector. The crucial challenge is, on the one hand, to positively change attitudes towards the prolongation of active life and lifelong learning and, on the other, to break those (sometimes unfounded) stereotypes about older people (Dudkiewicz and Sobiesiak-Penszko, 2011; Schimanek, 2011).

Against the growing interest observed at the organisational (or meso) level, current governmental public policy and public debate seem to omit or marginalise this specific type of activation in terms of voluntary work, concentrating first on the activation of inactive people in the labour market and on prolonging professional work. As the reasons for inactivity and the conditions for profit and non-profit activation seem to be basically the same, the solutions and propositions relative to the labour market might soon have an impact on the situation in the third sector as well. Public policy focusing on ageing and older generations is still an issue for the future in Poland, given that the existing solutions have mainly protective characteristics in the attempt to secure employment in older age.

Conclusions

This chapter has analysed the phenomenon of volunteering in older age in Poland at an individual, organisational and public policy level. The voluntary activity rate of seniors in Poland is among the lowest in Europe, for reasons that are quite different compared to young generations. First, they result from history, tradition and culture, as people aged 50+ lived for at least 30 years under a Socialist regime. This heritage is something that should not be underestimated, and can still be observed at the individual level: general inactivity, demanding attitudes, reluctance to do or lack of knowledge about voluntary work, and a distorted notion of volunteering due to the Socialist ideology. The predominant view of older age in the public opinion is far from an active image. It is rather a specific culture of inactivity in which senior volunteering does not exist. Older people are considered rather more often as passive objects of help and care than as active participants. A secondary factor is the current socio-economic conditions and life situation, which, for at least a significant proportion of older Poles, remain difficult. At the organisational level, we may reiterate the problem of limited possibilities. The third sector for seniors, consisting of NGOs that are able to meet the needs and aspirations of older volunteers, is still very small. Nevertheless, for a few years now, it has been developing, albeit slowly, and NGOs are the only actors that actually attempt to engage older people in volunteering. Public policy, however, does not support this form of activity in an effective way. For the last two decades, it has focused on the financial aspects of demographic changes and pension system reform. Policy makers still do not consider the third sector an important field of activity in older age.

Until recently, what NGOs had to offer to older people, apart from isolated examples of good initiatives, was rather narrow and focused more on big cities. It amounted to single initiatives by local leaders, but lacked systematic and broader actions. Recently, however, the situation has changed. Professionalisation and stabilisation of the third sector, EU priorities and funds, the media and a growing awareness of the challenges posed by an ageing society, have resulted in an increasing concern about the need for more active older people in the voluntary field. It is difficult to predict whether an increasing commitment by the labour market may phase in or crowd out older Poles from volunteering. The current older people's extremely low rates in both activities may suggest that the relationship between the two activities may not be wholly negative. On the other hand, informal family care may undermine volunteering by older people, and especially for women, since the family in Poland is still considered the principal care supplier. All this requires extensive reflection among all concerned parties in Poland, where there has so far been very little discussion about the consequences of an ageing population on the contribution of older people to civil society.

Note

[1] The terms 'formal' and 'informal volunteering' were defined in the SHARE documents and used in the analysis of SHARE data by Hank and Erlinghagen (2008).

References

Baczko, A. and Ogrocka, A. (2008) *Wolontariat, filantropia i 1%* [*Volunteering, philanthropy and 1%*], Warszawa: Stowarzyszenie Klon/ Jawor.

Bartkowski, J. (2003) *Tradycja i polityka. Wpływa tradycji kulturowych polskich regionów na współczesne zachowania społeczne i polityczne* [*Tradition and politics. The influence of regional cultural traditions on contemporary social and political activity*], Warszawa: Wydawnictwo Akademickie „Żak".

Bettio, F. and Verashchagina, A. (2012) *Long-term care for the elderly. Provisions and providers in 33 European countries*, Luxembourg: European Union.

Błędowski, P. (2002) *Lokalna polityka społeczna wobec ludzi starych* [*Local social policy towards older people*], Warszawa: SGH.

Bogacz-Wojtanowska, E. and Rymsza, M. (eds) (2009) *Nie tylko społecznie. Zatrudnienie i wolontariat w organizacjach pozarządowych* [*Not only voluntary. Employment and volunteering in non-governmental organisations*], Warszawa: Fundacja Instytut Spraw Publicznych.

CBOS (The Public Opinion Research Center) (2010) *Obraz typowego Polaka w starszym wieku* [*The image of a typical Pole in older age*], Warszawa: CBOS.

Centrum Wolontariatu (2008) *I ogólnopolskie badania wolontariatu pracowniczego* [*First Polish research on employee volunteering*], Warszawa: Centrum Wolontariatu.

Dudkiewicz, M. and Sobiesiak-Penszko, P. (2011) 'Starość w trzecim sektorze: aktywnie czy opiekuńczo?' ['Older age in the third sector: activity or protection?'], *Trzeci sektor*, vol 25, pp 28-36.

ESS (European Social Survey) (2008) Round 4 data, Data file edition 4.0, Norway: Norwegian Social Science Data Services (www.europeansocialsurvey.org).

Eurobarometer (2007) *Health and long-term care in the European Union* (http://ec.europa.eu/public_opinion/index_en.htm).

Eurobarometer (2011) *Active ageing* (http://ec.europa.eu/public_opinion/archives/ebs/ebs_378_fact_pl_en.pdf).

Eurostat (2011, 2012) http://epp.eurostat.ec.europa.eu/portal/page/portal/statistics/search_database

Fenger, H. (2007) 'Welfare regimes in Central and Eastern Europe: Incorporating post-communist countries in a welfare regime typology', *Contemporary Issues and Ideas in Social Sciences*, vol 3, no 2 (http://journal.ciiss.net/index.php/ciiss/article/view/45/37).

Ferge, Z. (2001) 'Welfare and "ill-fare" systems in Central-Eastern Europe', in B. Sykes, B. Palier and M. Prior (eds) *Globalization and European welfare states: Challenges and change*, Basingstoke: Palgrave, pp 127-52.

Gumkowska, M. and Herbst, J. (2008) *Polski sektor pozarządowy 2008* [*The Polish non-governmental sector*], Warszawa: Stowarzyszenie Klon/Jawor.

GUS (Główny Urząd Statystyczny) (2010) *Stowarzyszenia, fundacje i społeczne podmioty wyznaniowe w 2008 r* [*Associations, foundations and religious organisations in 2008*], Warszawa: GUS.

GUS (2012a) *Emerytury i renty w 2010 r* [*Pension and disability benefits in 2010*], Warszawa: Główny Urząd Statystyczny.

GUS (2012b) *Wstępne wyniki badania SOF-1 w 2010 roku* [*Preliminary results of the SOF-1 study in 2010*], Warszawa: Główny Urząd Statystyczny.

Halicka, M. and Kramkowska, E. (2011) 'Aktywność osób starszych i przykłady samoorganizowania się seniorów w Polsce' ['Activity of older people and examples of self-organisation of seniors in Poland'], *Trzeci sector*, vol 25, pp 36-44.

Hank, K. and Erlinghagen, M. (2008) 'Dynamics of volunteering', in A. Börsch-Supan, K. Hank, H. Jürges and M. Schröder (eds) *Health, ageing and retirement in Europe*, Mannheim: MEA, pp 239-46.

Herbst, J. and Przewłocka, J. (2011) *Podstawowe fakty o organizacjach pozarządowych. Raport z badań 2010* [*Basic facts about non-governmental organisations. Research report 2010*], Warszawa: Stowarzyszenie Klon/Jawor.

ISSP (International Social Survey Programme) (1997) 'Work Orientations II', Mannheim: ISSP (www.gesis.org/issp/issp-modules-profiles/work-orientations/1997).

Kamiński, R. (2008) *Aktywność społeczności wiejskich* [*Activity of agricultural communities*], Warszawa: IRWiR PAN.

Klon/Jawor (2008) *Indeks Społeczeństwa Obywatelskiego 2007* [*Civil Society Index 2007*], Warszawa: Stowarzyszenie Klon/Jawor.

Kotowska, I.E. and Wóycicka, I. (eds) (2008) *Sprawowanie opieki oraz inne uwarunkowania podnoszenia aktywności zawodowej osób w starszym wieku produkcyjnym* [*Care obligations and other conditions of increasing the labour market activity of people in older productive age*], Warszawa: Ministerstwo Pracy i Polityki Społecznej.

Leszczyńska-Rejchert, A. (2005) 'Organizacje pozarządowe w służbie ludziom starszym' ['Non-governmental organisations on duty for older persons'], in B. Kromolicka (eds) *Praca socjalna w organizacjach pozarządowych* [*Social work in non-governmental organisations*], Toruń: Akapit, pp 213-23.

Makowski, G. (ed) (2008) *U progu zmian. Pięć lat ustawy o działalności pożytku publicznego i o wolontariacie* [*On the threshold of change. Five years of the act on public benefit activity and volunteering*], Warszawa: Instytut Spraw Publicznych.

Makowski, G. and Schimanek, T. (eds) (2008) *Organizacje pozarządowe i władza publiczna. Drogi do partnerstwa* [*Non-governmental organisations and public authorities. Ways to partnership*], Warszawa: Instytut Spraw Publicznych.

MPiPS (Ministerstwo Pracy i Polityki Społecznej) (2008) *Dezaktywizacja osób w wieku około emerytalnym* [*Leaving activity in pre-retirement age*], Warszawa: MPiPS.

Pazderski, F. and Sobieszak-Penszko, P. (2012) *Wolontariat osób dojrzałych w Polsce* [*Volunteering of mature people in Poland*], Warszawa: Ministerstwo Pracy i Polityki Społecznej.

PGSS (Polski Generalny Sondaż Społeczny, Polish General Social Survey) (2008) http://pgss.iss.uw.edu.pl/

Principi, A. and Perek-Białas, J. (2011) *The reconciliation of employment and eldercare: A secondary data analysis*, Volkswagen Stiftung (www.carersatwork.tu-dortmund.de/download/Carers@work_SDA.pdf).

Przewłocka, J. (2011) *Zaangażowanie społeczne Polaków w roku 2010: wolontariat, filantropia, 1%* [*Social engagement of Poles in 2010: volunteering, philanthropy, 1%*], Warszawa: Stowarzyszenie Klon/Jawor.

PTS (Polskiego Towarzystwa Socjologicznego) (2008) *Diagnoza problemów funkcjonowania organizacji pożytku publicznego* [*Diagnosis of the problems of public benefit organisations*], Warszawa: Zakład Badań Naukowych PTS.

Racław, M. (2011) 'Mit w służbie rutyny – lokalne wymiary troski o osoby starsze' ['A myth on duty of routine – local dimension of attention of older people'], *Trzeci sector*, vol 25, pp 19-28.

Rosochacka-Gmitrzak, M. (2011) 'W stronę Hyde Parku i zarządzanie starością, czyli o aktywności polskich seniorów' ['Towards Hyde Park and old age management, or on the activity of Polish seniors'], *Trzeci sector*, vol 25, pp 44-50.

Rymsza, M. (2008) 'State policy towards the civic sector in Poland in the years 1989–2007', *Trzeci sector*, Special English Edition, pp 53-63.

SHARE (2006-07) *The Survey of Health, Ageing and Retirement in Europe* (www.share-project.org).

Schimanek, T. (2006) *Sytuacja osób powyżej 50-tego roku życia na rynku pracy oraz rola organizacji pozarządowych* [*Labour market situation of people 50+ and the role of non-governmental organisations*], Warszawa: Fundacja Inicjatyw Społeczno-Ekonomicznych.

Schimanek, T. (2011) 'Starzenie się społeczeństwa wyzwaniem XXI wieku' ['Population ageing as a challenge of the 21st century'], *Trzeci sector*, vol 25, pp 8-19.

Slany, K. (2002) *Alternatywne formy życia małżeńsko-rodzinnego w ponowoczesnym* świecie [*The alternative forms of marriage and family life in postmodern world*], Kraków: NOMOS.

Synak, B. (2000) *Polska starość* [*Polish old age*], Gdańsk: Wydawnictwo Uniwersytetu Gdańskiego.

Szatur-Jaworska, B. (2000) *Ludzie starzy i starość w polityce społecznej* [*Older people and older age in social policy*], Warszawa: Aspra-JR.

Turek, K. and Perek-Białas, J. (2011) *Opportunities for older people in the civil society. National report: Poland*, Kraków: Jagiellonian University.

USAID (United States Agency for International Development) (2009) *2008 NGO sustainability index for Central and Eastern Europe and Eurasia*, Washington: USAID.

ZUS (2011) *Ważniejsze informacje z zakresu ubezpieczeń społecznych w 2010 r* [*The most important information about social insurance in 2010*], Warszawa: ZUS.

NINE

Older volunteers in Sweden: a welfare state in transition

Per-Åke Andersson and Dominique Anxo[1]

Introduction

Non-profit volunteer organisations are well integrated into Swedish society, and play an important role in many different sectors. The voluntary sector was estimated to comprise around 50,000 organisations in 2009, with six million adult Swedes members in at least one voluntary organisation – this corresponds to around 80 per cent of the adult population. The organisations engaged 110,000 paid employees and 934,000 unpaid volunteers (Statistics Sweden, 2011). The voluntary sector's contribution to GDP (gross domestic product) is estimated at around 5 per cent (Wijkström and Einarsson, 2011).

The Swedish experience shows that a large voluntary sector is compatible with a homogeneous and egalitarian society with a strong and universal welfare state. Actually, the relationship between Swedish civil society and the Swedish state has been one of close cooperation. The collaboration between the Social Democratic Party, the labour movement, housing associations and consumer organisations during the rise of the Swedish welfare state is particularly notable. The presence and strength of the non-profit and volunteer sector can be attributed to the popular movement tradition, such as the labour and Socialist movements, as well as a reflection of the distinctive features of the Swedish welfare state.

The Swedish model is based on a strong political commitment to the goals of full employment and price stability, as well as to egalitarian ideals supporting processes of individualisation. It is based on the principle that all citizens have access to the same standard and quality of services independently of the individual level of income, that the individual, and not the family, is the basic unit not only of taxation but also of social benefits and social rights, and the full integration of women into the labour market (Anxo and Niklasson, 2006). Labour market participation is high for both men and women. The economic activity rate in 2011 for those aged 15-74 was 68 per cent for women and 74 per cent for men (Statistics Sweden, 2012). The Swedish family form can thus be characterised as a dual breadwinner/external care model, epitomised as a trend towards *de-familisation* (Esping-Andersen, 2003).

The characteristics of the welfare state have played an important role in how the volunteer sector is structured and has developed over time. Since the state is strongly involved in the provision of social services (childcare, education, health, elder care), and the financing of a generous and encompassing social protection system, the volunteer organisations are less active in the fields of social problems. Compared to other European countries, the Swedish volunteer sector in the field of social welfare appears, therefore, to be relatively small. Lundström and Svedberg (2003) suggest that the powerful expansion of the social democratic welfare state in Sweden discouraged non-profit involvement and voluntary organisation in these fields. Voluntary work in Sweden is predominantly self-centred/self-expressive rather than philanthropic.

As a new trend, however, it should be noted that the volunteer organisations have increased their activities within the field of social welfare over the past few years. The introduction of new public management (NPM) reforms in Sweden, together with an increased reliance on market competition, waves of deregulation and market-like arrangement, has implied changes for the non-profit and volunteer sector. Traditional welfare services, such as childcare, elder care and education, have been opened up for, among others, non-profit actors (Wijkström, 2004).

A large share of volunteering among the whole Swedish population corresponds to a rather high share of the population involved in volunteering in older age compared with most of the European countries. Even if volunteering in Sweden is mainly self-expressive, Swedish older volunteers are involved in both self-expressive (for example, in cultural and recreational activities), and altruistic (for example, in the social services and religion sectors) volunteering. Given the recent overall trend of increasing volunteering activities in social welfare, the role of older volunteers is supposed to increase, in the near future.

In light of this, the main objective of this chapter is to present the background, size, composition and enrolment of older people in the voluntary sector and possible developments of their volunteering in Sweden. This chapter starts with a short historical outlook and then discusses the legal framework. The next section presents data on the significance and magnitude of volunteer work with a special focus on older volunteers. Opportunities and restrictions for older volunteers are discussed in the third section. The fourth section discusses future scenarios followed by a concluding section.

The Swedish tradition of voluntary action

The voluntary sector has a long tradition in Swedish society, dating back as early as the 16th century. Its history is heavily influenced by its relation to the state and popular mass movements, with their emphasis on membership and activism (Lundström and Wijkström, 1995). Initially, most voluntary work was philanthropic, aiming at alleviating the effects of poverty on the homeless, those with a disability, those who were deprived, and so on. During the 19th century the sobriety movement grew strong, with major actors such as the Swedish Mission Association, a church organisation, founded in 1878, and the International Organisation of Good Templars (IOGT) founded in 1879. Child welfare was also increasingly recognised, and charity organisations initiated institutions, as orphanages and reformatories, for young people.

The sobriety organisations, together with the labour movement's organisations, consolidated the voluntary sector in Sweden in the 1880s. While the philanthropic organisations dominated the volunteer sector until the beginning of the 20th century, their social welfare activities declined in importance with the development of welfare state activities and the creation of a modern and universal social protection system (Lundström and Wijkström, 1995).

Instead, popular mass movements became the dominant feature of the volunteer sector. These movements included the free churches, the modern temperance movement, the labour movement (especially trade unions), consumer cooperatives, the sports movement and adult education institutes. Lundström and Wijkström (1995) suggest that the popular mass movement is a loosely defined type of organisation found in Scandinavian countries, based on the existence of a strong bond and mutual trust between the movement and the general public.

Throughout the last two decades, two significant developments are noticeable. First, the Swedish welfare state, social protection and tax system have undergone a series of transformations and reforms since the end of the 1980s. These reforms, aiming at strengthening 'work incentives' and fostering 'flexibility', could hardly be achieved without consequences perceived as 'rising inequality' (wider dispersion of wages, disposable income and wealth) and 'less security', in particular, a less generous social insurance system and a weakening of employment protection regulations. The structural reforms undertaken have also included a wave of deregulations, liberalisation and privatisations, aimed at exposing previously protected activities to competition. The implementation of these reforms has, to a large extent, involved the dismantling of previously existing public monopolies and an increase in private for-profit and non-profit suppliers. The striving for efficiency-enhancing competition has been manifested not only in a somewhat increasing role for private providers, but also in organisational reforms intended to achieve more competition between different agencies within the public sector, for example, between different schools, hospitals and universities, as well as productivity-enhancing organisational changes (rationalisation, downsizing, management by objectives, NPM and so on) (Anxo, 2013). Second, and perhaps as one of the consequences of this new climate of 'less security', membership in voluntary organisations of a popular mass movement type has significantly diminished. This is assumed to have a significant role on volunteering, since these memberships have traditionally been the bridge into it (Olsson et al, 2005).

Statistics Sweden (2011) estimates that voluntary organisations had an annual turnover of approximately SEK 210 billion (around 21 billion) in 2009. Around 66 per cent of revenues were membership fees, private donations, second-hand sales and sales of services to Swedish municipalities. Donations and transfers from the state corresponded to 34 per cent of total revenue. State funding can be in the form of core funding, activity grants, commission reimbursements and project grants. In addition, purchase of services by Swedish municipalities amounted to around SEK 14 billion, and occurred mainly within the education and social services areas.

Donations and transfers from the state are mainly concentrated in the following sectors: education and research, international, culture and recreation. Most dependent of the public sector are organisations active in the international sector. These voluntary organisations received 90 per cent of their revenue from the state in 2009. The corresponding figure for the education and research sector is 83 per cent. The Swedish state seems to be 'young-friendly' when it comes to donations and transfers to voluntary organisations. Associations with a large participation of older people such as pensioners' organisations, sobriety organisations, culture organisations and religious organisations are not being prioritised by the Swedish public sector (Statistics Sweden, 2011).

The legal framework

The Swedish legal system is based on common law. The volunteer or non-profit organisations are not regulated by an explicit and separate body of laws, and therefore their regulations and status are principally the outcome of courts 'and judicial decisions and case laws' (Lundström and Wijkström, 1995).

In Sweden non-profit organisations constitute legal entities that take principally two basic legal forms: either association or foundation. They are regarded as legal when their members have accepted the association's statutes, which usually takes place at a meeting at which the members elect a committee or board of directors. The statutes should contain the organisation's name, objectives and the set of rules stipulating how decisions will be taken. Members normally influence decisions through participation at the general assemblies.

A non-profit association has to pay income taxes and also social contributions if the association employs workers (payroll tax). But it can be favourably treated in respect of income taxation if the purpose and activities of the association are for the benefit of everyone. Membership is open and earnings cover expenses for activities. Swedish law provides no specific legal framework for older people participating in non-profit organisations as volunteers (Swedish Tax Agency, 2005).

The dimension of volunteer work

Using data from national surveys by Statistic Sweden on active volunteering in 1992, 1998, 2005 and 2009, Svedberg et al (2010) suggest that Swedes' commitment to voluntary work has been rather stable and robust during these years. Around 50 per cent of the Swedish population performed unpaid voluntary work – the participation rate varied between 48 and 52 per cent. The authors also note that this strong level of commitment to voluntary work can only be found in a few other countries.

Formal membership is an important feature of Swedish civil society. It is estimated that non-profit organisations have more than 25 million members out of a population of 9 million. Only around 20 per cent of the Swedish adult population was without formal membership in civil society organisations in 2009 (Statistics Sweden, 2011). The trend is declining, however, since only 10 per cent was without membership in the 1990s (Wijkström, 2004).

Voluntary organisations

Statistics Sweden (2011) estimates that there were around 50,000 voluntary organisations in Sweden in 2009. As many as 211,000 civil society organisations were registered, but only around a fourth had some basic economic activity. There is no comparable statistics over time, but the discourse in Sweden suggests that the sector is expanding, both in numbers of organisations and in importance. The sector engaged 110,000 paid employees and 934,000 unpaid volunteers in 2009. The unpaid volunteers correspond to 53,000 full-time workers.

Most organisations were active in the culture and recreation sector (37 per cent). Many associations were found in development and housing (10 per cent) and business and professional associations (8 per cent). The employment and volunteer structure follows the same pattern. The culture and recreation sector is the most important considering full-time employees (23 per cent) as well as contribution of volunteers (37 per cent). The education and research sector is the second most important in view of employees, while business and professional associations is the runner-up sector (Statistics Sweden, 2011).

The geographical dimension shows that the capital Stockholm is the most important – people living in the capital account for almost 50 per cent of members, 26 per cent of volunteer work and 41 per cent of full-time employees (Statistics Sweden, 2011). These figures seem to indicate that voluntary activity is more common outside the capital.

Wijkström and Einarsson (2011) suggest that the Swedish voluntary sector is undergoing a fast and significant change in line with the overall developments in society. First, a number of new organisations, both non-profit and for-profit, in welfare provision as in healthcare, social services and education, are being established. These organisations are seen as dedicated tools for welfare service provision by the state. Local governments as well as national government are engaged in expanding contracts to these organisations. Second, a number of new advocacy-type organisations are being established. Some of these are focused on global issues such as human rights and environmental groups, while others are special interest organisations in the field of healthcare. These organisations have professional and well-informed members and staff, and the voluntary sector is being rejuvenated. Wijkström and Einarsson believe that not more than 50 per cent of today's voluntary organisations have been active for more than 10 years.

Volunteers by sector, gender and age

As mentioned earlier, Swedish voluntary organisations have a large number of members, but not all are participating actively in the organisations' activities, although the participation rate is high. As shown by Table 9.1, the share of active volunteers of total population aged 16-84 has been stable, at around 50 per cent during 1998-2009. This implies that in 2009 around 3.5 million people provided voluntary work within third sector civil service organisations. Although the share of volunteering of the total population is relatively stable, some alterations can be noted across the various cohorts. First, during the last decade there was a significant decline in the participation of young men. The decline was less dramatic among young women. Second, while the participation of older men aged 65-74 lowered from 2005 to 2009, the rate for women in the same age cohort increased. Third, the participation of both men and women in the oldest age cohort increased.

Table 9.2 shows that as many as 40 per cent of the volunteering Swedes participated in the culture and recreation sector. The second most popular sector is development and housing, where almost 10 per cent of the volunteers worked.

From a gender perspective, men are on average slightly more active than women, and their participation rate is more stable over time.

Table 9.1: Share of the Swedish population volunteering in 1992, 1998, 2005 and 2009, by age and gender (%)

Age	Gender	1992	1998	2005	2009
16-29	Men	51	50	39	40
	Women	42	47	43	39
30-44	Men	61	55	59	64
	Women	51	57	60	54
45-59	Men	54	62	55	56
	Women	45	53	48	36
60-64	Men	44	54	56	54
	Women	38	38	45	38
65-74	Men	38	45	56	51
	Women	33	45	37	44
75-84	Men	–	–	32	38
	Women	–	–	24	32
Total	Men	52	53	53	54
	Women	44	50	49	43

Source: Svedberg et al (2010)

Women increased their rate of participation dramatically from 1992 to 1998 and 2005, but their participation went down again in 2009. The decline is evident in all age cohorts up to the age of 64. But older women have increased their participation. The largest gender differential occurs in the age cohort 45-59 in 2009, where only 36 per cent of women were volunteering compared to 56 per cent of men. The least difference is shown for the youngest cohort.

There are also gender differences in sectoral participation. Olsson (2008) shows that in 2005, men preferred to participate in sports associations (23 per cent), social organisations (20 per cent) and housing associations (9 per cent). In his study, Olsson defines social organisations as organisations that are active in social services, religion and education, as well as parent associations, women's associations and pensioners' organisations. The top three areas of volunteer participation for women were the same, but the ordering was slightly different: social organisations (30 per cent), sports associations (18 per cent) and housing associations (7 per cent). Most striking is that social organisations attract more women than men.

The average time spent on volunteer work has increased over time. In 1992, Swedish volunteers spent 13 hours per month on volunteer unpaid work, but in 2009 they participated with 16 hours per month (Svedberg et al, 2010).

Table 9.3 reveals that voluntary work in Sweden is more self-expressive than philanthropic. It is more common for Swedes to be involved in culture and recreation activities than in classical welfare provision activities in the social services sector. The Johns Hopkins Comparative Non-profit Sector Project estimated that the voice-to-service ratio in Sweden was as high as 107 per cent compared to, for

Table 9.2: Share of Swedish population volunteering in 2005, by sector (%)

Sector	%
Culture and recreation	39.9
Education and research	5.8
Social services	5.6
Environment	6.0
Development and housing	9.8
Law, advocacy and politics	8.5
International	2.8
Religion	8.5
Business and professional association, unions	5.0

Source: Authors' own calculations; Olsson (2008)

instance, 2 per cent in Ireland, 10 per cent in Germany and 58 per cent in the UK. Yet, the voice-to-service ratio was calculated as full-time staff (rather than as volunteers) employed in 'voice' organisations compared with employment (rather than volunteering) in 'service'

Table 9.3: Share of Swedish population volunteering in 2005, by age and primary area of activity (%)

	16-29	30-44	45-59	60-64	65-74	75-84
Culture and recreation						
Culture organisations	6	5	5	4	4	2
Sports associations	20	28	22	7	6	2
Outdoor life associations	2	3	5	3	5	0
Other hobby organisations	6	2	3	4	5	1
Automobile organisations	0	3	3	3	3	1
Pensioners' organisations	0	0	0	0	10	13
Immigrant associations	1	1	0	1	1	0
Women's associations	1	1	0	1	1	0
Education and research						
Parents' associations	1	11	5	0	0	0
Social services						
Humanitarian assistance	2	2	1	5	3	0
Disability associations	1	2	1	4	1	0
Sobriety associations	1	1	1	0	1	3
Independent orders	0	1	1	6	5	2
Voluntary efforts in public sector	3	4	3	2	1	0
Other social organisations	0	0	1	0	1	0
Environment	0	0	1	1	1	0
Development and housing						
Housing associations	2	9	11	12	6	3
Law, advocacy and politics						
Political party	1	1	2	5	1	1
International						
Peace organisations	1	1	2	5	1	1
Religion						
Swedish church parish	2	3	3	5	6	4
Other Christian parish	1	3	3	4	6	4
Business and professional associations, unions						
Cooperatives	0	5	3	3	1	0
Trade unions	1	5	6	8	1	0
Shareholders' associations	0	0	1	1	0	0

Source: Olsson et al (2005)

organisations. Voice organisations were active in civic and advocacy, environment, business and professional associations sectors. Service organisations are instead principally found in healthcare, social services and education (Wijkström, 2004). Svedberg et al (2010) suggest that voice organisations also continued to be important in 2009 for volunteer work. Almost 80 per cent of the volunteers participated in boards and/or did administrative work; only 19 per cent performed direct social efforts.

Table 9.3 displays the age distribution of volunteer work by type of activities for 2005. As shown by the table, a strong connection between age and participation in some type of organisations becomes visible. Sports associations attract mainly young people. People are active in parents' associations while their children attend schools. Participation in pensioners' organisations starts after the age of 65. While the major pensioners' organisations had more than 600,000 members, only 140,000 of these were active in 2005. Housing associations and trade unions are attractive to people from their middle ages to age of retirement. The trade unions also exhibit a large differential between total membership and active members. The trade unions had 3.4 million members, but only 280,000 were active volunteers in 2005.

There is a strong correlation between educational attainment and voluntary work. The higher the education, the larger the likelihood that a person performs unpaid volunteer work. Furthermore, white-collar workers are more inclined to volunteer than blue-collar workers. In addition, people with a higher income participate more in volunteer activities. These factors explaining participation in voluntary work have changed over time. Explanatory factors such as high education and high income were more important in the 1990s than in the 2000s, while parents' engagement in voluntary work became more important in the latter decade. Thus, a cultural and social inheritance seems to increase in importance (Svedberg et al, 2010).

As for considerations based on ethnicity, first-generation male immigrants participate to a smaller extent in the voluntary sector. While 53 per cent of Swedish males performed voluntary unpaid work, the corresponding number was 38 per cent for males born in other Nordic countries, 20 per cent for men from other European countries and 40 per cent for men from non-European countries. The participation of second-generation immigrants did not differ from the average (Olsson et al, 2005). The differences for female immigrants are less pronounced. Actually, Nordic female immigrants are more active (52 per cent) than the Swedes (49 per cent), while other female immigrants were slightly less active (37 per cent).

This leads us to consider that the prototypical Swedish volunteer is a man or woman in the midst of their career and well integrated into society. The person has children, is a native-born Swede and originates from a family with a tradition for civic engagement. In addition, the typical volunteer is well educated. As many as 32 per cent have a university education, 46 per cent secondary school and the remaining 22 per cent compulsory school only (Olsson et al, 2005).

Participation of older volunteers

In 2005, the prototypical older volunteer was 69 years of age. His/her educational status was relatively high, but slightly lower than for the average volunteer. As many as 63 per cent of older volunteers had merely compulsory school education, and 21 per cent had a university education. The older volunteers consider their health status to be good and they are outward-oriented in the sense that they often participate in informal networks and meet friends (Jegermalm and Jeppsson Grassman, 2009).

Olsson et al (2005) also show that although the rate of participation in volunteer activities among Swedes declines with age, older volunteers spend on average more time doing unpaid voluntary work. While the largest participation rate is found among Swedes in their middle age, they dedicate only 9 hours per month to volunteer activities. On the other hand, active pensioners between 60 and 74 years of age dedicated 20 hours each month.

Table 9.1 above shows that both men and women's participation falls when they get older, even if the participation rates of the oldest generations can be considered high compared with most of the European countries. In 2009, men's participation rate declined from 54 per cent (60-64 age cohort) to 38 per cent for the oldest cohort, 75-84. Women's participation actually increased to 44 per cent for the age cohort 65-74 from 38 per cent for the 60-64 cohort. Participation then fell to 32 per cent for the oldest ages.

Older volunteers are more involved in pensioners' organisations, church organisations, housing associations and sports associations (see Table 9.3). As many as 10-13 per cent of Swedes in the age group 65–84 volunteered for pensioners' organisations, indicating that volunteering among peers may fill in their desire of informal networking and of meeting friends (Jegermalm and Jeppsson Grassman, 2009), once retired. While there is a general tendency of a decrease in participation in most of the activities, an interesting exception is that volunteer participation in parishes stays about the same at all ages. This may mean that the effect of religiosity (or faith) on volunteering is greater than the age effect.

Naturally, people's interest in volunteering in different sectors depends on where they are in their life cycle. For instance, adults having children participating in sports activities appears to be an important factor explaining the active involvement of citizens in local sports associations. Thus prime adults are overrepresented in these associations and the lower participation rate for older citizens is not due to barriers. Life cycle interests explain in the same way the very limited volunteering in pensioners' organisations of citizens who have still not reached retirement age.

From an organisational point of view, Andersson et al (2011) interviewed representatives of nine volunteer organisations in Sweden, and all were very positive about involving older volunteers in their organisations, especially since they could provide important experience and knowledge. Yet some negative aspects linked to the involvement of older volunteers were also found (see also Chapter Eleven of this book). Specific age-related initiatives, for example, in the fields of recruitment, retainment, training, development, flexible practice, job design, well-being and generational relations, were not common in Swedish voluntary organisations.

The largest organisations involving older volunteers in Sweden are the Swedish National Pensioners' Organisation (PRO) and Swedish Pensioners' Association (SPF). PRO has more than 400,000 members. It was founded in 1942, when many developers of the major national popular movements at the turn of the century retired. SPF was founded in 1939 and has around 225,000 members. Both organisations are politically and religiously independent. They are typical interest organisations with an advocacy role in the sense that they look after the interests of senior citizens in various national matters such as pensions, right to work, housing, taxes and healthcare. The organisations also play an important role as social networks, since they have local chapters spread throughout the country, where senior citizens can meet new friends at social gatherings, travel, study, sing in choirs, exercise or take part in other activities.

Older people's participation in voluntary organisations: opportunities and restrictions

This section includes a discussion on past developments and the present situation concerning opportunities and restrictions in older volunteers' participation in the voluntary sector. The discussion is, of course, affected by ongoing modifications of the Swedish welfare state.

Opportunities and restrictions for volunteering for older people

Svedberg et al (2010) report that Swedes have become more positive about voluntary work. In 1995, 74 per cent considered engagement in the voluntary sector a good way of active participation in a democratic society. This percentage increased to 88 per cent in 2009. There is no information available if older people would have a different point of view, but we would find that very unlikely. Indeed, and as a matter of fact, senior citizens are becoming more active, more interested and more knowledgeable, and the winding down of interest occurs later and later in life, which has positive effects on their volunteering. The only hindrances to senior citizens' participation in the voluntary sector seem to be illness and disability, where there appears to be a self-selection process among the elders with a group of healthier older people active in providing volunteer services, while unhealthy retirees might be less active and more in need of social services. Jegermalm and Jeppson Grassman (2009) report that 80 per cent of the volunteers over the age of 60 considered themselves healthy. These volunteers were also socially active, belonging to networks and meeting friends and family on a regular basis.

Turning to the meso and macro levels, Sweden has a large vibrant civil society, and there are no legal restrictions on older people's engagement in the non-profit and volunteer sector. Participation of older people in volunteering (at least until the age of 74, when health problems are still absent), in all, does not diverge too much from the participation rates of other age segments of the population (see Table 9.1), and so neither policy makers nor voluntary organisations have felt a need for specific programmes for older volunteers. Nevertheless, recent developments of Swedish society (for example, the NPM reform) have fostered the role of volunteering in traditional welfare services, and this may indirectly strengthen the role of older volunteers in the future, since they tend to participate to a great extent in activities within the social services sector through, for example, independent orders, sobriety associations and parishes (Table 9.3).

Older people between employment and volunteering

Sweden has a strong work orientation. In 1996, almost 78 per cent of the Swedish population in the age cohort 50-65 claimed that they would enjoy having a paid job even if they did not need the money (ISSP, 1997). In 2011 the employment rate for Swedes aged 55-64 was 72 per cent, while it was 12 per cent for the age cohort 65-74. Men participated only slightly more in the labour market then women. Men aged 55-64 had an employment rate of 76 per cent compared to 69 per cent for women. The corresponding figure for Swedes aged 65-74 was 16 per cent for men and 8 per cent for women (Statistics Sweden, 2012).

Anxo and Ericson (2010) suggest that there are two central features in the exit pattern of older workers in Sweden: the high and continuous female participation rate and the similar gender employment profiles across the life course. When studying employment rates from 1995, the authors show that there is an increasing trend for older Swedes. The trend is most evident for workers in the age bracket 60-64, for both men and women. The increase is mainly due to changes in the pension system, where the state is encouraging the working population to postpone their retirement and maybe even to continue working part time after official retirement. Jegermalm and Jeppsson Grassman (2009) observed that of the older volunteers aged 60-84, 34 per cent reported that they still had gainful employment.

Considering the corresponding availability of older people to the voluntary organisations, there seems to be some counterbalancing effects. The ageing population in Sweden, together with the postponement of retirement and the increase of older workers' employment rates, may be supposed to have a negative affect on the volunteering of older people, but this should not be taken for granted. Indeed, the supposed negative effect is not visible in the activity rates of older volunteers presented in Table 9.1. Rather, Sweden presents high rates of both volunteering and employment rates at all ages, suggesting that perhaps support for older people to remain in paid work may have a positive impact on their volunteering (Warburton and Jeppsson Grassman, 2011), even if corporate employee volunteer programmes (that is, a way to reinforce the positive link between employment and volunteering) do not seem to be particularly widespread in Sweden. On the other hand, as also previously mentioned, older volunteers spend more hours on volunteer activities than younger ones. Thus another explanation may be that the overall positive effect of a healthier and more interested group of senior citizens may outweigh a supposed negative impact of the increase of the labour force participation of older workers.

Older people between family care and volunteering

The nature of the Swedish welfare model implies that few older people are caught between family care and volunteering, as the preferred type of elder care in Sweden is formal, with nursing homes/residential care and public/private service providers playing an important role (Eurobarometer, 2007). There is a tendency, however, that the public sector is moving away from more expensive residential care towards home care services. During the time period 2000-06, older people living in nursing homes went down 17 per cent to around 196,000, while public/private home service provision increased 19 per cent to 280,000 beneficiaries (National Board of Health and Welfare, 2007).

In 2009, only 5 per cent of the population took care informally of a person with special care needs in their home. The level of participation was similar for men and women, but while men spent 36 hours per month, women spent 153 hours (Svedberg et al, 2010). Thus, relative to this albeit limited Swedish population segment of informal caregivers, it may be women in particular who face difficulties in reconciling caregiving with other activities, including volunteering.

Improving the match between supply of older candidates with the demand of voluntary organisations: future perspectives

Andersson et al (2011) report that Swedish volunteer organisations do not experience difficulties in recruiting older volunteers with specific experience or knowledge. Thus, there is no current matching problem between needs and the availability of older volunteers. Developments on the Swedish civil society scene might change this situation. The non-profit sector is becoming more complex and dynamic. New organisations are being established, while older organisations are being transformed. New opportunities in welfare provision such as healthcare, social services and education are arising, and, on the one hand, as anticipated earlier (see p 209), this may be beneficial to the volunteering of older people. On the other hand, new advocacy types of organisations are being established, with demands on professional and well-informed members and staff (Wijkström, 2004; Wijkström and Einarsson, 2011). Thus, it is expected that non-profit organisations will demand more and more well educated volunteers, and a matching problem might occur for older volunteers in the future, in some sectors or activities, since they are those less educated ones, on average (see p 207).

Even if this possible future mismatch is not currently being addressed at the institutional level, some interesting insights on how to possibly manage it can be drawn at the organisational (or meso) level, using a parallel of what is being done to overcome this kind of mismatch in the labour market. In general, there are a number of companies in Sweden that are specialists in labour market matching, and there is, of course, no hindrance for these companies to also engage in match-making in the volunteer market. Indeed, recently, a non-profit organisation was established aiming at matching potential volunteers (by empowering them and improving their knowledge and capacities) with non-profit organisations. In this case, it is believed, however, that the establishment of this organisation was merely driven by the youth unemployment situation in Sweden: when traditional work is unavailable, young people become more interested in volunteering to have more social contacts and to improve their work situation. Yet similar initiatives may be established in the future, to also foster older people's involvement in volunteering.

Conclusions

The typical older volunteer is around 70 years of age. He/she is more educated than older non-volunteers, but less educated than younger volunteers. He/she has good health and is outward-oriented in the sense that he/she often participates in informal networks and meets friends. Older volunteers are mostly involved in pensioners' organisations, church organisations and other kinds of associations providing social services, housing and sports. Their participation rate is considered high compared with most of the European countries. Sweden offers more opportunities than restrictions for older people to be engaged in volunteer activities. The only hindrances seem to be illness and disability. Some self-selection process seems to be at play with a group of healthier older people being active while unhealthy retirees are less active.

Sweden has a large non-profit and volunteer sector that is well integrated into Swedish society. The majority of volunteer organisations are voice/self-expressive organisations and less philanthropic. It should be noted, however, that Swedish society is changing, and the current government seems to be willing to continue with the current policy of transforming the welfare state, in particular by opening up previously sheltered sectors to competition and allowing a greater diversity of providers of welfare services including non-profit organisations. That is, more welfare service-oriented associations are being established in areas such as childcare, care of older people and education. New special interest organisations are also being established in different fields, for example, in healthcare for people with various disabilities. This may have both positive and negative aspects to manage in the future, relative to the volunteering of older people. On the one hand, this may foster their volunteering since they tend to participate more than younger people in altruistic-type volunteering. On the other hand, these developments might indicate that the volunteer organisations will demand more well-educated volunteers in the future, providing a new challenge both for the organisations and for older volunteers.

In this context, the impact of the main external aspects on the volunteering of older people seems to be favourable. Sweden has a strong work orientation and presents high rates of both employment rates and volunteering. Thus, the current tendency that older people postpone their retirement may actually interact positively on their volunteering. On the other hand, family care of older people does not seem to affect the volunteering of older people, since care to older people is, to a great extent, guaranteed by formal services.

Note
[1] For research assistance, we thank Osvaldo Salas.

References
Andersson, P., Anxo, D. and Salas, O. (2011) *Opportunities for older people in the Swedish civil society: Experience from nine case studies*, Kalmar: CAFO, Linnaeus University.

Anxo, D. (2013) 'Early fiscal consolidation and negotiated flexibility in Sweden: A fair way out of the crisis', in D. Vaughan-Whitehead (ed) *The public sector shock*, Cheltenham: Edward Elgar, pp 301-19.

Anxo, D. and Ericson T. (2010) *Activity rates in the labour market and civil society: Sweden*, Working Paper 3, Kalmar: CAFO, Linnaeus University.

Anxo, D. and Niklasson, H. (2006) 'The Swedish model in turbulent times: decline or renaissance?', *International Labour Review*, vol 145, no 4, pp 339-71.

Esping-Andersen, G. (2003) *Why we need a new welfare state*, Oxford: Oxford University Press.

Eurobarometer (2007) *Health and long-term care in the European Union*, Special Eurobarometer 283/Wave 67.3, TNS Opinion & Social (ec.europa.eu/public_opinion/archives/ebs/ebs_283_en.pdf).

ISSP (International Social Survey Programme) (1997) 'Work Orientations II', Mannheim: ISSP (www.gesis.org/issp/issp-modules-profiles/work-orientations/1997).

Jegermalm, M. and Jeppsson Grassman, E. (2009) 'Caregiving and volunteering among older people in Sweden – Prevalence and profiles', *Journal of Aging & Social Policy*, vol 21, no 4, pp 352-73.

Lundström, T. and Svedberg, L. (2003) 'The voluntary sector in a social democratic welfare state – The case of Sweden', *Journal of Social Policy*, vol 32, no 2, pp 217-38.

Lundström, T. and Wijkström, F. (1995) *Defining the non-profit sector: Sweden*, Working Papers of the Johns Hopkins Comparative Non-profit Sector Project, No 16, Baltimore, MD: The Johns Hopkins Institute for Policy Studies.

National Board of Health and Welfare (2007) *Care and services to elderly persons 2006*, Stockholm (www.socialstyrelsen.se/Lists/Artikelkatalog/Attachments/9341/2007-44-2007443.pdf).

Olsson, L. (2008) *Frivilligt arbete bland äldre och hälsa – Medborgarundersökning* [*Voluntary work among older people and health – A national survey*], Vårdalstiftelsen: Ersta Sköndal Högskola.

Olsson, L., Jeppsson Grassman, E. and Svedberg, L. (2005) *Medborgarnas insatser och engagemang i civilsamhället – några grundläggande uppgifter från en ny befolkningsstudie* [*Citizen input and participation in civil society – Some basic information from a new population study*], Working Paper, Sköndalsinstitutet: Ersta Sköndal Högskola.

Statistics Sweden (2011) *The civil society – An assignment from the government with surveys from Statistics Sweden*, Stockholm (www.scb.se/statistik/_publikationer/OV9999_2010A01_BR_X105BR1101.pdf).

Statistics Sweden (2012) *Labour force survey 2011*, Stockholm (www.scb.se/Statistik/AM/AM0401/2011A01/AM0401_2011A01_SM_AM12SM1201.pdf).

Svedberg, L., von Essen, J. and Jegermalm, M. (2010) *Svenskars engagemang är större än någonsin* [*Swedes' commitment is stronger than ever*], Working Paper 68, Vårdalstiftelsen: Ersta Sköndal Högskola (www.esh.se/fileadmin/erstaskondal/ESH_Gemensamt/Arbetsrapporter/arbetsrapport_68.pdf).

Swedish Tax Agency (2005) *Handledning för stiftelser och ideella föreningar* [*Guidelines for foundations and nonprofit associations*], SKV 327, vol 6, Stockholm.

Warburton, J. and Jeppsson Grassman, E. (2011) 'Variations in voluntary association involvement by seniors across different social welfare regimes', *International Journal of Social Welfare*, vol 20, no 2, pp 180-91.

Wijkström, F. (2004) 'The role of civil society – The case of Sweden in international comparison', Paper presented at the 1st International Korean Studies Workshop on Civil Society & Consolidating Democracy in Comparative Perspective, Yonsei University.

Wijkström, F. and Einarsson, T. (2011) *Från nationalstat till näringsliv? Det civila samhällets organisationsliv i förändring* [*From state to business activities? The change of the organisation of civil society*], Stockholm: SSE Institute for Research and European Civil Society Press.

TEN

Older volunteers in the Netherlands: new challenges to an old tradition

Joop Schippers and Wieteke Conen

Introduction

When Esping-Andersen (1990) wrote his famous study on the different types of welfare states, he characterised the Netherlands as a member of the conservative, corporatist family of continental welfare states in Europe. Based on the image of the 1960s and 1970s, this qualification may have been correct. But during the 1980s one could already see the start of a process of the Netherlands drifting away from its continental anchors. During the 1990s it looked like the Netherlands evolved into a mixture of the social democratic and liberal welfare state model, turning the ideas developed by Giddens (1998) about a 'third way' into reality. However, after the turn of the century and the rise of populist right-wing political parties, the welfare state came under attack. During the last decade privatisation, market orientation and own risk and responsibility became leading notions with respect to the reorientation of the welfare state. Especially after the budget cut-backs related to the banking and Euro crisis during a long period after 2008 the Dutch welfare state – or what is left of it – will be hardly more than a shadow of what it used to be in the 1980s. In particular, there will be major cut-backs in the field of care, compelling people in need of help to rely more on family members or other people from their social networks.

Compared to other European countries, unemployment has been and still is relatively low, even though during 2012 it increased rapidly. Unemployment hits older workers particularly hard. From all vacancies filled during 2011, only 2 per cent went to people over 55 years old. So, older people becoming unemployed experience more and more that they are likely to remain unemployed for the rest of their life. A growing share of these long-term unemployed start to shift focus and make inquiries as to whether there is an option to do voluntary work. Even though this is unpaid work, it offers them the opportunity to do something useful in society, gives them a goal in life again, and adds to their social network.

Despite growing unemployment, labour market participation in the Netherlands is still high, especially for women. When it comes to the share of women in employment, the Netherlands is close to the Scandinavian frontrunner countries. Yet most women (two thirds to three quarters) work in part-time jobs. This used to allow women to take up family responsibilities quite easily, and also to spend much more time on voluntary activities. As the traditional breadwinner wages for men have almost completely disappeared, and individualisation has moved forward, it is now more or less the natural thing that families consist of two earners holding one-and-a-half to one-and-three-quarters of a job. Despite the growing participation of women in the Dutch labour market, there is still a considerable degree of labour market segregation. Many women work in care, education and public health, while the Netherlands has one of the lowest shares of women in technical jobs of all European Union (EU) and Organisation for Economic Co-operation and Development (OECD) countries.

Of course, this evolution has not passed by the voluntary sector. Many organisations that have lost (part, and often most of) their public subsidies during the last decade had to fire professionals on their payroll and became more dependent on voluntary workers. We see this, for instance, in museums, libraries, scouting and welfare organisations. Due to budget cuts many primary schools would not survive without parents helping with reading, lunch break supervision or even swimming lessons. Or at least, they would have to stick to core activities such as reading, writing and arithmetic. A similar picture can be drawn with respect to older people in need of care. Privatised home care workers only have a few minutes to wash people who are not able to take a shower independently. So again, it is volunteers who devote their time and attention to older people in need of care to guarantee them at least some quality of life. Even though this is not the largest voluntary sector in terms of participants and hours (as we show later, see p 226), it is the sector where the need for voluntary workers and the impact of voluntary work is the largest. In sport, the absence of volunteers to run a canteen would simply imply that there would be no drinks after a match. In schools and in care, the absence of volunteers could imply a breakdown in the sector.

What has not changed, despite the rough times the Dutch welfare state is going through, is the spirit of voluntary workers and the commitment of the Dutch population to spend part of their time on voluntary work. Throughout the period 1997–2008 the share of the 18+ population participating in organised voluntary work was around 45 per cent, with a slightly decreasing trend (from 47 per cent in 1997 to 43 per cent in 2008). During the same period the share of the adult population participating in informal help (mostly care) remained constant, at 30 per cent. Altogether, almost 60 per cent of the adult Dutch population participates in some form of voluntary work. However, other sources report different figures, and we come back to this later (see p 223). It is not known and recorded in the Netherlands how much voluntary work contributes to gross domestic product (GDP). The same holds for the number of voluntary organisations. As a matter of fact, most voluntary workers work in mixed organisations, that is, organisations that employ a number of paid employees and a number of voluntary workers. This mix ranges from organisations with only a few paid employees and mostly voluntary workers to organisations with mostly paid employees and only few additional voluntary workers.

Even though the share of people participating in voluntary work has been relatively stable, the hours spent on voluntary work has been affected by changes in the labour market. The most marked development of the last few decades in the Dutch labour market has been the emergence of the Dutch working wife and mother. It looks as if this increase in women's labour market participation has reduced women's opportunities to spend time on voluntary work. While the average number of hours for men remained the same over the period 2001–09, at 5.5 hours, women's hours spent on voluntary work dropped from 4.9 to 4.3 during the same period.

In the meantime, even though it is difficult to establish, there is some evidence that the role of voluntary work in society has changed over time. While in the past voluntary work was something that had to be done and was done primarily based on feelings of social responsibility and altruistic motives, it looks like enjoyment and 'expressing yourself' has become more important, at least if we take the increasing share of voluntary workers indicating that they *always* enjoy their voluntary activities as a proper indicator. That is, voluntary work in the Netherlands is on the verge of changing from being predominantly 'philanthropic/altruistic' to being predominantly 'self-centred/self-expressive' in nature. We discuss this issue into some more detail later. Here we can already mention that this tendency is particularly strong among older volunteers. Their participation in voluntary work has increased substantially over the last decade, especially for the two age categories, 65-75 and over 75 years old.

To a large extent people's participation in voluntary work reflects their life course position. While adolescents are overrepresented in voluntary youth work, and parents with young children in voluntary work at school and in sports organisations, older volunteers are often found in care, cultural, philosophical and religious organisations.

This chapter now continues with a brief description of the roots and history of voluntary work in the Netherlands and its current legal framework. In the second section we present statistics on participation in voluntary work in general and then focus on the participation of older people. In the third section we discuss opportunities and restrictions for older people's participation in voluntary work in the Netherlands, while the fourth section looks at future developments. The chapter ends with a conclusion.

The Dutch tradition of voluntary action

Volunteer work in the Netherlands has followed the pattern of pillarisation that is characteristic for politics, labour, care and education (see, for example, Lijphart, 1968). As part of the emancipation process that started in the middle of the 19th century, different religious groups developed their own institutional structures in society. With the start of the emancipation of the lower social classes and the growing social democratic movement during the first quarter of the 20th century, a social democratic pillar was erected next to the Roman Catholic and Protestant pillars. Each pillar included all relevant institutions for different stages of the life course: schools, hospitals, volunteer organisations, trade unions, political parties, papers, broadcasting companies, old age homes, and so on. So, if you were a Roman Catholic you could live your life completely within the Roman Catholic pillar. On Sunday you went to church, you read a Catholic newspaper, listened to the Roman Catholic radio service and sent your children to a Roman Catholic school or even university. If you belonged to the social democratic pillar you were member of the Social Democratic Party, went to a Socialist holiday camp in summer and spent your old age in an old-age home called 'Aurora'. As a result, volunteer work remained segmented along the lines of the Dutch pillars. And even as the pillar system more or less collapsed during the 1970s and 1980s, many Dutch volunteer organisations still bear the marks of their origin. Even though many of them have become 'neutral' organisations in a formal sense (with the articles of association no longer pointing to specific religious or political principles), most still 'breathe' their traditional values.

Because all pillars devoted themselves to keeping as many societal activities within their own control – and out of state control – voluntary work in the Netherlands has expanded enormously during the course of the 20th century. Voluntary work was also partly seen as an instrument to ensure cohesion within the pillar. If organisations belonging to the pillar looked after you in times of need, and offered you social support and 'cosiness', this lowered the risk of people turning their back on the pillar. So, traditionally, the Netherlands has a high level of volunteering compared with other European countries. Most volunteer work takes place on the level of NGOs (non-governmental organisations; in Dutch, *maatschappelijk middenveld*), and within relatively small organisations. From a governance perspective these organisations are independent of the government, but particularly during the construction period of the modern welfare state during the 1960s and 1970s many volunteer organisations (for instance, organisations dealing with the help of women who have been victims of sexual abuse or organisations helping ex-convicts to start up a new life) became more or less dependent on government subsidies, either from the national or local government. However, the trend towards reduction of the welfare state and the introduction of market principles in the world of volunteer work has (especially after 2003, when the government realised a first series of major budget cuts) resulted in a substantial reduction of government subsidies for volunteer organisations. Some of them have had to close or scale down, while others are still busy finding other sources of finance, for example, sponsoring by private firms and companies. One of the consequences of the budget problems of many NGOs is that the balance between paid professional workers and unpaid voluntary workers in these organisations has shifted, and organisations have to rely more on voluntary workers. As a result, the professionals have less time for coaching and counselling volunteers, and often the tasks, responsibilities and workload of voluntary workers has increased. This may particularly harm older voluntary workers if they depend more on the counselling and support of the professionals. Moreover, several organisations working with large numbers of voluntary workers had to decide to end their activities, because they were no longer able to pay their professional workers who constituted the backbone of the organisation and organised the activities of the voluntary workers (for instance, organisations promoting women's emancipation or organisations trying to combat older workers' discrimination). Of course, this problem is felt less in an organisation with a large number of professionals and a small share of voluntary workers.

The legal framework

The Netherlands does not have a specific law on volunteers or voluntary work. Yet a lot of laws designed for other purposes also apply to voluntary work and volunteer organisations. Organisations working with volunteers report that they have to deal with:

- fiscal laws, for example, when they want to reimburse volunteers' travel costs;
- the law on social benefits (*Algemene Bijstandswet*), for example, if a volunteer is on benefits and the organisation wants to award him/ her an allowance for all the time and effort the volunteer puts into the volunteer work. If the allowance exceeds a certain amount of money or is not 'labelled' properly, the volunteer runs the risk of losing part of his/her benefits (Pennings, 2001);
- the law on social support (*Wet Maatschappelijke Ondersteuning*) that grants people social support from local government. This law is relevant when voluntary work (partly) overlaps with professional services offered by/paid for by local government;
- the law on working conditions (*Arbo-wet*). Rules on safety, working hours and working conditions also serve to protect and apply to volunteers;
- the law on catering (*Horecawet*). This law applies, for example, in case a volunteer is behind the bar or working in a canteen or a kitchen with food;
- liability law. If a volunteer acts on behalf of the organisation and causes damage doing his/her work, the organisation is responsible (and will probably opt for a liability insurance);
- health and safety regulation, including, for example, rules on the use of tobacco and alcohol.

None of these laws and regulations makes a distinction with respect to age, and so they do have not a different impact on younger and on older volunteers.

For many organisations, complying with all these legal rules brings along a lot of administration and administrative burden. For a long time there has been discussion on whether all these laws and regulations must also apply to organisations working with volunteers. In many cases they have been developed for a professional setting and not for the informal setting of many volunteer organisations. Yet public authorities argue that, for example, when a volunteer is working with a group of children, the necessity of complying with all kinds of safety and protection rules is as important in case a professional is working with that same group. So in such cases the law does not allow any concessions to the 'normal' legal rules, and treats volunteer organisations the same as professional organisations.

A specific problem is the taxation of volunteer allowances (ANBI, 2010). According to many experts in the field, the fiscal exemption for these allowances is too low. In many cases volunteers have additional costs resulting from the voluntary work they do (for example, travelling costs or costs from special clothing/shoes, materials they use). Reimbursing these costs (completely) often results in allowances that exceed the exemption limit (Lankers, nd). This implies that the volunteers have to pay taxes over their allowance (Kollen, 2007). Consequently, they not only have to spend time on their voluntary work, but also their own financial means. In some cases it has been reported that volunteers had to give up their voluntary work because they could no longer afford it financially.

The dimension of volunteer work

Different statistical sources report different participation rates for voluntary work. The differences partly result from the use of (slightly) different questions and definitions, but also from the use of different samples of the population. Of course, one may get different answers depending on whether the question relates to voluntary work 'during the last year' or 'during the last week'. Moreover, asking for the main activity during a particular period of time may result in different findings than counting all forms of time use. Table 10.1 includes participation figures in voluntary work of the Dutch adult population for the first decade of the 21st century from different statistical sources.

The CBS (*Centraal Bureau voor de Statistiek* – Statistics Netherlands) figures from the statistics on living conditions in the Netherlands are closest to those frequently reported in Eurobarometer. We cannot explain why the figures from the Labour Force Survey are so much lower than those from the other studies. Even though the levels of participation in voluntary work differ between the various statistical sources over time, all sources show a rather stable picture.

Table 10.1: Participation of the Dutch population in volunteer activities (%)

Different studies	2001	2002	2003	2004	2005	2006	2007	2008	2009
GIN (Giving in the Netherlands)									
Percentage of the 16+ population that has participated in voluntary work for civil organisations during the last year		46		41		42		45	
SCP (2005) (Time Use Studies)									
Percentage of the 16+ population that has participated in voluntary work for civil organisations during the last year					30	32			
CBS (Statistics Netherlands, Living conditions in the Netherlands)									
Percentage of the inhabitants of the Netherlands of 18+ years that has participated in organised volunteer work	43	42	42	43				44	42
CBS (Statistics Netherlands, Labour Force Survey)									
Percentage of the inhabitants of the Netherlands of 18+ years who participate in voluntary work and indicate that they do this within an organisation	18	19	20	21	21	22	21	21	22

Voluntary organisations

In the Netherlands there is no registration of voluntary organisations, and their number is not known and recorded (see p 219). Voluntary organisations – just like other private firms, NGOs or publicly financed organisations – can have different legal statuses, varying from foundations or cooperations to different forms of corporation. So, from the legal form (and that is the only way organisations are registered in the Netherlands), one cannot tell whether and to what extent an organisation works with volunteers, and for this reason it is also difficult to get a clear picture of employees working in these kinds of organisation. As already mentioned, most organisations that work with voluntary workers can be characterised as mixed organisations: they employ both paid professional workers and unpaid voluntary workers. Of course, there are differences with respect to the role of voluntary workers. For instance, in a hospital or in a school paid professional workers do the majority of tasks. Voluntary workers have additional tasks, which usually do not involve the core business of the organisation. Yet voluntary workers are often characterised as the cement of organisations: without them filling the gaps between the bricks of the organisation, the quality of the organisation's performance would be far worse. In other organisations, such as a brass band or an association that organises the annual celebration of a carnival or the queen's birthday, the emphasis is on voluntary workers. Sometimes these associations work without or with only one or two professionals. However, the law does not make a distinction between organisations – be it associations, foundations, corporations – based on the question as to whether they do or do not employ voluntary workers only. As an association of voluntary workers they still have to sign a memorandum of association with a notary and register with the local Chamber of Commerce before they can act legally.

A good impression of the wide variety of organisations working with voluntary workers can be found at http://vrijwilligerswerk. startpagina.nl (voluntary work start page). This serves as a kind of meeting point for organisations in search of voluntary workers and voluntary workers looking for interesting voluntary 'jobs', and shows that voluntary organisations can be found throughout the country. Most organisations that post their job openings on this website belong to the welfare and care field. One should realise, however, that sports clubs, schools, political parties, religious organisations or unions can recruit voluntary workers from their own members, parents and so on, and may not need this web page.

Most voluntary organisations can be found in cities and larger villages, depending, of course, on the composition of the population. People with children tend to live more often in the highly urbanised western part of the Netherlands. So voluntary organisations related to education and sports are more often found there. The same holds for cultural voluntary organisations, often depending on higher educated volunteers. Logically, an organisation such as the traditional Federation of Rural Women, which originated from farmers' wives who wanted to exchange recipes and knitting patterns, but who also wanted to escape once in a while from the daily worries of their work, has more branches in the rural areas of the Netherlands.

Volunteers by sector, gender and age

Based on the Labour Force Survey by Statistics Netherlands, Table 10.2 summarises how many men and women of various age categories were active in voluntary work in different sectors in 2009. The table also includes the average number of hours participants spent per week on their voluntary work.

Table 10.2: Participants in voluntary work (n, ×1,000) and their number of hours (H) spent per week on volunteering in different sectors, by gender and age, 2009

	Total		School, youth work, scouting		Care and nursing		Sports, hobby, culture		Church, philosophy, religion		Union, political parties, action and lobby groups		Other		Share of volunteers (%)[a]
	n	H	n	H	n	H	n	H	n	H	n	H	n	H	
Men															
Total	1,368	5.5	185	4.1	125	5.5	641	4.8	255	4.5	63	5.7	257	5.8	22
18-25	104	5.1	25	5.5	.	.	56	4.1	10	3.7	.	.	13	7.2	15
25-35	152	4.4	30	3.6	6	6.3	75	3.9	23	4.4	5	5.6	24	4.6	15
35-45	253	4.0	46	2.6	11	5.0	127	3.8	35	3.9	7	3.9	45	4.0	20
45-55	298	4.7		3.5	21	5.1	162	4.3	46	3.5	13	4.5	44	5.2	24
55-65	291	6.8	26	5.3	37	6.1	133	6.2	56	5.1	19	4.8	64	6.2	27
65-75	193	7.7	15	7.1	32	4.8	69	7.1	60	5.6	11	7.2	43	7.3	29
75+	76	6.4	–	–	14	6.6	17	5.4	24	4.0	5	10.0	23	6.5	19
Women															
Total	1,470	4.3	344	3.0	307	4.1	370	3.7	329	3.6	41	3.6	292	4.3	23
18-25	91	3.8	22	3.9	10	5.0	38	2.8	14	3.2	–	–	12	4.1	13
25-35	164	3.1	49	2.9	16	2.4	45	3.1	30	2.6	–	–	34	2.8	17
35-45	343	3.0	167	2.2	34	2.5	82	2.9	59	2.6	6	2.4	56	3.0	28
45-55	311	4.2	67	3.2	58	4.2	96	3.8	71	3.3	10	3.7	53	4.1	26
55-65	290	5.6	27	5.7	94	4.5	67	5.0	70	4.8	9	4.2	66	5.1	27
65-75	186	5.3	7	3.8	67	4.4	32	4.2	56	3.5	5	5.3	53	5.7	26
75+	85	5.4	6	4.0	28	4.7	10	4.9	29	5.1	–	–	18	5.5	14

Note: [a] Percentages refer to the whole surveyed population of the same age.

Source: www.statline.nl

The table shows that the sports, hobby and culture sector is by far the largest when it comes to the number of voluntary workers, with over one million participants. The school, youth work and scouting sector, the church, philosophy, religion sector and that of other organisations are equally large, with between 500,000 and 600,000 voluntary workers. The care and nursing sector counts about 430,000 voluntary workers, while the union, political parties and action and lobby groups sector is the smallest, with just over 100,000 voluntary workers.

As with paid work in the labour market, voluntary work shows a high degree of gender segregation. Voluntary work at school is much more women's domain, in particular women aged between 35 and 55, than that of men. The same holds, even more so, for care and nursing, but here the focus is more on older women. To a large extent the sports, hobby and culture sector is a male domain. Within this broad sector there is segregation again between sport where men are overrepresented, and culture, which is much more a female domain.

As already mentioned in the introduction to this chapter, participation in voluntary work follows the average life course pattern of individuals. At younger ages they are busy with school or working on their career, so there is relatively little time for voluntary work. Among the younger generations the sports sector appears to be the most favoured one. After people have started a family, many women engage in voluntary work at school, while men make themselves available for various leisure activities, such as for the sports, hobby or culture sector. When the children grow older, women in particular become active in organised voluntary work in care, health or nursing and in organisations that are active in the field of religion and philosophy. One reason may be that their own parents or other relatives become infirm or ill, or the loss of older relatives may confront them with questions related to the purpose and meaning of life. In particular, these categories of voluntary work are most important for women. The figures on voluntary work in unions and political organisations confirm the picture that these organisations are still the strongholds of older males.

Next to the numbers of voluntary workers we have also included the average number of hours voluntary workers spend per week on their voluntary activities. Here one sees that men and especially women in the 'rush hour of life' have only limited time available for voluntary work. After the life stage where career and children compete for the scarce hours, there is more room for voluntary work, in particular among retired men. As most women never retire from their household duties, reaching the higher age brackets does not offer them as much additional time to spend on voluntary work as it does men. In particular, men's involvement in voluntary work for a union or some political organisation requires a lot of time.

In addition to the figures presented in Table 10.2, Table 10.3 includes figures on participation in voluntary work among the population by educational level, main activity, household type and degree of urbanisation.

The figures from Table 10.3 show that higher educated individuals and those working in management and white-collar jobs are more active in voluntary work than low educated individuals and people in blue-collar jobs. Unemployed and early retired workers have more time available for voluntary work, while those who are disabled may lack the capacity and energy to participate in voluntary work. Among households and families, traditional families are the main suppliers of voluntary work. This should not come as a surprise as we saw earlier that many women/mothers are doing voluntary work at school (in many cases probably the school their children attend). Single parents do not often have any time left to participate in voluntary work, as they are responsible for making a living and all the care and household tasks on their own. Furthermore, the table shows that participation in voluntary work is indeed related to the degree of urbanisation. In the country people engage more in voluntary work than in the cities and suburbs of the Netherlands.

After presenting in some detail the picture on voluntary work for the Netherlands for 2009, we would like to shed some light on developments over time. Figure 10.1 shows the development of the number of people participating in voluntary work for the period 2001-09, by age category. The upper panel shows the development for men, while the lower panel shows the development for women.

While the younger age categories show a relatively stable pattern, both men and women show a steady increase in the number of voluntary workers in the age categories 55-65 and 75+. Over the whole period the number of voluntary workers aged 65-75 also increased, but the increase is less spectacular and came to a halt for men after 2006.

If – despite all variety – one wants to characterise the prototypical volunteer in the Netherlands, one would probably see a higher educated mother with a part-time job, in her late thirties or early forties, husband present, living in a village somewhere in the country, doing voluntary work at her children's school. Maybe she is a 'reading mom' for three hours a week, who helps the young children learning

Table 10.3: Share of the Dutch population, 15-65 years old, participating in voluntary work, by education, main activity, family type and degree of urbanisation, 2009 (%)

Characteristic	%
Educational level	
Primary education	23
Basic vocational training	36
Basic secondary education	43
Higher secondary education or intermediate vocational training	45
Higher education (higher vocational training and university)	54
Main activity	
Management job	51
Other white-collar job	42
Self-employed	36
Skilled blue-collar job	34
Unskilled blue-collar job	34
Unemployed	47
Disabled	31
Early retired or in pre-pension scheme	51
Household type	
Single-person household	36
Single-parent family	31
Couple without children	39
Couple with children	50
Degree of urbanisation	
Very high	37
High	37
Moderate	44
Low	47
Very low	48

Source: www.statline.nl

to read, or maybe she looks after the schoolchildren who cannot go home during the lunch break, on the one or two days she does not work herself.

Participation of older volunteers

The prototypical *older* volunteer is probably a man in his early sixties, most likely recently retired from a white-collar job, with two grown-up children and a wife who does most of the housekeeping. He is active in an organisation in the field of sports or leisure, maybe the

Figure 10.1: The development of the number of people participating in voluntary work in the Netherlands, by gender and age, 2001-09 (×1,000)

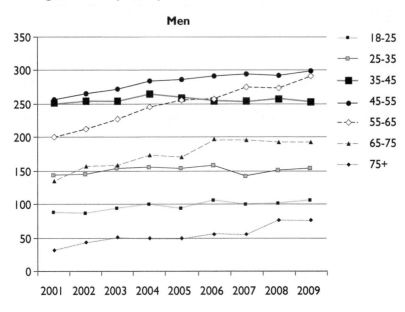

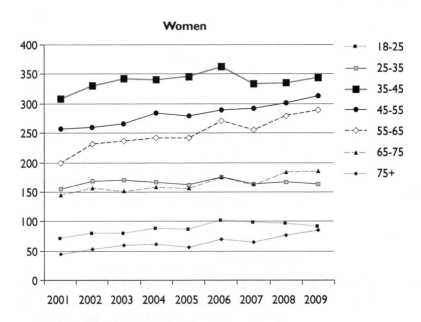

Source: www.statline.nl

tennis club or the association that organises the annual fair on the square in the middle of the village. On average he spends almost a day a week on voluntary work. Older women in particular are engaged in care, nursing activities and religious organisations.

This image of an older volunteer in the Netherlands is no coincidence. On the one hand, it reflects developments on the supply side of 'the market for volunteers'. Around the turn of the century the first of the large post-war baby-boom cohorts reached the age of 55. Many members of these cohorts retired at some point during the first decade of the new century. So they are a group with plenty of time on their hands for voluntary work. When they entered the labour market in their late teens or early twenties, many of them got a job in an office. Many dirty and heavy jobs in manufacturing in the Netherlands were taken over by machines, while employment increased in trade, banking, commercial services and the public sector, including education. So many of them did not suffer from bad working conditions and are still in good health. Moreover, they have reasonable pensions that allow them a lifestyle where they do not have to count every cost. And because this age group is healthy and still has a substantial life expectancy, that is increasingly higher for every vintage that reaches the age of 65 (Bruggink, 2009), they find it worthwhile investing in new contacts, maybe developing new skills and looking for new goals in life after a labour market career of 30-40 years.

On the other hand, as already pointed at in the introduction to this chapter, many organisations in sectors such as sports, culture, care and religion are in need of extra hands. Budget cuts mean they have had to reduce the share of professional workers to a minimum, but a lot of tasks still need to be done. So experienced retirees with various skills and a lot of time available come in handy. Altogether, the demand for high skilled voluntary workers has increased, and voluntary workers are no longer just the 'hands' who put out the chairs ready for the local choir's concert, selling tickets at the entrance and serving coffee and tea during a break.

Older volunteers – men and women – may have been active in voluntary work during earlier stages of their life. Retirement might be a natural moment for reorientation on the kind of voluntary work that best suits their stage of the life course. For many people reaching the official retirement age of 65, after which they receive their first pension benefits, brings a moment of reflection. And if it is not reaching the age of 65 that provokes some reflection it might be the birth of a first grandchild or the loss of one's last parent. So it should not come as a surprise that for older volunteers' activities that have to do with care, nursing, religion, history or philosophical issues become relatively important. And other older volunteers continue their activities for their football club or the music hall they joined when they were still teenagers. The general picture shows that volunteers are primarily involved with volunteer work that fits the stage of their life course.

Over the years older volunteers, in particular those beyond official retirement age, seem to enjoy their voluntary work more than younger volunteers. Moreover, the overall share of volunteers who agree with the statement that they 'always' enjoy their voluntary work has risen over the years (see Table 10.4).

Looking from an organisational perspective one cannot say that (even some) organisations are specifically targeting older volunteers. Depending on the nature of the voluntary work, of course, some organisations attract more older volunteers, while others attract more younger volunteers, as already seen in Table 10.2. As a matter of fact, targeting any specific age category would be a violation of the Dutch law against age discrimination. This law not only refers to paid labour, but also to voluntary work. However, when it comes to actual recruitment, many organisations working with volunteers show a bias in favour of older volunteers. This bias can primarily be explained from limitations on the supply side. Many voluntary workers find their way to organisations through 'hear say'. They meet someone at a birthday party, in the pub or at some festival or meeting of the organisation, show an interest in the organisation's activities and are asked to join. In practice, this often implies that an organisation with older voluntary workers will attract older voluntary workers (this may

Table 10.4: Share of volunteers who always enjoys their voluntary work (%)

Age	1999	2000	2001	2002	2003	2004	2007	2008
18-25	62	58	59	61	65	56	67	68
25-35	59	59	57	63	55	59	63	66
35-45	56	56	59	61	56	63	70	70
45-55	59	59	62	57	58	56	67	71
55-65	67	63	61	69	65	67	73	71
65-75	72	67	64	64	79	71	71	81
75+	63	na	76	69	79	80	77	75
Total	61	60	60	62	61	62	69	71

Note: na = not available.

Source: www.statline.nl

apply, for example, to organisations operating in the care and nursing, church, philosophy and religion sectors), while an organisation with younger volunteers will probably recruit younger voluntary workers. In addition, there is the process of self-selection: some voluntary workers may prefer an organisation where they can cooperate with people from their own age.

Older people's participation in voluntary organisations: opportunities and restrictions

When we look at the factors that have determined opportunities for participation of older people in voluntary work over the past decades, several developments come into mind: the – for the Netherlands – historically low, but increasing participation of older people in paid work and the emancipation of women making their way into the labour market. But another development that calls for attention is the changing nature of much of the voluntary work itself. At the individual level one may point to the fact that everyone in society, including older people, seem to be ever more busy. Another development is the changing family network: fewer siblings and parents who live longer. In this section we discuss these opportunities and restrictions in some more detail.

Opportunities and restrictions for volunteering for older people

Looking from the individual perspective, older people's better health could contribute to their opportunities to engage longer and until higher ages in voluntary work. That same better health, however, is also brought forward by the government as an argument to raise the official retirement age, thereby possibly restricting again older people's opportunities to engage in voluntary work. Older people who are in good shape are also inclined to spend more time travelling and on sport. Many retirees enjoy travelling, may buy a boat or a house in the country. Some enjoy their work so much that they take up another job or engage in self-employment. This again also limits their time available for voluntary work. As increasing life expectancy not only offers additional healthy years, it would be a mistake to think that older people's opportunities to engage in voluntary work will increase just as fast as life expectancy. Given the smaller number of siblings of successive generations on the one hand, there are fewer relatives to care for than in the past. As such this would increase the opportunities for participating in voluntary work. On the other hand, if a relative is in need of care and support, the circle of potential carers is smaller, and this may limit opportunities for participation in voluntary work. In any case, since altruistic motivations seem to have a considerable role in driving Dutch older volunteers (Principi et al, 2012), the care sector may potentially also offer volunteer opportunities to older people, and women in particular. For each individual, the balance may be different.

At the organisational level coordinators of voluntary work report that, just as in the domain of paid labour, the work has been changing, especially during the last decade. Three major developments call for attention. The first is the emergence of ICT (information and communications technology). If someone works in the library as a volunteer (s)he will have to adapt to the fact that the books are no longer registered on small cards in a card tray, but can only be found when accessing the library computer. If, as an older person, you have not had the opportunity to learn how to use a computer as part of your daily work routine, it might be a barrier if a volunteer job requires computer skills. A second change in the nature of voluntary work is the high level of professional requirements also requested in voluntary organisations. In branches of industry such as institutional care, childcare, culture (think again of the library, museums) and recreation work, standards have increased tremendously. Many professional jobs require some kind of education and a certificate to prove that you have the right skills. As the director of SCP (The Netherlands Institute for Social Research), one of the major policy advisers of the Dutch government, puts it: 'Quite some demands are requested from volunteers: to become a treasurer of a bigger voluntary organisation you almost need a professional financial background'.[1] Related to this professionalisation is the third development, the emancipation of 'clients'. Many clients, patients or visitors of the volunteer organisations are well educated busy professionals. They have learned to stand up for themselves and they have got used to professional service levels in all corners of society. In the Netherlands in particular this 'empowerment of the client' has developed so much that people are likely to complain – and often loudly. It requires the professionals' utmost to prevent a client losing his or her head. That is why nowadays bus drivers, desk clerks, doorkeepers and a whole range of other workers have to have training in 'how to deal with difficult clients'. In such a world not every volunteer worker may find it easy to join the volunteer organisation. Fortunately, even in the Netherlands this is more the exception to the rule, but it is a tendency that makes it increasingly less likely that people, and especially older people, will join in voluntary work.

As already mentioned, the increase in the official retirement age in the Netherlands (to 67 years by the end of this decade) will potentially limit the availability of (full-time) volunteers. Reduction of pension income may work in the same direction, as a growing share of people beyond official retirement age may want to earn additional money in the paid labour market. We have also already mentioned the growing individualisation and abolishment of breadwinner wages (and breadwinner social security benefits), which compels younger generations of women to earn their own living. This may also limit opportunities for voluntary work. Limited growth of the economy and continuous budget cuts will result in growing unemployment during the rest of the current decade, offering more people time to engage in voluntary work. It will depend on the regulations regarding unemployment benefits and welfare to what extent (long-term) unemployed people will actually be allowed to participate in voluntary work. In the Netherlands there are no volunteer programmes run by the government, or other measures to support volunteer work.

Older people between employment and volunteering

In the Netherlands, during the period 1970-95 the average age at which workers actually retired fell from almost 65 (the mandatory retirement age) to below the age of 60, with some sectors of industry or occupations offering the opportunity to retire at 55, and participation rates of 50+ workers sinking to as low as 20 per cent for men between 60 and 65. The rather low participation rates paired with a not so high work orientation in the Netherlands, since only 48.6 per cent of people aged 50-65 agreed or strongly agreed with the statement 'I would enjoy having a paid job even if I did not need the money' (ISSP, 1997). As Figure 10.2 shows, this tendency has reversed since the mid-1990s.

Despite this increase in the participation of older people in paid work, this has not resulted in a decrease in participation in voluntary work (as already seen in Figure 10.1). However, even though between 2001 and 2009 the share of older men and older women between 55 and 65 participating in voluntary work went up from 24 to 27 per cent (so there is no gender difference), the average number of hours spent on voluntary work slightly declined: from 7.4 hours a week to 6.8 hours a week for men and from 6.2 hours a week to 5.6 hours a week for women. So it looks as if increasing participation in paid work does not affect the share of older people active in voluntary work, but is itself reflected in the number of hours they have available. Here it

Figure 10.2: Participation rates in paid work of older workers, by gender, 1971-2008 (%)

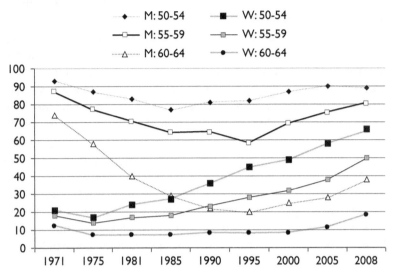

Source: Authors' own calculations based on information from Statistics Netherlands (different years)

should be noted that many women and older men work in part-time jobs, which also allows them to spend some time on voluntary work.

Volunteering in older age may be driven by corporate efforts to promote it among employees, yet in the Netherlands a very limited number of private firms offer their employees (of all ages) the opportunity to work as a volunteer some days a year.

Older people between family care and volunteering

While longevity has been increasing, many people in their fifties or sixties still have to care for an older generation of people in their eighties or nineties. The reverse of smaller numbers of siblings is that you cannot share the care with a large number of kin. Yet the presence of an extensive network of formal, public (health) care – even though it has been eroding as a result of budgetary cuts – means that the increasing numbers of 80+ people do not currently constitute a threat to older people's voluntary work, but possible future developments in this respect should be monitored. In the Netherlands formal long-term care services are largely available to people aged 65+, as recent data show that 21.1 per cent of them receive home care while 6.5 per cent are in residential care (Huber et al, 2009). This makes the

Netherlands one of the European countries with the highest provision of long-term care services for older people. This is in line with elder care values, since 81 per cent of the Dutch population thinks that the best option for an older parent living alone and in need of regular help is that service providers should visit their home and provide them with appropriate care (Eurobarometer, 2007).

Another dimension of the lower number of siblings that might be especially relevant for future generations of older voluntary workers is the increasing importance of fellow volunteers as network members. If you do not have any siblings or only siblings living far away, participating in voluntary work may become more relevant as an opportunity to build a new network in old age.

Furthermore, with the emergence of the working mother in the Netherlands there has been a growing demand for childcare. An increasing share of parents bring their young children to a professional childcare centre, but often for only two or three days a week. During the other days they care for their young children themselves or they ask their parents (in law) to step in. Many grandparents enjoy this 'golden occasion'; for many grandfathers it is an opportunity to make up for their absence, in the literal or figurative sense, while their own young children needed care. The large increase in public childcare facilities over the last decade has mitigated the demand for grandparents' childcare. Consequently, even this grandparental task has not been a serious threat to older people's participation in voluntary work. Moreover, the number of grandchildren per grandparent is still declining.

Improving the match between supply of older candidates with the demand of voluntary organisations: future scenarios

There are two major threats to the match between the supply of older voluntary workers and the demand from organisations wanting to hire volunteers. The first threat, relevant for voluntary organisations, lies at the supply side, that is, with older people who will make a decision on whether or not to engage in voluntary work, what kind of voluntary work and for how many hours. As already mentioned (see p 233), as older people become more healthy and wealthy, their scope of opportunities increases. So organisations that want to attract or hold on to voluntary staff have to compete with an increasing range of alternative forms of time use by older people. A growing share of retirees has had interesting and challenging jobs. So many of them are also likely to prefer interesting and challenging work as volunteers. Unfortunately, not all voluntary work falls into this category. Sometimes it is repetitive or involves simple tasks such as clearing out a dishwasher and making coffee. To attract older volunteers, organisations should emphasise that volunteering may increase their social contacts. Indeed, one major point of attraction of participation in voluntary work, especially as people get older (75+ and beyond), is the social network function already mentioned, and the idea of contributing something to society. One may speculate that demographic developments (fewer siblings, a higher divorce rate) may give rise to more older people feeling lonely and 'useless'. Voluntary organisations might be one of the answers to this development. And indeed they might capitalise on the role they could play in older people's life and invest in this role. In the meantime, the voluntary work still has to be done. Earlier we mentioned the pressure many volunteer organisations are under these days to perform at an almost professional level.

The second threat is the austerity of the Dutch welfare state. This threat will manifest itself in several ways:

- In 2012 Parliament agreed to increase the official retirement age stepwise to 67 by 2023, and older workers will be pushed to continue working until the official retirement age. In addition, women will be encouraged to work more hours, that is, to extend their small part-time job into a larger one. This will leave older people with less time to spend on voluntary work. And even if the share of voluntary workers may not decline (see p 235), increased participation in paid work may have a negative impact on the number of voluntary hours.
- Budgetary cuts in health, social support and childcare may prompt people (often family members) to take up more tasks in these fields themselves.
- A further reduction in the budgets of volunteer organisations will increase demand for volunteers, and in particular, for experienced retired professionals. It may also reduce organisations' possibilities of coaching and counselling (new) volunteers. This may be particularly discouraging for lower educated volunteers.

So there seem to be a need that at the institutional level, there should be more attention on the consequences of what has just been said above on volunteering in general and the volunteering of older people in particular, in this current era which is characterised by a European call for active ageing.

Of course one can only speculate about the extent of the effects of the general tendencies just mentioned, because there are still a large number of uncertainties: how will paid employment develop? Will additional budgetary cut-backs be necessary? How will older people and organisations adapt to changing conditions?

Governments *should* be sensitive to the role voluntary organisations could play, not only for the supply of (additional) services in care, health, culture, sports or education, but also for the well-being of older voluntary workers who participate in these organisations. However, with the cold wind of budget cuts blowing all over Europe, and the Netherlands in particular, it is not so clear if in the near future there will be renewed room for additional investments in professionals coaching older voluntary workers, or for fiscal facilities reimbursing the costs of older people in participating in voluntary work.

Conclusions

The Netherlands is a country with traditionally high rates of participation in voluntary work. Major changes in its welfare state regime over the last two decades has shown that the supply of voluntary work is relatively 'inelastic' (as economists like to call it); it is not strong in responding to policy changes. As a matter of fact, the number of older volunteers has been, and is still, increasing. This may reflect the increasing longevity and better health situation of the 50+ population. The typical Dutch older volunteer is a man in his early sixties, well educated, active in an organisation in the field of sports or leisure, or a woman engaged in care, nursing activities or a religious organisation.

Yet new challenges are arising. Increasing time pressure (from work, family obligations or other leisure activities) appears to have resulted in a small decline in the number of hours older people have available to participate in voluntary work. Higher demands with respect to the quality of voluntary work, less capacity for coaching (new) volunteers and competing claims on older people from various domains of life constitute a puzzle for the future of voluntary organisations, for which there is no easy solution. It will require their utmost creativity to match organisational demands and the needs and preferences of older people to entice them into engaging in voluntary work. Just as in paid employment, it looks as if there is a particular need for tailor-made solutions. And just as in the paid labour market, organisations and their managers have a major responsibility to integrate the talents of older people. Despite the higher retirement age and the growing necessity for older people to take care of their relatives, older volunteers will be available (after retirement, when they have no one to take care of or because their care tasks are relatively small), but the challenge lies with organisations, and not primarily with the government, since this does not seem to be 'a priority' for government, to integrate them in a proper way that satisfies both the increasingly complex organisational needs and older volunteers' preferences to be active, to contribute something to society and to be part of a network of a congenial group.

Note
[1] As quoted during the 2010 ASPA (Activating Senior Potential in Ageing Europe) national focus group meeting, 'Opportunities for older people in the civil society'.

References
ANBI (Algemeen Nut Beogende Instelling) (2010) *Vrijwilligersregeling, vacatiegelden en onkostenvergoedingen door ANBI's [Arrangements for volunteers, fee attendance money and allowances for expenses by ANBIs]* (www.anbi.nl/anbi-info/vrijwilligers-bestuurders).

Bruggink, J.W. (2009) 'Ontwikkelingen in (gezonde) levensverwachting naar opleidingsniveau' ['Trends in (healthy) life expectancy by educational level'], *Bevolkingstrends*, 4e kwartaal, Den Haag: Centraal Bureau voor de Statistiek.

CBS (Centraal Bureau voor de Statistiek) (Statistics Netherlands), Labour Force Survey, different years.

CBS (Statistics Netherlands) (different years) *Living conditions in the Netherlands*, Voorburg: Centraal Bureau voor de Statistiek.

Esping-Andersen, G. (1990) *The three worlds of welfare capitalism*, Cambridge: Polity Press.

Eurobarometer (2007) *Health and long-term care in the European Union*, Special Eurobarometer 283/Wave 67.3, TNS Opinion & Social (ec. europa.eu/public_opinion/archives/ebs/ebs_283_en.pdf).

Giddens, A. (1998) *The third way: The renewal of social democracy*, Cambridge: Polity Press.

Giving in the Netherlands (different years) Database established by Vrije Universiteit Amsterdam, Center for Philanthropic Studies (www.giving.nl).

Huber, M., Rodrigues, R., Hoffmann, F., Gasior, K. and Marin, B. (2009) *Facts and figures on long-term care: Europe and North America*, Vienna: European Centre for Social Welfare Policy and Research.

ISSP (International Social Survey Programme) (1997) 'Work Orientations II', Mannheim: ISSP (www.gesis.org/issp/issp-modules-profiles/work-orientations/1997).

Kollen, F.C. (2007) *De vereniging in de praktijk* [*The practice of the association*], Deventer: Kluwer.

Lankers, E. (no date) *Werken in de sport: vrijwillig of betaald* [*Working in sports: Voluntary or paid*], Roosendaal: WOS (Werkgeversorganisaties in de Sport – Employers' Organisations in Sports).

Lijphart, A. (1968) *The politics of accommodation: pluralism and democracy in the Netherlands*, Berkeley, CA: University of California Press.

Pennings, F.J.L. (2001) 'Vrijwilligerswerk en sociale zekerheid' ('Voluntary work and social security'), in P.Vlaardingerbroek (ed) *Via het vrijwilligersstatuut naar een betere status voor de vrijwilligers*, Tilburg: Bureau juridisch PAO, pp 43-55.

Principi, A., Chiatti, C., Lamura, G. (2012) 'Motivations of older volunteers in three European countries', *International Journal of Manpower*, vol 33, no 6, pp 704-22.

SCP (The Netherlands Institute for Social Research)/CBS (Centraal Bureau voor de Statistiek) (2005) *Tijdbestedingsonderzoek* [*Time use studies*], The Hague: Sociaal en Cultureel Planbureau/Centraal Bureau voor de Statistiek.

Part III

OPPORTUNITIES AND RESTRICTIONS FOR OLDER VOLUNTEERS

Case studies in European voluntary organisations

ELEVEN

Voluntary organisations' characteristics and practices towards older volunteers

Andrea Principi and Jolanta Perek-Białas

Introduction

This chapter is the first of three that focus on the 73 case studies carried out among European voluntary organisations on opportunities and restrictions for older volunteers from an organisational perspective. From an active ageing perspective, the overall aim of the three chapters is to understand whether voluntary organisations are inclusive enough to accept older people as volunteers, if they appreciate older volunteers in terms of available skills and resources, and if they are willing and prepared to invest in them through pro-active strategies and measures. Furthermore, we look to determine whether negative stereotypes and prejudices towards older volunteers may be present among voluntary organisations. This is important to really understand, because voluntary organisations represent the 'demand' of voluntary work, yet very little is known about their policies, opinions and behaviours towards older volunteers. Thus, these three chapters constitute the main innovative aspect of this volume. They deal with the *meso* level, and relevant to the conceptual framework employed in this volume as described in Chapter Two are questions such as: do voluntary organisations employ or plan to employ special measures in order to recruit and retain older volunteers for as long as possible? What is actually being offered to older volunteers by these organisations? How do voluntary organisations perceive the consequences of an increasingly older workforce and of informal family care on the contribution of older people as volunteers?

The methods used in these three chapters are described in detail in Chapter One. It is useful here to remember that the activity sector and age structure of the volunteer workforce were the main criteria adopted for selecting voluntary organisations to be included in this study. The final sample is described in Table 11.1 (in-text citations of organisations through the three chapters are based on what is reported in note a).

The three chapters are conceived as reporting results from case studies that deal respectively with the following: the internal management of older volunteers in terms of policies, behaviours or attitudes (this chapter); how the welfare mix conditions the way in which older people's labour market participation and care obligations have an impact on both the participation of older volunteers and organisational activities (Chapter Twelve); and voluntary organisations' orientations towards responding to future societal changes through volunteers' age management practices (Chapter Thirteen).

An interesting approach towards studying the internal management of older volunteers in terms of policies and behaviours (the aim of this present chapter) is to adopt a human resources (HR) 'age management' perspective. The 'age management' concept is well established relative to work on the labour market (Naegele and Walker, 2006), which has been defined as organisational 'initiatives designed to combat age barriers, either directly or indirectly, and providing an environment in which each individual is able to achieve his or her potential without being disadvantaged by their age' (Walker and Taylor, 1998, p 3). These initiatives are intended to increase opportunities for older people in employment. And yet, we want to understand if they are employed not just by companies but also by voluntary organisations in an attempt to manage their volunteer workforce. Thus, the main purpose of this study is to identify possible age management practices vis-à-vis volunteers in voluntary organisations. We consider age management practices as all those organisational formal and informal policies or behaviours that emerged from the interviews, thereby implying an intentional or unintentional management of volunteers on the basis of their (older) age. This topic was studied by means of information gathered from interviewed organisational representatives on policies and practices regarding older volunteers, or specific initiatives (for example, a project, programme or measure) designed for older people as volunteers.

Organisations may exhibit very different characteristics between them that could have a direct impact on the way they manage their work and their workforce (Mintzberg, 1983). For example, voluntary organisations may provide or carry out very different services or activities, be more or less professionalised, have different sizes, and volunteers of different ages and gender compositions. Thus, we argue that organisational policies, including those for the sake of managing

Table 11.1: Description of the investigated voluntary organisations

No	Name[a]	Sector	Main services	Number of volunteers	Share of older volunteers (H/L)[b]	% of female volunteers (approx)
			THE NETHERLANDS			
1	Nivon Hunebed and De Kleine Rug	Culture and recreation	Hosting guests in nature houses	1,500	H	60
2	Gilde Zeist	Culture and recreation	Transfer of knowledge, skills and experience through guided tours, lectures, counselling, mentoring, and so on	6,000	H	50
3	Kasteel de Haar	Culture and recreation	Guided tours in the castle; events for children and adults	65	H	50
4	Hospice Utrecht and Thuis Sterven	Health	Caregiving and support to the dying and their family and friends	81	H	90
5	Ronald McDonald House Utrecht	Health	Temporary accommodation for parents of ill children, patients of the children's hospital	75	L	91
6	2 Studies on nursing homes[c]	Health	Care for the nursing homes' patients	40,000	H	90
7	PKN Pro Deo Utrecht	Social services	The largest Protestant church in the Netherlands, provides all kinds of support to people in need	80	H	55
8	Portes	Social services	Community centres offering activities in about 25 facilities to improve life conditions and everyday surroundings for people of all ages	1,000	L	75

(continued)

Table 11.1: Description of the investigated voluntary organisations (continued)

No	Name[a]	Sector	Main services	Number of volunteers	Share of older volunteers (H/L)[b]	% of female volunteers (approx)
			THE NETHERLANDS (continued)			
9	Cliëntenbelang	Social services	Advocating the interests of individuals in the areas of care and social services, as well as labour and income	10	L	70
			ENGLAND			
10	Volunteer Reading Help Northamptonshire (VRH)	Education and research	Helping schoolchildren improve their reading skills	120	H	84
11	Workers' Educational Association (WEA)	Education and research	Adult education provider	About 1,000	H	Not available[d]
12	The Waterways Trust	Culture and recreation	Preservation and protection of the nation's waterways	220	H	34
13	Shakespeare Birthplace Trust	Culture and recreation	Manages and maintains Shakespeare's birthplace and four other heritage sites linked with Shakespeare and his family	300	H	60
14	Royal National Institute of Blind People (RNIB)	Social services	Information, support, advocacy and advice to the two million Britons who are blind or partially sighted	3,100	H	44
15	The Scout Association	Social services	Activities for the development of young people in achieving their full physical, intellectual, social and spiritual potentials	100,000	L	43

(continued)

Table 11.1: Description of the investigated voluntary organisations (continued)

No	Name[a]	Sector	Main services	Number of volunteers	Share of older volunteers (H/L)[b]	% of female volunteers (approx)
			ENGLAND (continued)			
16	Women's Royal Voluntary Service (WRVS)	Social services	Personal and practical support to older people to help them live independent lives and to stay active in the community; other services include retail and patient support in hospitals	47,000	H	82
17	Community Service Volunteers (CSV)	Development and housing	Offers volunteering opportunities mainly in the field of education, social services and environment, and provides training for disadvantaged people to gain employment	165,666	L	Not available[d]
			GERMANY			
18	Kunstverein Bremen	Culture and recreation	Art association and a museum	65	H	74
19	SV Werder Bremen	Culture and recreation	Soccer sports club	320	L	33
20	Bücherhallen Medienprojekte Hamburg	Culture and recreation	Supply of books and reading services to disabled older people	124	H	75
21	Lohner Tafel	Social services	Supply of foodstuffs to people in need	100	H	84
22	Integrationslotsen Duisburg	Social services	Integration network to support non-natives	69	L	64

(continued)

Table 11.1: Description of the investigated voluntary organisations (continued)

No	Name[a]	Sector	Main services	Number of volunteers	Share of older volunteers (H/L)[b]	% of female volunteers (approx)
			GERMANY (continued)			
23	Caritas Dachverband	Social services	Provision of low-threshold services and support at the federal, state and local level	500,000	H	79
24	Seniorpartner in School	Education and research	Helping pupils solve conflicts with teachers, contributing to a better learning atmosphere at school	183	H	75
25	Zeitzeugenbörse	Education and research	Providing historical witnesses and biographically based experiences to pupils and other interested groups	200	H	52
26	Ausbildungspaten Recklinghausen	Education and research	Mentoring programmes for young people during the transition from school to professional work	100	H	50
			SWEDEN			
27	The Swedish Church	Religion	Mentoring to young people, church services, sales in second-hand shops	About 18,000	H	75
28	Mission Covenant Church Lerum	Religion	Activities for young people in particular, but also social and cultural activities for older people	150	L	50
29	Salvation Army	Religion	Helping people with difficulties, for example, disadvantaged groups, disabled people, drug and alcohol addicts, and so on	800	H	70

(continued)

Table 11.1: Description of the investigated voluntary organisations (continued)

No	Name[a]	Sector	Main services	Number of volunteers	Share of older volunteers (H/L)[b]	% of female volunteers (approx)
			SWEDEN (continued)			
30	Ria Lerum	Social services	Advice and information on alcohol-related issues to people who are exposed to high risk of social exclusion	45	H	70
31	Stockholm City Mission	Social services	Social work mainly focused on disadvantaged groups (homeless people, drug and alcohol addicts, disabled people, and so on)	About 360	H	75
32	Children's Rights in the Society West Region	Social services	Support to children and young people in distress; a link between children, adults and the community	90	L	90
33	Amnesty International Gothenburg	International	Actions to prevent and stop abuse of human rights and demand justice for those whose rights have been violated	220	L	70
34	Save the Children Gothenburg	International	Activities for children's rights	100	L	70
35	Red Cross Sweden	International	Support to people in distress	About 40,000	H	75
			DENMARK			
36	Vejgaard Historic Association	Culture and recreation	Collection of documents from the local area issuing publications, and management of excursions	9	H	0

(continued)

Table 11.1: Description of the investigated voluntary organisations (continued)

No	Name[a]	Sector	Main services	Number of volunteers	Share of older volunteers (H/L)[b]	% of female volunteers (approx)
			DENMARK (continued)			
37	Aalborg Senior Sport	Culture and recreation	Sports activities for seniors	190	H	Not available[d]
38	Dgi North Jutland	Culture and recreation	Gymnastic and sports association	142	L	40
39	Tenants Association Aalborg	Development and housing	Attending to tenants' interests in relation to landlords, public authorities and policy makers	14	L	71
40	Gistrup Cable Service Provider	Development and housing	Cable services	8	H	25
41	9220 Aalborg East	Development and housing	Activities with a main focus on jobs and education, social integration, communities and health	365	L	60
42	DaneAge Aalborg	Social services	Support to the rights and interests of senior citizens	162	H	61
43	Cross Church Army Aalborg	Social services	Provides social services to the frailest and most marginalised people, such as people with mental ill health, homeless people, addicts, and so on. Its activities include drop-in centres, shelters, house shares, community work and therapy for addicts and burdened families	6,000	H	90

(continued)

Table 11.1: Description of the investigated voluntary organisations (continued)

No	Name[a]	Sector	Main services	Number of volunteers	Share of older volunteers (H/L)[b]	% of female volunteers (approx)
			DENMARK (continued)			
44	DanChurchAid Aalborg	Social services	Helping poor people abroad; the work conducted in Denmark mainly includes fundraising, advocacy and information	Primary network: about 500; coordinators of national fundraising campaigns: 900; fundraising: 23,000; second-hand shops: 3,500	H	Second-hand shops: 90%; Remaining volunteers: 50%
45	Red Cross Army	International	Sales in second-hand shops, companionship and 'nørklere' (knitting and crocheting various things, such as dolls)	20,000.	H	80
			ITALY			
46	Associazione per l'Autogestione dei servizi e la solidarietà (AUSER)	Social services	Services for older people: personal services, telephone company and light home care (social care) services. Civic services to the community: socialisation and cultural expressive activities	37,738	H	45

(continued)

253

Table 11.1: Description of the investigated voluntary organisations (continued)

No	Name[a]	Sector	Main services	Number of volunteers	Share of older volunteers (H/L)[b]	% of female volunteers (approx)
			ITALY (continued)			
47	Unione Nazionale Italiana Volontari pro Ciechi (UNIVOC)	Social services	Services for blind people. Companionship and support in different daily and leisure-cultural activities to foster social inclusion of the blind	2,000	H	57
48	Tenda di Abramo	Social services	Reception centre for people with severe economic and social hardships; accompaniment and support to guests looking for accommodation or work	249	L	54
49	Associazione per il volontariato nelle unità locali dei servizi socio sanitari (AVULSS)	Health	Services provided mainly in hospitals (companionship and light social health services), but also in nursing homes, prisons, facilities for disabled people and private homes	10,353	H	83
50	Associazione Nazionale Pubbliche Assistenze (ANPAS)	Health	First health aid (transport) in emergency health situations, and social transport for people with health problems	90,000	L	36
51	Associazione Volontari Italiani Sangue (AVIS)	Health	Blood provision (for example, to hospitals) through voluntary, free-of-charge, periodical and anonymous blood donation	1,156,286	L	30

(continued)

Table 11.1: Description of the investigated voluntary organisations (continued)

No	Name[a]	Sector	Main services	Number of volunteers	Share of older volunteers (H/L)[b]	% of female volunteers (approx)
			ITALY (continued)			
52	Associazione Nazionale delle Università della Terza Età (UNITRE)	Culture and recreation	Third age university that also provides cultural voluntary activities carried out by students (for example, in museums); conferences and meetings; publications	4,000	H	70
53	Teatro Aperto	Culture and recreation	Promotion and dissemination of cultural initiatives (theatrical performances in particular)	62	H	40
54	Unione Italiana Sport per Tutti (UISP)	Culture and recreation	Sports and sport-related leisure and cultural activities	50,070	L	30
			POLAND			
55	Polski Komitet Pomocy Społecznej (PKPS)	Social services	Professional help, substantive and organisational support, restoring hope and sense of security to people in difficult situations, for example, poor, old, disabled, homeless, lonely and abandoned people	About 400	H	85
56	Fundacja Samaritanus	Social services	Organisation of senior activation centres whose activities are addressed to the local community (information services, counselling, active help and advocacy, and so on)	16	H	85

(continued)

Table 11.1: Description of the investigated voluntary organisations (continued)

No	Name[a]	Sector	Main services	Number of volunteers	Share of older volunteers (H/L)[b]	% of female volunteers (approx)
			POLAND (continued)			
57	Mali Bracia Ubogich (MBU)	Social services	Services to prevent and combat the marginalisation of older people	About 300	H	80
58	Lekarzy Nadziei Cracow	Social services	Social and medical assistance to people in need in clinics for the homeless and the poor, charity points, and so on	14	H	50
59	Integracyjne Razem	Culture and recreation	Self-support groups providing free services for old, disabled, poor, socially excluded people, and children in the local community	15	H	85
60	Espar 50+	Culture and recreation	Promotion of physical activity of older people: gerontological prevention to improve the quality of life of seniors	10	L	90
61	Ja Kobieta	Education and research	Mobilisation of people 50+ to improve the quality of life of older people, in order to counteract discrimination based on age, gender stereotypes, and so on	25	H	90
62	Senior na Czasie	Education and research	Preventing marginalisation and activation of middle-aged and older people, by implementing measures promoting active and healthy lifestyles	5	L	80

(continued)

Table 11.1: Description of the investigated voluntary organisations (continued)

No	Name[a]	Sector	Main services	Number of volunteers	Share of older volunteers (H/L)[b]	% of female volunteers (approx)
			POLAND (continued)			
63	Akademia Pełni Życia	Education and research	Educational activities, such as computer and language courses, and so on	20	H	65
			FRANCE			
64	Lire et Faire Lire (LFL)	Culture and recreation	Reading workshops for children delivered by seniors in school or extracurricular settings	11,901	H	90
65	Fédération Française de la Retraite Sportive	Culture and recreation	Organisation and self-leading of various sports activities for retired people	2,000	H	Not available[d]
66	Chemins de fer du Creusot	Culture and recreation	Managing the tourist railway in a park and promoting the park using attractions, leisure activities and entertainment	51	H	20
67	Fédération Française de la Randonnée Pédestre	Culture and recreation	Practising and promoting hikes	20,000	H	75
68	Fédération Nationale des Associations de Retraités (FNAR)	Law, advocacy and politics	Lobbying and expertise to advocate rights, material and moral interests of seniors and their legal successors	400	H	10
69	Association Force Ouvrière Consommateurs	Law, advocacy and politics	Inform, advise and represent consumers in a spirit of independence and solidarity	400	H	50

(continued)

Table 11.1: Description of the investigated voluntary organisations (continued)

No	Name[a]	Sector	Main services	Number of volunteers	Share of older volunteers (H/L)[b]	% of female volunteers (approx)
			FRANCE (continued)			
70	Association Générale des Intervenants Retraités-Abcd	Social services	Activities of solidarity, for example, accompaniment towards employment, companionship, literacy, support to economic, cultural and human development	3,124	H	38
71	Petits Frères des Pauvres	Social services	Accompaniment to sick, at the end of life and isolated people	8,500	H	70
72	Association Emmaüs	Social services	Accommodation and social accompaniment	350	H	50
73	Solidarités Nouvelles face au Chômage	Social services	Jobseekers' accompaniment, development jobs creation, voicing of opinions in public debate	1,200	H	48

Notes:
[a] In this column, the words underlined have been used to cite the organisations through Chapters Eleven to Thirteen;
[b] H = rather high or above average; L = rather low or below average. Average is meant as the total share of older volunteers (50+ years) among all volunteers in the country;
[c] Case study based on the following studies: Scholten, C. and van Overbeek, R. (2009) *Een solide basis: onderzoek naar vrijwilligerswerk en verantwoorde zorg*, Vilans: Januari, and Elferink, J. and Scholten, C. (2009) *Met pensioen als vrijwilliger: onderzoek naar de inzet van oudere vrijwilligers*, Vilans: MOVISIE, November;
[d] Even after a request for an estimate of the organisational representatives.

older volunteers, may be conditioned and influenced by these characteristics. And so, a second aim of this chapter is to determine whether certain organisational characteristics are associated with certain age management practices among volunteers.

Nevertheless, age management policies may be affected not only by such organisational characteristics, but also by the attitudes towards older volunteers among organisational decision-makers. For instance, it was found that age discrimination in employment could depend on stereotypes about age and other age barriers (Sargeant, 2006). Thus, we consider it important to examine opinions held by organisational representatives on older volunteers, and whether (or not) some form of age barriers may be present among voluntary organisations.

The chapter is structured as follows: the next section presents the main organisational characteristics to be looked at in the analysis, and how they are related to the sample of voluntary organisations being investigated. In the third section, organisational 'age management practices' are described and related, to the extent that it was possible, to the characteristics of voluntary organisations. Then, the fourth section provides an overview of opinions among organisational representatives on older volunteers, as well as reflections on the main organisational barriers to volunteering in older age. The chapter ends with some concluding remarks.

Characteristics of organisations under study

This section illustrates the main characteristics to be considered in the analysis of the voluntary organisations under scrutiny. In particular, we take into account the activity sector, the number of volunteers employed by the organisation and the age and gender balance of the volunteer workforce (see Table 11.2). We expect that according to different characteristics, voluntary organisations may have different ways of coping with an aged volunteer workforce, that is, this may play a role in shaping organisational practices for older volunteers.

In the sample of organisations investigated, in both philanthropic and non-philanthropic organisations, the share of older volunteers was mainly high (in 69 and 76 per cent of the organisations, respectively), whereas with respect to the volunteers' gender, contrary to non-philanthropic ones, most philanthropic organisations had a higher share of female volunteers. The share of female volunteers was about 50 per cent in organisations mainly composed of older volunteers and in young-profiled organisations (data not shown).

Table 11.2: Characteristics of the voluntary organisations under study (n)

	Sector[a]		Number of volunteers[b]			% of older volunteers[c]		% of female volunteers[d]		
	n=73		*n=73*			*n=73*		*n=69*[e]		
	Philan-thropic	Non-philan-thropic	L	M	H	L	H	L	M	H
The Netherlands	6	3	5	0	4	3	6	0	4	5
England	3	5	0	3	5	2	6	3	1	2
Germany	3	6	4	4	1	2	7	1	3	5
Sweden	9	0	3	3	3	4	5	0	1	8
Denmark	4	6	3	4	3	3	7	3	2	4
Italy	6	3	1	1	7	4	5	4	3	2
Poland	4	5	7	2	0	2	7	0	2	7
France	4	6	1	3	6	0	10	3	3	3
Total	39	34	24	20	29	20	53	14	19	36

Notes: [a] We made a distinction in this sample between organisations that provide mainly philanthropic or altruistic services to needy people (sectors: social services, health, religion and international) and organisations providing mainly non-philanthropic and more self-expressive services and activities (sectors: culture and recreation, education and research, development and housing, law, advocacy and politics); [b] Low (L) = 0-100, Medium (M) = 101-500, High (H) = 501 or more; [c] L = rather low or below average, H = rather high or above average. Average is meant to be the total share of older volunteers (50+ years) among all volunteers in the country; [d] Low = up to 44%, Medium = 45-65%, High = 66% or more; [e] Unavailable in four voluntary organisations.

Important organisational features also include the size (for this we based our estimation on the number of volunteers in the organisation, number of users and the magnitude of the organisational yearly turnover; information on this is reported in more detail in Principi and Lamura, 2011) and the number of paid staff in the organisation (Principi and Lamura, 2011). The degree or presence of the latter aspects, together with the kind of services provided (see Table 11.1), may also give a proper picture of the degree of professionalisation in the organisation, which is another key characteristic to consider in the analysis of organisational policies.

In the following section we explore whether organisational practices of the volunteers' age management can be found in the voluntary organisations being investigated, and whether (some) organisational characteristics may play a role in shaping the said volunteers' age management initiatives.

Volunteers' 'age management'?

Age management of the workforce is a familiar concept to for-profit organisations (that is, companies). Studies on this topic underlined that initiatives could be found in a number of possible dimensions and phases of the working life, as, for example, recruitment, health and well-being, flexible working practices, training, transition to retirement, and so on (see, for instance, Naegele and Walker, 2006). Through our study, our aim was to understand if and how this concept of 'age management' applied to the volunteer workforce in the organisations being investigated.

Officially, the majority of the investigated organisations did not seem to pursue any explicit strategies of age management in relation to their volunteers. More precisely, it was found overall that in the organisations under study the entire traditional concept of human resources management (HRM) concerning the volunteer workforce was not well established. HRM offices were found in large voluntary organisations, but they did not usually have any connection with volunteers, dealing only with paid staff. This applies less to large Italian organisations under study, since in that country paid staff were hardly found among voluntary organisations.

Given the growing professionalisation of the volunteer sector (Warburton and Cordingley, 2004), it may be expected that HRM could increasingly focus on managing volunteers rather than dealing only with paid workers. The remaining part of this section provides evidence of volunteers' age management practices in the following dimensions: recruitment, intergenerational exchange, training, flexibility, redeployment, exit policies and comprehensive approach. These concepts emerged in the organisations being analysed from interviews with their organisational representatives. As a matter of fact, in the investigated organisations, it was possible to recognise some organisational 'age management' practices, and to classify them according to the key dimensions of age management as identified through the case study methodology for employees working for the labour market (Walker and Taylor, 1998; Naegele and Walker, 2006).

Recruitment

Some informal actions (rather than real planned strategies) that indirectly refer to age management were found among the investigated organisations. In particular, several of them reported the wish to obtain a more suitable age mix of volunteers. This meant that, on the one hand, older-age profiled organisations sometimes felt a lack of younger volunteers, whereas, on the other hand, younger-age profiled ones felt at times the need to involve a larger number of older volunteers. The study highlighted the presence of both mechanisms.

Several studied organisations composed mainly of older volunteers complained about a lack of younger volunteers and would often invest to increase the participation of the latter. As to the specific reasons for this, organisational representatives reported the following:

- a wish to rejuvenate the organisation and increase voluntary staff in order to remove a certain fragility within the organisation (Hospice);
- for renovation purposes, and to better address the needs of some users (2 Studies);
- to resolve concerns about the future supply of volunteers, given the relatively high mean age of current ones (WEA, WRVS);
- need for knowledge, skills and a better understanding of younger people on some issues, for example, legal regulations and new technologies (MBU, Lekarzy Nadziei, Razem, Akademia);
- to balance and complement existing older volunteers in terms of skills, energy and time (Waterways);
- because older people are no longer fit enough to perform all tasks (Kunstverein, Lohner);
- because younger volunteers have the potential to stay in the organisation for a longer period of time, thereby allowing some of the older volunteers to retire (Gistrup);
- to promote and increase intergenerational engagement (WRVS);
- because the best dynamic is found in groups with mixed ages (Salvation Army).

Interestingly, most of the organisations that expressed this wish for a more suitable age balance were characterised by a high share of female volunteers, suggesting that older volunteer men tend to prefer a more intragenerational exchange.

Despite the clear intention to move in this direction, little evidence was found in terms of concrete organisational strategies to achieve age balance, although the following was found in some medium and large organisations:

- a project with 16- to 24-year-olds achieved a more balanced mix in terms of age, experience and skills, and gave young people the

opportunity to develop in personal terms and in technical areas (Waterways);
- investment of specific funds to attract younger volunteers (WEA and Nivon);
- organisation of youth conferences every three years, aiming to attract young people into the organisation (AVULSS);
- programmes with clearly defined goals and a limited time frame to appeal to young people (Caritas).

In most cases, attracting younger volunteers to this kind of organisation was not an easy task, and often the actions failed, according to respondents from certain philanthropic organisations. As some Swedish representatives put it, if there were too many older volunteers, it might be difficult to attract younger ones (Save the Children), and this remains a critical issue (Salvation Army).

This difficulty is clearly evident at AVULSS, an Italian organisation actively trying to attract more younger volunteers, but with meagre results. Some responsibilities for the failure were attributed to the older volunteers themselves, who may have shown resistance and too little desire to communicate their experiences. A key responsibility for this failure is the kind of activity the organisation carries out, which is judged as 'not appealing' by younger volunteers. Organisations also ascribed this failure to the lack of time that younger and very busy people have (AUSER, AVULSS, and some German organisations).

The fact that organisations, where older volunteers were mainly present, tried to involve more younger people does not necessarily mean that the recruitment and contribution of older volunteers were not considered to be equally important. Indeed, some of them give outright preference to applicants aged 55 and over to carry out their activities, probably due to their greater experience (Seniorpartner), which could be exploited in the organisation according to the desired professional competences (DanAge), such that recruitment programmes addressing older citizens are now being developed (Salvation Army) as well as special training for project managers and best practice for recruitment (WRVS).

There were also some examples of initiatives through which certain organisations, made up mainly of young volunteers, were striving to involve older ones, as in the following:

- establishment of a 'group on the accessibility to volunteering' to attract underrepresented categories of volunteers, including older ones (ANPAS);

- '60 plus' initiative: the association sent letters to all members over 59 years of age to learn about their interests and their potential for civic commitment. In light of the replies, the organisation set up new sports groups, organised cultural tours, and so on (Werder);
- concrete efforts towards even representation concerning age (Children's Rights, some organisations in England).

Intergenerational exchange

The desire to have a more balanced age structure for the volunteer workforce in terms of their recruitment may of course be linked to the desire to pursue intergenerational exchange among volunteers. To add information to the rather scarce knowledge in the current literature on this topic concerning the reciprocal benefits that may be derived from the possibility of volunteers of different generations working together, our study found that the situation in the studied organisations could be considered favourable, since in most of them younger and older volunteers generally tended to carry out the same tasks and activities. Evidence in support of intergenerational understanding, empathy and collaboration is certainly present in some large English organisations such as the CSV, whose representatives stated that promoting intergenerational engagement was fine because 'it is a value in itself', or WRVS, whose Heritage Plus project was designed to bring together different generations of volunteers through documenting their own and their community's history. In the same direction is UNITRE's project focusing on younger volunteers teaching ICT skills to older volunteers as a way of intergenerational exchange, and the German Caritas' participation in the intergenerational Volunteer Services programme, aimed at attracting voluntary activity from both pensioners and young people in transition from the education system to employment. In a small Italian organisation that mobilises a considerable number of volunteers rather than paid staff, it was observed that when activities are shared between volunteers belonging to different age groups, the older ones in particular show greater satisfaction (UNIVOC).

Large organisations that may heavily rely on paid staff can think of solving work problems through an intergenerational exchange. Thus, intergenerational cooperation may be possible whenever older volunteers have or acquire age-associated difficulties (for example, with hearing or some tasks that are physically demanding), since these inconveniences may be reduced by a younger fellow volunteer worker (Ronald).

The intergenerational exchange seems to be critical, especially for tasks such as being 'members of the board', a leading position characterised by the traditional predominance of older men (for example, Scout, and some Italian organisations), but in which some organisations are striving to involve more young people (and more women). Some Polish organisations, for example, underlined that as an older person leaves the organisation, there must be someone who will take over and continue its mission and initiatives. Thus, mixed-age boards were often preferred, yet not so easy to implement in practice. The same occurred in some Italian organisations. In two of them with mainly male volunteers, older volunteers are concentrated in leading positions, and in these organisations it is not so clear whether it is younger volunteers who are reluctant to be involved in managerial functions or older managers who refuse to step aside (AVIS, UISP).

Training

In the studied organisations, training is usually addressed to volunteers of all ages without a specific age dimension. Nevertheless, this activity is also described as very important in organisations where older volunteers constitute the majority (for example, Razem, AVULSS, Retraite Sportive, LFL, Solidarités).

In this kind of organisation, participation in training is voluntary, but in some cases it becomes a 'must', especially when a specific task cannot be taken up before training has been completed (Seniorpartner). AVULSS' representatives reported that older volunteers particularly lack ICT competence and need to be trained in it. Regarding how far training can be achieved, it was usually provided in the form of training-by-doing under supervision (Caritas), by means of brochures and written work instructions (Zeitzeugenbörse), as well as courses, conferences and meetings. In this way, older volunteers were able to broaden their horizons, and feel that their competences improved through volunteering (Senior Sport). Providing training was judged to be helpful in counteracting the possible withdrawal of volunteers.

Retention strategies: flexibility and redeployment

Most of the studied organisations wanted to retain their older volunteers for as long as possible. To achieve this, some of them, made up mainly of older volunteers, had introduced more flexible possibilities towards performing certain tasks in order to take into account the possible changing circumstances of older volunteers, such as, for example, temporarily interrupting membership when needed and facilitating readmission afterwards (Caritas, Bücherhallen). Furthermore, since older volunteers generally have more time to volunteer, they could be considered to better fit certain flexible characteristics that organisations are requesting more and more, such as, for example, being available on demand around-the-clock (2 Studies). Flexible working practices are considered important for solving potential conflicts among people in relation to volunteer activity. Thus, for the studied organisations it was crucial to find an adequate intensity level of engagement. According to a young-profiled Swedish organisation, composed mainly of women volunteers caught between work, raising children and volunteering, this flexibility was crucial (Save the Children).

Relative to older volunteers, the most often mentioned reasons identified by organisations for giving up voluntary work were changes in 'family circumstances' (for example, to care for a spouse or a parent, duties as grandparents, and so on) or in the 'volunteers' interests'. In these cases, to avoid the withdrawal of older volunteers, an appropriate retention strategy could be to offer a new task to older volunteers. This seemed to be important in some organisations composed mainly of older volunteers, as for the following two French organisations. Frères created a body ('Fioretti', that is, 'little flowers') to deal with older volunteers becoming dependent on others or having worsening health conditions. The organisation tried to find and create new activities to maintain their commitment, and in a few years the number of older volunteers in the organisation had doubled. Another similar example is provided by Retraite Sportive, which set up an Old Age Commission with the task of studying and formulating proposals for reducing the negative effects of ageing (which were likely to discourage certain members), with the aim of retaining all retired people within the activities of the organisation. Even some young-profiled organisations pursue the retention of older volunteers when capacities and needs change with redeployment in another manageable task. For example, to help adult volunteers and thus retain them longer, Scout had established 'adult support services' with the tasks of advising and guiding volunteers with formal appointments in areas such as recruitment, induction, training and review of adult volunteers. In the case of small organisations with few older volunteers, their involvement in the decision-making processes through regular meetings and good communication quality was also considered a good retention strategy (Integrationslotsen).

'Exit policies'

With regard to 'exit policies', there is generally no strict law or regulation that prescribes the age beyond which doing voluntary work is no longer allowed. Still, in some cases, such a rule could be found at the organisational level. In 2004, for example, Scout abolished its mandatory retirement age of 65 for volunteers with formal appointments as part of its commitment to diversity and equal opportunities. Hardly any of the studied organisations wanted its volunteers to retire because of ageing, but the professionalisation process had sometimes introduced certain reviews in large organisations with a modest number of older volunteers that could also be intended as 'exit policies'. At the English Scout, for example, there is a procedure for reviewing volunteers which would formally allow those who were in an advanced age to reconsider their commitment and/or change to less active roles. The words are chosen carefully so as not to offend, but the implication is clear. Similarly, at the Dutch Ronald, from the age of 70, every year during the annual performance interview, the manager discusses with the volunteer the appropriateness of keeping on with volunteering.

'Succession planning' has instead been introduced at the French Retraite Sportive, comprised mainly of older volunteers, where for each position, and particularly those of responsibility, a deputy is appointed in order to reduce the problems associated with absence. With this initiative, inconveniences linked to a lack of replacement of older managers due to possible sudden death, health problems or relocation are avoided. In any case, individual 'retirement decisions' in most of the investigated organisations are mainly and strongly linked with worsening health or physical conditions and changed capabilities, thus making the tasks too demanding, rather than ageing per se.

Comprehensive approach

A comprehensive approach to age management means dealing with the quality of HR management from recruitment to exit. Good practice in comprehensive approaches is characterised by, for example, an emphasis on preventing age management problems and a focus on the entire working life and all age groups, not just older workers (Naegele and Walker, 2006). This implies considerations on the good quality of 'the volunteer cycle' without focusing solely on older volunteers. This aspect was found important, for example, at the large English WRVS, which has a policy for a 'people engagement cycle', starting at the pre-recruitment phase and continuing with volunteers' retainment as supporters after their withdrawal from active volunteering.

Less structured examples in this direction were found in other organisations which could be summarised in two main organisational actions: (a) to select the best suited candidate according to the organisational needs and thereby preventing possible future problems; and (b) to take care of the selected volunteer in a better way during the volunteering experience.

The main channel to identify candidates used by the studied organisations was word-of-mouth, but in certain cases they could be identified among members, as in a French sports association where the most dynamic and healthy members could be selected to become volunteers (Retraite Sportive).

Some large organisations underlined that selecting the best-suited volunteers is more important than accepting all-comers, and one reason behind it could be that a work organisation needs expert volunteers for specific tasks. Interviewed representatives of the English Waterways underlined the importance of the selection procedure, because 'if you get the wrong person, they are with you for 10 years and the business will go downhill'. Thus, it seems that as a more professional framework evolves, organisations increasingly have to think about the necessary tasks to be done and allocate volunteers regardless of their preferences. A selection process took place in a number of investigated organisations (particularly in the more professionalised ones) in different countries. This process may consist of an initial interview (Nivon, Hospice, Frères), and this interview is also useful for finding a match between the organisation's needs and the person's interests and capacities (Werder). In some cases, organisations were required to provide selected candidates with compulsory training sessions before officially allowing them into the organisation (Seniorpartner, AVULSS, City Mission). The French Frères invests several months and resources to channel new volunteers' talents through a proper course before volunteering. Introduction programmes for settling into the work and being familiarised with the organisations were normal in the Dutch organisations Cliëntenbelang and PKN.

In order to contribute towards creating a good atmosphere, at Dgi and Senior Sport, a 'greeting group' is in charge of making sure that new members feel welcome. Other ways to support a good quality volunteer cycle are training, accompaniment and regular meetings to organise activities. They are fundamental not only for new volunteers, as neglecting this aspect might be fatal for an organisation in the long term, since problems of loose bonding between volunteers and the organisation may arise (Integrationslotsen, Zeitzeugenbörse, Ausbildungspaten).

We conclude this section by considering that even if the age management concept is not widespread in voluntary organisations, it has to be said that some of these organisations have started to adopt age management considerations to manage their volunteer workforce, both to improve their performance and to increase opportunities for older volunteers. While this section has addressed opportunities for older volunteers, the following explores the main barriers to volunteering.

Age discrimination in voluntary organisations?

Age management has to do with removing age barriers, and this may be linked to negative opinions and stereotypes of older volunteers, among other barriers. The aim of this section is to investigate the main organisational opinions of older volunteers and the barriers for volunteering in older age.

Organisational opinions of older volunteers

All the above-presented organisational 'age management' practices may be affected by opinions and stereotypes of older volunteers, especially as perceived by organisational decision-makers (Henkens, 2005; Principi et al, 2012). Indeed, organisational representatives mentioned both positive and negative concerns that might at least indirectly affect policies and practices towards older volunteers. When we inquired specifically over this, representatives of organisations with a high share of older volunteers in particular demonstrated appreciation for their older volunteers, considering them useful and reliable, for without them, they would simply no longer be able to operate (AUSER, AVULSS, UNITRE, Red Cross Army, WEA). In general, older volunteers were valued as those with more time and a greater commitment. At Nivon, for example, many were active after retirement for more than 20 or even 30 years, so in a way they grew older in the organisation. They were also appreciated for their great sense of availability, life experience, skills and knowledge, respect and authority. Other recognised strengths by the investigated organisational representatives included the fact that they can easily work autonomously, taking responsibility for their own projects (Gilde), as well as being pro-active (WRVS). According to representatives of some younger-profiled organisations, older volunteers have more sense of duty and less monetary claims (Werder). They do not usually make cost-benefit analyses of their time investments, as the younger people do, and have the attitude of giving something to the organisation instead of only trying to get something out of it (Integrationslotsen).

Besides the majority of positive opinions, however, some negative perceptions were also reported, mainly in relation to stereotypes that could potentially lead to discriminatory practices. Indeed, some of the interviewed people confirmed that older volunteers are less willing to change things, have too little will to exchange their experience due to a lack of trust in the younger generation, and so are less capable of learning new things and in general suffer from worse health and psychological conditions. Last but not least, according to representatives of two organisations, older volunteers are not always cooperative.

Main barriers to volunteering in older age

We have argued that opportunities might be conditioned by barriers such as organisational age-related negative perceptions, that may in turn be an indicator of possible age discrimination. From this, it can generally be said that when concrete actions to provide opportunities to older volunteers are missing, and negative opinions of older volunteers are overwhelming, this may well represent a barrier to greater involvement by older volunteers. More specifically, in the studied organisations, few practices were observed that could also be quite clearly labelled as discriminatory against older volunteers. For example, in a large young-profiled German organisation, older volunteers were not admitted to a corporate social responsibility programme. The director evaded questions on that programme, so the exact reason can only be proffered as a possible lack of identification models for the rather young public. In 2004 the English Scout abolished the mandatory retirement age of 65 for volunteers, even though in another English organisation members and volunteers over the age of 85 are currently not covered by the organisation's insurance policy. Thus, there seems to be a need to combat age barriers towards volunteering through an appropriate awareness campaign to improve the 'image' of older people, not only at the organisational level, but at all levels. For example, their image may be usually quite 'negative' in the media (MBU), or even self-perceived as such at the individual level. Interestingly enough, when older people (especially those aged 70 or more) introduced themselves during their first contact, a question they commonly asked to a large English organisation supporting children in schools with literacy was: 'Am I too old?' (VRH). A considerable role in this game may be played by the current 'professionalisation' trend of the voluntary sector. Although professionalisation may mean more attention to induction and training opportunities, it also contributes to excluding lower educated, unqualified and less healthy people, that is, mainly older volunteers (Principi et al, 2012). For example, for some DanChurchAid activities the lack of English skills could become an exclusion mechanism; and at Integrationslotsen, older volunteers become less suitable when they have a worse command of foreign languages than younger people. Similarly, at Seniorpartner and Ausbildungspaten, both with a high share of older volunteers, people with a higher educational level were preferred as they could serve as mentors for younger people as well as being generally regarded as more loyal. Professionalising volunteering often means carrying out appraisals of volunteers, a praxis that, as already anticipated, may be negative for older volunteers. For example, some of the investigated organisations had competence charts, because this helped them decide which volunteer could be deployed for which task (2 Studies). So, to a certain extent, volunteers are increasingly being treated in a similar manner to paid staff. As a matter of fact, one further key aspect of professionalisation is the role of paid staff employed by voluntary organisations. It is thus important to understand the relationships between paid staff and the volunteer workforce, and in particular the older volunteer workforce, over whether barriers still stand in the way of older volunteers due to a not-so-ideal relationship with paid staff.

Large organisations that rely to a greater extent on employees and on only a few volunteers who are mainly older (that is, where paid workers have the power to recruit volunteers), may try to solve these problems by limiting the presence of volunteers in the organisation (as in the case of Kasteel). Another argument to support this view is that it is difficult to prescribe or forbid volunteers from doing anything, as they are not paid staff (Lohner).

In some voluntary organisations, including older-profiled ones, volunteers felt that the staff merely considered them (that is, the volunteers) as people who should serve them (that is, the staff), and not the other way around (Tenants, DaneAge, 2 Studies, AVULSS). Furthermore, according to some interviewed people, sometimes employees perceive volunteers as essentially having the more pleasant jobs (2 Studies), or feel that their job security is impaired by the presence of volunteers (Caritas). On the same issue, in some Swedish organisations with a high share of older volunteers, trade unions have raised some questions over whether an increase in volunteer work might result in a reduction in the number of paid employees (City Mission and Swedish Church).

Conclusions

Based on the 'age management' concept established in relation to the work of the labour market, and defined as 'organisational initiatives designed to combat age barriers, either directly or indirectly, and providing an environment in which each individual is able to achieve his or her potential without being disadvantaged by their age' (Walker and Taylor, 1998, p 3), the main aim of this chapter was to determine whether volunteers' age management practices could be found among the investigated European voluntary organisations. As a matter of fact, we have identified, as described earlier, some organisational age management practices in the following areas: recruitment, intergenerational exchange, training, flexibility, redeployment, exit policies and comprehensive approach. So we can say with some certainty that even if most of the voluntary organisations did not officially pursue any age management strategy, organisational initiatives based on volunteers' age were not unknown. This means that some voluntary organisations are currently striving to adjust work tasks to meet the needs and preferences of older volunteers by means of special measures in order to recruit and retain them for as long as possible.

Yet age management practices have been implemented by organisations with different features, and we argued in the introduction to this chapter that organisational features might influence these practices. Indeed, some characteristics were found to play a prominent role in shaping such practices. It was found, for example, that the identified practices have not always had all the positive features implied in Walker and Taylor's definition (1998). Age management with 'positive features' seems to be found more clearly in organisations composed mainly of older volunteers that implemented some initiatives in line with the active ageing concept, intended as 'a comprehensive strategy to maximise participation and well-being as people age' (Walker, 2002, p 130). In concrete terms, this means, for example: flexibility to facilitate readmission after a period of care for a spouse or a parent or after grandparenting; redeployment to maintain commitment and reduce the negative effects of ageing; and succession planning with the aim of retaining older volunteers to prevent problems associated with their possible absence. Another distinctive trait is a wish to involve and have relationships with volunteers from the younger generation. Yet despite some efforts in this direction, intergenerational relationships between volunteers seem difficult to realise, particularly in philanthropic organisations, probably because they imply activities that may not appeal to younger volunteers.

Despite age management initiatives in line with the active ageing concept were mainly found in organisations composed mainly of older volunteers, some of these initiatives were also found in organisations composed mainly of younger volunteers. For example, some of the latter aimed to recruit more older volunteers to have a more balanced age structure for the volunteer workforce, since a better age-mix of such a workforce was considered valuable.

The situation seems to show some difficulties for older volunteers in organisations with a considerable degree of professionalisation (that is, mainly large ones with a high level of paid staff, and sometimes organisations with mainly younger volunteers). Even if good practices are not missing from this kind of organisations (see, for example, the 'people engagement cycle' at WRVS, an organisation composed mainly of older volunteers), volunteers' age management practices seem to be first oriented towards maintaining a suitable quality of work and solving work problems. This is not a negative aspect in itself, since a more professionalised volunteer sector would necessarily mean a more professionalised volunteer workforce. This is also clearly indicated in the increasing importance given by these organisations to a very selective recruitment process in order to identify the best suited candidates. However, this may sometimes imply certain uncomfortable or penalising practices for older volunteers, as, for example: difficulties in being recruited; allocation to a non-attractive task; or being 'dismissed' as a result of a periodical review.

A further issue discussed in this chapter was age discrimination in voluntary organisations, particularly with respect to opinions held by organisational representatives on older volunteers, as well as other possible organisational age barriers. In general, we found that especially (although not exclusively) organisations composed mainly of older volunteers held positive opinions of the latter, and even considered them reliable, available, experienced and skilled. These kinds of organisation also exhibited fewer age barriers, while the more professionalised ones tended, to a higher extent, to exclude older volunteers from certain activities or manifested some kind of age barrier.

On the whole, the study indicates that even if some age management practices could be found among European voluntary organisations, the majority of the investigated organisations were still unfamiliar with the concept of 'age management'. At the organisational level there is still a need to remove direct and indirect negative perceptions of older people as volunteers. This should be considered in a context of growing professionalisation of the voluntary sector which may tend to exclude older people, that is, generally people with less individual resources. It would seem that the more there are paid and professionalised staff among these organisations, the more they tend to solve work problems at the expense of older volunteers, leading to the latter's further alienation, for as pointed out by one respondent, they might have difficulties in seeing themselves within the context of a 'professional' organisational environment (DanChurchAid).

References

Henkens, K. (2005) 'Stereotyping older workers and retirement: the managers' point of view', *Canadian Journal of Aging*, vol 24, no 4, pp 353-66.

Mintzberg, H. (1983) *Structure in fives: Designing effective organizations*, Upper Saddle River, NJ: Prentice-Hall.

Naegele, G. and Walker, A. (2006) *A guide to good practice in age management*, Dublin: European Foundation for the Improvement of Living and Working Conditions.

Principi, A. and Lamura, G. (2011) *Opportunities for older people in the civil society: International report*, Ancona: National Institute of Health and Science on Aging.

Principi, A., Lindley, R., Perek-Bialas, J. and Turek, K. (2012) 'Volunteering in older age: an organizational perspective', *International Journal of Manpower*, vol 33, no 6, pp 685-703.

Sargeant, M. (2006) *Age discrimination in employment*, Aldershot: Gower Publishing.

Walker, A. (2002) 'A strategy for active ageing', *International Social Security Review*, vol 55, no 1, pp 121-39.

Walker, A. and Taylor, P. (1998) *Combating age barriers in employment: A European portfolio of good practice*, Luxemburg: Office for Official Publications of the European Communities.

Warburton, J. and Cordingley, S. (2004) 'The contemporary challenges of volunteering in an ageing Australia', *Australian Journal on Volunteering*, vol 9, no 2, pp 67-74.

TWELVE

Organisational reflections on the impact of working and caring on older volunteering

Robert Lindley and Andrea Principi

Introduction

Voluntary organisations are conscious of the fact that volunteers have other potential roles, notably, as members of the paid labour force, as informal carers (particularly to family members), and in other forms of informal support to family and community. But this does not mean that all are concerned about the implications of these roles. An organisation in whatever country or sector of activity may be currently experiencing no volunteer recruitment difficulty at all, so its attention is drawn to other matters of policy and practice. Indeed, in general, the voluntary organisations taking part in this study were pre-occupied with managing and funding their present activity rather than with the long-term supply of volunteers. However, within their responses were various lines of thinking that indicate a more nuanced assessment of the implications of external labour market situations and the impact of demographic change on the timing and pattern of caring responsibilities.

Following the theoretical approach adopted in the book as a whole and outlined in Chapter Two, this chapter deals, primarily, with what is termed the 'meso level', namely, the situations and perceptions of voluntary organisations. The focus is on *older* volunteers and the *external conditions* affecting their volunteering, *as viewed currently by the voluntary organisations*. The external conditions considered are those that act on the propensities and opportunities to volunteer and that affect the operations of the organisation through the influence of working and caring activities. This is in contrast to internal conditions created by voluntary organisations themselves.

The external conditions may be related to the notion of the 'welfare mix' used in Chapter Two that refers to the 'interactions/divisions of responsibilities' between the market and institutional conditions that comprise the external environment – family, labour market, care system and voluntary sector. So this chapter, in part, deals with how voluntary organisations, in effect, view the impact of the 'welfare mix' on older volunteering – that is, how the latter is conditioned by the former.

Previous research on the impact of work and informal care on the volunteering of older people has concentrated much more on the individual level, namely, volunteers or potential volunteers, than on those who might recruit and deploy them. The imbalance in available empirical evidence also applies to the relative efforts devoted to theorising. If we focus further on older people, these disparities remain: as reviewed in Chapter Two, there is a significant body of research on older volunteers whereas there is little that addresses the views of the voluntary organisations themselves.

For instance, activity and continuity theories (Havighurst, 1961; Maddox, 1968) stress the scope for maintaining activity with later ageing, and encourage expectations based on theories and evidence of how best this might be achieved. This is in contrast to the pessimism/realism inherent in the earlier disengagement theories of the ageing process (Cumming and Henry, 1961). Thus we may note that participation in volunteering is positively associated with participation in employment since paid workers have more individual and social resources, and this is conducive to volunteering (Wilson and Musick, 1997). Moreover, in most European countries retirement ages are increasing, as are the employment rates of older workers (OECD, 2011). However, scarcity theory (Marks, 1977) points to the potential difficulties of coping with multiple roles and the possibility that informal family care responsibility will crowd out volunteering.

However, these perspectives are drawn from research on individuals. We do not know how voluntary organisations perceive the consequences for their activities of an increasing involvement of older people in the labour market, or if organisations are seeking partnerships with companies to increase their older volunteer force among employed people. Similarly, we do not know how organisations regard the effects of informal family care on older volunteering; this may be particularly crucial for organisations providing social care, an activity that may overlap with informal family care. Thus, this chapter gives priority to filling these gaps in knowledge by addressing the organisational rather than individual point of view.

This chapter draws on 73 'case studies' carried out in voluntary organisations operating in eight different European countries in order to illustrate different examples of how they assess the impacts of external conditions on the volunteering of older people and the effects of these on the organisations themselves.

The methodological position of the chapter is that the case studies are vehicles for identifying generic types of behaviour without making claims for representativeness. To aid identification of the organisations, there is sometimes reference to the country of location. Moreover, this may go further to mention an aspect of the national socio-economic policy environment that is likely to be part of the explanation of the views of the particular voluntary organisations being considered. Generalising from a relatively small number of cases to making statements about national patterns should, obviously, be avoided. However, explaining a given case or group of cases fully may naturally allude to features of the national environment that are likely to be part of that explanation without implying that all potential cases would be similarly affected. This chapter does do this to some extent, but the interaction between older volunteering and country 'welfare mixes' is primarily a matter for the concluding Chapter Fourteen of this volume.

Thus, in light of the above, this chapter seeks to bring more balance to the body of evidence available on volunteering, by extending our knowledge of the perspectives of voluntary organisations. Basically, it addresses the following four main research questions relating to the working–caring–volunteering nexus involving older people;

1. How do voluntary organisations regard the implications of longer working lives for their volunteering environments, for example, through people's underlying attitudes to volunteering, to what they have to offer and to when to make the time commitment?
2. What is the experience of voluntary organisations in collaborating with private and public sector employers that seek directly to foster volunteering by their employees?
3. How do voluntary organisations perceive the impact of an increasingly older population and the requirement for more informal family care on the contribution of older people to volunteering?
4. Regarding informal family care, what further considerations arise for those voluntary organisations that specialise in the provision of social care?

Thus, the following section turns to examine how volunteering situations are affected by the labour force participation of older people (the first two questions). The third section is devoted to the experiences and diagnoses of voluntary organisations relating to the impact of family care responsibilities on older volunteering (the third and fourth questions). The final section brings together the implications of the previous two sections for what are the principal generic dilemmas that face voluntary organisations. This is done by addressing how far the apparent 'logic of competition', between time for volunteering, working and informal caring, applies in practice.

The labour market

Labour force participation of older workers

Volunteering and work: orientating the discourse

Based mainly on a quantitative approach, a considerable body of emerging evidence suggests that older people still in paid work are more likely to volunteer than those outside paid work (see, for example, Erlinghagen, 2010). This does not mean, however, that voluntary organisations may not feel the intensification and/or the extension of the working lives of older people as a threat that may have the consequence of reducing the supply of volunteers.

Before referring to specific issues and illustrating their importance in the context of particular case studies, it is worth making some generic statements that apply to most of the cases and/or their wider environments:

- The perceptions of voluntary organisations about trends in older labour force participation and employment rates and of their actual or potential impacts on the behaviour of their organisations may be plausible enough, but it cannot be assumed that they are necessarily based on sound analyses.
- The propensity to volunteer is highest among those in employment, and among those with higher qualifications and/or skilled jobs and these two (overlapping) groups are growing in most countries. Evidence for this comes from survey analyses; these usually allow for differences in health among participants, so that the positive relationship between volunteering and working is a direct one and is not simply explained by a common positive relationship that each has with degree of good health (or of absence of limiting disability).

- Hours-related increases in older people's employment rates may come about without changes in formal retirement ages, through increases in hours of work in pre-retirement or post-retirement situations, where retirement is defined as taking a pension from one's main employment. This will be the case, especially where pension schemes impose no limitation on working for pay after retirement.

- Where retirement is actually delayed, this may be thought likely to shorten or 'squeeze' the period left for volunteering, but whether it does so depends on what is happening to the length of healthy active life and on the patterns of interests and priorities that older people display through it.

- There is some evidence (to be discussed later) that the 'new seniors' differ from previous cohorts at the same stage in their attitudes to volunteering, in that the kinds of commitment they give are less binding and more measured in terms of compatibility with their individual goals.

- There is a strong gender dimension to how working, caring and volunteering interact. For some voluntary organisations, this is of explicit and central concern; for others it is implicit and apparently of uncertain significance to them (to be discussed later).

The above observations have a bearing on a number of issues considered by voluntary organisations and covered in this and the following section. At the outset, however, we might note that, taking a *country cross-section* among a sample of developed nations, there is certainly not a negative relationship between participating in the labour market and volunteering. Indeed, volunteering rates are higher among those countries with higher employment rates (Warburton and Jeppsson-Grassman, 2011). Moreover, *within* the countries covered in the present volume, there are also no such negative relationships *over time*.

Volunteering and work: the quantitative dimension

It is easy to exaggerate differences in country-sector situations and their external conditions and changes in different factors over time, while ignoring the fairly common overall background. Many respondents recognised this, and referred to the extent of the *potential* pool of retired older volunteers simply because they do, in general, have more time to allocate as they wish, compared with younger and middle-aged people with developing families and careers to attend to (Univoc, Teatro, Nivon, Gilde, Red Cross Army, DaneAge, DanChurchAid, Lekarzy Nadziei, WEA). This does not mean that actual – as opposed to potential – volunteering patterns are not radically different.

Moreover, older people's volunteering can be offered in more flexible forms (for example, by filling hosting vacancies at short notice in the case of Kasteel) and even in some cases on demand (as in 2 Studies). However, from some cases, there were complaints about volunteers negating this advantage, by committing themselves to multiple volunteering activities that then constrained their availability. Retired volunteers may then be no more flexible than labour market participants.

At the same time, there have been rigidities on the organisation's side that look out of place, given changes in the external environment. Particularly noteworthy is the self-imposed constraint adopted by Retraite Sportive, where volunteers were requested to comply with a condition that they should not be active in the labour market. In light of the increase in the legal retirement age in France, this condition was under review (at the time of interview with the organisation) in order to broaden the target volunteer population. On the other hand, another management reaction was to regret the legal reform allowing people to hold a job and be paid a pension, which would give younger retired people a financial incentive to find paid professional activity rather than to work as volunteers (Randonnée).

As regards the extent of change, some scepticism about the underlying trends was expressed by a small minority of respondents – for example, managers' personal experiences of having been made redundant as older workers and their lack of belief generally in employers' willingness to actively engage with seniors' potential coloured the responses of a Dutch environmental leisure service (Nivon). They believed that much had to change within organisations and in the minds of employers before people would be able to be employed at higher ages. In other cases, respondents admitted they were not really aware of the labour market developments around them and the possible implications for their organisations, or simply had no opinion (Portes and most of the Danish cases).

Leaving scepticism or lack of opinion aside, the demographics can be interpreted by some organisations in quite straightforward terms. Those involving both older volunteers and providing services to older people may indicate an underlying lack of concern because population ageing increases the 'younger-older' cohorts before it increases the 'older-older' cohorts: the supply of potential volunteers, therefore, receives a boost before the demand from clients needing care expands (Seniorpartner). The effects of demographic change on volunteer supply in relation to demand are seen to be modest.

However, few of the respondents took comfort from such 'demographic dynamics'. An equally straightforward view is that increased labour force participation will have a negative effect on volunteer supply; this was held particularly by organisations drawing mainly on older volunteers and providing altruistic services: Swedish Church, Mission Covenant, Salvation Army, City Mission, Red Cross Sweden. The Italian AUSER organisation took a similar view and another, UNIVOC, saw it as particularly penalising organisations heavily dependent on older volunteers. It was these organisations that were most likely to be analysing trends and looking for possible solutions. In contrast, organisations with a high share of younger volunteers as, for example, Save the Children and Children's Rights, saw no such negative effect, the former because they believed that their volunteer work depended on 'engagement' and not time availability, and the latter because most volunteers were younger anyway, and in employment. Other organisations, most of whose volunteers are, in any case, in employment, tend also to regard the increase in employment rates among older people as not constituting a problem.

Nonetheless, some organisations are concerned because they depend more on older women in part-time employment whose work intensity may increase to the point where it does encroach on their availability for volunteering; in others, substantial reductions in the pool of potential (women) volunteers were already in evidence (Caritas).

Alongside these current problems faced by some organisations are the reflections from an organisation that was in no such difficulty but was wary of their recent experience of greater enrolment of volunteers as a result of the economic crisis; many older people had lost their jobs, retired or had had their working hours reduced and had volunteered. These organisations did not want to rely on this effect for the medium-to-long term, when it was hoped that the economy and employment would recover and higher employment rates might begin to have some negative effects on volunteer supply (UNITRE).

Other organisations had noticed that rising labour force participation was having an effect on volunteering among older people, even though they themselves were not experiencing recruitment difficulties as a result, nor did they anticipate doing so. While not referring to a 'shortening' effect, the age at which some seniors were volunteering had risen from 60 to 62-65 (Senior Sport). Phases of post-retirement activity were identified in terms of spending the early two or three years catching up on doing things that had not been possible during a busy working life, followed by a period of feeling somewhat at a loose end, which led to some retirees turning to volunteering (WRVS).

For organisations with a very broad 'older' age group engaged in volunteering, the specifics of gradual increases in formal retirement ages by three years or so, however, would seem to be much less pressing – yet organisational reactions could be quite different. Gilde, with volunteers aged between 50 and 70, saw the prospect of 90 per cent of their volunteers being 'busy in the labour market' if future policy scenarios came about. This led them to advocate volunteering as part of the transition between regular working life and active retirement. Yet the volunteer coordinator at Kasteel, working with 50+ plus volunteers, saw no such difficulty just because the retirement age was rising and more recruits were 67 rather than 65.

While it is possible to envisage a shifting of the volunteering phase of a person's life in time following the shifting of retirement ages with no loss of volunteering effort in the long run, this would still imply at least a one-off drop in the supply of volunteering as this process is taking place. Moreover, not only is there a lag, following retirement, before someone might turn to volunteering, but there is also likely to be a lag in the effects of increased work intensity in later life, with or without an actual extension to working life. Those who approach retirement with volunteering in mind through a wish to 'get involved', have new experiences and learn new skills may feel differently if they have spent longer at work. These sentiments that may be keenly felt at 60 could be less pressing at a later age. Some organisations that were trying to attract older volunteers in order to achieve more balanced age structures worried that they might miss the best moment when seeking to recruit them (ANPAS).

Thus, although there are good reasons for monitoring the prospects for the supply of older volunteers, most of those cited by the case study organisations were much less concerned about the *volume* of supply but rather reflected *qualitative* considerations.

Volunteering and work: the qualitative dimension

Whether there are age-related propensities to volunteer, the above tends to ignore the fact that retirement may change the terms and timing of volunteering, but many people are already volunteering, and it is more a question of adjusting the extent and pattern of commitments, rather than deciding to volunteer or not to volunteer. The qualitative aspects apply to these as much as to new volunteers. Those receiving most comment from the organisations and considered below, were: (i) the attitudes of volunteers and the nature of their volunteering; (ii) the place of women; (iii) the qualifications and professional experience that potential volunteers could offer; and (iv) the development of knowledge and skills relating to the volunteering roles.

(i) On the nature of volunteering available, a number of the organisations pointed to changes in attitudes among the new seniors as being more important than any increase in labour force participation (although the two may be linked to some degree to a common effect). Reference was made to the more individualistic approaches that affected the willingness to volunteer, what to offer and how regularly. This was particularly underlined by voluntary organisations providing altruistic services (as, for example, Cross Church and Red Cross Army), probably since individualistic approaches tend to drive older people mainly towards self-expressive volunteering or other activities. In a rather different context, Gistrup, with a mainly older volunteer force, also faced what it felt to be a reduction in potential volunteers because of a lack of time and interest.

(ii) As regards the place of women in the volunteering system, a number of organisations cited their concern at the observed or expected effects of rising labour force participation among older women when they were the dominant volunteer group (and also typically most subject to family caring pressures). Others, however, alluded to the under-utilisation of women's capabilities, acquired through women taking advantage of greater educational and occupational opportunities, yet given limited scope when it came to volunteering, where they were assigned traditional roles. In France, for example, the fact that older men are more likely to be volunteering in responsible positions than women is explained by the relative lack of occupational experience of retired women (Poussou-Plesse et al, 2010). But rather than leaving this problem to resolve itself, at least in part, since the imbalance in experience is declining with successive generations, Retraite Sportive adopted a more pro-active approach. It created a special commission to reflect on methods of promoting access for women to responsible posts at all levels. Through its work, the committee examined the various social, cultural and structural obstacles, as well as time management considerations, which constituted the principal hurdles to participation by women.

In some of the Italian and German organisations too, concern was expressed at the lack of women in leading roles. A rather different emphasis here from that of the French one given above is indicated by the ANPAS respondent – pointing to the greater difficulty for women in reconciling family and volunteering activities, increasing as it does with age (see p 288), rather than the lack of women with suitable experience.

(iii) While the external labour market context can influence patterns of volunteering, so can the qualifications and professional experience that potential volunteers can offer. In general, the respondents in virtually all countries acknowledged, at least implicitly, that there was a fairly benign relationship between, on the one hand, external growth in education, training and skilled work experience that potential volunteers were able to offer and, on the other hand, the evolving requirements of voluntary organisations. Indeed, the quality of supply has probably grown faster than the quality of demand, as indicated by the earlier point in relation to the under-utilisation of the skills of women volunteers. There is, however, a less favourable effect of this, in that people with greater capabilities to offer may be discouraged from volunteering where they see their potential contribution being un(der)-recognised.

(iv) While the (internal) 'age' management of volunteers and the development of voluntary organisations was the subject of Chapter Eleven, an external labour supply effect on their behaviour was alluded to by a number of the organisations interviewed. This is the constraint on them resulting from a lack of suitably qualified people to work in a sector that is seeking to professionalise its operations in several areas. Again, the current employment crisis may lead more qualified people to apply for work in this sector, rather than volunteer to get some worthwhile experience to add to their CVs, while still pursuing jobs with conventional private or public sector employers.

Employers: meeting business needs and social objectives

The attitudes of voluntary organisations to more conventional business organisations derive from a number of factors. Here the focus is on how different relationships or linkages between voluntary activity and the corporate level may have an impact on volunteering by older Europeans. First, there may be sponsorship relations in which the voluntary body receives donations of money, supplies of an organisation's products or services and other resources (for example, business equipment), and accepts volunteer assistance; second, a voluntary organisation may provide charitable supporting functions, which it can legitimately carry out for a conventional business or, more usually, a public service; and third, a voluntary organisation may supply services under contract, again usually to a public service and ostensibly via normal commercial relations, where the voluntary body may have competed against other such bodies or commercial suppliers in order to secure the business.

As regards the first type of linkage, the growth of corporate social responsibility programmes has included corporate volunteering activities (or employee volunteer programmes), where employees are given time off (paid or unpaid) during the working day to volunteer for specific purposes. This is particularly prevalent in the US but is also significant, if modest in scale, in certain EU member states as, for example, Denmark, the UK and France (see Chapters Four, Six and Seven, respectively). A milder form of commitment may come through the employer being especially flexible in allowing individual employees who wish to volunteer to do so without complications arising over making up the working time lost (AVULSS). Indeed, in Italy, AVULSS was very concerned about the effects of extensions to working life and was seeking to strengthen enforcement of the 1991 Law no 266, which gives workers who are members of voluntary organisations an entitlement to take advantage of flexible working times, in order to carry out voluntary activities, allowing for the needs of the company.

Examples of companies offering employees as volunteers to organisations were found in the Netherlands (Gilde), and there are similar initiatives in England, at RNIB and VRH. Similarly, the Ronald charity attracts various forms of support from profit-making organisations. Instead of a team-building day in the open air, a group of employees of one company helps out with chores; or a personnel officer of Dutch Railways gives advice to the charity's manager about personnel management.

A somewhat different corporate motivation comes into play in schemes that introduce into a retirement programme a period of employment that may involve being deployed in work for a voluntary organisation before retiring (Gilde, WRVS).

While these initiatives were seen as positive, they were often created at the margins of a company's human resources (HR) activity and could be weakened or withdrawn – for example, if the company experienced new business conditions and the implicit subsidies involved began to appear unaffordable or tied up too much management time. Those voluntary organisations involved with them, however, did not seem very concerned about the loss of this support in the event of the supplying organisation facing financial difficulties that would lead them to withdraw the programme.

Indeed, anticipating potential problems may lead to mediating action: the project manager in the Bücherhallen assumed that the financial crisis would reduce the amount of money received from sponsors, but the organisation aimed to compensate for that by commissioning volunteers to engage in fundraising and selling books in flea markets.

The second kind of linkage comes through voluntary organisations providing charitable services, usually to public or quasi-public bodies (for example, supplying people to act as hospital information guides for patients and families, serving refreshments and offering transport to and from hospital appointments; helping children to read; voluntary work on public heritage projects). In some of these cases, there is the potential for substituting volunteering for conventional jobs, at least to a degree. In general, voluntary organisations did not regard this as being very significant at all – but see below in relation to those providing care services.

The attitudes of voluntary organisations or, more generally, the 'voluntary practitioner community' towards taking on tasks under the third category, supplying paid-for services, appear to derive from a complex mix of different elements. These include, especially, culture (for example, what should be the responsibility of the individual or family to provide and/or fund and what should be expected from publicly funded services), activities relating to advocacy in the arena where political priorities are debated and recognition of social imperatives that provoke some citizens to respond actively on a voluntary basis to apparent social need.

Concern can also derive from the view that some of these tasks should be carried out by employees, and not volunteers, and that the latter are taking paid work from the former. This is less likely to be the reaction when employment levels in the organisation are stable or rising. But when job cuts are a consequence of reductions in public spending, this becomes a more difficult issue. In point of fact, few voluntary organisations referred to this as an external challenge to the legitimacy of their activities.

Informal and structured care provision: the impact on volunteering of older people

After the analysis in the previous section of the relationship between work and volunteering of older people, this section deals with the organisational perspective on the linkage between informal care and volunteering. It is divided into two parts: the first reports on how the organisations studied perceived the relationship between informal family caregiving in relation to older relatives and, more broadly, of family members (such as helping adult children in raising grandchildren) and volunteering in older age; the second focuses on those organisations that are primarily active in the care sector, with the additional issues that arose in their case.

Older volunteers as family caregivers: organisational perceptions

The views of voluntary organisations form the primary source for analysis but, as observed in the previous section regarding the effects on volunteering of the labour force participation of older people, it is not assumed that they are necessarily cogent or based on extensive analysis. These views are, however, important as perceptions that are likely to guide the behaviour of the key actor at the centre of this study.

We can say that, while in general the voluntary organisations perceived family caregiving as a recurrent activity, this did not worry all such organisations. For instance, at Scout, with a relatively high proportion of younger volunteers, there were many individual examples where increased family/elder care responsibilities affected volunteering, but it did not have an impact on the organisation as a whole. Even at WRVS, taking on caring responsibilities for grandchildren or an older family member was one of the most common reasons for older people to drop out of volunteering, but they could join the charity again after a couple of years, when care duties were over (this also applied in some of the Italian organisations).

Moreover, several organisations did not have particular problems in recruiting (older) volunteers, so the potentially negative impact of informal caring on volunteering was not felt to be a major issue. Furthermore, although our case study methodology does not allow generalisation, we should not be surprised that voluntary organisations operating where informal family caregiving is not widespread were not concerned about its influence on volunteering by older people (for example, the Danish and Dutch organisations).

Nonetheless, some organisations seemed to be directly affected by the influence of family caregiving on their volunteer workforce, and considered this to be a major problem. Ausbildungspaten, for example, regularly experienced cessation of individual volunteering due to volunteers' family care situations. And representatives of some Swedish organisations believed that any greater need for informal family care would reduce the number of volunteers available, as people substituted informal caring for volunteering. Similar situations applied in Italy to ANPAS, UNIVOC and UNITRE. In the German Caritas and Lohner representatives' opinion, this effect extended to the recruitment of new volunteers. Indeed, organisations were more inclined to see the downside for volunteer supply of a major growth in demand for elder care, responsibility for its informal provision mainly falling on women in an environment where the role of the family in informally caring for older people is a strong one. This particularly applies to those organisations with proportionately more older people among their volunteers.

Again, while emphasising the distinction between explaining a case partly by reference to the national policy and socio-economic environment and generalising to the national level from the level of the case, we may refer to the absence of concern about the effects of informal family care on volunteering among the Polish organisations interviewed. It is reasonable to hypothesise that this stemmed from a combination of the deep-rooted role of informal family care that is taken for granted in that country, combined with the extremely low role of volunteering apparent.

Care provision by voluntary organisations: intersections with informal caring

This section focuses on the implications of informal caregiving for those organisations that are primarily active in the care sector. Thus, narrowing the discussion further to focus on voluntary organisations providing social and health services (not just to older people but to other parts or all of the population) identifies part of the voluntary sector that clearly expects there to be a strong growth in the underlying demand for its services. Most of all, this relates to increases in life expectancy, albeit accompanied by rising healthy life expectancy.

Here, we confine the discussion to how informal caring by volunteers intersects with the work of voluntary care organisations and the broader care system. Three aspects of this are explored: (i) the relationship between volunteers as informal carers and their role in voluntary care organisations; (ii) the evolution of the care system and its consequences for volunteers and voluntary organisations, as seen by the latter; and (iii) voluntary organisations and public policy.

The relationship between volunteers as informal carers and their role in voluntary organisations

The potential effects of increased family care roles on volunteering behaviour have been discussed above in broad terms. Some more specific issues should be added. First, increased experience of caring may mean that certain volunteer caring roles become less attractive to people because they represent a reinforcement of what they contend with at home. Children's Rights points to the fact that it is not simply a question of availability of time; contacts with children in distress are psychologically stressful and an increase in the home caring workload would reduce the number of volunteers. In the same vein, the respondent from the Italian UNIVOC, which provides social services to blind individuals, worried that a person caring for a dependent family member could not consider voluntary work within the social and health services as a 'safety valve', since they would be more or less pursuing similar activities to those carried out at home. They believe that people would presumably try to 'have a break' in a different form of volunteering.

However, there is another perspective offered by Children's Rights itself, which identifies a potentially positive aspect: greater personal involvement in informal caregiving might entail a positive externality for volunteer organisations because citizens may become more prone to engage in civic organisation in the future. More specifically, the WRVS which provides, among other things, care services for older people, observed that it gained 'quite a few volunteers' whose parents had received support from the organisation and who joined WRVS after they had died, wanting 'to give something back' as the organisation had been 'very helpful in their family circumstances'. Thus, in a way, they repaid the support their parent had received.

Recently in the Netherlands, a foundation with about 25 care homes has provoked debate by proposing that such an altruistic follow-up might be turned into a way of helping to cover the costs of care more predictably, by preferring clients who bring their own

289

volunteer with them; this is achieved by introducing a condition into the contract for elder care that the family would supply a minimum number of volunteered hours per week, in return for their relative being accepted as a resident.

Finally, despite the rather pessimistic Italian view mentioned earlier, as exemplified by UNIVOC, the Italian AVULSS joins Sweden's Children's Rights and the English WRVS in believing that there are positive aspects present where carers engaged in informal 'voluntary work' at home may be taking a first step to volunteering in the formal social or health sector.

The evolution of the care system and its consequences for volunteers and voluntary organisations

The majority of the investigated organisations providing care services employ mainly older volunteers and mainly women. There is a problematical element here in that male service users tend to prefer to be cared for by men (AVULSS). In light of this, two strategies identified were to recruit more men (for example, the Italian AVULSS) and young-middle-aged volunteers (2 Studies, Hospice, PKN, Swedish Church, MBU, Lekarzy Nadziei, WRVS).

One reason for involving more young volunteers is that voluntary work in these organisations often involved physically demanding work (Lohner, 2 Studies, Ronald).

Nevertheless, organisations were finding it difficult to meet these objectives, since young volunteers and men in general, seem to be less attracted by care activities. Furthermore, in some voluntary organisations with older age profiles (for example, Caritas), existing volunteers may not be so eager to integrate new volunteers from non-traditional groups.

While the lack of balance between the demographic (age and/or gender) dimensions of volunteer supply and demand is evident in the above, it is accompanied by a corresponding one among employed care staff. Stimulating the supply of male workers, whether employees or volunteers, is a matter for public policy to wrestle with, rather than to be left simply to individual organisations.

Against the above background, there are other important ingredients that different voluntary organisations must deal with. In some cases, organisations were struggling to recruit volunteers for specific tasks, such as visiting lonely older people (DaneAge and Red Cross Army). While measures to reduce the impact of this exist, for example, through helping such people to become less isolated, these do not remove the need for 'person-to-person' contact.

However, many of the voluntary organisations saw a more general issue when reflecting on their external environment, even if it also stemmed from the impetus to develop their organisations to meet changing internal aspirations to improve their performance. This is their need for more professional and competent volunteers (Lekarzy Nadziei, Emmaüs and Frères), whereas, in some organisations, the main perception was that this could not be met through the current profiles of older volunteers, as, for example, in some organisations investigated in Denmark (DanChurchAid, 9220 and Cross Church), even if older volunteers played a major role in this field.

Voluntary organisations and public policy

Most of the voluntary organisations studied believed that the demand for the care services they provide had been growing and would continue to do so in future. Most received funding from the state, at the national, regional and/or local level, and some from the European Union (EU). Some of this funding was (more or less) continuous, some contingent on formal contract performance and some time-limited, in accordance with the programmes of which it was a part. For those organisations that relied on these sources of funding (particularly the last two), sustainability was a continual concern, even if the underlying demand was rising, simply because the purchasing power of the state was not keeping up with it. Thus, even before the western financial crisis broke in 2008, all governments were struggling to devise plans to deal with a rising health and social care bill, at the same time as trying to improve the quality of care and quality of life of older citizens.

The aftermath of the economic crisis has not just involved matters of finance. During the last decade in particular, certain types of external regulation, depending on the country, have impinged on the voluntary care sector.

The Dutch context can be taken as a case in point. Here, volunteer supply is not a problem but the country has not been immune from the European economic crisis. Municipalities, having the responsibility to make policies for voluntary work, have sought to encourage free-of-charge volunteering in the health sector, since the crisis in the short run within the healthcare sector involves major shortages of professional carers (2 Studies).

Thus, in a situation requiring an expansion of services by the voluntary sector (Hospice Utrecht), there is also an increase in demand for more professionalised older volunteers. Exemplifying this pressure is the growing practice, according to 2 Studies, to work with competence charts for volunteers, which help them to understand which volunteer can be deployed for which task. A role in professionalising volunteer work is also played by the need to meet similar standards for volunteers to those for employees concerning safety and hygiene.

While the above issues are already in the centre of the big picture, there are others that appear at the margins, where the perception of the 'challenge' to voluntary organisations is given another twist. Rising informal family care may not only compromise the capacity of some voluntary bodies to meet the growing demand for care, given its potential impact on the supply of volunteer carers. It may also compete with established volunteer bodies in providing that care; at its simplest, more informal caring may mean less work and funding to bid for by voluntary service providers than would otherwise have been the case (as noted, for example, by the Salvation Army in Sweden).

The situation can be complex, however. Governments have been exploring (indeed, experimenting on a large scale, in some cases) with different approaches to caring that generally favour services in the home and improving the financial and other support for family carers. Thus, rather than seeing the increase in informal family care as, in some way, potentially reducing the funded demand for the services of voluntary care organisations, some organisations assessed the position from a different perspective. They believed that the demand for their current services would not decrease but would, instead, be supplemented by needing to provide assistance to family carers – the Italian AUSER, for example, pointed to this, but was concerned that it would not be able to meet increasing demand for such support.

Furthermore, at a time when it may seem that the scenario for voluntary organisations appears quite promising, given the calls for more engagement of volunteers in the care sector to save public money, the state may not allocate adequate resources for competency development to improve the quality and organisation of voluntary work to the level needed (as observed by DanChurchAid). Thus, care organisations were coming under great pressure to deal with a decrease in public funding when demands on their activity were growing (for example, Caritas and Lohner, providing goods from clothing and food banks).

Conclusions

It is clear that socio-economic changes are leading to competition for the time of those who *might* volunteer. The activities of three (overlapping) groups are most involved: greater participation by women in the labour force; extended working lives of older people; and greater engagement of the 'young-older' in informal caring for elderly relatives who are living longer (albeit with greater healthy life expectancy) and grandchildren whose parents (mothers) are working more substantially in the labour market.

Two of these forces stem from the rising attainments achieved in the education and training systems, especially prior to entering the labour market. This has been particularly dramatic for women, buttressed by positive changes in attitudes and equal opportunities employment legislation, and has contributed to their higher employment rates; but it has also contributed, along with the expansion of occupations in the intermediate and higher levels of the occupational hierarchy, to older people staying on longer in employment.

This final section draws on the key findings of the previous two sections relating to the research questions posed at the start of the chapter in order to offer some more general reflections on the situations facing voluntary organisations, referring to the analytical deficit, the qualitative dimension and competing concerns in their operation vis-à-vis the external environment.

An analytical deficit

Voluntary organisations view external challenges regarding their abilities to recruit and manage an effective volunteer force through a mix of concerns that are not always accompanied by helpful analysis. There is a tendency to blur distinctions between:

- their ability to meet current demand as opposed to future demand;
- funded demand and the underlying demand that includes unmet need;
- the different sources of the challenge, however defined: rising demand for the services they provide; an absolute decline in the supply of volunteers; and a rising supply of volunteers, but one that is failing to keep pace with the rising demand for them;
- the qualitative dimensions to the match between volunteer demand and supply.

This uncertainty is not particularly surprising, given the contrast between the lack of regular information available on developments in the 'market for unpaid volunteers' and the considerable volume of labour market information and analysis available to conventional employers, dealing with questions of the demand and supply of paid labour in both quantitative and qualitative terms.

Most voluntary organisations are not used to thinking in the above terms, yet are increasingly having to develop the capacity to do so.

When it comes to those areas of voluntary work that overlap with or complement public services, especially in health and social care, the limited knowledge and understanding that voluntary organisations have of their external environments is compounded by the approaches taken by most governments. As shown in the earlier country chapters (Part II), public authorities achieve only periodic understandings of the situations in the voluntary sector through the reports of ad hoc review committees, yet they often adopt bold positions setting out various contributions they want the voluntary sector to make to social welfare.

This analytical deficit is at its greatest in the case of the welfare of older citizens, in contrast to the efforts made to assess childcare situations or mainstream healthcare provision.

The importance of the qualitative dimension

Woven into the discussion of external influences on volunteering are organisational expressions of concern about the *capabilities of the older volunteers available*. These are quite sensitive to their cultural histories and current situations. But whether organisations state them baldly in terms of 'quality of volunteers', or in more nuanced terms, these expressions boil down to three essential messages. First, there is a need to improve organisational performance through professionalising the management of volunteers and their relationships with the roles of employed staff. Second, while there is a need for volunteers to carry out traditional tasks, there is also a need for them to tackle more demanding functions. And third, in pursuing the latter, organisations should capitalise both on the rising supply of better qualified people approaching retirement and on the higher propensity of such people to volunteer.

Competing concerns: working–caring–volunteering–funding

This chapter has explored the views held by voluntary organisations on the current and potential impacts of *labour force participation* and *informal family caregiving* by older people on their abilities to meet the demand for their voluntary services. These relate to the first and third questions, respectively, of the four posed in the introductory section. We find that organisational perceptions differ according to the structure of their volunteer force (organisations involving older and women volunteers saw greater difficulties), the nature of the activity (organisations providing 'altruistic' services seemed to feel more vulnerable) and, to some extent, the 'welfare mix' of which they are a part.

Overall, organisational views are dominated by short-term considerations in which the effects of rising employment rates among older people seem to be regarded as being less important than the effects of their growing responsibilities for caregiving.

The first question led to a second about *interactions with private and public sector organisations via employee volunteering*: the small number of cases offering insights into these no doubt reflects the fact that this is still a relatively marginal phenomenon in Europe compared with the US. However, there is scope for further development, for example, through linkages to the retirement transition where phasing out of paid work might be accompanied by phasing in of some or more volunteering, with resourcing from the employer.

Thus, regarding the fourth question, relating to the *particular experiences of those voluntary organisations that specialise in social care*, these are doubly affected by such developments: they usually rely greatly on older people and women as volunteers, the two groups most affected by the rise in both labour force participation and informal caring. In addition, where people engage in family caregiving, voluntary organisations recognise that this may replicate too much the demands that volunteers do or would experience. On the other hand, it is acknowledged that informal caring can be conducive to the *later* resumption or take-up of care-related formal volunteering.

It is difficult to anticipate what the implications of the financial crisis are ultimately going to be for volunteering in general and that of older people in particular. Voluntary organisations often receive funding from the state of one kind or another. Restraints on public spending are likely to affect their work, even their viability. Yet it is just at such times of austerity, with cut-backs in public provision and funding of care services that voluntary organisations come forward to support the needy members of the population. It remains to be seen what may happen in the future – that is a matter for the next chapter. Meanwhile, *if the current views of the organisations are extrapolated*, it is probably true to say that they expect that the effects of this stringency in public finance on the future operations of voluntary organisations – on both the demands they experience and their capacity to meet them – will exceed the labour market effects on volunteer supply.

However, there is also a sense from this research that voluntary organisations are beginning to see a rather different volunteering environment emerging, whether through changing preferences, labour market opportunities/constraints, or family imperatives. These external conditions will increasingly impinge on organisational styles and strategies and on the experiences of the older volunteer.

References

Cumming, E. and Henry, W.E. (1961) *Growing old*, New York: Basic Books.

Erlinghagen, M. (2010) 'Volunteering after retirement', *European Societies*, vol 12, no 5, pp 603-25.

Havighurst, R.J. (1961) 'Successful aging', *The Gerontologist*, vol 1, no 1, pp 8-13.

Maddox, G.L. (1968) 'Persistence of life style among the elderly: a longitudinal study of patterns of social activity in relation to life satisfaction', in B.L. Neugarten (ed) *Middle age and aging: A reader in social psychology*, Chicago, IL: University of Chicago Press, pp 181-3.

Marks, S.R. (1977) 'Multiple roles and role strain: some notes on human energy, time and commitment', *American Sociological Review*, vol 42, no 6, pp 921-36.

OECD (Organisation for Economic Co-operation and Development) (2011) *Pensions at a glance 2011: Retirement income systems in OECD and G20 countries*, Paris: OECD Publishing.

Poussou-Plesse, M., Petit, M. and Mascova, E. (2010) *Opportunities for older people in the civil society: National report (France), Part 2 – Case studies*, ASPA Project, Deliverable 5.1, Paris: École des Hautes Études en Science Sociales.

Warburton, J. and Jeppsson-Grassman, E. (2011) 'Variations in voluntary association involvement by seniors across different social welfare regimes', *International Journal of Social Welfare*, vol 20, no 2, pp 180-91.

Wilson, J. and Musick, M. (1997) 'Who cares? Towards an integrated theory of volunteer work', *American Sociological Review*, vol 62, no 5, pp 694-713.

THIRTEEN

Organisations' age management of older volunteers: pointing to the future

Joop Schippers and Andrea Principi

Introduction

In the two previous chapters we presented information on the current situation of voluntary organisations: their characteristics, their policies towards older volunteers and their perception of older volunteers. The social environment of voluntary organisations, however, is changing and will continue to change over the next few decades. This may pose new challenges as well as offer new opportunities for volunteering. Demographic change, for instance, may result in a lower supply of care by younger generations and a greater pressure on older people to care for frail members within their own family circle, which will presumably have a negative effect on the supply of older volunteers. Population ageing, however, is also associated with increasing longevity and better general health among older people. This, in turn, may increase the number of potential recruits for voluntary organisations. This potential growth in the number of volunteers, however, may be confined by a European-wide trend to increase the mandatory retirement age. Moreover, future generations of older people will be better educated and higher educated people are inclined to stay in the labour market longer. Thus, future prospects in the supply of older volunteers are highly uncertain.

In light of the trends described above, this chapter focuses on the way voluntary organisations look at and deal with uncertainty about future developments. No matter whether voluntary organisations have or do not have formal age management strategies or policies, they will have to cope in any case with these changes and uncertain developments. That is why the main aim of this chapter is to identify future-oriented ideas, plans or initiatives initiated by the voluntary organisations.

As will become clear in the course of this chapter, some organisations explicitly took this future perspective into account, while others were less focused on this. Most had no current organisational policies and practices regarding older volunteers in place, nor did they have any future policies in development. This does not necessarily imply, however, that the policies of these organisations did not offer a proper future perspective. Compared to Chapters Eleven and Twelve, however, in this chapter we try to connect the mentioned expected changes and developments to organisational policies, and to read their potential impact for the future. To this purpose, we include exemplary results from the organisations in the eight different countries, selecting them from the empirical data collected. The 'line of our story' does not include judgements in terms of 'good' and 'bad' practice, but rather tries to describe as accurately as possible – from the limited information we have on organisational policies – how the voluntary organisations looked at and were going to deal with the future. Given the nature of the methodology employed (case studies), information is treated qualitatively.

In the following, we first provide an overview of how the voluntary organisations defined and perceived future age management issues in their own organisations. Were they worried about the future supply and availability of older volunteers in light of the mentioned developments? And did they think they should and could manage the future role of older volunteers in their organisations? In the next section we examine the more prominent intentions that are developing in various organisations to cope with the changing environment. This also allows us to identify examples of age management that are dealing with potential future developments. The fourth section focuses on organisations' suggestions and ideas concerning the desired future supportive government policies, while the final section concludes this chapter.

Organisations' perceptions of future age management issues

The organisations showed a wide variation in terms of what they considered relevant issues from an age management perspective. On the whole, as already observed in Chapter Eleven, age management in strict terms did not seem to be regarded as a priority by many of the voluntary organisations, even though several of them believed that a balanced age structure might have positive effects, and some considered a balanced volunteers' age mix as a desirable goal. Indeed, for some voluntary organisations the overall lack of volunteers represented a major problem, while others were still primarily worried about how to best match supply and demand of (older) volunteers, or the continuity of their participation. As in many cases future perspectives are linked to the aims organisations have set and to initiatives they have undertaken in the past, in this section we analyse how this is likely to have an impact on future strategies, identifying to what extent the voluntary organisations foresaw future problems related to older volunteers, and whether they expected to develop or consider age management policies to cope with these problems.

Changes related to older individuals

For some organisations, the leading idea about why they should engage in some kind of age management for volunteers in the future was the increased longevity and ongoing ageing of the population. This process may imply the development of both positive and negative organisational views about volunteering in older age. What is important here is that organisations identified increased longevity as one of the main challenges for future development of the volunteer workforce. Seen in a positive way, increased longevity means that the average age and the share of older volunteers will grow, and so will their supply. This was clearly underlined by one German representative, who expected future cohorts to have a period of 30 years of volunteering after the end of their working life, compared to 6-10 years in the past (Seniorpartner). Population ageing was, in this sense, evaluated positively, especially by organisations that relied mostly on older volunteers. Most organisations, however, reported a rather 'neutral' feeling about this: they did not think this would have a negative or positive impact on their activities, while only a few organisations thought that population ageing might have a negative impact. This was the case for those that had made some efforts to increase the supply of younger volunteers but that had already had difficulties in recruiting them, and were now afraid of finding it increasingly hard to attract suitable young candidates. As some interviewees put it, if there is a tendency among older volunteers to stay active over a longer period of time, it becomes more important for organisations to pay attention to recruiting 'the right' person, since "if you get the wrong person, they stick with you for 10 years" (Waterways). This illustrates more a relevant attitude than an actual or future policy, but also illustrates how closely current and future policy perspectives are connected. Furthermore, even if older people are in general increasingly healthier than previous cohorts of peers, according to some organisations a progressive ageing of volunteers would also increase the need to pay more attention to their health and physical abilities, as health inequalities among voluntary workers might increase (UISP, Retraite Sportive). As some volunteers might reach a very old age, the risk of higher absenteeism due to illness was also mentioned (Kunstverein), even though this was believed to have only a moderate impact on organisations.

This apparently supportive scenario of older people living longer and having more time to volunteer was undermined by their own changing attitudes and preferences concerning volunteering. Many older adults might not settle for simple voluntary tasks, but ask for more challenging and varied commitments (Senior Sport). Consequently, some organisations realised that something should be done to face potentially negative developments in this respect. Indeed, while most of the investigated organisations appreciated older people's large time availability, some reported a tendency among older volunteers to be available only to a limited extent (Ronald).

As today's older Europeans are on average healthier and wealthier than previous generations, their aspirations are higher, too, as they want to undertake and can afford long journeys or to buy a cottage somewhere in the country where they stay occasionally. This means that they are not always available on a regular basis. Related to this point was the organisations' observation that the coming generations are increasingly opting for 'loose ties' (Caritas): they want to participate in a project for a limited period of time and then commit themselves to something else. What they did not want was a permanent relation with one specific voluntary organisation. Taken together, these two tendencies resulted in some voluntary organisations being worried about the stability of their pool of older volunteers, and this may be supposed to affect mainly organisations with a high share of older volunteers. For example, some of them expected and complained that in the future they would have to work with a smaller group of permanent volunteers, supplemented with a larger circle of temporary volunteers for particular projects, whose recruitment may require a lot of time and effort (2 Studies). This is one of the reasons why comparing older volunteers to older workers is not appropriate in all respects. As one representative of an English organisation mainly composed of older volunteers said, volunteers can walk away at any time, saying that they no longer want to engage in what they are doing, so "it is all about making the volunteer want to stay and to be part of your organisation" (WEA). For several organisations older volunteers' motivational issues were thus becoming the focal point for their age management strategies.

Changes related to organisational needs

In almost all organisations investigated it was increasingly evident that there was a growing need to provide highly professional services through volunteering. Even though voluntary organisations could not quantify this development in terms of different educational categories they might need, some of them did realise already that this might constitute a growing problem in the future. The older the volunteers become, the less likely it is that they would automatically have the (physical) capacities, skills and abilities required for this high performance. This put voluntary organisations in a similar position as 'ordinary' employers: did they want or could they afford to invest in improving older volunteers' capabilities and/or could/did they want to assign the less 'productive' older volunteers to easier tasks requiring lower qualifications? This observation may to some extent modify the image of voluntary organisations belonging to a kind of 'sheltered' sector of society and the economy, where there is a place for everyone, irrespective of one's competencies and capabilities and where, according to the Olympic ideal, participating prevails over gaining. Organisational needs may develop in such a way that in the future there will be not enough room for everyone, as some potential older volunteers may not pass the 'productivity hurdle'.

Changes related to the surrounding society

Recent societal developments may be seen by organisations as threats for future volunteering by older people. This applies, for example, to the role of paid work in the labour market and obligations related to informal family care, as well as to the economic downturn that Europe is currently experiencing. Since in the future both mothers and older workers are likely to remain more often in the labour market, even when they have respectively young children and grandchildren, some voluntary organisations felt that they would have to compete with older people's double role of being both grandparents and paid workers. Several organisations (Kunstverein and Waterways), operating in countries that have already increased the official retirement age, feared that the growth in the number of older volunteers resulting from increasing longevity would be pruned away by this increased retirement age, especially if this followed the trend of national life expectancy. Other organisations (UNITRE) complained that, if an older person had to choose between spending time in caring for grandchildren or on voluntary work, usually the first is expected to take priority.

In addition to these issues highlighted by our study, recent literature shows an increasing risk of competing claims on older people's time due to a growing age gap between successive generations, resulting from the fact that more and more European women are postponing motherhood (Beets et al, 2011). While the age gap between generations had fallen to less than 25 years in the 1960s, today the age at which mothers give birth for the first time has increased to over 30 (and even later for highly educated women). Consequently, grandchildren may be born when their grandparents are well in their sixties (Geurts, 2012). Another important factor is represented by the economic crisis. On the one hand, this may be seen as fuelling the future voluntary sector, since governments may increasingly rely on voluntary activities given the overall climate characterised by budget cuts and by people feeling stimulated to commit in volunteering (Lohner, Scout); on the other hand, however, the crisis itself may prevent governments from adequately supporting even the volunteer sector (and thus older volunteers) in the future, and thus from guaranteeing suitable services (Waterways, Bücherhallen).

From what has been reported above, it is possible to conclude that, even if the need for future 'official age management' initiatives in a strict sense was not yet being perceived as urgent by organisational representatives, most of the future challenges related to an ageing volunteer workforce were not unknown to the organisations. In the light of this, some organisations were indeed going to cope with them through specific future strategies and actions, as illustrated in the following section.

Volunteer age management: insights on future attitudes, strategies and policies

Only a few of the voluntary organisations under study were engaged in future-oriented age management, primarily because they did not feel the need for special future policies or initiatives in this area. For example, the Danish organisations 9220 and Gistrup argued that they did not aim to implement age management because they wanted to recruit on a broader scale, since age as such was not an important issue for them. Some organisations, as for example, Tenants, thought that the lack of strategic planning about volunteers' age could be considered a consequence of an 'old-fashioned' management approach in voluntary organisations, or might even result from the non-existence of management. Indeed, often the way voluntary organisations had come into existence, developed and grown over the years did not call for any form of age management, so there was simply no tradition in this field. In both cases, the result is the same: a passive attitude with respect to age management.

On the contrary, those organisations that currently have 'age management' strategies in place could pose questions on this in a future perspective. The old-profiled Italian organisation AVULSS, for example, pointed out two main alternative explanations in this respect, in the attempt to elucidate its failure to involve more younger volunteers. The first attributed this failure to the organisation, judging it as too passive; the second ascribed it to general external aspects, such as, for instance, a general tendency of lower commitment to voluntary organisations. The way to answer the crucial question to what extent age management strategies are future-proof can lead to two basically opposite conclusions and future behaviours, that is, a more active organisational attitude in the former case, and a more passive one in the latter. And indeed, our study shows that both examples of what we can call 'a passive attitude' and an 'active attitude' about future age management initiatives were found (as illustrated below), showing in particular that organisations with a higher degree of professionalisation generally tended to adopt an active rather than a passive attitude.

Passive attitude

The Italian organisation UISP is an example of a passive attitude. It saw itself as a passive actor, since the organisation was convinced that the main cause for the low interest of younger volunteers lay in external economic factors rather than with its organisational efforts. Organisational representatives argued that if young people have to deal with unemployment and are putting all their efforts into looking for a job, they will hardly find time to volunteer. In a similar vein, this organisation argued that, in case of a further worsening of the Italian pensions' levels and requirements, older volunteers might be lost as well, as they would have to start looking for paid activities to supplement their old-age pensions. In such a context, this organisation did not feel particularly encouraged to undertake age management strategies in the future.

Active attitude

Other organisations, however, thought that it is more up to them to attract more older volunteers and to manage them in appropriate ways, planning therefore to apply some form of age management for the future. At the English WEA, for example, rather than pushing this issue to policy makers, it was argued that it was important 'to engage with people on their terms at a local level', and to develop their confidence so that they can engage in matters that interest them, pointing to older people's personal needs and motivation. This represents an organisational challenge to better understand people's driving forces and skills, in order to strengthen their abilities, for instance, in using information and communication technologies (ICT), thus enabling them to start deploying them and becoming more proficient. In sum, several organisations were striving to make the voluntary work more attractive to (older) volunteers, in order to recruit and retain them, by explaining to them that they could be useful in the organisation even in older age (AVIS). The following examples show which forms these efforts are concretely taking, and can be considered as organisations' 'future intentions' of age management of volunteers.

Organisational orientations in a future perspective

In the Swedish Mission Covenant's opinion, different strategies to meet the needs of the ageing population had to start from the actual needs of older people themselves. For example, one of the most relevant was that of breaking older citizens' isolation through social and cultural activities, an area in which this organisation believed it could play a major role.

Dutch organisations operating in the healthcare sector (mainly composed of older volunteers) are experiencing shortages of professional staff, and therefore plan to rely mostly on volunteers in the future (2 Studies). For this reason, they are exploring what the wishes of the 'new volunteering style' are (for example, of young seniors with a more hedonistic lifestyle, who do not want to commit themselves for continuous and long-term civic responsibilities). In the same way, the English WEA's coordinators are focusing on *responding more effectively to the demands for support coming from volunteers* and to the quality of their experience, in order to ensure that their deployment and retention will be (more) effective.

On the other hand, different Danish investigated organisations are planning or implementing actions linked to the age management of volunteers. Dgi's future plans and objectives will be focusing on developing more arrangements for retired people. In order to retain and attract more seniors, Dgi plans to work on the organisation's culture, as seniors are sometimes perceived to be difficult to engage in a voluntary organisation, because it becomes too formal and somehow too 'posh'. Hence, Dgi plans to clarify the difference between paid and voluntary staff, the former being necessary to take care of the overall administrative work. Moreover, the organisation underlines that the paid staff are supposed to service and support volunteers – and not the other way around. This way, *volunteers should be able to focus more on the content and interesting aspects of work*, thus making volunteering more attractive for seniors.

DaneAge's future intentions are to *strengthen their voluntary leaders by organising management training*. This will be arranged in collaboration with the volunteers themselves and will focus on improving their abilities to motivate and qualify voluntary workers. DaneAge has also initiated a pilot project about recruitment of younger senior volunteers (50-65 years), through five local committees that have been working on ways to *improve the dialogue with potential members in this age group*. This process made it clear to the committees that, in order to recruit and attract this target group, it is necessary to rethink the role of volunteering, as people who are (still) active in the labour market had the energy and found it meaningful to use their competencies to volunteer. The organisation is now working on easier ways to inform new volunteers of the different tasks and dimensions of volunteering, indicating how much time they can expect to spend on each activity. Finally, it has considered how to retain volunteers through different kinds of development interviews.

DanChurchAid future plans are focused around the question of how to best retain volunteers. One aspect of their plan is to *focus on a good quality of voluntary work*, since this is seen as necessary to motivate seniors to spend their time as volunteers. This organisation found it important to broaden the perspective of volunteering, by informing older people about the flexible opportunities offered by this kind of engagement in terms of time and tasks that could be performed, for example, by showing that voluntary work could be everything from 4 to 400 hours annually. In addition, the organisation needed to accommodate the tendency that volunteers do not necessarily (want to) engage in the same activity year after year, so that volunteers may be facilitated in shifting between different forms of voluntary work over time.

Just as in the paid labour market, *flexible working opportunities* were also expected to mitigate the influence of external aspects in the voluntary sector. Among the investigated organisations, some English ones in particular seem to give high priority to this factor in the future, in order to offer people more opportunities to engage in voluntary work. One example is RNIB, which also aims to achieve a more intensive commitment from existing volunteers, whereas Scout, while using the same strategy, expects instead a less intensive commitment, due to a shortage of adult volunteers. To foster flexibility is also an aim of WRVS, whose representatives thought that the 'new' older volunteers are more likely to opt for flexible volunteering in roles where they could continue to use the professional skills they had acquired during their working lives. These 'new' older volunteers were not expected to give their time routinely forever, but rather wanted to volunteer for 'chunks' of their time to fit in with their current life stage.

Beyond flexible working practices, the same organisation has planned to introduce in the near future a structured dialogue between volunteers and the manager about the contribution of each volunteer. Held on an annual basis, these conversations will also *pay attention to the individual's changing capabilities and needs*, for example, related to changing health conditions or changes in the family situation (the birth of a grandchild or the death of a partner). The need for a conversation with volunteers about their future role was also felt by WEA, in particular when health or disability-related issues set in, which affected the work the volunteers were able to do. The role played by the changing physical conditions of older volunteers was also considered by Werder in Germany, which is considering offering older volunteers in the sports clothing sector, who are no longer able to carry out activities where they have to stand, to move to activities that could be performed sitting (such as, for instance, sewing).

An *increasing acceptance of the 'fixed-term project' idea* can be noticed in most of the German voluntary organisations included in the study, which seemed to have a similar approach or strategy with respect to age management. Indeed, their older volunteers became more involved in the development and coordination of new projects and received training for new tasks, thus showing the importance of volunteering for these non-profit organisations. In this context, positive individual effects for older volunteers were likely to be experienced, such as more appreciation and acceptance as well as increased qualifications. Project work, according to the examples given, was not necessarily temporary, but established new ways for civic commitment. As older volunteers did not seem to leave the studied organisations once the projects were over, project work might therefore be seen as a promising way to improve future recruitment and retention of older volunteers.

As far as the 'end of the volunteer career' is concerned, to prevent possible problems related to this aspect at organisational level, and so to help align service provision with volunteer supply, the English WRVS is going to develop a new task force with local service managers and middle management, to *facilitate succession planning*, taking into account the likelihood of people retiring from volunteering. Thanks to this, in the future managers will be able to look in a much more focused way at services, for example, by providing projections such as that according to which 'the age range in service is X and we anticipate that over the next 5 years a Y percentage of older volunteers might retire, so that we are looking how we might replace them'.

Organisational desires with respect to supportive government policies

The future of volunteering in older age is of course not only linked to individual and organisational attitudes and behaviours, but also to external aspects, including institutional policies. The investigated organisations, even in different countries, appeared to be hardly aware of the existence of supportive institutional policies (such as, for instance, national or local programmes to promote volunteering in older age). Yet several suggestions for the future were advanced at this governmental/macro level by organisations, sometimes broadening the issue beyond the scope of age management, as summarised in the following.

Several voluntary organisations pointed to the fact that governments and public authorities could help to increase the *visibility* of the voluntary work of older people, for example, with an annual prize for volunteers (ANPAS, Ronald). A good example in this respect is the Dutch tradition, according to which a substantial share of the royal honours that are awarded annually on the occasion of the queen's birthday go to people who have been active in voluntary work.

Next to visibility, several organisations pointed out the necessity of institutional intervention for granting a stronger *recognition* of voluntary work in the future. If the value of volunteering in older age is recognised whole-heartedly, for example, through social credits such as free-of-charge transport cards (AUSER), or by acknowledging the skills gained through volunteering by means of a widely accepted award (Scout), this might represent a positive incentive for people to join voluntary organisations. It is still now the case that older volunteers have to pay for the materials they use themselves, no matter how low their income level.

Many organisations also favoured broadening the *political perception* of voluntary work. In the eyes of many politicians, voluntary work is indeed still too often viewed as primarily or only a form of social work, in some countries more than in others. As a consequence, little priority is given to investment in voluntary work, for example, in terms of human capital (such as competency development). Too little investment may have negative drawbacks on the quality of voluntary work (DanChurchAid). An Italian organisation underlined that politicians' main interest in voluntary organisations was not to enhance the human capital of volunteers, but to make sure the organisation provided a socially needed service (UNIVOC). Some German organisations noticed that this argument seemed especially important in fields and domains where the state had withdrawn, whereas it had been hitherto responsible (Werder, Caritas).

Another desire expressed by some organisations for the future was to extend the right to *training at all ages*. Some interviewed people considered it inappropriate that the target set by the European Council of Lisbon in 2000, which intended to guarantee lifelong learning to adults, was defined only up to the age of 64 (the target set for 2010 was the participation of 12.5 per cent of people aged between 25 and 64), thus discriminating against all people over 64. In contrast to this decision, in Italy AUSER promoted a petition to introduce a law to recognise the right to lifelong learning at all ages. Also related to the training issue is the claim from some organisations that the government should support their training infrastructure. After all, argued some German organisations, the government benefited from all the voluntary work that was done, so these public benefits justified some public investments too (Caritas, Ausbildungspaten).

Many organisations working with volunteers shared the opinion that the *information* on volunteer opportunities in older age also needs to improve in the future. In some countries, such as the Netherlands, voluntary organisations had organised a website where volunteers could look for vacancies in the domain they would like to volunteer in and where they could also register, so that organisations might find them. However, hosting and mastering such a website requires investment in both time and money, especially if the website is to be kept up to date. Moreover, older people may be reluctant to use the internet, so mediation by institutions may be useful in this respect. Furthermore, public services are sometimes not aware of the opportunities to volunteer, or even provide incorrect information.

A problem evidenced by some English voluntary organisations, for example, was that potential unemployed volunteers were informed at the job centre that they could not volunteer while receiving unemployment benefit, despite the contrary being the case (Scout, WRVS).

In several countries, voluntary organisations worried and complained about the short-term focus of public policies. Even though in some countries the government now and then made financial means available for projects to support voluntary work, these projects usually lacked *sustainability*. For example, in the two editions of the Polish Seniors in Action programme, almost 70 projects activating people 50+ were awarded to increase the extremely low social engagement of (older) people in this country but, by the time the projects got into their stride, government support had already finished. In Germany, the cancellation of funds after the expiration of the state-supported project run by Caritas resulted in the loss of the infrastructure that had been created for the project, because there was no funding available for its maintenance. And Ausbildungspaten also criticised the lack of sustainability beyond usual project funding schemes.

Moreover, several organisations argued that in the future governments could do more to promote an *intergenerational culture* (AVULSS). In many countries the policy focus and also the media's attention are much more concentrated on the younger than on the older generations – following the motto 'young is in, old is out' – thus providing a very contradictory message with respect to current active ageing policies.

Beyond this, some organisations recommended the creation of *specific volunteer programmes for older volunteers*, such as the Italian Voluntary Service (see Chapter Three). In this case, given the little token involved to remunerate this activity, a further extension of this initiative could also be useful to face the problem of the expulsion of 'young-older people' from the labour market (AVIS), even though this may raise concerns as to whether this kind of (paid) social engagement can really be considered a form of volunteering or not.

A broadly shared desire for the future among voluntary organisations was the commitment by institutions *to help more in reinforcing the positive link between work in the labour market and volunteering*. Several suggestions were advanced to this aim, since the working period and especially the last part of the working career were deemed important for older people's engagement in volunteering. Someone voiced measures to allow a gradual transition from work to volunteer activities, for instance, by paying some additional imputed retirement contribution

(Tenda), or allowing the companies to 'move' managers to voluntary organisations, thus allowing them to receive their salary while they were volunteering (AUSER), or envisaging time off or a given number of working hours they could spend in voluntary activities (Scout, Gilde). Other suggestions in this context were to provide training courses (where not already available) in the final stage of the working career (for instance, 30 hours per year), to be attended during working hours without any loss of earnings. The aim of such courses should be to inform people on voluntary work – including aspects such as its meaning and its implementation at local level – and to clarify that, through volunteering, people after retirement were less likely to be left alone (UISP). Another suggestion by an Italian organisation was to send newly retired people a letter when they received their first pension wage, with a message such as: 'Think about your future, place yourself at others' disposal: be a volunteer' (ANPAS).

Conclusions

This chapter concludes the part of our study devoted to the investigation of volunteering in older age through case studies carried out in European voluntary organisations (that is, the meso level). While Chapters Eleven and Twelve dealt with the current situation, this chapter has focused on the future perspectives of formal volunteering by older people.

The logic of this chapter has been that the social environment of voluntary organisations and of older people is rapidly changing, and this will have a heavy impact on the future volunteering of older people. As mentioned in the introduction of this chapter, population ageing, better health conditions of older people, increased longevity and better education in older age may all be linked to an expected increase in older people's participation in a series of different activities. These activities may include, for example, informal family care to older people, work in the labour market or other leisure activities. This causes uncertainty about future features of volunteering by older people. Voluntary organisations can play a key role in reducing this uncertainty. Therefore, we have explored the meso level, and relevant to the conceptual framework employed in Chapter Two, is, for example, a question such as: are voluntary organisations adjusting work tasks to meet the preferences and dispositions of older volunteers? From an active ageing perspective, it may be expected that voluntary organisations will offer new participatory opportunities for older adults, since active ageing holds the promise that older adults are allowed to participate in voluntary organisations for as long as they are able to and wish to do so. However, as has been argued in Chapter One, sometimes expectations may be highly unrealistic, at it may be unsure whether a greater potential supply of older volunteers will be met by a greater potential demand.

Thus, in this chapter, the first step was to understand whether the interviewed voluntary organisations' representatives could make a link between the expected and mentioned changes, and volunteering by older people in their organisations. Were they worried about the future supply of older volunteers, and, if so, did they think they should deal with volunteers' age management? The result is that in general, future age management of volunteers did not seem to be a priority for most of the voluntary organisations. Yet earlier in this chapter we observed that across Europe some voluntary organisations were aware of the main societal changes and of at least some of the possible consequences for volunteering by older people. On the one hand, they were aware that in the future there might be a higher supply of and a longer commitment by older volunteers, and in particular organisations mainly composed of older volunteers might benefit from this. On the other hand, they were also aware that older volunteers would be healthier than in the past and better educated. Consequently, this might bring about a change of preferences in terms of tasks and commitment (to the benefit of other activities), and a less stable volunteer workforce. All this, in a climate of economic crisis with a policy call for more volunteering, but with less funds to accommodate this, leaving it mainly to voluntary organisations to decide whether or not to invest in older volunteers.

Consequently, the second step has been to understand if voluntary organisations intend to invest substantially in older volunteers in the future, through age management policies. That is, whether they intend to reduce the negative effects of the expected changes, and to enjoy the positive ones. By exploring their (formal and informal) future plans, we have shown that this decision is not represented by digital 'yes/no' variables telling whether a voluntary organisation is busy thinking about its future and the role of future older volunteers, but rather reflected in (part of) the opinions they expressed and (some of) the age management strategies they had already implemented or were considering to implement. Results, however, have been rather encouraging from an active ageing perspective, since some organisations intended to actively respond to future societal changes by capitalising on the interests of older volunteers by engaging with them on their terms, by assigning them activities of interest to them, by fulfilling the wishes of older volunteers in the 'new style' (for example by specifying how much time they could expect to spend in which activities), or by focusing on the more interesting aspects of the work. More concretely, this would also mean paying much more attention to training and flexibility in terms of tasks, hours spent volunteering and duration of the volunteer experience (for example, considering intervals of time to spend in other activities such as leisure or family care duties, and between different volunteering experiences). Some respondents admitted that this would imply an organisational change of mentality or 'culture'. In this perspective, older volunteers would be central actors in the future for voluntary organisations, to the benefit of the (good) quality of organisational activities.

Most interestingly, some organisations underlined that, given the evolving nature of current and future challenges, all this should be continuously managed over time, considering the changing capabilities and needs of older volunteers, and planning succession and knowledge transfer in the volunteer roles.

While recognising themselves as the main actors in this play, at the same time voluntary organisations wanted to be much more supported at the institutional level in this task, as observed earlier. This support should involve in particular visibility, recognition, training, information and the integration of policies concerning voluntary work with labour market and welfare policies. The current economic crisis threatens, however, to leave this wish largely unmet for a long time to come, at least in the most financially affected countries.

Generally speaking, in this chapter we have learned that for voluntary organisations, older volunteers' motivational issues are becoming the central point of their age management strategies. In general, age management in voluntary organisations is likely to become more important in the future, in order to match the supply of older volunteers with the demand from organisations, both in a quantitative and in a qualitative way, given that the increasing complexity of this match may require (further) professionalisation of the age management, and so of volunteering.

References

Beets, G., Schippers J. and te Velde, E.R. (2011) *The future of motherhood in Western societies: Late fertility and its consequences*, Dordrecht: Springer.

Geurts, T. (2012) *Grandparent–grandchild relationships in the Netherlands. A dynamic and multigenerational perspective*, Amsterdam: Vrije Universiteit.

Part IV

CONCLUSIONS

FOURTEEN

Conclusions: enhancing volunteering by older people in Europe

Andrea Principi, Giovanni Lamura and Per H. Jensen

Introduction

As observed in Chapter One, 'active ageing' represents an overarching aim of current European Union (EU) policies. Defined as the process 'of optimising opportunities for health, participation and security in order to enhance quality of life as people age' (WHO, 2002), it should be intended as an effort to maximise participation and well-being as people age, at the individual, organisational and societal level (Walker, 2002). According to this perspective, the current ageing of the European population can be seen in a positive way, since the capacity to perform activities at an advanced stage of age has sharply increased in recent years. A current 70-year-old or even an 80-year-old corresponds to a person 15 or 20 years younger living a century ago, and in this sense, European society is not actually ageing, but rather 'rejuvenating' (Giarini, 2009). In recent years, policy makers and the scientific community have increasingly recognised that, through active ageing, older people can greatly contribute to society, thus active ageing benefits society as well as older individuals in terms of better health and life satisfaction (Walker, 2011). This implies a striving to increase the participation of older people in a range of social activities within and outside the labour market. Volunteering is an important field in which active ageing can be realised, and several policy efforts in this direction have recently been undertaken by the EU, through activities planned within the European Year of Volunteering and the European Year of Active Ageing and Intergenerational Solidarity, in 2011 and 2012 respectively. But how can the formal volunteering of older people be enhanced in Europe, a rather variegated continent formed by the co-existence of different welfare regimes, with peculiar welfare mixes and legal frameworks? Although in the past a considerable number of studies have dealt with the issue of volunteering in older age (see, for example, Fischer and Schaffer, 1993; Morrow-Howell et al, 2001; Warburton and Cordingley, 2004), these studies have seldom offered a European comparative perspective on this issue, and analyses have hardly ever considered the micro, meso, macro and structural levels in a single study, with empirical evidence mainly lacking at the meso (or organisational) level.

In the light of this background, and in accordance with the conceptual framework discussed in Chapter Two and the results of Chapters Three to Thirteen, the main aim of this concluding chapter is to attempt to comparatively explain volunteering by older people in Europe, by considering all levels of interaction. In this perspective, the indicators used to 'explain' volunteering in older age (for example, in terms of size and composition) represent the dependent variables constituting the thread throughout the elements employed to build our conceptual framework, as presented in Figure 14.1. The basic assumption is that five major factors concur to explain the volunteering of older people in Europe: (1) older people's individual characteristics and predispositions (micro level); (2) voluntary organisations (meso level), that represent the demand for older volunteers and structure older people's voluntary work opportunities; (3) the interaction and division of tasks between welfare-producing institutions (that is, the welfare mix); (4) governmental policies implemented in this field (macro level); and (5) the specific welfare regime.

The latter – with its ideology and set of cultural values and beliefs – includes all other dimensions considered in our conceptual framework, so that in this chapter the welfare regime is treated as a background element to comparatively understand the phenomenon of volunteering in older age. The possibility of comparing voluntary organisations (meso level) by country is limited, however, due to the methodology used in our study, since the restricted number of cases investigated in each nation prevents us delivering country-specific messages. Based on this analysis, a further aim of this chapter is to give an answer to the overall question of this volume raised in Chapter One: under what circumstances can volunteering function as a real basis for the self-fulfilment and social integration of older adults in Europe? That is, given that voluntary work allows older adults to remain active, enjoying social recognition and integration that contributes to their physical, social and mental well-being throughout their lives (Walker, 2002), what are the main policy challenges at a country level, to possibly enhance volunteering by older people?

Figure 14.1: Conceptual framework of volunteering in older age

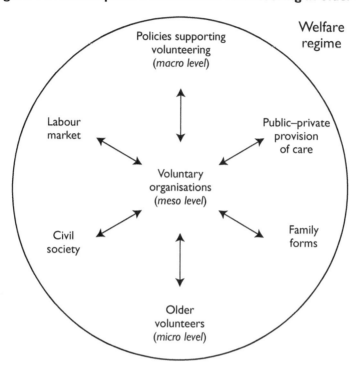

As visualised in Figure 14.1, the elements explaining the volunteering of older people in a given regime are bi-directionally connected to each other through their link with voluntary organisations, so that all of them concur to influence volunteering patterns in older age. Yet to present the results in a sequential way, in this chapter we suggest following a particular logic: in the next section we outline the characteristics of the welfare regimes included in the study, that is, the set of cultural values and beliefs that primarily characterise them. In the third section the volunteering of older people is associated with the type of interaction taking place between welfare-producing institutions (that is, the welfare mix), intended as a consequence of the peculiar welfare regimes' characteristics. The fourth section deals with older individuals' cultural orientations, characteristics and predispositions to volunteer in a given regime. In the fifth section volunteering in older age is discussed from the perspective of voluntary organisations and linked to the previous two sections, since voluntary organisations represent the key level to understand how to match the *demand* of older volunteers (which is also subject to the kind of contribution that voluntary organisations make to the welfare mix)

with the *supply* of older volunteers (which depends on their individual predispositions). In the sixth section the volunteering of older people is analysed in association with the policy frameworks existing in the different regimes, and the chapter ends with some concluding remarks on how volunteering by older people may be enhanced in Europe.

Main characteristics of the welfare regimes included in the study

Since the voluntary sector is embedded in a welfare regime with its cultural and ideological context, the first step of our analysis is to describe the characteristics of the welfare regimes of the countries included in our study: Denmark, England (data are shown for the UK, when unavailable for England), France, Germany, Italy, the Netherlands, Poland and Sweden. As mentioned in Chapter Two, culture, values and belief systems are the basic organising principles shaping choices made by individuals and institutions. Since cultural events can persist over a long time, to understand these cultural values we have to assume a historical perspective, paying particular attention to the period in which modern welfare states were born. According to this view, each welfare regime is characterised by (or embedded in) historically rooted cultural differences that explain contemporary situations and differences. This implies a shared conception of what is good and desirable in a specific culture, and this understanding justifies beliefs, actions (that is, strategies) and goals at the individual and societal levels (Schwartz, 2008). This also determines what the 'right' relation between the different welfare-producing institutions, including the voluntary sector, 'should' be. Scholars have conceptualised and measured the 'division of labour' between different welfare-producing institutions (state, labour market, family, the voluntary sector) in different ways. These include the degree of *de-commodification*, intended as state intervention to allow individuals to be independent from the market (Esping-Andersen, 1990), and that of *de-familialisation* (Bambra, 2004), intended as the degree to which individuals, especially women, are able to participate in society (through work, volunteering or other activities) and can thus be independent from the family. Table 14.1 attempts to summarise the main properties of the welfare regimes under study here.

Although in 1990 Esping-Andersen recognised three main regime models (social democratic, liberal and conservative), his and other scholars' later work argued that there are reasons to add new regime types to these three initial typologies, and relevant for our study are

Table 14.1: Characteristics of welfare regimes included in the study

Regime	Main characteristics
Social democratic	Cultural homogeneity (no immigration) during industrialisation and absence of internal conflicts, favouring social democratic movements striving for decommodification to allow workers to be mobilised (by making them independent from the market) for solidaristic actions. Presence of strong level of decommodification in terms of state intervention in welfare provision to individuals through universal benefits, and related development of a strong voluntary sector in self-expressive activities
Liberal	The industrial development between the 19th and the 20th centuries strengthened the private market because of the workers' good economic conditions and concomitant strong position of the middle class in terms of power, at the expense of the working class. This resulted in a means-tested, 'residual' assistance with low state benefits and a major role played by market solutions. Consequently, the voluntary sector has a tradition in social welfare delivery
Conservative	Persistence of craftsmen, farmers and small businesses during industrialisation led to the consolidation of security and support mechanisms on the basis of professional corporations. Influence of the Catholic Church to preserve traditional family structures. Principle of subsidiarity, which left ample space to the voluntary sector, with state support playing a role when the family is in need. In this context the voluntary sector collaborates with the state through a close relationship
Mediterranean	Unlike the corporatist states, weak democratic institutions during the process of industrialisation and consequent state-centred and fragmented social care tended to crowd out the voluntary sector. Cultural tradition of family care of older relatives influenced by the Catholic Church, resulting in a family-based welfare model with very limited public responsibilities, in which the voluntary sector developed marginally, and in particular to integrate weak state-centred welfare services
Post-Communist	Influence of the former Communist regime makes economic growth difficult, and inequality in distribution of resources among the population. Concomitant influence of the Catholic Church, and strong familism. In this it bears some resemblance to the Mediterranean model, but financial constraints are more severe. The Communist government almost totally eliminated the voluntary sector from social life, and it is currently underdeveloped

Sources: Information from Part II of this volume; Esping-Andersen (1990); Ferrera (1996); Salamon and Anheier (1998); Holden (2003); Bambra (2004); Fenger (2007); Warburton and Jeppsson Grassman (2011)

the Mediterranean (or Southern) model (Ferrera, 1996) and the post-Communist model (Fenger, 2007).

With regard to the categorisation of the countries included in our study according to these five regimes (as described in Table 14.1), Sweden and Denmark belong to the social democratic model, England to the liberal one, Germany to the conservative model, Italy to the Mediterranean model and Poland to the post-Communist one (following the terminology adopted in Chapter Eight, in the following we refer to a post-Socialist regime for Poland). While in the previous cases the categorisation is quite clear, for the Netherlands and France (both of them originally included by Esping-Andersen in the conservative regime) this is less so as they have somewhat changed over time. The national chapters, Three to Ten, provide an in-depth understanding of the single welfare regime's roots and of the related voluntary action taking place in each country. However, it is worth underlining that, first, the concept of 'welfare regime' should not be interpreted as static and, second, that some countries can be considered to be more 'core' to certain regime types than others, so that regime membership might in some cases be disputed (Bambra, 2007, p 336). This may depend on important country distinctions within regimes, as argued for the conservative type (Warburton and Jeppson Grassman, 2011), or even on more recent substantial changes in policy goals. From its conservative anchors, due to a policy process started in the 1980s, the welfare regime characterising the Netherlands has evolved into a mixture of the social democratic and the liberal welfare state model, where the population has maintained a strong propensity for voluntary action, as historically fertilised by the high social cohesion within pillars (see Chapter Ten for a detailed explanation of the Dutch phenomenon of *pillarisation*). Instead, the French welfare regime seems to be evolving towards a liberal model (see Chapter Seven) in which the widespread sense of solidarity and citizenship has fuelled the voluntary sector, leading it to a partnership with the state that in the past 30 years has evolved from an institutional oversight to a contractual partnership based on a shared responsibility for social investment, similar to that characterising the liberal model (Archambault, 1996). Important changes have also been occurring in Poland, since in order to overcome its structural difficulties, this country seems to have been moving towards a liberal-residual regime type, even though a clear type of welfare regime has not yet been fully developed (see Chapter Eight).

In the following we consider, as far as possible, these mentioned regimes' developments, in order to take them into account for analysing volunteering in older age using a comparative approach.

The impact of the welfare mix on volunteering by older people

There is a strong link between the welfare regime's characteristics and the other elements considered in our conceptual framework. Starting from the welfare mix, intended as the set of interactions between the state, the market, the family and the voluntary sector, we argue that a specific welfare regime includes a specific welfare mix, and that different welfare mixes are associated differently with volunteering of older people, by influencing both the demand and the supply of older volunteers. More specifically, we want to understand how the volunteering of older people is associated with the employment rate of older workers, and with the diffusion of employee volunteer programmes in companies, since the latter create volunteer opportunities for older workers to join voluntary initiatives and to continue them even after retirement. Another useful indicator is the type of established care regime, that is, whether it is informal (not regulated), semi-formal (cash-for-care) or formal (home help/institutional care) (Anttonen and Sipilä, 1996; Geissler and Pfau-Effinger, 2005). The family form also plays a role in this, in its possible different connotations: male breadwinner/female full-time carer; male breadwinner/female part-time carer (and part-time worker); dual breadwinner/external care (Lewis, 1992; Pfau-Effinger et al, 2009). By considering these aspects, it makes it easier to understand how care work is divided between the family and the state, and the related possibility for older people to participate in the labour market and in particular in volunteer activity. For this reason, in order to explain the size and the composition of volunteering by older people, the mentioned indicators are associated in each country with volunteering rates among older people (and in the total population) as well as with the prevalent type of voluntary work (if altruistic or self-expressive), as visualised in Table 14.2.

The data summarised in Table 14.2 allow us to start with the general observation that the regimes with the highest share of volunteering in older age (but also among the whole population) are the social democratic and the liberal ones (Sweden, Denmark, the Netherlands and the UK). Volunteering in older age is less widespread in the conservative regimes (Germany and France), and rather weak in the

Table 14.2: Volunteering in older age in different European welfare mixes

Regime	Country	Labour market		Care		Voluntary sector		
		Employment rate, 55-64[a]	Employee volunteer programmes	Predominant type of elder care	Family form	Prevalent type of voluntary work[b]	Volunteering rate, all population	Volunteering rate, 65-74[c]
Social democratic	Sweden	++	Few	Formal	Dual breadwinner/external care	Self-expressive	+++	+++
	Denmark	+	Yes	Formal	Dual breadwinner/external care	Self-expressive	++	++
Social democratic-liberal	Netherlands	+	Few	Formal	Male breadwinner/female part-time carer	Self-expressive	+++	+++
Liberal	UK	+	Yes	Semi-formal/informal	Male breadwinner/female part-time carer	Self-expressive	++	++
Conservative-(liberal)	France	–	Yes	Semi-formal	Dual breadwinner/external care	Both typologies	/	+ –
Conservative	Germany	+	Few	Semi-formal/informal	Male breadwinner/female part-time carer	Both typologies	+	+
Mediterranean	Italy	– –	No	Semi-formal/informal	Male breadwinner/female full-time carer	Both typologies	–	–
Post-Socialist-(liberal)	Poland	– –	No	Informal	Dual breadwinner/female full-time carer	Both typologies	–	–
	EU27	47.4					20.0[d]	na[e]

Notes and sources: + more than the European average; – less than the European average; / around the European average. Information from Part II of this volume; [a] Eurostat (2013, data for 2011); [b] If self-expressive or altruistic, expressed by the number of volunteers involved in self-expressive volunteering (for example, volunteering in the sports, culture or recreational sectors), compared to the number of volunteers involved in altruistic volunteering (for example, volunteering in the social services or health sectors); [c] We concentrated on the younger-old age group, that is, when older people are assumed to be healthy and free from disabilities. After 75 years, participation in voluntary activities decreases in all countries, mainly due to health problems and physical limitations; [d] McCloughan et al (2011); [e] Data not available for Europe, + and – are based on comparisons with the volunteering rate of all the population in the country and with the volunteering rates of 65- to 74-year-olds in the other countries under study.

Mediterranean (Italy) and post-Socialist (Poland) regimes. This is at least partly explained by the regimes' characteristics that, as described in the previous section, give rise to different welfare mixes. For example, a positive association between the employment rates of older workers and the volunteering rates of older people can be seen. This is not, however, an age-related issue, since such a trend is true for the total population (and not only for its older members). Indeed countries such as Sweden and Denmark, in which political commitment has been historically devoted to full employment (Stephens, 1996), show high rates of volunteering. A reason for this is that work leads to an increase in social relationships that are conducive to volunteering. This means that politically pursuing an increase in employment rates in older age could also have a positive impact in terms of strengthening volunteering among older people, as already observed (Warburton and Jeppsson Grassman, 2011). This is in line with the concept of active ageing at all levels, and with the aims of the European and (most) national policies currently aiming at postponing retirement age.

However, as the work–volunteering nexus is not separate from the familiar sphere, it is also important to understand to which extent older people are able to participate in the labour market and in volunteering activities, in light of their involvement in informal care duties. This mainly concerns the participation of women, especially since mature and older women carry out informal care to older family members and experience major problems in reconciling paid work with unpaid care activities (Principi et al, 2012a). As a matter of fact, the evidence from the national situations described in this volume shows that while participation rates in volunteer activities are rather similar for both genders in most countries up until adult age, in mature and older age, the participation of women seems to decrease. From Table 14.2 one can see that family forms encouraging participation in the labour market (such as the dual breadwinner/external care and male breadwinner/female part-time carer models) are associated with high volunteering rates. The same general conclusion can be drawn by examining the (linked) predominant type of elder care, since the provision of formal elder care is associated with a context of high participation in the labour market and of family forms allowing such participation, as well as with high rates of volunteering. In Italy, a country characterised by low volunteering rates, a large cash-for-care scheme is available, albeit not so generous as to allow families to be fully free from care duties (despite the growing trend of employing migrant care workers for carrying out these tasks, often under undeclared terms; see Di Rosa et al, 2012).

In some countries, however, specific peculiarities still need to be better understood. For instance, despite a not particularly high share of volunteering in older age, the current French family form is described as an example of dual breadwinner/external care model (see Chapter Seven). This may be surprising, since France has a tradition of informal care, and employment rates (even of women) are not particularly high. Yet the French welfare state is under transformation, and the recently introduced long-term care cash-for-care scheme aims to formalise family care, by providing additional resources in the form of regulated domestic care work. This means that this formalisation is directly linked to employment policies (Da Roit and Le Bihan, 2010), by shifting family care from the informal to the formal level, so that the French family model can now be more precisely classified as a dual breadwinner/external care model, with an expected positive impact in the near future on labour force participation, especially of older women. Another specification concerns the Polish family form, which has been recently evolving into a dual breadwinner/female full-time carer model. This means that Polish women mainly work, but they simultaneously continue to be the chief person in charge of family care and of its organisation, being helped in this task by other family members while they are at work. Yet employment rates are rather low in this country, as are volunteering rates.

Welfare mix characteristics also have a relationship with the prevalent type of voluntary work, since they can drag the voluntary sector in a specific direction. According to the prevalent type of interactions taking place between social actors (state, market, family and so on), volunteering may assume mainly self-expressive or mainly altruistic forms. From Table 14.2 it can be argued that when the formal provision of elder care services is predominant, volunteering tends to be mainly self-expressive in its nature, rather than altruistic. This can be explained by the fact that in highly de-commodified welfare states, the public actor, rather than the volunteer sector, is mainly responsible for the provision of welfare services, and as a consequence volunteer activities mainly develop in self-centred activities. Yet, while it is possible to clearly recognise this pattern in the social democratic regime, this evaluation is more blurred in others. That is, in countries where the predominant type of elder care is not formal, the diffusion of the altruistic type of volunteering is higher, but not that high as to be considered really 'prevalent'. Indeed in the UK volunteering seems to be mainly self-expressive, despite the relevant role it plays in the country's social welfare delivery.

A last point of analysis concerns employee volunteer programmes. Collaborations between companies and the voluntary sector – in terms of employees donating time or similar patterns – are not common in Europe, contrary to what happens, for instance, in the US. Yet, as shown by data reported in Table 14.2, in some European countries the first steps have been taken in this direction, even if they are still far from being fully developed, as so far they do not seem to have had a meaningful impact on the volunteering of older people.

Individual dispositions of older volunteers

The characteristics of the welfare regime influence not only the nature of the relation between the different welfare-producing institutions, but they also contribute to construct and frame identities and guide individual behaviour (Pierson, 1993), including older people's attitudes and decisions towards the voluntary sector. As a consequence, one might imagine the existence of a strong link between individual values and the characteristics of the welfare mix. In this section, the size and composition of volunteering by older people are analysed by exploring individual attitudes.

To this aim, the volunteering rate among older people can be associated with individual preferences concerning the best solution for the care of older parents (choosing between formal and informal care options), and with the work propensity of people aged 50-65 (see Table 14.3). We may hypothesise that, within a given welfare regime, there might be a direct relationship between individual orientations and welfare mix characteristics, so that individual expectations on care services for older parents are directly related to the predominant type of elder care; and that older individuals' disposition to work is directly related to the employment rate of older workers. All this may affect the propensity of volunteering in older age in a supply-side perspective (that is, the number of older volunteers).

Related to elder care values, with the help of both Tables 14.2 and 14.3, we can observe in general that indeed, when individual orientations reflect a higher propensity for the use of formal services (rather than of informal family care by children), the role of such formal services in the welfare mix is more relevant, and this also corresponds to higher volunteering rates.

Although a similar association can be partly observed even between work orientation and employment rate, this relation is not always clear. In the Netherlands and the UK both the employment rate (see Table 14.2) and the volunteering rate of older people are rather high, but

Table 14.3: Individual cultural orientations and size of volunteering by older people in different European welfare regimes

Regime	Country	Older parents should be cared for by services[a]	Older parents should be cared for by children[b]	Work orienta-tion, 50-65[c]	Volunteer-ing rate, 65-74
Social democratic	Sweden	++	– –	++	+++
	Denmark	++	– –	++	++
Social democratic-liberal	Netherlands	++	– –	– –	+++
Liberal	UK	+	–	–	++
Conservative-(liberal)	France	+	–	– –	+ –
Conservative	Germany	/	/	+	+
Mediterranean	Italy	/	/	– –	–
Post-Socialist-(liberal)	Poland	–	+	+	–
	EU27 (%)	37	54	60.9	

Notes and sources: [a] Percentage of people who answered 'Public or private service providers should visit their home and provide them with appropriate help and care' or 'They should move to a nursing home' to the following question: 'Imagine an elderly father or mother who lives alone and can no longer manage to live without regular help because of his or her physical or mental condition. In your opinion, what would be the best, first option for people in this situation?' (Eurobarometer, 2007); [b] Percentage of people who answered 'They should live with one of their children' or 'One of their children should regularly visit their home and provide them with the necessary care' to the same question as before (Eurobarometer, 2007); [c] Percentage of 50- to 65-year-olds who agreed or strongly agreed with the following statement: 'I would enjoy having a paid job even if I did not need the money' (ISSP, 1997).

work propensity per se is rather low. In the Netherlands this may be due, perhaps, to a long tradition of early exit schemes in past years, while the situation in the UK might rather be due to a partly unmet call for more long-term care services for older people (see Table 14.3). Indeed, care services provided to the older UK population are not so widespread, meaning that well-off older people may prefer to care for older relatives, rather than to work. In Poland, on the contrary, both the employment rate and volunteering rate of older people are low, while work propensity is rather high, so that older Polish people would rather prefer to work more. This is in line with the developing family form in Poland (that is, the dual breadwinner model), although this clashes with the Polish state's financial constraints and difficulties in creating work opportunities. In addition, the strong family-based welfare approach prevents many older Poles from accessing the labour market, with negative effects also on the voluntary sector.

In conclusion, the relation between individual cultural orientations and the size of volunteering in older age reflects, and is generally in line with, the country's main welfare mix characteristics. Yet in the case of discrepancies between individual orientations and welfare mix characteristics, the size of volunteering in older age in a given country seems to be more decisively affected by the latter (as shown, for instance, by the Dutch case, where we find both high rates of volunteering and employment among older people, despite their low individual work propensity). This may be interpreted in the sense that, in general, welfare mix characteristics might be stronger than individual will.

To better understand the nature of older people's voluntary work and its variation in different regimes, we can now explore older people's individual dispositions towards voluntary activities. In particular, the aim is to understand whether older volunteers are inclined to do mainly altruistic rather than self-expressive volunteering, and whether a prototypical older volunteer in a given country differs from a prototypical younger volunteer.

From analysis of the national situations, it is quite interesting to note that older volunteers' individual characteristics and dispositions are rather similar across countries. As already witnessed by a voluminous body of studies, in all countries older volunteers seem to have a very good position in terms of socio-economic resources (even if the position of younger volunteers is even better in this respect), such as high education, income, qualification, social contacts and good health conditions. Even if the nature of the present study does not allow us to analyse in detail longitudinal aspects, older volunteers can generally be described as 'young volunteers who have grown old'. Furthermore, even if in most countries there is a general tendency to devote more time to volunteer activities in older age due to the greater amount of time available after retirement, there seem to be a few exceptions: in Italy, time devoted to volunteer activities is about the same at all ages, and in Germany, older volunteers seem to be involved more sporadically, probably due to the effect of some policy limitations (see later in this chapter).

To understand older volunteers' dispositions towards voluntary work and the possible differences from those characterising younger volunteers, in Chapters Three to Ten we described the single countries' 'age-prototypical volunteers'. We found very few deviations from the general European 'rule', depicting 'prototypical volunteers' as those engaged in self-expressive activities (women being more inclined to altruistic work), and 'prototypical older volunteers' as those more oriented to altruistic activities (especially women, again, men having a stronger propensity to work as board members).

This has repercussions in two different directions when considering the preferences and dispositions of older volunteers. On the one hand, if we look at participation *within sectors*, as demonstrated by previous literature (Warburton and Cordingley, 2004; Morrow-Howell, 2007), compared to younger volunteers there is a tendency for older ones, and especially for older women, to prefer an altruistic-type of volunteering (that is, providing help to people in need, being engaged in the social services or health sectors), often between peers. On the other hand, if we look at participation *within age groups*, it is surprising to note that, at least in the 'younger-old' age group, numerically speaking, the bulk of older volunteers may still be involved in self-expressive activities in most of the countries under study, although younger volunteers prevail in these activities. This interest of older volunteers for self-expressive activities is also underlined in most country profiles of older volunteers.

This (growing) interest towards self-expressive volunteering can be related to a cohort effect. Current older volunteers are more educated, qualified and healthy than previous cohorts of older volunteers, so in all countries they are motivated to volunteer by a mix of factors that are both altruistic and ego-related. The following are among the most relevant: to realise solidarity by helping other people; to increase social contacts by meeting people and making friends; to carry out useful, interesting and pleasant activities; to make one's life more meaningful; a wish to change things; to have a new goal or role in life after a long career in the labour market; or to give 'something back' to society. This cohort effect is expected to have an even stronger impact on future (potential) older volunteers, since they will be increasingly educated, qualified and healthy, and are therefore expected to be pushed by more ego-related motivations to volunteer and, probably, be more inclined to carry out self-expressive volunteering.

Volunteering in older age: assuming the perspective of voluntary organisations

Voluntary organisations are the point of contact between demand and supply of volunteering in older age. On the one hand, according to the different activities that voluntary organisations carry out, their demand for older volunteers may be related to the welfare mix, in particular to the role they play in it. On the other hand, the supply of older volunteers, qualitatively speaking, depends on their individual predispositions and motivations. We now analyse the match between the two sides in two steps: first, by using information from the national descriptions (see Part II of this volume), we scrutinise what kind of voluntary organisations mainly attract older volunteers and how they achieve this; and second, by using the results from the case studies (as reported in Chapters Eleven to Thirteen), we explore what they are concretely doing and what they should do to support volunteering in older age, that is, to enable older volunteers to be and to remain involved. Since the case study methodology employed hardly allows a generalisation of results at a country level, the organisational perspective in this case is presented transversally across countries.

As illustrated above, older volunteers are more often associated with the altruistic type of volunteering than younger volunteers, so it may be expected that organisations providing altruistic services are those that mainly target older volunteers. This is of course the case, as witnessed in the national profiles' descriptions, even if it might not be a real 'free organisational choice'. In fact, when these kinds of organisations try to involve younger volunteers, they often fail, ascribing the failure mainly to the lack of interest by younger people towards altruistic activities. Yet we have learned from the different national experiences that other kinds of organisations and tasks also attract older volunteers, and that the best way to catch their attention is through word-of-mouth. This is the case for organisations with an advocacy role, as, for example, pensioners' organisations in Sweden, in France and in Italy, or of those carrying out some kind of cultural and recreational activity. Chapter Six reports Europe's perhaps most interesting and structured case of a specifically designed organisational effort to involve older volunteers: the UK's Retired and Senior Volunteer Programme (RSVP), hosted as an independent free-standing programme within the Community Service Volunteers (CSV). This programme involves thousands of volunteers aged 50+ in a wide range of activities. From what has been said, it can be argued that organisations attracting mainly older volunteers may sometimes be 'reserved' for older volunteers, for example, pensioners' organisations, or other kinds of organisations involving an exchange with peers, even in the recreational field. In general, however, older people's organisations seem to be present mainly in Italy, France and Sweden. Therefore it is in these countries that individuals may potentially become volunteers for the first time in older age, assuming that those who volunteer for a long time would usually continue to do so in the same organisation where they started in previous life stages.

From the evidence emerging from the case studies, it appears that to enable older people to be recruited and retained as volunteers, voluntary organisations seem to deal with three main factors: supply of older volunteers; organisational needs; and capitalising on older volunteers' strengths.

Supply of older volunteers: to plan their future activities, voluntary organisations need to consider individual factors linked to the supply of older volunteers. As already argued, the ageing of the European population and its increased longevity may potentially imply a larger supply of older volunteers. Since there is an EU interest in active ageing policies, this might mean that this increased supply may be better exploited to the benefit of the society and of older individuals themselves. These individuals are healthier and better educated, their interests and attitudes are changing, and they want to fulfil their dreams in later life. Furthermore, older people are even more involved in the labour market, and in some countries still strongly involved in informal care of older family members. Yet, as we have seen in the previous section, older volunteers may have specific preferences and motivations, so they need to find the 'right' way to meet both individual preferences and organisational needs.

Organisational needs: evidence from the case studies shows that the main needs of voluntary organisations are to maintain and possibly improve the quality of their work and to ensure the services they provide, and voluntary organisations know that older volunteers may help a lot in meeting both these needs. To cope with this situation, voluntary organisations may rely on two (even concurrent) strategies: on the one hand, asking for help from policy makers; on the other, investing themselves in older volunteers. As seen in Chapter Thirteen, voluntary organisations mainly ask policy makers for the following: to provide more visibility to the voluntary work of older people; stronger recognition and political perception of voluntary work; improved access to information on volunteer opportunities in older age; specific volunteer programmes for older volunteers that can be sustained over time; and interventions to reinforce the positive link between work for the labour market and volunteering, by supporting employee volunteer programmes. All this, however, is taking place in the light of an economic crisis which means, on the one hand, a growing call for voluntary action in service provision and, on the other, less funds for the voluntary sector overall. In particular, this latter cruciality obviously affects voluntary organisations involved in service provision (see Chapter Twelve).

This brings us to the conclusion that the real challenge for organisations is represented by their capacity for investing in and exploiting the voluntary older workforce. Yet voluntary organisations often seem to be mainly concentrated in fulfilling their own aims in the short term, without sufficient capacity to think of their management in the long term, and without using appropriate in-depth analyses. They are, however, aware that, to maintain or improve the quality of their services, they need more professional and competent (older) volunteers, and this may also involve some kind of organisational barriers to volunteering in older age. In a context of growing professionalisation, voluntary organisations may indeed tend to solve work problems by favouring the use of paid staff rather than referring to older volunteers. Other barriers may derive from a distorted perception of social changes experienced by older people: as seen in Chapter Twelve, some organisations think that an increasing involvement of older people in the labour market might be negative for their propensity to volunteering, despite wage work being positively associated with volunteering (at least, in terms of participation, if not of intensity). As a consequence (as illustrated in Chapter Thirteen), some organisations may be rather passive in approaching potential older volunteers, since general external aspects are considered as decisive, and they do not feel motivated to try to solve the recruitment problem.

Capitalising on older volunteers' strengths: a quite different model (as indicated in Chapter Eleven) is that proposed by some organisations, which are concretely doing something to support older volunteers by explicitly capitalising on them. These organisations recognise that older volunteers have several strengths: they are highly experienced and with specific knowledge related to their former work career; they are reliable; they are available, also in terms of time; they have social skills; and they are highly committed. In light of this recognition, several voluntary organisations have thus implemented initiatives to capitalise on older volunteers: some, mainly composed of younger volunteers, implemented, more or less formally, measures to *recruit* older volunteers, for example, by establishing a 'group on the accessibility to volunteering'; by sending letters to older members asking for their interests in volunteering (and creating activities accordingly); or by aiming for a more age-balanced composition. Even if, in general, most voluntary organisations do not seem to be ready to fully exploit older volunteers' potential, we have seen that some organisations have begun to structure their activity by trying to improve older volunteers' experience and to *maintain their commitment*. This is done by planning five main strategic directions (see Chapter Eleven for more details), based on the following:

- more intergenerational exchange between volunteers;
- more training to improve skills;
- more flexible voluntary work (through facilitated readmissions when wished, or scheduling tasks by taking into account new needs), to meet the potential new needs of older volunteers in terms of changing interests, the need to care for a relative or as a grandparent;
- redeployment, for instance, by creating new activities to deal with older volunteers with worsened health conditions or when these volunteers become dependent;
- an interest for a 'people engagement cycle' (Principi et al, 2012b), through an internal global policy starting at the pre-recruitment phase and continuing until volunteers' retainment as supporters, after their withdrawal from active volunteering.

So, the human resources (HR) age management concept – so well known among companies (Naegele and Walker, 2006) – is not widespread, but it is becoming manifest also among voluntary organisations. It is expected to become more common in the future, once voluntary organisations acknowledge that they are able to improve their performance through volunteers' age management, at the same time allowing older people to optimise their opportunities for health, participation and security, and to enhance their quality of life (WHO, 2002). Yet age management strategies may sometimes 'cross the frontier' of these positive terms, looking like rather discriminatory practices. A few of these cases were found mainly in some large and professionalised voluntary organisations, with a rather high extent of paid staff, often composed mainly of younger volunteers. These cases prove that sometimes organisations continue to treat older volunteers as 'outdated', rather than being willing to invest in the improvement of their skills and capacities, and to exploit their interests and strengths. This is often the case when recruitment processes are too focused on the necessary tasks to be done, rather than on older candidates' preferences and competences, or when older volunteers are reviewed and 'allowed to reconsider their commitment'.

Policies on volunteering: what is the impact on older people's participation?

At the macro level, public policies may create opportunities or restrictions for the formal volunteering of older people, since they affect individuals' lives and society as a whole, including voluntary organisations and the welfare mix. Public policies are decisive in affecting social dynamics (in the particular case under study, the volunteering of older people), and constitute a key level to activate initiatives able to foster the volunteering of older people in different countries. Thus we can argue that the phenomenon of volunteering in older age is also a result of a specific constellation of policy choices in each country.

In this light, it is certainly useful to analyse the association between activities carried out at the policy level (such as, for instance, laws on volunteering in older age, the policy debate on this issue and funding patterns) and volunteering rates among older people. Other important aspects to scrutinise in order to understand whether policies to sustain the volunteering of older people are effective or rather need improvement are volunteering trends, especially after retirement age (that is, 65 years).

The experience of the social democratic regime (Sweden and Denmark) and of the social democratic-like Dutch regime – where volunteering rates remain stable over time and do not drop after the age of 65 (see Table 14.4) – demonstrates that high and stable rates of self-expressive volunteering can coexist with very limited efforts at the policy level (which in these countries promotes no laws or policies or shows any 'active' policy interest in volunteering, at any age, except for funding). In all countries (apart from Poland), volunteering is to some extent funded by the state, even if the recent economic crisis has had a negative affect on the public provision of funds for the voluntary sector. While in Sweden and Denmark public funds seem to be provided mainly for self-expressive volunteering, in the Netherlands it is mainly service-oriented organisations that are fuelled by the state (such as those helping women victims of sexual abuse or similar associations). Since older people usually express a preference for altruistic rather than self-expressive volunteering, this may imply that in Sweden and Denmark public funds may be oriented to support the volunteering of younger rather than older people, even if, as observed earlier, self-expressive voluntary activities have lately been exerting a growing appeal for older volunteers too.

Table 14.4: The impact of policies on volunteering in older age in different European welfare regimes

		Policies					Volunteering		
Regime	Country	Specific laws on volunteering (Y/N)	Special laws on volunteering in older age (Y/N)	Special policies on volunteering in older age (Y/N)	Is volunteering of older people in the current political agenda? (Y/N)	Public funds mainly for volunteering...	Volunteering trend[a]	Volunteering rate, 65-74	After 65 years (and up to 74 years) volunteering rate...[b]
Social democratic	Sweden	N	N	N	N	Self-expressive	=	++	Remains quite stable
	Denmark	N	N	N	N	Self-expressive	+	+	Remains quite stable[c]
Social democratic-liberal	Netherlands	N	N	N	N	Altruistic	=	++	Remains quite stable
Liberal	UK	Y	N	Y	N	Altruistic	=	+	Remains quite stable
Conservative	Germany	N	N	Y	Y	Altruistic	+	+	Decreases
Conservative-(liberal)	France	Y	N	N	Y	Both typologies	=	+	–	Remains quite stable
Mediterranean	Italy	Y	Y	Y	Y	Self-expressive	+	–	Decreases
Post-Socialist-(liberal)	Poland	Y	N	N	N	(no funds granted)	+	–	Decreases

Notes: Information from Part II of this volume; Y = yes, N = no; [a] If in the last few years the volunteering rate among the population is increasing (+) or rather stable (=); after 65 years the volunteering rate decreases, increases or remains the same; [c] This stability in Denmark is assumed based on the Swedish experience (that is, the two countries belong to the same social democratic regime). This is because data for Denmark are available only for the whole age bracket 66+, showing a decrease of participation rates when compared to the previous considered 50-65 age bracket. But this drop in participation is assumed to be mainly ascribed to a low participation of 75+ individuals, while participation between 66 and 74 years remaining rather stable. [b] Whether, when compared to the previous age group,

As noted above, in Italy and Poland older people's volunteering is less widespread, although showing a growth trend (especially among older Italians), parallel to decreasing rates of participation after 65 years. A further similar characteristic of these two countries is that both have specific laws regulating volunteering. This may mean that, at the policy level, too detailed regulations on volunteering may be confusing and counterproductive to the growth of the voluntary sector, as also evidenced by the opposite experience reported by the social democratic regimes. Yet there are also differences between these two countries. In Poland public funds are unavailable, while in Italy it is mainly self-expressive volunteering that enjoys most of public funds. What is surprising is that, in Italy, low levels of volunteering in older age are linked with considerable attention on this matter at the policy level in terms of special laws and policies to increase volunteering in older age, and a marked current policy interest around volunteering in older age. If we look at this in a positive way, in recent years the volunteering of older people is growing in Italy, and since this apparent strong policy interest is very recent, more concrete positive results of it might be expected in the near future. If we look at this in a negative way, this policy interest expresses mainly intentions, with nothing to ensure that it will turn into more concrete facts.

We have observed that older people volunteer more frequently in the UK rather than in Germany and (especially) in France. However, these countries seem to have some similar characteristics at the policy level, the first being the absence or very limited legislation on volunteering (in England, charitable organisations are just envisaged and defined; in France, the legal framework is very old, dating back to 1901). Yet in the UK the volunteering rates of older people are high and do not decrease after 65 years of age (actually, rates seem to slightly increase). This may be partly due to the considerable extent of public funds made available to support altruistic volunteering, but also and perhaps primarily to a long tradition of policies aimed at promoting the volunteering of older people in the UK. The pattern in Germany seems to have similar characteristics, although volunteering rates seem to decrease after the age of 65, despite policy efforts to support volunteering in older age, and public funds promoting mainly altruistic volunteering. This may be surprising to some extent, but the reason for this could lie in the fact that German policies usually only fund older volunteers' activities for a limited period of time, without a clear idea of how to ensure their sustainability. Furthermore, in some cases policies were interrupted because they had not achieved the expected results in terms of older people's participation (see Chapter Five). In

France, a country that is characterised by a 'medium' participation rate in volunteer activities, volunteering shows a stable trend, and does not decrease after 65 years of age. Public funds are rather high and enjoyed by both altruistic and self-expressive volunteering, but there are no real special policies to involve older people in volunteering. Yet in France there seems to be recent interest at the policy level in increasing the volunteer engagement of older people, although this has not been too effective up to now, as this effort is mainly depicted as 'communication stunts' (see Chapter Seven).

Enhancing volunteering in older age in Europe

As we have seen, formal volunteering by older people in Europe depends on the interwoven action of various elements operating at the micro, meso, macro and structural levels. Across countries, high employment rates, widespread de-familialisation and the provision of formal long-term care services are associated with high levels of volunteering. At the same time, however, different welfare systems have led to different situations in single countries. Social democratic, liberal and conservative regimes show higher levels of volunteering by older people than Mediterranean and post-Socialist ones. A first, immediate, question is whether, by acting on some of the elements that we have considered, volunteering by older people may be possibly extended and enhanced, also in countries currently showing a medium or even high level of volunteering rates among older people. This is of primary importance in an active ageing perspective: in this era of growing population ageing, the major European federation of older people's organisations (that is, AGE Platform Europe) is aiming for more recognition and promotion of volunteering activities in later life (AGE, 2007), to the benefit of older individuals in terms of self-fulfilment and social integration, and of society overall.

So, under what circumstances can volunteering by older people be enhanced? At a meso level, our study delivers a cross-cutting message to European voluntary organisations deriving from the results of the case studies, as well as some country-specific considerations at a policy level, which are summarised below.

With regards to *voluntary organisations*, if they want to activate older people to volunteer in the future, it is fundamental for all countries (but also for policy makers) to carefully consider the current and future cohorts of older volunteers, with their large spectrum of different motivations and dispositions, who are and will be attracted not only by altruistic activities in health and social services, but also by self-expressive, recreational and educational tasks and interests. Furthermore, to properly 'ride the wave' of European demographic trends, this should be considered a priority by voluntary organisations carrying out self-expressive activities. *Voluntary organisations should be aware that, by considering the preferences and motivations of older volunteers, they will benefit from the strengths they recognise in older volunteers themselves:* lots of experience and knowledge related to their former work career, high social skills, reliability, availability and commitment. *As with companies in the labour market, voluntary organisations should capitalise on older volunteers through age management policies and practices,* that is, initiatives designed to combat age barriers, either directly or indirectly, and to provide an environment in which each individual is able to achieve his or her potential without being disadvantaged by their age (Walker and Taylor, 1998, p 3). Age barriers in this sector may be represented by age-biased selection processes or by more or less direct invitations to step aside at a certain age, which is particularly true of large and professionalised voluntary organisations. By adopting an age management approach, voluntary organisations could more properly also deal with the challenges posed by overall decreasing public funds to the voluntary sector.

Moreover, voluntary organisations may have a distorted interpretation of social changes. For example, some of them consider a longer working life a threat for volunteering by older people, although the contrary seems to be true. Voluntary organisations may then see companies as competitors, rather than as potential partners, through the establishment of *employee volunteer programmes* (or corporate volunteering, or employer-supported volunteering). These programmes are seldom implemented in Europe, the UK being the more advanced country in this regard. Nevertheless, in light of the evidence emerging from North America, these programmes should be considered as important tools to introduce voluntary activities to older workers. Appropriate information should therefore be granted to voluntary organisations, in order to help them better understand how they can best benefit from such programmes.

The latter suggestions should actually also be addressed to national policy makers, who of course represent crucial actors in tackling the challenges emerging in this area. Thus, the comparative approach embodied by our study allows us at this stage to summarise these *main policy challenges, which are likely to be faced by different European countries* to enhance volunteering in older age in the future. Keeping in mind the huge complexity characterising this topic, and in light of the conceptual framework employed and of the reported findings (recapitulated in Table 14.5), we can state that in *Italy* and *Poland* the main challenge is how to increase participation rates not only in the volunteer sector, but also in the labour market, through employment policies able, among other things, to also develop part-time opportunities for those who are unemployed (since, as we have seen, this is also beneficial to volunteering). In both countries the labour market participation of both older people and women is expected to increase, due to the recent raising of retirement age and its planned levelling for both genders, but the gap compared to most European countries remains considerable. A greater commitment to pursue de-familialisation – another factor associated with volunteering – might also be desirable in these two countries, through the already mentioned extension of part-time work and also by improving and rationalising long-term care provision (as current financial constraints make it unrealistic to aim at increasing the resources to be spent in this sector, at least in the short term). However, the existence of too detailed special regulations on volunteering in both countries may prevent this sector from growing. Furthermore, while in Italy policies on the volunteering of older people are very recent and, at least so far, not very effective on older people's social behaviour, in Poland more interest and policies are needed around the issue of volunteering in older age than what has occurred so far.

Compared to Southern and Eastern European countries, *Sweden*, *Denmark* and *the Netherlands* seem to be in a rather privileged position,

Table 14.5: Main areas of policy challenges for volunteering in older age in Europe

Regime	Country	Employ-ment rates	Formal care and care benefits	Laws on volunteer-ing	Policies supporting older volunteers
Social democratic	Sweden				x
	Denmark				x
Social democratic-liberal	Netherlands				x
Liberal	UK		x		
Conservative	Germany		x		x
Conservative-(liberal)	France	x	x		x
Mediterranean	Italy	x	x	x	x
Post-Socialist-(liberal)	Poland	x	x	x	x

thanks to their well-developed welfare state and the relative wealth of service provision deriving from it. Yet in these countries no specific policies seem to exist to directly enhance the volunteering of older people per se (but only as volunteering in general), so this issue is not in the national political agendas, despite EU calls for strengthening national active ageing policies. This seems to suggest that the volunteering of older people in these countries could perhaps be enhanced further, by acting at the policy level with measures more directly addressing older volunteers as such. In the *United Kingdom*, a call for more long-term care services emerged from our study, as a possible sign of demand not being fully satisfied in this area, with a supposed negative impact on the propensity to volunteer by older people. It can therefore be expected that, by improving long-term care service provision, volunteering by older UK citizens might also be stimulated, although this cannot be considered a priority in today's UK political agenda. In *Germany* and *France* one of the main challenges is likely to be related to the poor effectiveness and sustainability of policies to promote volunteering by older people, as current measures do not seem to be effective enough in this respect. In both countries, similarly to that observed for the UK context, volunteering in older age might also benefit from an improvement in the provision of formal care services, particularly in the home care sector (Rodrigues et al, 2012). In France, an additional positive effect might come from interventions aimed at promoting the employment of older workers and part-time opportunities for currently unemployed older adults.

We cannot conclude this volume without mentioning its several *limitations* and calls for future research. One of these is that, at the individual level, we have studied how the choice to become an older volunteer is socially structured, leaving out from our investigation a more specific focus on aspects such as the intensity of volunteering in terms of time or frequency. In addition, a more structured cross-country comparison of the multidimensional phenomenon of individual motivations to volunteer in older age (Clary et al, 1998) should be strengthened, due to a substantial lack of large and comparable datasets on this aspect. Moreover, while we are fully aware that older people are a non-homogeneous group, we have mainly concentrated on the younger-old group, whereas it is necessary to study volunteering more in-depth when physical or health limitations can arise, that is, particularly after 75 years of age. Furthermore, longitudinal aspects are not included in this study, thus future investigations on these aspects are needed to better understand the long-term dynamics of volunteering along the life course. Another main limitation deriving from the chosen research methodology is that the findings emerging from the case studies carried out at the organisational level cannot be generalised at a country level, so, even if it was possible to grasp the main aspects of volunteering in older age in organisations, we were not able to provide clearer country-specific indications concerning voluntary organisations. Despite these limitations, this volume represents to the best of our knowledge the first organic attempt at explaining volunteering by older people in Europe in its complexity and at different levels of analysis. Thus we hope that it might contribute to establish a solid starting point for future comparative research on this topic.

References

AGE (2007) *Healthy ageing: Good practice examples, recommendations, policy actions*, Brussels: The European Older People's Platform.

Anttonen, A. and Sipilä, J. (1996) 'European social care services: is it possible to identify models?', *Journal of European Social Policy*, vol 6, no 2, pp 87-100.

Archambault, E. (1996) *The nonprofit sector in France*, Manchester: Manchester University Press.

Bambra, C. (2004) 'The worlds of welfare: illusory and gender blind?', *Social Policy and Society*, vol 3, no 3, pp 201-11.

Bambra, C. (2007) 'Defamilisation and welfare state regimes: a cluster analysis', *International Journal of Social Welfare*, vol 16, no 4, pp 326-38.

Clary, E.G., Snyder, M., Ridge, R.D., Copeland, J., Stukas, A.A., Haugen, J. and Miene, P. (1998) 'Understanding and assessing the motivations of volunteers: a functional approach', *Journal of Personality and Social Psychology*, vol 74, no 6, pp 1516-30.

Da Roit, B. and Le Bihan, B. (2010) 'Similar and yet so different: cash-for-care in six European countries' long-term care policies', *Milbank Quarterly*, vol 88, no 3, pp 286-309.

Di Rosa, M., Melchiorre, M.G., Lucchetti M. and Lamura G. (2012) 'The impact of migrant work in the elder care sector: recent trends and empirical evidence in Italy', *European Journal of Social Work*, vol 15, no 1, pp 9-27.

Esping-Andersen, G. (1990) *The three worlds of welfare capitalism*, Oxford: Polity Press.

Eurobarometer (2007) *Health and long-term care in the European Union*, Special Eurobarometer 283/Wave 67.3 – TNS Opinion & Social (ec.europa.eu/public_opinion/archives/ebs/ebs_283_en.pdf).

Eurostat (2013) *Employment – Labour Force Survey adjusted series* (t_lfsi_emp) (http://epp.eurostat.ec.europa.eu/portal/page/portal/statistics/search_database).

Fenger, H. (2007) 'Welfare regimes in Central and Eastern Europe: incorporating post-communist countries in a welfare regime typology', *Contemporary Issues and Ideas in Social Sciences*, vol 3, no 2, pp 1-30.

Ferrera, M. (1996) 'The "southern" model of welfare in social Europe', *Journal of European Social Policy*, vol 6, no 1, pp 17-37.

Fischer, L.R. and Schaffer, K.B. (1993) *Older volunteers: A guide to research and practice*, Newbury Park, CA: Sage Publications.

Geissler, B. and Pfau-Effinger, B. (2005) 'Change of European care arrangements', in B. Pfau-Effinger and B. Geissler (eds) *Care arrangements in Europe – Variations and change*, Bristol: Policy Press, pp 3-19.

Giarini, O. (2009) 'The four pillars, the financial crisis and demographics – Challenges and opportunities', *The Geneva Papers*, vol 34, no 4, pp 507-11.

Holden, C. (2003) 'Decommodification and the workfare state', *Political Studies Review*, vol 1, no 3, pp 303-16.

ISSP (International Social Survey Programme) (1997) 'Work Orientations II', Mannheim: ISSP (www.gesis.org/issp/issp-modules-profiles/work-orientations/1997).

Lewis, J. (1992) 'Gender and the development of welfare regimes', *Journal of European Social Policy*, vol 2, no 3, pp 159-73.

McCloughan, P., Batt, W.H., Costine M. and Scully, D. (2011) *Participation in volunteering and unpaid work. Second European Quality of Life Survey*, Dublin: European Foundation for the Improvement of Living and Working Conditions.

Morrow-Howell, N. (2007) 'A longer worklife: the new road to volunteering', *Generations*, vol 31, no 1, pp 63-7.

Morrow-Howell, N., Hinterlong, J. and Sherraden, M. (eds) (2001) *Productive ageing: Concepts and challenges*, Baltimore, MD: The Johns Hopkins University Press.

Naegele, G. and Walker, A. (2006) *A guide to good practice in age management*, Dublin: European Foundation for the Improvement of Living and Working Conditions.

Pfau-Effinger, B., Flaquer, L. and Jensen, P.H. (eds) (2009) *Formal and informal work: The hidden work regime in Europe*, New York and London: Routledge.

Pierson, P. (1993) 'Policy feedback and political change', *World Politics*, vol 45, no 4, pp 595-628.

Principi, A., Lindley, R., Perek-Bialas, J. and Turek, K. (2012b) 'Volunteering in older age: an organizational perspective', *International Journal of Manpower*, vol 33, no 6, pp 685-703.

Principi, A., Lamura, G., Sirolla, C., Mestheneos, L., Bień, B., Brown, J., Krevers, B., Melchiorre, M.G. and Döhner, H. (2012a) 'Work restrictions experienced by midlife family caregivers of older people: evidence from six European countries', *Ageing & Society*.

Rodrigues, R., Huber, M. and Lamura, G. (eds) (2012) *Facts and figures on healthy ageing and long-term care*, Vienna: European Centre for Social Welfare Policy and Research.

Salamon, L.M. and Anheier, H.K. (1998) 'Social origins of civil society. Explaining the non-profit sector cross-nationally', *Voluntas*, vol 9, no 3, pp 213-48.

Schwartz, S.H. (2008) 'Causes of culture: national differences in cultural embeddedness', in A. Gari and K. Milonas (eds) *Quod erat demonstrandum. From Herodotus' ethnographic journeys to cross-cultural research*, Athens: Atrapos Editions, pp 1-11.

Stephens, J.D. (1996) 'The Scandinavian welfare states: achievements, crisis and prospects', in G. Esping-Andersen (ed) *Welfare states in transition. National adaptation in global economies*, London: Sage Publications, pp 32-65.

Walker, A. (2002) 'A strategy for active ageing', *International Social Security Review*, vol 55, no 1, pp 121-39.

Walker, A. (ed) (2011) *The future of ageing research in Europe: A road map*, Sheffield: University of Sheffield.

Walker, A. and Taylor, P. (1998) *Combating age barriers in employment: A European portfolio of good practice*, Luxemburg: Office for Official Publications of the European Communities.

Warburton, J. and Cordingley, S. (2004) 'The contemporary challenges of volunteering in an ageing Australia', *Australian Journal on Volunteering*, vol 9, no 2, pp 67-74.

Warburton, J. and Jeppsson-Grassman, E. (2011) 'Variations in voluntary association involvement by seniors across different social welfare regimes', *International Journal of Social Welfare*, vol 20, no 2, pp 180-91.

WHO (World Health Organization) (2002) *Active ageing: A policy framework*, Geneva: WHO.

Index

Note: The following abbreviations have been used – *f* = figure; *n* = note; *t* = table

welfare mix and 32
see also under individual countries
Voluntary Organisations, National Council
for (NCVO) (England) 124
Voluntary Service (*servizio civile*) (Italy) 51,
53
'Voluntary services of all generations'
(Germany) 104
Voluntary Social Work, Centre for
(Denmark) 82
volunteer centres 36, 161
volunteer cycle 267
Volunteer Effort, Danish Committee on 73
Volunteer Fire Brigades (Poland) 178, 185
volunteer programmes *see* employee
volunteer programmes
Volunteer Survey (Germany) 97, 98*t*, 99,
100, 101
Volunteering, EU Year of (2011) 4
Volunteering, National Strategy for the
Promotion of (Germany) 104
Volunteering in the Third Age (VITA)
(England) 133
Volunteerism, Law on Public Benefit
Activity and (2003) (Poland) 177
volunteers and volunteering 7, 35–6, 103
by sector 53, 54*t*, 55*t*, 56*t&f*, 57
competing commitments 295–6
complexity of factors for 10–11, 22, 26–7
conceptual framework 119, 316, 317*f*
definitions of 11–12, 21–2, 49, 176, 177
individual dispositions 316, 325, 326*t*,
327–8
information on 308–9, 312
main barriers in old age 270–2
strengths of 331–2
vrijwilligerswerk.startpagina.nl (voluntary
work start page) (Netherlands) 225

W

Walker, A. 272
Warburton, J. 37
WEA 304, 306
Welfare, Ministry of (Denmark) 74–5
welfare mix 22, 23*t*, 24, 25, 32–4, 36, 37,
295
employment and 275–6, 277
Germany 94, 110, 111
impact on volunteering by older people
316, 321, 322*t*, 323–5, 327, 328–9
welfare regimes 9, 22, 23*t*, 24–5, 36–8, 120,
121, 173
altruistic voluntary work 322*t*, 324, 327,
328, 329, 334*t*
employment and 322*t*, 323, 325, 326*t*
impact of policies 334*t*
individual cultural orientations 326*t*
main characteristics 316, 317*f*, 318, 319*t*,
320–1
see also under individual countries
welfare state 8–9, 10, 11, 33

Denmark 71, 72, 73, 74, 83–4, 86
France 149
Germany 94, 96
Italy 47, 48, 49
Netherlands 217, 238, 239
Sweden 197, 198, 199–200, 211, 212–13
well-being 4, 6, 238, 272, 300, 315, 316
active ageing 22, 25, 27, 31, 59, 103
England 120, 132, 139, 141
France 160
Poland 173
Sweden 208
Werder 249*t*, 306
Wet Maatschappelijke Ondersteuning (law on
social support) (Netherlands) 222
WHO *see* World Health Organization
Wijkström, F. 199, 202
Williams, C.C. 71
Wilson, L. 85
Windebank, J. 71
women 281, 293, 301, 323
Denmark 76*t*, 77, 78, 81, 82
England 121, 128, 130, 136, 140
France 156, 157, 159, 164, 165, 283
Germany 93, 99, 100, 101, 102*t*, 105, 107,
108, 284
informal family care 47, 62, 63, 288, 290
Italy 54, 55*t*, 56*f*, 57, 284
motherhood and 302
Netherlands 218, 219, 226*t*, 227, 228,
230*f*, 233, 235, 236, 239
percentage of volunteers 246–58*t*, 259,
260*t*
Poland 173, 180, 189, 191, 324
retirement 61, 65
Sweden 197, 198, 203*t*, 204, 206, 207,
210, 211, 266
Women's Royal Voluntary Service (WRVS)
130, 249*t*, 262, 264, 267, 273, 306, 307
informal family care 287, 289, 290
worker mutual aid societies 151
World Health Organization (WHO) 3, 4, 6

Y

Year of Volunteering (2011) (European
Union) 21, 133, 166, 315
younger volunteers 139, 154, 181, 200
age management 262–3, 264, 265, 270,
273, 281, 299
altruistic volunteering 329
Denmark 73–4, 79, 86, 305
Italy 53, 303